# Houghton Mifflin
# Reading

# Expeditions

**Senior Authors**
J. David Cooper
John J. Pikulski

**Authors**
David J. Chard
Gilbert Garcia
Claude Goldenberg
Phyllis Hunter
Marjorie Y. Lipson
Shane Templeton
Sheila Valencia
MaryEllen Vogt

**Consultants**
Linda H. Butler
Linnea C. Ehri
Carla Ford

HOUGHTON MIFFLIN                    BOSTON

Cover photography Nick Vedros, Vedros & Associates.

Acknowledgments begin on page 689.

Printed in the U.S.A.

ISBN: 0-618-61942-9

2 3 4 5 6 7 8 9 10 VH 11 10 09 08 07 06

# Expeditions

# Theme 1

# Nature's Fury

4

**Theme Wrap-Up**

## Check Your Progress

# Focus on Genre

# TALL TALES

# Give It All You've Got

# Give It All You've Got

## Theme Wrap-Up
## Check Your Progress

# Voices
## of the
# Revolution

## Theme Wrap-Up
# Check Your Progress

11

# Theme 4

# Person to Person

Theme Wrap-Up

## Check Your Progress

# PLAYS

# One Land, Many Trails

# One Land, Many Trails

**Theme Wrap-Up**

## Check Your Progress

# AUTOBIOGRAPHY

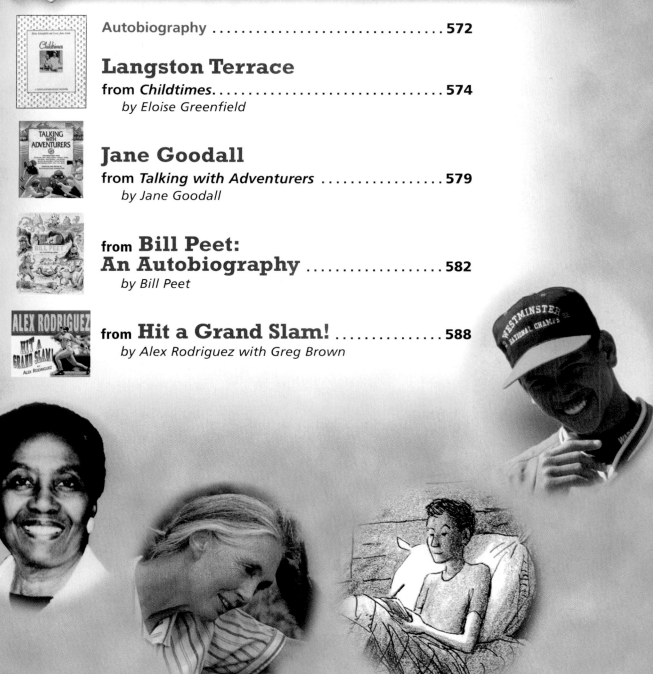

# Theme 6

# Animal Encounters

# Nature's Fury

Now the house of wind is thundering.
Now the house of wind is thundering.
As I go roaring over the land,
the land is covered in thunder.

— *from "Wind Song" (Pima)*

# Nature's Fury

## with Warren Faidley

Are you ready to face nature at its most explosive? Start with a letter that just blew in from storm chaser Warren Faidley!

**Dear Reader,**

I chase storms — anywhere, anytime.

I pursue tornadoes, lightning, hurricanes and other natural disasters. I capture the events on film and video.

In this theme you'll get a taste of my adventures on the job. You'll also encounter other examples of nature's power, from earthquakes to blizzards.

One of the biggest storms I have chased was Hurricane Andrew in August of 1992. Andrew hit South Florida with winds of over 160 miles per hour.

It was both exciting and frightening to be in the middle of a "category 5" storm, the biggest of all hurricanes.

I had to be very careful. The rain hit so hard it stung. Large trees were uprooted and debris flew through the air.

Huge waves crashed inland, bringing boats and wreckage toward me.

I had to use all of my experiences as a storm chaser to survive. I wore safety glasses to protect my eyes, and I kept my camera equipment in waterproof cases.

When the storm passed I was safe.

I was also a little tired and wet.

You won't have to worry about the wind and rain as you read the selections in this theme. Just enjoy the forces of nature on display!

Sincerely yours,

# Step Into the Storm

As a storm chaser, Warren Faidley *chooses* to go out into tornadoes and hurricanes. Have you ever been caught in a storm or in some other example of nature gone wild? Think about that experience as you read the selections in this theme, which are shown below. Try putting yourself into the different situations in the selections. Sometimes the storm you read about can be as exciting as the storm you were in!

Internet

To learn about the authors in this theme, visit Education Place. **www.eduplace.com/kids**

## Background and Vocabulary

**Earthquake Terror**

PEG KEHRET
author of *Terror at the Zoo*

Genre **Realistic Fiction**

### Key Vocabulary

devastation
earthquake
fault
jolt
undulating
upheaval

**Vocabulary Reader**

The San Francisco **Earthquake** by Rob Arego

*e* • **Glossary**

# BUILDUP TO A SHAKEUP

**What forces cause the earthquake in *Earthquake Terror*? The answer lies deep underground.**

## Pressure Builds

Pressure has been building along a deep crack in the earth's crust, the San Andreas Fault in California. The rock on one side of the **fault** is pushing against the rock on the other side, until . . .

## Earthquake!

Too much pressure! The rock on each side of the fault slips with a **jolt** . All that released energy causes the ground to go **undulating** for miles. The **upheaval** may cause terrible **devastation** to anything standing.

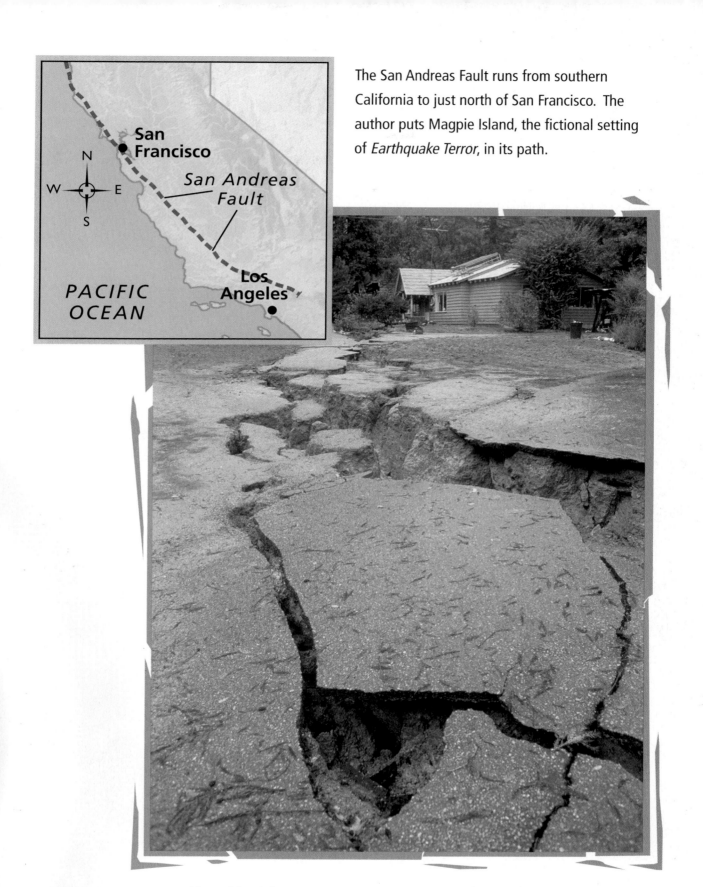

The San Andreas Fault runs from southern California to just north of San Francisco. The author puts Magpie Island, the fictional setting of *Earthquake Terror*, in its path.

A road in California's Santa Cruz Mountains, south of San Francisco, shows extensive damage from the "World Series Earthquake" that struck part of the San Andreas Fault in October, 1989.

PEG KEHRET
author of *Terror at the Zoo*

EARTHQUAKE
TERROR

It started as an adventure—
and turned into a nightmare

## Strategy Focus

Think about the selection title and cover illustration. What do you **predict** Jonathan will do to protect himself and his younger sister when a powerful earthquake strikes?

A family vacation begins peacefully in the woods of Magpie Island. Then Jonathan and Abby's mom breaks her ankle, and their dad has to rush her to the hospital. He promises to return in three hours, leaving Jonathan, age twelve, in charge of his six-year-old sister, whose legs are partially paralyzed. Moose, the family's dog, is with them. But Jonathan is uneasy.

In his mind, Jonathan could see his father unhitching the small camping trailer. He pictured the car going along the narrow, winding road that meandered from the campground through the woods. He saw the high bridge that crossed the river, connecting the island campground to the mainland.

He imagined his father driving across the bridge, faster than usual, with Mom lying down in the back seat. Or maybe she wouldn't lie down. Maybe, even with a broken ankle, she would wear her seat belt. She always did, and she insisted that Jonathan and Abby wear theirs.

Moose cocked his head, as if listening to something. Then he ran toward the trail, sniffing the ground.

"Moose," Jonathan called. "Come back."

Moose paused, looked at Jonathan, and barked.

"Come!"

Moose returned but he continued to smell the ground and pace back and forth.

"Moose wants Mommy," Abby said.

Moose suddenly stood still, his legs stiff and his tail up. He barked again.

"Silly old dog," Abby said.

He knows something is wrong, Jonathan thought. Dogs sense things. He knows I'm worried about Mom. Jonathan patted Moose's head. "It's all right, Moose. Good dog."

Moose barked again.

"I'm hot," Abby said. "It's too hot to eat."

"Let's start back. It'll be cooler in the shade and we can finish our lunch in the camper."

Maybe he could relax in the camper. Here he felt jumpy. He didn't like being totally out of communication with the rest of the world. Whenever he stayed alone at home, or took care of Abby, there was always a telephone at his fingertips or a neighbor just down the street. If he had a problem, he could call his parents or Mrs. Smith next door or even nine-one-one.

Here he was isolated. I wouldn't do well as a forest ranger, Jonathan thought. How do they stand being alone in the woods all the time?

He rewrapped the uneaten food, buckled the backpack over his shoulders, and put the leash on Moose. The goofy way Moose was acting, he might bolt down the trail and not come back.

Jonathan helped Abby stand up and placed her walker in position. Slowly, they began the journey across the sand and into the woods, to follow the trail through the trees.

Jonathan wished he had worn a watch. It seemed as if his parents had been gone long enough to get partway to town, but it was hard to be sure. Time had a way of evaporating instantly when he was engrossed in an interesting project, such as cataloging his baseball cards, or reading a good mystery. But time dragged unbearably when he was in the dentist's office or waiting for a ride. It was hard to estimate how much time had passed since his parents waved good-bye and walked away. Forty minutes? An hour?

Abby walked in front of him. That way he could see her and know if she needed help, and it kept him from going too fast. When he was in the lead, he usually got too far ahead, even when he tried to walk slowly.

While they walked Jonathan planned what he would do when they got back to the camper. As soon as he got Abby settled on her bed, he would turn on the radio and listen to the ball game. That would give him something to think about. The San Francisco Giants were his favorite baseball team and he hoped they would win the World Series.

Jonathan noticed again how quiet it was. No magpies cawed, no leaves rustled overhead. The air was stifling, with no hint of breeze.

Moose barked. Jonathan jumped at the sudden noise. It was Moose's warning bark, the one he used when a stranger knocked on the door. He stood beside Jonathan and barked again. The dog's eyes had a frantic look. He was shaking, the way he always did during a thunderstorm.

"What's wrong, boy?" Jonathan asked. He reached out to pet Moose but the dog tugged toward Abby and barked at her.

"Hush, Moose," Abby said.

Jonathan looked in all directions. He saw nothing unusual. There were still no people and no animals that would startle Moose and set him off. Jonathan listened hard, wondering if Moose had heard something that Jonathan couldn't hear.

Abby stopped walking. "What was that?" she said.

"What was what?"

Jonathan listened. He heard a deep rumbling sound in the distance.

Thunder? He looked up. The sky was bright and cloudless. The noise came closer; it was too sharp to be thunder. It was more like several rifles being fired at the same time.

Hunters! he thought. There are hunters in the woods and they heard us move and they've mistaken us for deer or pheasant. Moose must have seen them or heard them or possibly smelled them.

"Don't shoot!" he cried.

As he yelled, Jonathan felt a jolt. He stumbled forward, thrusting an arm out to brace himself against a tree. Another loud noise exploded as Jonathan lurched sideways.

He dropped the leash.

Abby screamed.

A bomb? Jonathan thought. Who would bomb a deserted campground?

The noise continued, and the earth moved beneath his feet. As he felt himself lifted, he knew that the sound was not hunters with guns. It was not a bomb, either.

Earthquake! The word flashed across his brain as if he had seen it blazing on a neon sign.

He felt as if he were on a surfboard, catching a giant wave, rising, cresting, and sliding back down again. Except he was standing on dry land.

"Jonathan!" Abby's scream was lost in the thunderous noise. He saw her fall, her walker flying off to one side as she went down. Jonathan lunged forward, arms outstretched, trying to catch Abby before she hit the ground. He couldn't get there fast enough.

The ground dropped away beneath his feet as if a trapdoor had opened. His legs buckled and he sank to his knees. He reached for a tree trunk, to steady himself, but before his hand touched it, the tree moved.

Jonathan's stomach rose into his throat, the way it sometimes did on a fast elevator.

Ever since first grade, when the Palmers moved to California, Jonathan had practiced earthquake drills in school each year. He knew that most earthquakes occur along the shores of the Pacific Ocean. He knew that the San Andreas fault runs north and south for hundreds of miles in California, making that land particularly susceptible to earthquakes. He knew that if an earthquake hit while he was in school, he was supposed to crawl under his desk or under a table because injury was most likely to be caused by the roof caving in on him.

That was school. This was Magpie Island. How should he protect himself in the woods? Where could he hide?

He struggled to his feet again. Ahead of him, Abby lay whimpering on the ground. Moose stood beside her, his head low.

"Put your hands over your head," Jonathan called.

The ground shook again, and Jonathan struggled to remain on his feet.

"I'm coming," he shouted. "Stay where you are. I'm coming!"

But he did not go to her. He couldn't.

He staggered sideways, unable to keep his balance. He felt as if he were riding a roller coaster standing up, except the ground rocked back and forth at the same time that it rolled up and down.

A clump of small birch trees swayed like dancers and then fell.

The rumbling noise continued, surrounding him, coming from every direction at once. It was like standing in the center of a huge orchestra, with kettle drums pounding on all sides.

Abby's screams and Moose's barking blended with the noise.

Although there was no roof to cave in on him, Jonathan put his arms over his head as he fell. The school's earthquake drills had taught him to protect his head and he did it the only way he could.

Earthquake.

He had never felt an earthquake before and he had always wondered how it would feel. He had questioned his teacher, that first year. "How will I know it's an earthquake?" he asked. "If it's a big one," the teacher said, "you'll know."

His teacher had been right. Jonathan knew. He knew with a certainty that made the hair rise on the back of his neck. He was in the middle of an earthquake now. A big one.

The ground heaved, pitching Jonathan into the air.

Jonathan hit the ground hard, jarring every bone in his body. Immediately, the earth below him moved, tossing him into the air again.

As he dropped back down, he saw the trunk of a giant redwood tree tremble. The huge tree swayed back and forth for a few moments and then tilted toward Jonathan.

Frantically, he crawled to his left, rushing to get out of the tree's path.

The roots ripped loose slowly, as if not wanting to relinquish their century-long hold on the dirt.

As Jonathan scrambled across the unsteady ground, he clenched his teeth, bracing himself for the impact.

The tree fell. Air whizzed across Jonathan as the tree trunk dropped past, and branches brushed his shoulder, scratching his arms. The redwood crashed beside him, missing him by only a few feet. It thudded down, landing at an angle on another fallen tree. Dirt and dry leaves whooshed into the air, and then settled slowly back down.

The earth shuddered, but Jonathan didn't know if it was from the impact of the tree or another jolt from the earthquake.

With his heart in his throat, Jonathan crept away from the redwood tree, toward Abby. Beneath him, the ground swelled and retreated, like ocean waves. Twice he sprawled facedown in the dirt, unable to keep his balance. The second time, he lay still, with his eyes closed. How much longer would this go on? Maybe he should just lie there and wait until this earthquake was over.

"Mommy!" Abby's shrill cry rose above the thundering noise.

Jonathan struggled toward her again, his heart racing. When he finally reached her, he lay beside her and wrapped his arms around her. She clung to him, sobbing.

"We'll be okay," he said. "It's only an earthquake."

Only an earthquake. He remembered magazine pictures of terrible devastation from earthquakes: homes toppled, highways buckled, cars tossed upside down, and people crushed in debris. Only an earthquake.

"We have to get under shelter," he said. "Try to crawl with me." Keeping one arm around Abby's waist, he got to his hands and knees and began crawling forward on the undulating ground.

"I can't!" Abby cried. "I'm scared. The ground is moving."

Jonathan tightened his grip, dragging her across the ground. A small tree crashed beside them. Dust rose, filling their noses.

"I want Mommy!" Abby shrieked.

He pulled her to the trunk of the huge redwood tree that had uprooted.

"Get under the tree," he said, as he pushed her into the angle of space that was created because the center of the redwood's trunk rested on the other tree.

When Abby was completely under the tree, Jonathan lay on his stomach beside her, with his right arm tucked beneath his stomach and his left arm thrown across Abby. He pulled himself in as close as he could so that both he and Abby were wedged in the space under the big tree.

"What's happening?" Abby sobbed. Her fingernails dug into Jonathan's bare arm.

"It's an earthquake."

"I want to go home." Abby tried to push Jonathan away.

"Lie still," Jonathan said. "The tree will protect us."

The dry forest floor scratched his cheek as he inhaled the pungent scent of dead leaves. He felt dwarfed by the enormous redwood and tried not to imagine what would have happened if it had landed on him.

"Moose!" he called. "Come, Moose."

Beneath him, the ground trembled again. Jonathan tightened his grip on Abby and pushed his face close to hers. A sharp crack rang out beside them as another tree hit the ground. Jonathan turned his head enough to peer out; he saw the redwood branches quivering from the impact.

What if the earthquake caused the redwood to move again? What if it slipped off the tree it rested on and crushed them beneath it? Anxiety tied a tight knot in Jonathan's stomach.

The earth shuddered once more. Abby buried her face in Jonathan's shoulder. His shirt grew wet from her tears. The jolt did not seem as severe this time, but Jonathan thought that might be because he was lying down.

Moose, panting with fear, huddled beside Jonathan, pawing at Jonathan's shoulder. Relieved that the dog had not been injured, Jonathan put his right arm around Moose and held him close.

As suddenly as it had begun, the upheaval stopped. Jonathan was unsure how long it had lasted. Five minutes? Ten? While it was happening, time seemed suspended and Jonathan had thought the shaking might go on for days.

The woods were quiet.

He lay motionless, one arm around Abby and the other around Moose, waiting to see if it was really over. The air was completely still. After the roar of the earthquake, the silence seemed both comforting and ominous.

Earlier, even though there were no other people in the area, he'd heard the magpies cawing, and a squirrel had complained when Jonathan tossed a rock.

Now he heard nothing. No birds. No squirrels. Not even wind in the leaves.

He wondered if his parents had felt the quake. Sometimes, he knew, earthquakes were confined to fairly small areas.

Once Grandma Whitney had called them from Iowa. She had seen news reports of a violent California earthquake less than one hundred miles from where the Palmers lived.

"Are you all right?" Grandma cried, when Mrs. Palmer answered the phone. "Was anyone hurt?"

Grandma had been astonished when none of the Palmers knew anything about an earthquake.

After several minutes of quiet, Jonathan eased out from under the tree. He sat up and looked around. Moose, still trembling, licked his hand.

Jonathan put his cheek on the dog's neck and rubbed his ears. He had chosen Moose at the animal shelter, more than six years ago. The Palmers had planned to get a small dog but the moment Jonathan saw the big golden retriever, who was then one year old, he knew which dog he wanted.

Mrs. Palmer had said, "He's too big to be a house dog."

Mr. Palmer said, "I think he's half moose."

Jonathan laughed and said, "That's what I'll name him. Moose."

His parents tried unsuccessfully to interest Jonathan in one of the other, smaller dogs, before they gave in and brought Moose home.

Despite his size, Moose was a house dog from the start, and he slept beside Jonathan's bed every night. They played fetch, and their own version of tag, and Jonathan took Moose for long walks in the county park. In the summer, they swam whenever they had a chance.

When Abby had her accident and Jonathan's parents focused so much of their attention on her, Moose was Jonathan's comfort and companion.

Now, in the devastation of the earthquake, Jonathan again found comfort in the dog's presence. He let go of Moose and looked around. "Wow!" he said, trying to keep his voice steady. "That was some earthquake."

"Is it over?" Abby's voice was thin and high.

"I think so."

He grasped Abby's hand and pulled her out from under the tree. She sat up, apparently uninjured, and began picking leaves out of her hair.

"Are you okay?" he asked.

"My knee is cut." She touched one knee and her voice rose. "It's bleeding," she said, her lip trembling. "You pushed me under the tree too hard."

Jonathan examined her knee. It was a minor cut. He knew that if he made a fuss over it, Abby would cry. He had seen it happen before; if his mother showed concern about a small injury, Abby got practically hysterical, but if Mom acted like it was no big deal, Abby relaxed, too. It was as if she didn't know whether she hurt or not until she saw how her parents reacted.

"It's all right," he said. "If that tiny little scrape is all you got, you are lucky, and so am I. We could have been killed."

"We could?" Abby's eyes grew round.

Quickly Jonathan said, "But we weren't, and the earthquake is over now."

## Meet the Author
# Peg Kehret

**Favorite outfit:** Jeans and sweatshirt

**Favorite dish:** Spaghetti

**When not writing:** Reads, plays her player piano, bakes bread, volunteers at The Humane Society

**Home:** An eighty-year-old house in the state of Washington with apple and pear trees, blueberry and blackberry bushes, and a big vegetable garden

**Popularity:** Kehret has won children's choice awards in fifteen states. Twice a year she and her husband travel across the country in their motor home so that she can speak in schools and meet her readers.

**More Kehret books:** *Volcano Disaster, Blizzard Disaster, Nightmare Mountain, The Richest Kids in Town, Shelter Dogs: Amazing Stories of Adopted Strays*

## Meet the Illustrator
# Phil Boatwright

**Lone Star boyhood:** Boatwright grew up in Mesquite, Texas, a suburb of Dallas.

**Favorite children's book:** *Treasure Island*, by Robert Louis Stevenson

**Favorite illustrators:** Gennady Spirin, Jerry Pinkney, John Collier, and N. C. Wyeth

**Tips for success:** "You have to love to draw, take all the art classes possible, read all the art books available, and study the artists you admire."

*Internet*

For more information about Peg Kehret and Phil Boatwright, visit Education Place. **www.eduplace.com/kids**

45

# Think About the Selection

1. How does the author create suspense before the earthquake hits? Find examples from the story.

2. Summarize what Jonathan does to protect himself and Abby from the earthquake.

3. Sometimes the author interrupts the action with events that happened earlier. Do you think this adds to the story? Why or why not?

4. What did you learn about the fault that runs through the island?

5. How would you describe Jonathan's relationship with his sister? Give examples from the selection that show how they feel about each other.

6. Jonathan thinks about how time goes fast when he's excited or interested, and slowly when he's not. Give examples of that from your own life.

7. **Connecting/Comparing** Do you think *Earthquake Terror* is a good way to begin a theme called *Nature's Fury*? Why or why not?

**Narrating**

# Write an Adventure Story

Use what you learned about Jonathan and Abby in *Earthquake Terror* to write an adventure story with them as characters. Your story can tell how they escape from another natural disaster, such as a fire, a flood, or a storm.

**Tips**

- **Begin by thinking about the problem the characters face and write down details.**
- **Show how the characters feel.**
- **Include details of the setting.**

# Demonstrate Earthquake Safety

On pages 35 and 36 of the selection, Jonathan remembers what he learned in school about earthquake safety. Use that information to demonstrate for classmates what to do in case an earthquake strikes.

# Deliver a Newscast

With a partner, present a newscast about the earthquake on Magpie Island. You might wish to take on the roles of a television anchorperson and an on-the-scene reporter. Use information from the selection to give details.

### Tips

- **Plan the order in which you will present your information.**
- **Write notes on cards or slips of paper.**
- **Use exact details.**

*Internet*

# Post a Review

Write a review of *Earthquake Terror.* Tell others what you liked or didn't like about it. Visit Education Place. **www.eduplace.com/kids**

**Genre**

## Science Article

**Skill: How to Read a Science Article**

*Before you read . . .*

❶ Look at the title, captions, and illustrations.

❷ Identify the **topic** and ask what you already know about it.

❸ Predict what you will learn in the article.

*While you read . . .*

❶ Identify the **main idea** and **supporting details** in each paragraph.

❷ When you don't understand something, ask yourself questions and then reread.

# El Niño

by Fred Pearce

**In the winter of 1998,** heavy rains caused mudslides in California that washed houses off cliffs. Ice storms on the eastern seaboard from Maine to Quebec downed so many power lines that thousands of people had to live in the dark and cold for weeks. Indonesia's rain forests got no rain, and the months of dry weather turned the forests into the world's largest pile of firewood. At the same time, the worst drought in a hundred years hit neighboring New Guinea, killing crops and leaving some of the most isolated people on Earth starving. On the other side of the globe, lack of rain left the water level in the Panama Canal so low that large ships couldn't make it through.

**Mudslides in California**

Early 1998 also saw intense storms in places not used to them. Kenya suffered the worst floods in 40 years — in the middle of the *dry* season. Neighboring Uganda was cut off for several days, when both road and rail links were washed away. In South America, floods made half a million Peruvians homeless along a coastline that often has no rain for years at a time. Neighboring Ecuador said it would take 10 years to repair the damage. And in northern Tibet, the worst snow in 50 years starved or froze to death hundreds of Mongol tribesmen.

Was it just bad luck that there was so much bad weather in so many parts of the world at around the same time? Fifty years ago, most people would have said yes.

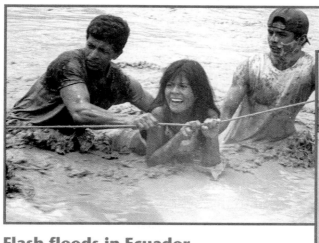

**Flash floods in Ecuador, South America**

**Floods in Kenya, East Africa**

**Forest fires in Indonesia, Southeast Asia**

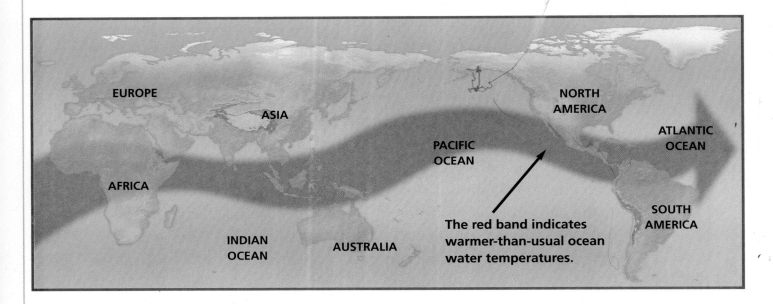

The red band indicates warmer-than-usual ocean water temperatures.

But today, meteorologists (scientists who study weather) blame most of 1998's weather disasters on a giant blip in the weather system called *El Niño.* Many years ago, Spanish-speaking Peruvian fishermen noticed that the fish suddenly disappeared whenever warm waters flowed in from the west. They called the warming El Niño ( Spanish for "the child") because it usually happened around Christmas. El Niño is caused by a sudden shift in the winds and ocean currents in the Pacific Ocean that pushes a layer of warm water across the ocean, taking weather systems with it.

El Niño is rather like a wave in your bathtub, only the tub is huge and the wave takes months to go from one end to the other. The huge bathtub in this case is the Pacific, the world's largest ocean.

Most of the time, winds and ocean currents at the equator move from east to west across the Pacific — from the Americas to Asia. The winds and currents push the ocean's water toward Asia. After a few years of this, the sea level around the islands of Indonesia is actually over a foot higher than on the American side. This can't go on forever. And it doesn't. Eventually, like a wave reaching the far end of your bathtub, the water bounces back, moving toward the Americas. Scientists have clocked this wave moving about 125 miles a day.

The water around Indonesia is the hottest in the world — usually warmer than 80° F, which is as warm as many swimming pools. As the wave moves toward the Americas, it spreads a layer of the warm Indonesian water across the ocean. And because ocean currents and winds are connected, the Indonesian weather follows, too. This means that the heavy rains that normally hit Indonesia for most of the year get moved thousands of miles east, soaking the Pacific Islands and normally dry coastlands from Peru to California. Meanwhile, normally wet Indonesia and its surrounding areas suffer drought.

No one is really sure how long El Niño has been around. Dan Sandweiss of the University of Maine has found telltale signs of sudden El Niño-style floods in old *sediments* in Peru. (Sediments are the solid stuff that settles out of water at places like the mouth of a river.) When it doesn't rain, few plants grow, and there isn't much pollen in the sediments. But when El Niño occurs in these normally dry regions, more plants grow and more pollen shows up. From the amount of pollen in the sediments, Sandweiss can tell that "El Niño has been around for at least 5000 years. Before that there seems to have been a gap."

El Niño isn't just about some rainstorm in California in 1998; it's about wild weather around the world through recorded history.

## Episode Two: La Niña Strikes Back!

El Niño typically lasts some 18 months, and usually returns every three to seven years, probably when enough warm water has built up again in the western Pacific. But when El Niño's warm water retreats, it's sometimes followed by a *cool* water wave. Scientists call this cooling of the Pacific *La Niña*. La Niña's effect on the weather is harder to predict than El Niño's. But during La Niña years, the normal weather in some regions becomes *exaggerated*: it gets extra wet in wet Indonesia, extra dry in dry Peru. That's also when we get big droughts in the American Midwest. The great Dust Bowl drought of 1930s America is thought to have been caused by a decade of La Niña-like conditions.

**Photo by Arthur Rothstein,**
***Dust Storm, Cimarron County, 1936.***

# A Description

A description is a picture in words that helps the reader share the writer's experience. Use this student's writing as a model when you write a description of your own.

## By the Sea

The **beginning** tells what the description is about.

    My grandfather has an apartment that we visit every summer for a few days. My favorite place is a beach where my family goes to play and walk along the shore.

**Imagery** lets readers visualize how something looks, sounds, smells, tastes, and feels.

    When the weather is nice, the sky is blue and the clouds are pure white. The ocean is greenish blue and when the waves crash, the foam is white. Along the water's edge, there are clam shells, crabs, baby shrimp, and once my brother found a starfish! The seagulls walk around like scavengers, looking for clams and crabs to eat. Sometimes I feel like a seagull, because we are both walking around trying to find something special. The seaweed washes up along the shore. It's green and long, and when it wraps around your leg it is ticklish. When we play in the water, we are always careful of the jellyfish. Some are red and some are clear, but they all sting.

**Similes** give the reader a clear mental picture.

When the weather is cloudy and stormy, the skies are gray and the waves crash along the shore. It sounds like thunder or like a roaring lion. We don't walk along the shore during a storm, but we can watch from the boardwalk.

The prettiest part of the day is when the sun sets over the bay. It seems as if every time we look up, the colors in the sky change. At first, there is pink, blue, and some green. Then the colors darken to red, orange, blue-gray, and purple. Finally the sky goes dark blue and the sun sets.

I love my grandfather's beach house!

A good description puts **details** in time order, in spatial order, or in order of importance.

A good **ending** wraps up the description.

## Meet the Author

**Dena S.**
**Grade:** five
**State:** New York
**Hobbies:** ice skating, singing, and basketball
**What she'd like to be when she grows up:** a singer

## Background and Vocabulary

Eye of the Storm
STEPHEN KRAMER
PHOTOGRAPHS BY
WARREN FAIDLEY

**Eye of the Storm:
Chasing Storms with
Warren Faidley**

Genre  **Nonfiction**

### Key Vocabulary

collide
funnel clouds
lightning
rotate
sizzling
tornadoes

Vocabulary Reader

Day of the
**Tornadoes**
by Gary Miller

e ● Glossary

# Photographing
# Wild
# Weather

**Eye of the Storm** tells about Warren Faidley, professional weather photographer and storm chaser.  Here's a look at where he goes and the dangers he faces on the job.

## The Risks

### Lightning Danger

▶ Lightning heats the air around it to a **sizzling** 50,000 degrees Fahrenheit.

▶ Each bolt carries hundreds of millions of volts of electricity.

▶ Lightning kills an average of 100 people each year in the United States.

# The Route

Every spring, Warren brings his cameras to "Tornado Alley" in the central United States, where warm and cool air **collide** to form **funnel clouds** that might become **tornadoes** . For the summer, Warren returns to his home state of Arizona to photograph **lightning** storms.

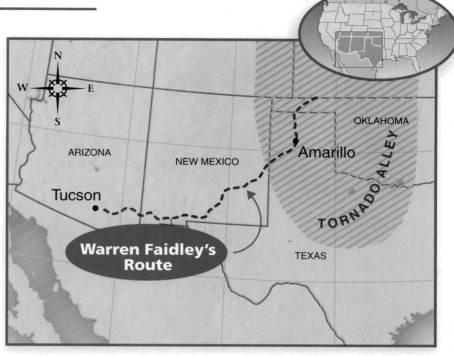

ARIZONA

Tucson

NEW MEXICO

OKLAHOMA

Amarillo

TORNADO ALLEY

TEXAS

**Warren Faidley's Route**

## Tornado Danger

▶ The winds inside a killer tornado may **rotate** at jet speed — spinning up to 300 miles per hour.

▶ Tornadoes kill an average of 80 people per year in the United States.

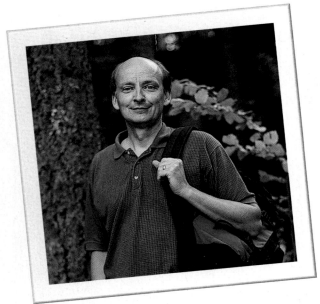

## Meet the Author
# Stephen Kramer

Stephen Kramer teaches at an elementary school near Vancouver, Washington. He has written several other books on nature topics, such as *Avalanche, Caves, Tornado,* and *Lightning.* *Lightning* features the photographs of Warren Faidley.

## Meet the Photographer
# Warren Faidley

Warren Faidley's dramatic weather photographs appear not only in books, but in movies, videos, calendars, magazines, and museums. Faidley also served as a consultant and cinematographer for the movie *Twister.* He and his cat, Megamouth, live in Tucson, Arizona.

**Internet**

For more information about Stephen Kramer and Warren Faidley, visit Education Place. **www.eduplace.com/kids**

# Eye of the Storm

## CHASING STORMS WITH WARREN FAIDLEY

### STEPHEN KRAMER

#### PHOTOGRAPHS BY
#### WARREN FAIDLEY

## Strategy Focus

Warren Faidley's job takes him all over the country, getting close-up shots of dangerous storms. As you read the selection, think of **questions** about his job to discuss with your classmates.

## Storm Chasing

In the evening shadows, a dusty black truck rolls along a dirt road. A rattlesnake feels the vibrations, lifts its head, and crawls off into the rocks. Giant saguaros sprout from the hillsides, arms held high. Somewhere in the distance, a cactus wren calls. But Warren Faidley isn't looking for rattlesnakes, saguaros, or cactus wrens.

He stares through the windshield, eyes glued to a cauliflower-shaped cloud. Behind the cloud, the setting sun turns the sky the color of a ripe peach. Warren has been watching this cloud, and hoping, for almost thirty minutes. The truck heads toward a hill with a clear view of the sky.

Suddenly, a jagged bolt of lightning shoots from the cloud.

"That's it," says Warren.

The truck speeds to the top of the hill and Warren jumps out, arms full of photographic equipment. His fingers fly as he unfolds tripods, mounts his cameras, and points them toward the cloud. Before the road dust has settled, the cameras are clicking.

For twenty minutes, lightning erupts from the cloud. Warren moves back and forth between the cameras — peering through viewfinders, changing film, switching lenses. Tomorrow, when the film is developed, Warren will know whether he had a successful night. In the meantime, he stands and watches, hoping his cameras are capturing the spectacular lights and colors of the evening thunderstorm.

## Watching the Sky

From earliest times, people have watched the sky. Astrologers used the positions of the stars to predict the future. Storytellers used rainbows, winds, the sun and moon to weave tales about the past. Farmers, shepherds, and sailors have all watched the clouds, wondering what tomorrow's weather will be like.

The spectacular storms that sometimes appear in the sky have helped to make weather one of the most mysterious of all natural forces. Myths and legends from around the world describe the fear and awe people felt as they watched lightning explode from a cloud or a tornado appear on the horizon, or listened to the howling winds of a hurricane.

For some people, storms have an irresistible call. These storm chasers head for the mountains, prairies, or seacoasts whenever weather conditions are right.

People chase storms for many reasons. Some storm chasers are scientists, who use video cameras, Doppler radar, and other instruments to learn about what happens in a tornado or a thunderstorm. Photographers follow storms to try to capture the beauty of wind and sky on film. Still other people chase storms in order to catch a brief glimpse of the awesome power of nature.

## Warren Faidley: Storm Chaser

Warren Faidley lives in Tucson, Arizona, with a one-toothed cat named Megamouth. He has been interested in storms for almost as long as he can remember.

Warren still remembers the tremendous thunderstorms he saw as a boy in Tucson. Tucked safely in bed, he watched the lightning and listened to the thunder. After the storms had passed, he fell asleep to the smell of wet creosote bushes outside his window.

Warren also had his first encounter with windstorms when he was a boy. Dust whirlwinds — spinning columns of wind that look like small tornadoes — often formed in the dusty vacant lots of his

neighborhood. One day Warren decided to put on safety goggles and a heavy jacket, and ride his bike into the center of a dust whirlwind. He'll never forget the excitement he felt when he rode through the wall of swirling winds:

"The inside was still and almost dust free. The light was orange, filtered, I guess, by the wall of dirt that was spinning around me. This rotating wall was filled with all kinds of debris, including tumbleweeds and newspaper pages. Looking up, I could see the very blue sky."

## Becoming a Storm Chaser

Warren hadn't always planned to be a storm chaser. He enjoyed studying science in school, and he loved being outside. But he didn't really become interested in taking pictures of the sky until he was working as a photographer for a newspaper.

Warren began by trying to take pictures of lightning from the balcony of his apartment. Although the pictures didn't turn out very well, he soon found himself spending more and more time taking pictures of lightning on summer evenings. Warren read everything he could about weather, and he began to dream about making a living as a weather photographer.

The storm that started Warren's career arrived in Tucson long after the end of the summer thunderstorm season. On that October afternoon, Warren glanced out the back window of his apartment and saw the sharp edges of the storm cloud. He grabbed his equipment, loaded his car, and drove toward a highway underpass on the east side of town.

When Warren reached the underpass, lightning was flashing just a few miles from it. Snatching up his equipment, he scrambled up the steep bank toward a dry ledge where he could set up his cameras. As he set up his tripods, a huge lightning bolt leaped from a cloud about a mile away, striking the ground next to an air traffic control tower.

But the storm was moving quickly. Suddenly, the air was filled with wind and rain, cutting off the view of any lightning to the east. Warren looked overhead and saw small lightning bolts leaping between the clouds. He knew there was about to be another large bolt — and he was pretty sure that the next big flash would be to the west, on the other side of the underpass.

Warren knew he had to get to the other side of the underpass right away. There wasn't enough room between the ledge and the top of the underpass to walk upright, so he scooted along on his knees. He grabbed hold of overhead rain gutters to keep his balance in the darkness.

Suddenly, Warren stuck his hand into a tangle of thick cobwebs. He quickly pulled his hand back. Then he pointed his penlight toward the ledge and gutters. The whole walkway was lined with webs, and rainwater washing through cracks in the concrete overhead was driving out hundreds of angry black widow spiders!

*Ka-boom!* A huge bolt of lightning flashed overhead. Warren knew the next bolt would strike somewhere on the west side of the underpass, and he knew he had one chance to capture it. Pushing ahead in the darkness, he used the legs of his tripod as a broom, sweeping aside the cobwebs and trying to brush off any spiders that landed on his clothes.

Near the end of the underpass, and clear of the spider webs, he decided to set up his cameras. The air was sizzling, and Warren could feel that something was about to happen. He slid a few feet down the rough concrete embankment, using his hands and the soles of his shoes as brakes. When the cameras were set up, Warren quickly wiped the raindrops off the lenses. Then he moved back up the slope to a safer place to wait.

Seconds later, he heard a loud crackling, and at the same time he saw a blinding flash of pure, white light. It sounded as if the sky were being torn apart. Next came the boom of a thunderclap roaring through the underpass. It had the energy of a bomb blast, and it lifted Warren's body right off the ground.

Warren lost his hold on the slope and began sliding downhill toward his cameras. He knew that he had to close the shutters on them without bumping the tripods — or the film with the lightning would blur and be ruined. Using his hands and feet and the seat of his pants as brakes on the concrete, Warren slid to a stop just above his tripods. Carefully, he reached up and closed the shutters on the cameras. Then he looked down at his palms and saw that they were covered with blood.

Warren stayed under the underpass long after the storm had passed, thinking about what had just happened. He knew the lightning strike had been close, because when he closed his eyes he could still see its jagged outline.

The next morning, when Warren had his film developed, he was astonished by what he saw. In the center of one of the rolls was an incredible image of a lightning bolt hitting a light pole in front of some metal storage tanks. The picture had been taken from less than four hundred feet. Warren knew that he was holding the closest good picture ever taken of a lightning bolt hitting an object.

The lightning picture changed Warren's life. It was analyzed and written about by Dr. E. Philip Krider, a lightning scientist at the University of

Arizona. *Life* magazine printed the picture, calling Warren a storm chaser. *National Geographic* called, wanting to film a special program about his work. The *National Enquirer* ran an article about Warren, calling him a "fearless spider-fighting photog." He even got a call from a Japanese game show that wanted to feature him on a TV program in which contestants try to guess a mystery guest's occupation. Warren began making enough money from selling his pictures that he could think about being a full-time storm chaser.

## What Happens to Warren's Photos After He Takes Them?

You've probably seen some of Warren's photographs. His pictures of lightning, tornadoes, and hurricanes have appeared in books, magazines, newspapers, advertisements, and scientific films. One of his lightning pictures was even used on stage passes for rock concerts by singer Paul McCartney.

Warren's business is called a stock photo agency. It's like a library of sky and storm photographs. People pay him for the use of his photos.

Suppose, for example, that you are a magazine editor. If you need a lightning photo for an article, you could go out and try to take a picture of lightning yourself. But you might have to wait a very long time for the right kind of storm, and unless you have lots of practice your lightning photograph probably won't be very good.

An easier way of getting a good lightning photo is to write to Warren. He'll send you samples, and you can select the one you like. Then, after sending Warren a fee, you can use the photo in your magazine.

When Warren began selling his lightning photos, he found that people were also asking for pictures of tornadoes and hurricanes. He didn't have photographs of these kinds of storms, so he read everything he could find about tornadoes and hurricanes — and he made plans to photograph them as well.

## Storm Seasons and Chasing

Storms are caused by certain kinds of weather patterns. The same patterns are found in the same areas year after year. For example, every spring, large areas of cool, dry air and warm, moist air collide over the central United States. If the winds are right, tornado-producing thunderstorms appear. That's why tornadoes in the south central United States are most likely to happen in spring. During July and August, shifting winds push moisture from the south up into the Arizona desert. When the cool, moist air is heated by the hot desert, storm clouds form. That's why Tucson has summer thunderstorms. In the late

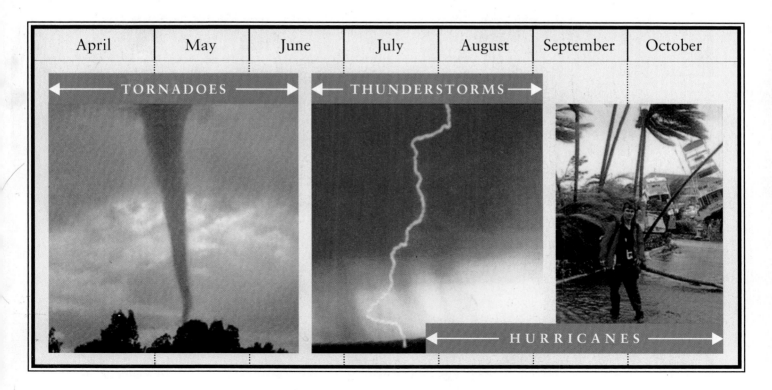

| April | May | June | July | August | September | October |

summer and early fall, when oceans in the northern Atlantic are warmest, tropical storms form off the west coast of Africa. A few of these turn into the hurricanes that sometimes batter the east and gulf coasts of North America.

Because Warren is a storm chaser, his life also follows these weather patterns. Each spring, Warren goes on the road, traveling through parts of the United States likely to be hit by tornadoes. During the summer, he stays near Tucson so he can photograph the thunderstorms that develop over the desert. In the late summer and fall, he keeps an eye on weather activity in the Atlantic Ocean, ready to fly to the east coast if a hurricane appears.

## Chasing Tornadoes

One of Warren's favorite tornado photos is a picture he took near Miami, Texas. Most of the sky is filled by the lower end of a huge storm cloud. A tornado hangs from the cloud, kicking up dust from the empty prairie, while the blue and yellow sky seems to go on forever.

In some ways, this wasn't a difficult picture for Warren to take. He's an experienced photographer. But before he could shoot this picture, he had to be in the right place at the right time — and that's what makes photographing tornadoes such hard work.

On a spring day, dozens of thunderstorms may develop over thousands of square miles in Texas, Oklahoma, and Kansas, but usually only a few will produce tornadoes. Since many tornadoes are on the ground only a few minutes, they will disappear before Warren can photograph them unless he is nearby. Other times, he will follow a promising storm, only to have it head off into an area where there are no roads. Tornadoes may be hidden by falling rain, making it impossible to take a picture of them. Still other storms may produce tornadoes at night, when it's too dark for Warren to take pictures and too dangerous for him to be out chasing because he can't see what's happening.

A successful tornado photographer needs patience, a good understanding of weather, up-to-the-minute forecasts, and lots of experience watching the sky. Even so, days, weeks, or even whole years can go by without a chance to see a tornado.

Every spring, Warren makes a trip to an area called Tornado Alley. This area stretches from northern Texas up into Oklahoma, Kansas, and Missouri. Warren and his tornado chase partner, Tom Willett, spend about six weeks tracking down giant storms and searching for tornadoes.

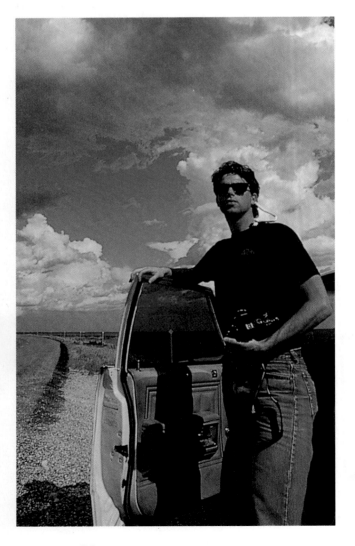

Getting ready to go tornado chasing takes lots of time and work. Warren checks all his cameras and buys plenty of film. He makes sure he has up-to-date copies of road maps for all the states he'll be traveling through. He arranges for friends to take care of Megamouth.

Finally, toward the end of April, Warren and Tom stow all their equipment in Shadow Chaser, Warren's black four-wheel-drive vehicle. Warren designed Shadow Chaser to help him find tornadoes and chase them safely. It is packed with electronic equipment, including radios, radio scanners, and a weather center that can take many different kinds of measurements. Shadow Chaser has emergency flashing lights, a long-range cellular phone, and special cabinets for storing equipment. It even has a front-mounted video camera that can make videotapes through the windshield.

As Warren and Tom drive toward Tornado Alley, their hopes are high. They know that they'll cover thousands of miles before returning to Tucson. They know they'll chase storms that never produce tornadoes and they'll probably hear about nearby tornadoes they can't get to in time. But with hard work, careful study of weather data, and a little luck, sometimes they'll have a day like the one they had on May 5, 1993.

## Tornado Chase Diary: May 5, 1993

Warren keeps a diary, in which he writes about his storm chases. Here are some of the things that happened on May 5, 1993, a remarkable day.

### Amarillo, Texas — Morning

I awaken in a motel in Tornado Alley. As I walk to the window to peek out the drapes, I remember that last night's weather forecast showed that this might be a good chase day. Tom climbs out of bed and turns on The Weather Channel.

Later in the morning, Tom and I get the Shadow Chaser ready for the day. I test the radios, check under the hood, make sure the tires are inflated and the lights and wipers are working. We clean, pack, and return each piece of equipment to its usual place. During a chase, there isn't time to look around for a roll of film or lens for a camera.

Finally, we check out of the motel and head for a nearby restaurant for breakfast. Then we drive into town to fill the gas tank and get a few supplies.

### National Weather Service Office — Early Afternoon

We arrive at the Amarillo office of the National Weather Service. Here I get an update on local weather conditions, as well as a chance to see a satellite picture

of the area. I use current weather information to draw a map of where today's thunderstorms are likely to form. The reports are saying that there is a moderate chance of severe weather in our area, and some of the thunderstorms will probably produce tornadoes. Since the storms aren't expected to develop until later in the afternoon, we take some time off and drive to a nearby garage to have the oil changed in Shadow Chaser.

A couple hours later, we're back at the National Weather Service office to make our final chase decisions. It's beginning to look like the area north of town is our best bet. We pull out the highway maps and start looking at possible routes.

As we leave town, I call a friend and fellow chaser who gives weather reports for a local TV station. He confirms that severe storm clouds are building right where we're headed. He also says that a news team from his station is already headed there.

## Near Panhandle, Texas — Late Afternoon

The sky is hazy, but in the distance we can see the tops of anvil-shaped storm clouds. We stop the truck to pick up the TV report. My forecaster friend is on. He's pointing to an area on his map about fifty miles north of our location. "It looks like we're going to have some severe storms in this area!" he says. We get back into the truck and drive north.

## Near Gruver, Texas — Early Evening

The overcast skies clear enough to show a giant thunderstorm just ahead. Then our radio scanner locks onto a message from the TV crew's chase unit. "There's a large funnel cloud coming from this storm," says the message. While the crew describes its location, I look at the map. "They're only eight miles from here," I tell Tom. "Let's go and find it!"

As we approach Gruver, we see the red TV van parked on the side of the road. A cameraman is pointing his camera at a huge, gray-white funnel cloud hanging from the base of a dark cloud. As Tom parks the truck, I use the radio to call in a weather report to the National Weather Service station in Amarillo. The funnel cloud pulls back up into the storm.

We head north, following the storm. As we drive, watching the back of the storm, we can see the clouds darkening and beginning to rotate. The white clouds at the top of the storm take on the shape of a giant mushroom. I'm excited, but I'm worried too. I know that anyone in the path of this storm is in terrible danger.

We follow the storm down the highway. Gradually, it turns and heads back toward the road. We pull over and wait for the storm to cross. While we're waiting, a large semi truck pulls up beside us. The driver opens his window and leans out.

"Hey, are you guys tornado chasers? Is that a tornado forming? Is it safe for me to drive under it?"

"We're not sure if it's going to turn into a tornado, but I'd wait here and let it pass," I answer.

We all watch as the swirling mass crosses the highway. A small funnel cloud reaches down from the storm cloud — and then quickly disappears. I reach for the microphone and call Amarillo:

"This is Warren. I'm about eight miles north of Gruver, just west of Highway 207. Tom and I are looking at a large cloud mass that is organizing and rotating."

"Roger, Warren," replies the spotter coordinator. "We're watching the same area on radar. Thanks."

Now we begin to worry about losing the storm. There aren't very many roads in this area, and most of them run north–south or east–west. Since most storms don't continue for long in these directions, following a storm is a little like playing a huge game of chess. Tom loads his cameras back into the truck while I check the road map.

We make our way along a tangle of unmarked farm roads a few miles from the Oklahoma border. Since the storm is on our west side, and it's moving northeast, we can safely stay quite close to the updraft without getting in the direct path of a tornado.

### Near the Oklahoma/Texas Border — Evening

We keep an eye on the swirling clouds as we drive along. Suddenly, from the center of the clouds, a large white funnel appears.

"Look, Tom! Another tornado!" I exclaim. "That thing is less than a mile away!"

I reach for the microphone and call in another report. The funnel cloud begins to stretch. Soon it looks like the trunk of a huge elephant, wiggling over the green fields below. Then it touches down, officially becoming a tornado. When the funnel touches the ground, wispy little vortices appear around the main cloud of wind. As these mini-tornadoes spin, they kick up dust of their

own. I grab the microphone and send another message to the spotter coordinator:

"We're about three or four miles south of the Texas/Oklahoma state line," I explain. "And we're looking at a large, multivortex tornado on the ground."

Just inside the Oklahoma state line, the road turns slightly toward the northwest. The tornado begins to cross the road a little ahead of us. We stop to try and get some pictures, but the light isn't good. It's hard to see the tornado clearly against the background of the cloud. The air is hazy, and another storm to the west is blocking the sunlight.

"We've got a great tornado here," I say to Tom, "but the light is terrible." We load our gear back into the truck and roll down a bumpy dirt road, looking for better light, while the tornado swirls along beside us.

As Tom drives, he keeps glancing at the tornado. Suddenly he yells, "Warren! There's another tornado forming!" I peer through the window and see a debris cloud forming, sucking up soil from a field.

"Wow," Tom says. "Look what it's doing to that fence!" We watch as it rips a section of barbed-wire fence out of the ground and scatters it across the field. The small area of spinning wind, with no visible funnel cloud above, tears across the fields.

"Slow down, Tom," I say. "I can't see the funnel cloud connected to that thing — and we sure don't want to get hit by it." A few seconds later, the debris cloud disappears.

We follow a maze of unmarked dirt roads until we reach a dead end. As we turn around and drive back toward the highway, we watch as the edges of the storm cloud wrap around the tornado, hiding it from sight. Many sightings of "our" tornado, as well as others in the area, are being reported over the radio. I'm happy to hear that so far the tornadoes haven't hit any populated areas.

### East of Guymon, Oklahoma — Evening

It's about 7:30 p.m. when we pull back onto the highway. As we head east, we see a long, thin tornado crossing the road a few miles ahead.

"I bet that's our tornado," I tell Tom. "It looks like it's weakening. We've got to shoot it now!" When Tom stops, I jump out the door, set my camera on the hood to steady it, and go through another roll of film. As we watch, the funnel pulls back up into the dark clouds.

### West of Hooker, Oklahoma — Evening

Traveling along the highway, we're joined again by the crew from the TV

station. Down the road, I see a huge wedge-shaped tornado on the ground.

"Stop!" I yell to Tom. Tom hits the brakes and we stare through the windshield. The tornado looks like it's about seven or eight miles from us, moving away, although the fading light makes it hard to be sure. As we watch, the funnel slows down, and then it disappears. We continue on and I spot another tornado. This one looks like a long stovepipe.

"This is incredible," I say to Tom. "We've got two large thunderstorms here, and they're dropping tornadoes everywhere!"

The stovepipe tornado swirls into the clouds before we can get close enough for pictures. As we watch it disappear, I realize that it's getting too dark for any more photos. I know the storms are still active, and I'm worried that the fading light could hide any newly forming tornadoes. Chasing any more tornadoes today would be too dangerous.

### Near the Oklahoma/Kansas Border — Evening

As the last of the light disappears, we see two more tornadoes in the distance. One is headed north, rolling into Kansas. As we drive back to Amarillo, we listen to news reports on the radio. "With as many tornadoes as we have had on the ground tonight," says a reporter, "it's a miracle that none of them have hit a town. We do have at least one report of a farm being destroyed, with no injuries so far. But beyond that, we have been extremely fortunate."

### Amarillo, Texas — Night

It's 11:00 p.m. by the time we finally pull back into the motel parking lot. As Tom and I unload Shadow Chaser, we're still shaking our heads about what we've seen. The tornadoes we saw caused some damage, but there have been no reports of any deaths or injuries. That makes it easier to celebrate our seven-tornado day.

75

# Responding

## Think About the Selection

**1.** Think about Warren Faidley's decision to ride his bike into a whirlwind. What does this action tell you about him?

**2.** Do you think Warren would face any danger in order to get a spectacular storm shot? Use facts from the selection to support your answer.

**3.** How did the section headings of *Eye of the Storm* help you understand the selection? How did the calendar on page 65 help you understand Warren's job?

**4.** On page 62, the author writes, "The air was sizzling" before Warren took his famous underpass photograph. What do you think he means?

**5.** Would you want to accompany Warren on a storm chase? Why or why not? If so, which kind of storm would you want to see up close, and why?

**6.** Warren's interest in storms led to his career as a weather photographer. What interests do you have that might lead to a career?

**7. Connecting/Comparing** Compare Warren's risk from tornadoes and lightning with Jonathan's risk in *Earthquake Terror*. How are their situations alike and different?

## Write a Job Description

Think about what a storm chaser does. Then write a job description for a storm chaser. Include the character traits and skills a storm chaser should have. Note any special equipment a storm chaser should be able to use.

**Tips**

- List the job requirements in two categories: traits and skills.
- In the skills category, include special equipment.

## Math

# Estimate Mileage

Estimate the number of miles Warren Faidley drove from his home to where he began his tornado chase diary for May 5, 1993. Use the map on page 55, a ruler, and this scale — one inch equals 300 miles.

## Viewing

# Compare Photographs

Choose two photographs from the selection and write a caption that compares and contrasts them. Choose two lightning photographs, two tornado photographs, or one of each kind. Tell about both the details and the mood of each photograph.

# Take an Online Poll

Have you ever seen a lightning strike or a tornado? What kind of storm have you been in? Do you enjoy books about the weather? Take our online poll and let us know. Visit Education Place. **www.eduplace.com/kids**

Genre

**Biography**

**Skill: How to Read a Sequence Chart**

❶ Read the **title** of the sequence chart. It tells what **process** is being shown.

❷ Read the **steps** in the process by following the **arrows** from top to bottom or left to right.

❸ Look for **order words**, such as *next, then, resulting,* and *now.*

# STORM WARNING

**Mishelle Michaels was formerly a weather forecaster at 7 News in Boston. When TV viewers tuned in, they saw the result of a long day of data collection and weather analysis — the job of the meteorologist.**

Forecasters like Mishelle rely on information collected at thousands of points around the world. These "eyes" and "ears" that scout the weather include radar, satellites, surface sites, and weather balloons.

Mishelle Michaels, meteorologist, analyzes computer models to prepare for her evening broadcast.

# Collecting the **Data**

Weather satellites 22,000 miles up take photographs of clouds to show the movement of weather systems.

Surface observing sites report the current weather conditions every hour of every day of every year.

Through a network of NEXRAD (Next Generation Radar) stations, radar images display the motion and intensity of rain or snow.

Weather balloons take measurements of the atmosphere from ground level to thousands of feet above the earth.

The National Weather Service's supercomputer then processes this information, making sixteen billion calculations per second.

The resulting charts and weather images are made available to meteorologists around the United States to help them create their forecasts.

# Analyzing the Weather

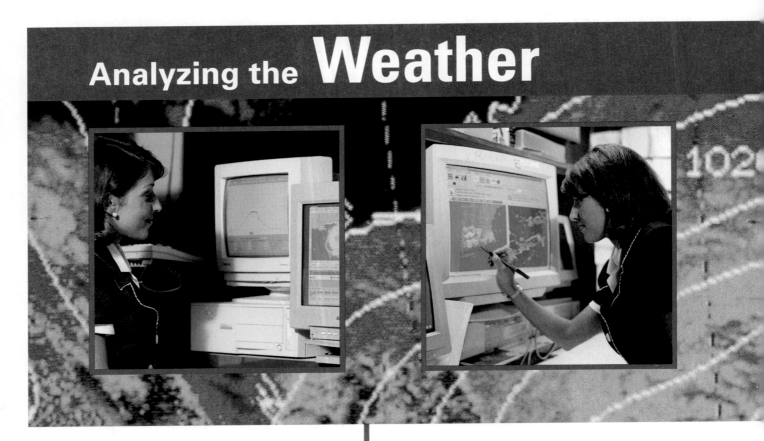

## Reviewing Conditions

To begin her forecast, Mishelle checks the current conditions — temperatures, winds, and weather patterns — for the city of Boston, its surrounding communities, and much of New England.

## Observing Radar Images

Enhanced Doppler radar provides Mishelle with images of thunderstorms moving toward Boston from the west. Next Generation Radar can detect dangerous shifts in wind direction that may result in tornadoes.

Meteorologists analyze the many charts and images that the National Weather Service provides. But that is only part of the studying and interpreting they have to do before they can create a forecast. The data gathered from the radar and satellites requires the explaining abilities of the meteorologist so that it makes sense to the rest of us.

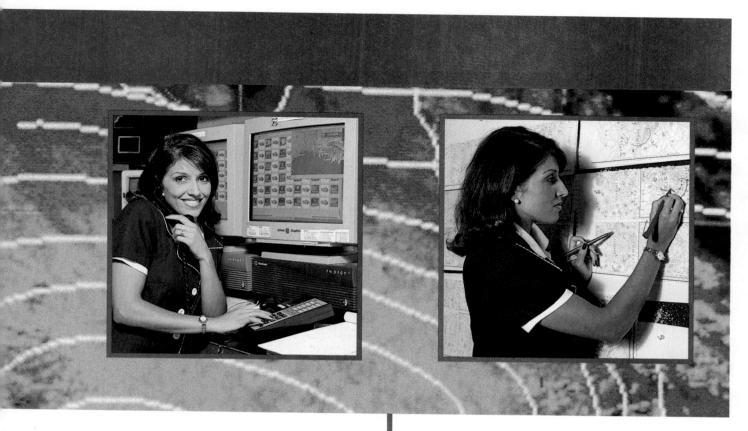

## Hearing from Weather Watchers

Local volunteers of all ages phone in detailed weather reports from their communities. These observations are often invaluable in helping Mishelle put together the pieces of the forecasting puzzle.

## Analyzing Computer Models

By analyzing weather charts and maps created by the National Weather Service from computer models, Mishelle develops a four- to five-day forecast for Greater Boston and New England. She relies on her education and experience to accurately predict how the atmosphere will change.

### Career File

# Meteorologist

Are you interested in following the weather professionally? You'll need a four-year college degree in Meteorology or Atmospheric Science. It also helps if you enjoy . . .

- watching clouds and chasing storms (from a safe distance)
- the challenge of problem-solving
- communicating your knowledge with others

Meanwhile, contact your local television station about becoming a volunteer weather observer.

*Volcanoes*

**Genre** Nonfiction

### Key Vocabulary

cinders
crater
crust
lava
molten

**Vocabulary Reader**

*e* **Glossary**

# The World of Volcanoes

From Hawaii to the Pacific Northwest, from Guatemala to Iceland, Seymour Simon's *Volcanoes* will take you on a world tour. You'll see more than mountain peaks. The heart of the story is about the part of the earth that's deep underground, where the heat turns the earth's **crust** into **molten** rock.

**Mauna Loa**
Molten rock erupts as flowing **lava** from Hawaii's Mauna Loa.

**Mount St. Helens**
One of many volcanoes in the Pacific Northwest, Mount St. Helens cooled down to form a hard lava dome in its **crater** .

**Surtsey**
An undersea volcano near Iceland created a new island, Surtsey.

**Fuego and Acatenango**
These volcanoes in Guatemala are built of **cinders** and ash.

VOLCANOES

SEYMOUR SIMON

In this selection, Seymour Simon gives you lots of information about volcanoes and how they form. As you read, **monitor** your understanding, and reread or use the photos and the map to **clarify**.

Throughout history, people have told stories about volcanoes. The early Romans believed in Vulcan, their god of fire. They thought that Vulcan worked at a hot forge, striking sparks as he made swords and armor for the other gods. It is from the Roman god Vulcan that we get the word *volcano*.

The early Hawaiians told legends of the wanderings of Pele, their goddess of fire. Pele was chased from her homes by her sister Namaka, goddess of the sea. Pele moved constantly from one Hawaiian island to another. Finally, Pele settled in a mountain called Kilauea, on the big island of Hawaii. Even though the islanders tried to please Pele, she burst forth every few years. Kilauea is still an active volcano.

In early times, no one knew how volcanoes formed or why they spouted fire. In modern times, scientists began to study volcanoes. They still don't know all the answers, but they know much about how a volcano works.

Our planet is made up of many layers of rock. The top layers of solid rock are called the crust. Deep beneath the crust, it is so hot that some rock melts. The melted, or molten, rock is called magma.

Volcanoes are formed by cracks or holes that poke through the earth's crust. Magma pushes its way up through the cracks. This is called a volcanic eruption. When magma pours forth on the surface it is called lava. In the above photograph of an eruption, you can see great fountains of boiling lava forming fiery rivers and lakes. As lava cools, it hardens to form rock.

A volcano can be two things: a hole in the ground that lava comes through, or a hill or mountain formed by the lava. Mount Rainier in the state of Washington is a volcano even though it has not erupted since 1882.

Not far from Mount Rainier (top, right) is Mount St. Helens (bottom, left). Native Americans and early settlers in the Northwest had seen Mount St. Helens puff out some ashes, steam, and lava in the mid-1800s. Yet for more than a century, the mountain seemed quiet and peaceful.

In March 1980 Mount St. Helens awakened from its long sleep. First there were a few small earthquakes that shook the mountain. Then on March 27 Mount St. Helens began to spout ashes and steam. Each day brought further quakes, until by mid-May more than ten thousand small quakes had been recorded. The mountain began to swell up and crack.

Sunday May 18 dawned bright and clear. The mountain seemed much the same as it had been for the past month. Suddenly, at 8:32 A.M., Mount St. Helens erupted with incredible force. The energy released in the eruption was equal to ten million tons of dynamite.

The eruption of Mount St. Helens was the most destructive in the history of the United States. Sixty people lost their lives as hot gases, rocks, and ashes covered an area of two hundred thirty square miles. Hundreds of houses and cabins were destroyed, leaving many people homeless. Miles of highways, roads, and railways were badly damaged. The force of the eruption was so great that entire forests were blown down like rows of matchsticks.

Compare the way Mount St. Helens looked before and after the eruption. The entire top of the mountain was blown away. In its place is a huge volcanic crater. In 1982 the mountain and the area around it were dedicated as the Mount St. Helens National Volcanic Monument. Visitor centers allow people to view the volcano's astonishing power.

**V**olcanoes don't just happen anyplace. The earth's crust is broken into huge sections like a giant cracked eggshell. The pieces of the crust are called plates. The United States, Canada, and Mexico and part of the North Atlantic Ocean are all on the North American plate. Almost all the volcanoes in the world erupt in places where two plates meet.

Down the middle of the North Atlantic Ocean, two plates are slowly moving apart. Hot magma pushes up between them. A chain of underwater volcanoes runs along the line where the two plates meet. Some of the underwater volcanoes have grown so high that they stick up from the ocean floor to make islands.

Iceland is a volcanic island in the North Atlantic. In 1963, an area of the sea near Iceland began to smoke. An undersea volcano was exploding and a new island was being formed. The island was named Surtsey, after the ancient Norse god of fire.

Ten years after the explosion that formed Surtsey, another volcano erupted near Iceland. It was off the south coast of Iceland on the island of Heimaey. Within six hours of the eruption, more than 5,000 people were taken off the island to safety. After two months, hundreds of buildings had burned down and dozens more had been buried in the advancing lava. Then the volcano stopped erupting. After a year's time, the people of Heimaey came back to reclaim their island with its new 735-foot volcano.

Most volcanoes and earthquakes are along the edges of the large Pacific plate. There are so many that the shoreline of the Pacific Ocean is called the "Ring of Fire." But a few volcanoes are not on the edge of a plate. The volcanoes in the Hawaiian Islands are in the middle of the Pacific plate.

A million years ago, magma pushed up through cracks in the Pacific plate. Over the years, eruption followed eruption. Little by little, thin layers of lava hardened, one atop another. Thousands of eruptions were needed to build mountains high enough to reach from the deep sea bottom and appear as islands.

The largest Hawaiian volcano is Mauna Loa. It is seventy miles long and rises thirty thousand feet from the ocean floor. It is still growing. Every few years, Mauna Loa erupts again.

Hawaiian volcano lava usually bubbles out quietly to form rivers or lakes, or spouts a few hundred feet in the air in a fiery fountain. Hawaiian volcanoes erupt much more gently than did Surtsey or Mount St. Helens. Only rarely does a Hawaiian volcano throw out rock and high clouds of ash.

Steam clouds billow as a flow of hot lava enters the sea. Hawaii is constantly changing as eruptions add hundreds of acres of new land to the islands. In other parts of the shoreline, old lava flows are quickly weathered by the waves into rocks and black sand.

Hawaiian lava is thin and flows quickly. In some lava rivers, speeds as high as thirty-five miles per hour have been measured. In an eruption in 1986, a number of houses were threatened by the quick-moving lava. Fire fighters sprayed water on the lava to slow down its advance.

When lava cools and hardens, it forms volcanic rocks. The kinds of rocks formed are clues to the kind of eruption. The two main kinds have Hawaiian names. Thick, slow-moving lava called *aa* (AH-ah) hardens into a rough tangle of sharp rocks. Thin, hot, quick-moving lava called *pahoehoe* (pah-HO-ee-ho-ee) forms a smooth, billowy surface.

Earth scientists have divided volcanoes into four groups. Shield volcanoes, such as Mauna Loa and Kilauea, have broad, gentle slopes shaped like an ancient warrior's shield.

Cinder cone volcanoes look like upside-down ice cream cones. They erupt explosively, blowing out burning ashes and cinders. The ashes and cinders build up to form the cone shape. The cinder cone volcano to the near left erupted in Guatemala, Central America, in 1984. The cinder cone volcanoes in the background are still smoking from earlier eruptions.

Most of the volcanoes in the world are composite or strato-volcanoes. Strato-volcanoes are formed by the lava, cinders, and ashes of an eruption. During an eruption, ashes and cinders fall to the ground. The eruption quiets down and lava slowly flows out, covering the layer of ashes and cinders. Further eruptions add more layers of ashes and cinders, followed by more layers of lava. Mount Shasta (above) in California and Mount Hood in Oregon are strato-volcanoes. They are still active even though they have not erupted for many years.

The fourth kind of volcano is called a dome volcano. Dome volcanoes have thick, slow-moving lava that forms a steep-sided dome shape. After an eruption, the volcano may be plugged with hardened lava. The plug prevents the gases from escaping, like a cork in a bottle of soda water. As the pressure builds up, the volcano blows its top, as Mount St. Helens did. Lassen Peak in California is a dome volcano that erupted violently in 1915. You can see the huge chunks of volcanic rock near the summit.

round the world there are many very old volcanoes that no longer erupt. These dead volcanoes are called extinct. Crater Lake in Oregon is an extinct volcano. Almost seven thousand years ago, Mount Mazama in Oregon erupted, sending out a thick blanket of ashes that covered the ground for miles around. Then the entire top of the volcano collapsed. A huge crater, called a caldera, formed and was later filled with water. Crater Lake reaches a depth of two thousand feet, the deepest lake in North America.

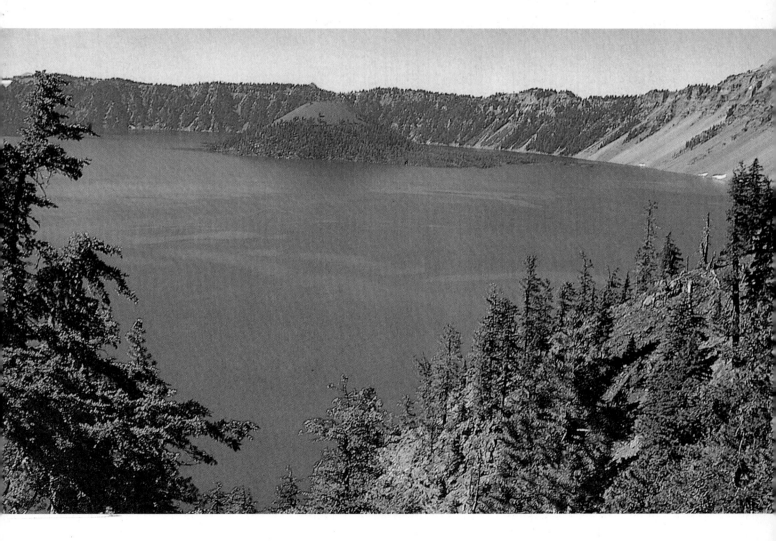

After a volcano erupts, everything is buried under lava or ashes. Plants and animals are nowhere to be found. But in a few short months, life renews itself. Plants grow in the cracks between the rocks. Insects and other animals return. Volcanoes do not just destroy. They bring new mountains, new islands, and new soil to the land. Many good things can come from the fiery explosions of volcanoes.

# Meet the AUTHOR

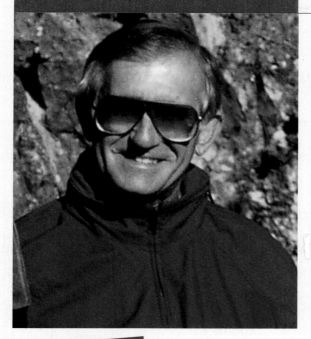

# Seymour Simon

"**M**any of the books I write are really in the nature of guidebooks to unknown territories. Each territory has to be discovered again by children venturing into it for the first time."

"**I**'m always working on several books at the same time. I may be writing a book and researching another book and writing for information about a third book and thinking about plans for still a fourth book."

## FACT FILE

- Graduated from the Bronx High School of Science
- President of the Junior Astronomy Club at New York's Museum of Natural History
- Taught science and creative writing in New York City public schools, 1955–1979
- First published work: a magazine article about the moon
- Author of more than two hundred books in thirty years

**Simon's range of interests shows in his titles, such as:** *Our Solar System, The Universe, Tornadoes, Sharks, Gorillas, Out of Sight: Pictures of Hidden Worlds, The Paper Airplane Book,* and the *Einstein Anderson, Science Detective* series.

 Internet

For more information about Seymour Simon, visit Education Place.

**www.eduplace.com/kids**

VOLCANOES

# Think About the Selection

1. Why do you think people have used folktales to explain volcanoes?

2. Find examples in the selection of both the helpful and harmful things that volcanoes do.

3. Why do you think earthquakes often happen just before volcanoes?

4. Of the different volcanoes mentioned in the selection, which one impressed you the most? Why?

5. Which word best describes a volcano for you: *beautiful, scary, exciting, ugly,* or some other word? Explain why.

6. What do you think would be the best and worst things about studying volcanoes for a living?

7. **Connecting/Comparing** Compare the conditions that cause a volcanic eruption with those that cause a tornado. Think about how, where, and when they happen, and how much warning people have.

**Explaining**

# Write a Travel Brochure

Use information from the selection to create a travel brochure for a tour of the world's volcanoes. Explain where the tour will go and what volcanoes you will see.

## Tips

- Fold a sheet of paper into three panels.
- Describe the tour on the inside panels and illustrate the outside panels.
- Check your spelling and capitalize all proper nouns.

## Science

# Create a Poster

Use information from Seymour Simon's *Volcanoes* to make a poster. You might show how magma rises to erupt as lava, or show the four different kinds of volcanoes.

## Social Studies

# Create a Fact File

With classmates, create a volcano fact file. Using the information in *Volcanoes*, each person chooses a country or state, such as Iceland or Hawaii, and lists the volcanoes for that place, along with a brief description of the volcanoes and a small map.

**Bonus:** Find information about the volcanoes of a country not mentioned in the selection, such as Italy or Japan. Add a fact file about that place.

### Internet

# Go on a Web Field Trip

Connect to Education Place and explore a weather center, science museum, and other places to observe nature's fury. **www.eduplace.com/kids**

**Genre**

### Folktales

**Skill: How to Read a Folktale**

❶ Notice that the **characters** are simple — good or bad, wise or foolish.

❷ Notice that the **action** moves quickly, in brief episodes.

❸ Look for information about the **country** the folktale comes from.

# THE PRINCESS AND

A Mexican Folktale

*Not far from Mexico City, two mountains, only five miles apart, rise more than 17,000 feet into the sky. One is an inactive volcano, Ixtaccihuatl (ees-tah-SEE-wah-tul). Its outline is said to resemble that of a sleeping woman. The other is Popocatépetl (poh-puh-CAT-uh-pet-ul), an active volcano that regularly sends up clouds of smoke and ash. This ancient Mexican folktale tells the story of how the two companion volcanoes came to be.*

**M**any centuries ago, there was an Aztec emperor who had a good and beautiful daughter named Ixtaccihuatl.

One day the emperor received word that his enemies were preparing to attack his lands. He called his brave young warriors to the

# THE WARRIOR

palace and said, "Since I am old, I can no longer lead you in battle. Name the bravest warrior among you to serve as the chief of our Aztec army. If he can defeat the enemy and establish peace in the land, I will give him my throne and my daughter's hand in marriage."

"Popo is the bravest, strongest warrior. He should be our chief!" shouted all the warriors but one.

"Very well. Popocatépetl, you are the chief," said the emperor. "May the gods lead you to victory."

One among the warriors was very jealous of Popocatépetl. This warrior thought that he himself should be the chief. But he didn't say a word to anyone about his thoughts.

It was a great secret that Popocatépetl and the emperor's daughter had fallen in love. Before leaving for battle, the young chief went to the garden to say good-bye to his beloved princess.

"I will soon be back, my love," said the youth to the princess. "Then we will be married."

With these words, Popocatépetl left for a long and brutal war. No one fought as bravely as the young Aztec chief.

At last the Aztec warriors defeated their enemies and prepared to return to the capital. The jealous warrior was the first to leave. He ran so swiftly that he reached home two days before the others. Immediately he announced that Popocatépetl had been killed and that he himself had been the hero of the final battle. Thus he claimed the right to be the next emperor and the husband of the princess.

The poor princess! She felt she would die of sadness.

The emperor, too, was saddened by Popo's death, for he believed the warrior's story.

The next day at the palace, the people prepared a great celebration to honor the wedding of the princess and the jealous warrior. Suddenly, the princess cried out, "Oh, my poor Popocatépetl!" And she fell dead to the floor.

At that moment, the Aztec warriors entered the palace. Popocatépetl ran to the emperor and announced, "We have returned. Now the princess and I can get married."

There was a great silence. Everyone turned to look at the princess.

At the sight of his beloved, the youth ran to her side and began to cry. He took her in his arms, saying, "My precious, I will be with you until the end of time."

Then the brave chief carried her body to the highest mountains. He laid her gently in a bed of beautiful flowers and sat down beside her.

Days passed. Finally, one of the good gods transformed the warrior and the princess into two volcanoes. Ixy remains quiet. But from time to time, Popo trembles and tears of fire flow from his heart. Then all of Mexico knows that Popo is crying for his beloved princess.

# Check Your Progress

In this theme you have read about nature's most powerful displays, from earthquakes to lightning to volcanoes. Now read and compare two new examples of nature's fury and practice your test-taking skills.

Start by looking back at the letter from Warren Faidley on pages 23–24 of your book. Think about how his account of his experiences during Hurricane Andrew gets you ready for looking at nature in a new way.

As you read the next two selections about a tornado and a blizzard, compare the way they show people coping with the power of nature.

# Read and Compare

**Realistic Fiction**

In a small town, three boys are at home alone during a monster tornado.

Try these strategies:
Question
Evaluate

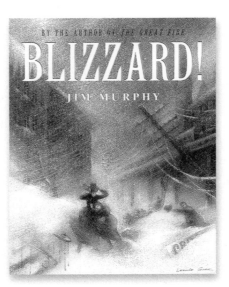

**Nonfiction**

Read about the terrible Blizzard of 1888 in New York City.

Try these strategies:
Summarize
Monitor and Clarify

**Strategies in Action**  *Make use of all your reading strategies as you read the selections.*

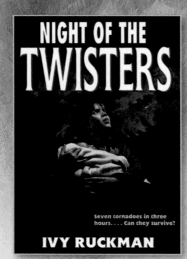

Seven tornadoes in three
hours.... Can they survive?

# NIGHT OF THE TWISTERS

BY IVY RUCKMAN, ILLUSTRATED BY MIKE ADAMS

**A siren has been sounding a tornado alert for the town of Grand Island, Nebraska. Dan Hatch's parents are away, leaving Dan and his friend Arthur alone in the house with Dan's baby brother, Ryan. While Arthur listens to the radio, Dan checks on Ryan. Maybe the storm will blow over, he thinks as he leaves Ryan's room.**

Quietly, I closed the door behind me.

That's when the lights started flickering.

In the hallway, I practically had a head-on with Arthur, who was coming at me real fast. The look on his face scared me.

"There's no . . . there's no . . ."

"What?"

"There's no radio reception anymore. It just went dead! This guy. . . . He kept saying, 'Tornado alert, tornado alert!' Then it went dead."

We rushed back to the living room. The TV was flashing these big letters that filled the entire screen: CD . . . CD . . . CD . . .

"What's it mean?" Arthur cried.

"Civil Defense Emergency!" I whirled around. "I'm getting Ryan!"

The lights flickered again.

At the same time we heard these really strange sounds that stopped us in our tracks. They were coming from the bathroom and the kitchen. Sucking sounds. The drains were sucking! I felt this awful pulling in my ears, too, as if there were vacuums on both sides of my head.

"I've got to go home!" Arthur cried all of a sudden, bolting for the door.

I ran after him. "You're not — you can't!" I grabbed the back of his T-shirt, hauled him around, and pushed him toward the stairs. "Get down there. I have to get Ryan! Now go!"

I don't know what I'd have done if he hadn't minded me. We were catching the fear from each other, and even though the siren was screaming on and off again, so I didn't know what it was telling us, I knew we had to take cover fast.

The lights went out for good just before I reached Ryan's room.

I smashed face first into Ryan's butterfly mobile. That's how I knew I was at the crib. I felt for him, got my hands under his nightshirt and diaper, rolled him over. I lifted him, but we didn't get far. He was caught in the mobile, his arm or his head ... I couldn't see ... I couldn't get him loose....

"Mom!" I yelled, though I knew she wasn't there.

I tried to lay him down again, but he was so tangled, part of him was still up in the air. He started to cry.

"Wait, Ryan, I'll get you out!" But I couldn't.

Finally, holding him with my left arm, I climbed onto the side of the crib. My right hand followed the string up the mobile, way up to the hook. I yanked it loose. The whole thing came crashing down on top of us as I jumped backward off the crib.

The plastic butterfly poking me was poking Ryan, too, but I didn't care. The tornado was close, and I knew it. Both my ears had popped, and I had this crazy fear that those drains, sucking like monsters now, would get us if the storm didn't.

Arthur was at the bottom of the stairs, waiting. He'd found the flashlight! I jumped the last half-flight to the floor.

"Hurry!" I screamed. I swung into the doorway of the bathroom, with Arthur right behind me. We crouched under the towel rack.

"Shine it here, on Ryan," I gasped. "He's caught in this thing." By now Ryan was kicking and screaming, and his eyes were big in the light.

106E

Once we got the mess of strings free of Ryan's sweaty nightshirt, Arthur kicked the mobile against the wall by the toilet.

"I have to go home!" he cried. "They won't go to the basement. Mama never does."

The beam of light bounced around the blackness of the bathroom as Arthur scrambled to his feet, but I grabbed and held on to him.

"You can't go!  It's here!  Can't you feel it?"

The siren quit again as I pulled him back down and threw my leg over him. The flashlight clattered to the floor and rolled away from us.

We heard it next. The lull. The deadliest quiet ever, one that makes you think you might explode. The heat in that room built until I couldn't get my breath.

Then I began to hear noises. A chair scraping across the kitchen floor upstairs.

"Your mom's back!" Arthur said, pushing at my leg.

I knew it wasn't my mother moving the chair.

The noises got worse.  It seemed as if every piece of furniture was moving around up there . . . big, heavy things, smashing into each other.

A window popped.

Crash! Another.

Glass, shattering — everywhere — right next to us in the laundry room.

I pulled a towel down over Ryan and held him tight. If he was still crying, I didn't know it because I was feeling the sucking this time. It was like something trying to lift my body right up off the floor.

Arthur felt it, too. "We're going to die!"

Ten seconds more and that howling, shrieking tornado was upon us.

"The blanket!" I screamed at Arthur's ear.

He pulled it down from the countertop and we covered ourselves, our hands shaking wildly. I wasn't worrying about my mom then or my dad or Mrs. Smiley. Just us. Ryan and Arthur and me, huddled together there on the floor.

The roaring had started somewhere to the east, then came bearing down on us like a hundred freight trains. Only that twister didn't move on. It stationed itself right overhead, making the loudest noise I'd ever heard, whining worse than any jet. There was a tremendous crack, and I felt the wall shudder behind us. I knew then our house was being ripped apart. Suddenly chunks of ceiling were falling on our heads.

We'll be buried! was all I could think.

At that moment, as plain as anything above that deafening roar, I heard my dad's voice: The shower's the safest place.

I didn't question hearing it. Holding Ryan against me with one arm, I began crawling toward the shower stall. I reached back and yanked at Arthur's shirt. Somehow we got inside with the blanket. Another explosion, and the glass shower door shattered all over the bathroom floor.

We pulled the blanket over our heads. I could feel Ryan's heart beating through his undershirt against mine. Outside those places where our bodies touched, there was nothing but terror as the roar of that tornado went on and on. I thought the world was coming to an end, had come to an end, and so would we, any minute.

Then I felt Ryan's fat fingers close around one of mine. He pulled my hand to his mouth and started sucking on my finger. It made me cry. The tears ran down my cheeks and onto his head. With the whole world blowing to pieces around us, Ryan took my hand and made me feel better.

Afterward, neither Arthur nor I was able to say how long we huddled there in the basement shower.

"A tornado's forward speed is generally thirty to fifty miles an hour," the meteorologist had told us.

Our tornado's forward speed was zero. It parked right there on Sand Crane Drive. Five minutes or ten, we couldn't tell, but it seemed like an hour. Roaring and humming and shrieking, that twister was right on top of us. I'll never be that scared again as long as I live. Neither will Arthur.

# BLIZZARD!

## BY JIM MURPHY

On March 12, 1888, one of the most destructive blizzards in history struck the eastern United States from Virginia to Maine. By the following day, snow, wind, and ice posed great danger for people trying to go back to work, especially in the city of New York.

In New York City and Brooklyn, the early-morning commuters were shocked when they saw the East River. It looked like a solid sheet of ice.

People immediately rushed to the riverbanks and began to speculate on how thick the ice might be and whether it was safe to walk on. Up close, the distance across looked immense and the ice was clearly not a single sheet, but many big and small ice floes jammed together. No one rushed to be first on the ice.

It was then that a Brooklyn boy of eighteen lowered a ladder onto the ice. Cautiously he climbed down, then proceeded to jump up and down several times. As he came back toward his ladder, he announced that "She's safe as the United States Mint!"

Instantly, many onlookers announced that they wanted to cross the ice bridge. On the Brooklyn side, the boy gladly held his ladder as one hardy soul after another came down, though he made it clear that the fee to use his ladder would be five cents.

"His pockets bulged with coins," one observer noted. "Soon a long file of pedestrians surely numbering at least two hundred were slowly edging toward the Manhattan shore." Similar business operations were set up on the Manhattan side, and in no time at all, the ice swarmed with people.

Another group of ice-crossers also appeared. The unnamed observer recalled that "all the dogs in Brooklyn . . . came barking and bounding onto the [ice] field as well. The pooches were of all sizes, shapes, and varieties. . . . Perhaps they, too, had sensed the drama and historic import of the occasion."

More than just men and dogs crossed the ice bridge. Several women were spotted making the journey, while hordes of boys slid down the icy pilings and raced across the expanse. And at least one horse was hoisted over the side in a sling-harness and ridden to Brooklyn by its owner.

Police on both sides of the river tried to halt the stream of adventurers, but with little success. Other ladder entrepreneurs had appeared, and now there were more spots where a person could get onto the ice than policemen to block them.

Not everyone had an easy crossing. Many slipped on the treacherous ice or were blown over by the still-fierce wind. A few of the elderly adventurers had to be carried to shore. For over an hour and a half, people and animals paraded from one shore to the other. While no one kept an official count, the policemen on duty that day estimated that between 1,500 and 3,000 walked across the river.

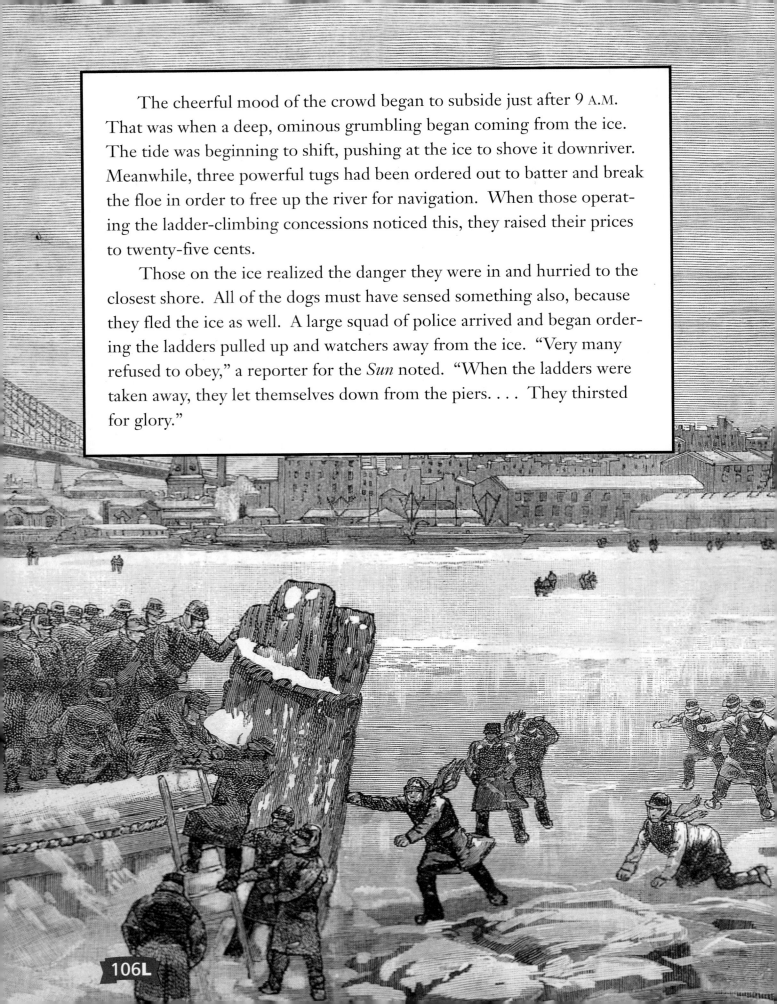

The cheerful mood of the crowd began to subside just after 9 A.M. That was when a deep, ominous grumbling began coming from the ice. The tide was beginning to shift, pushing at the ice to shove it downriver. Meanwhile, three powerful tugs had been ordered out to batter and break the floe in order to free up the river for navigation. When those operating the ladder-climbing concessions noticed this, they raised their prices to twenty-five cents.

Those on the ice realized the danger they were in and hurried to the closest shore. All of the dogs must have sensed something also, because they fled the ice as well. A large squad of police arrived and began ordering the ladders pulled up and watchers away from the ice. "Very many refused to obey," a reporter for the *Sun* noted. "When the ladders were taken away, they let themselves down from the piers. . . . They thirsted for glory."

Just then, the tide turned and began exerting immense pressure down-river. The giant cake of ice began to move very slowly. "There were over a hundred persons on the ice at this moment," the *Sun* reporter went on. "Most of them broke into a run. Loud were the cries [by those on the riverbank] to get to the shore."

When the ice broke free and began moving seaward, there were between forty and fifty people still on it. The ice came close to the Fulton Ferry pier and some of the stranded tried to grab hold, but the pilings were too slippery. They were close enough that the *Sun* reporter could see that "some exchanged cool jokes with those on the docks. One quietly asked to have a tug sent down for him; another requested a stove; still another shouted that he'd cable from Europe. . . . One man sank down on his knees and prayed."

The ice inched along and collided with a collection of piers on the New York City side. There was a horrible crunching sound as ice met wood, and then the floe came to a shivering stop. In the few minutes it was lodged there, men on the docks lowered down ladders and ropes and managed to pull almost everyone up to safety. Then the floe broke free and continued downriver.

There were still a number of men trapped on smaller chunks of ice heading toward New York Bay and the open sea. Three bobbed about near the Brooklyn shore, while five were close to Manhattan.

The *Sun* reporter took up the story of the three Brooklyn men. "The ice cracked merrily. Then it bulged up, separated and each young man was launched upon a separate cake of ice. The men shouted frantically and waved their arms. . . . Two of the men were on neighboring ice cakes. One finally made a dangerous jump to the cake nearer the shore on which the other stood. The crowd shouted approval, [and] told them to keep their hearts."

A rope with a rock attached to it was eventually tossed to these men and they were hauled to shore and rescued.

"The other young man, who was irreproachably dressed and carried a satchel, was on a cake scarcely twenty-five feet in diameter. He ran from edge to edge, till each time he nearly slipped in the water, and showed such terror that terror was communicated to those on shore."

Farther and farther out the desperate man drifted, and many watchers felt he would be lost. Then the tugboat *S.E. Babcock* managed to plow through a large chunk of ice and swing in close enough for the man to be brought on board.

Meanwhile, the five men near Manhattan were floating out rapidly. Three were on a rather large slab of ice, while two were each on cakes that the *Sun* reporter said were "the size of door mats."

First, a tug nudged the large floe into shore until it hit a wharf and the three men leaped off. Then the tug went after the two last floaters. When they were finally hauled up and safe "the thousands of men on the riverside and the Bridge yelled their applause in rounds of cheers and screams."

# Think and Compare

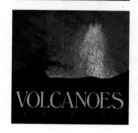

1. Compare the danger of the tornado in *Night of the Twisters* with the danger of the ice floes in *Blizzard!* What do the two situations have in common? How are they different?

2. How well-prepared do you think people were in 1888 to face a natural disaster compared with people today? Explain.

3. Compare what you learned about tornadoes in *Night of the Twisters* and in *Eye of the Storm*. Which selection seems scarier or more realistic? Use examples to tell why.

4. Compare Dan with Jonathan in *Earthquake Terror*. How are the characters alike and different?

5. How have *Night of the Twisters* and *Blizzard!* added to or changed your feelings about nature at its most dangerous?

**Strategies in Action** Which reading strategies did you use most while reading this theme? How did they help?

# Write a Weather Report

Write a paragraph telling about a fictional thunderstorm, blizzard, or tornado. Include details about what will happen and how people can stay safe.

**Tips**

- Think about the damage the storm might cause to land and buildings.
- Think about the movement in the storm, such as its speed and direction.
- Think about how long the storm will last.

# ✓ Choosing the Best Answer

To answer a multiple-choice test question, you need to decide which is the best answer. A test about *Night of the Twisters* might have this question.

---

**Read the question. Choose the best answer and fill in the circle in the answer row.**

1. When Dan realizes that the tornado is getting close, what is the first thing he does?

   **A**  He closes Ryan's door.

   **B**  He goes to get Ryan.

   **C**  He sends Arthur downstairs.

   **D**  He crawls into the shower stall.

   | ANSWER ROW 1 | Ⓐ ● Ⓒ Ⓓ |
   |---|---|

---

**1** **Understand the question.**

Find the key words. Use them to understand what you need to do.

> I think the key words are *realizes* and *first*. I need to find out what Dan does right after he realizes that the tornado is coming.

## 2 Look back at the selection.

Think about where to find the answer. You may need to look in more than one place. Skim the selection, using the key words.

I go to the part where Dan sees the CD warning on TV. That's when he knows the tornado is close by.

## 3 Narrow the choices. Then choose the best answer.

Find the choices that are clearly wrong. Have a good reason for choosing an answer. Guess only if you have to.

A happens too early to be right, and D happens too late. C could be right, but Dan goes to get Ryan *before* he sends Arthur downstairs. So I choose B.

TALL TALES

# Tall Tales

Out on the frontier of the 1800s, American settlers liked to **exaggerate**. They created heroes and heroines who were larger than life and did **amazing** deeds. The result was a new kind of story — the tall tale.

Tall tales are still told today. After you read these examples, add to the **tradition** and write your own!

## CONTENTS

> *As loggers changed the landscape of America in the 1800s, they told tales about a giant lumberjack of incredible strength. Paul Bunyan quickly became a folk legend from Maine to the Pacific Northwest.*

# Paul Bunyan, the Mightiest Logger of Them All

Retold by Mary Pope Osborne
Illustrated by Chris Van Allsburg

It seems an amazing baby was born in the state of Maine. When he was only two weeks old, he weighed more than a hundred pounds, and for breakfast every morning he ate five dozen eggs, ten sacks of potatoes, and a half barrel of mush made from a whole sack of cornmeal. But the baby's strangest feature was his big, curly black beard. It was so big and bushy that every morning his mother had to comb it with a pine tree.

Except for that black beard, the big baby wasn't much trouble to anybody until he was about nine months old. That was when he first started to crawl, and since he weighed over five hundred pounds, he caused an earthquake that shook the whole town.

The baby's parents tried putting him in a giant floating cradle off the coast of Maine; but every time he rolled over, huge waves drowned all the villages along the coast.

So his parents hauled the giant toddler to a cave in the Maine woods far away from civilization and said good-bye. His father gave him a fishing pole, a knife, some flint rocks, and an axe. "We'll think of you often, honey," his mother said, weeping. "But you can't come back home — you're just too big."

That's the story of how Paul Bunyan came to take care of himself in the Maine woods. And even though he lived alone for the next twenty years, he got along quite well.

In those times, huge sections of America were filled with dark green forests. It would be nice if those trees could have stayed tall and thick forever. But the pioneers needed them to build houses, churches, ships, wagons, bridges, and barns. So one day Paul Bunyan took a good look at those trees and decided to invent logging.

"Tim-ber!" he yelled, and he swung the bright steel axe his father had given him in a wide circle. There was a terrible crash, and when Paul looked around, he saw he'd felled ten white pines with a single swing.

After that Paul traveled plenty fast through the untamed North Woods. He cut pine, spruce, and red willow in Minnesota, Michigan, and Wisconsin. He cleared cottonwoods out of Kansas so farmers could plant wheat and oaks out of Iowa so farmers could plant corn.

When next heard of, Paul was headed to Arizona. He dragged his pickaxe behind him on the trip, not realizing he was leaving a big ditch in his tracks. Today that ditch is called the Grand Canyon.

When Paul got back from the West, he decided to start a logging camp. Word spread fast. Since all the woodsmen had heard of Paul Bunyan, thousands of them hurried to Paul's headquarters at Big Onion on the Big Onion River in Minnesota to be part of his crew.

"There's only two requirements," Paul announced to the men who'd gathered to apply for the job. "All my loggers have to be over ten feet tall and be able to pop six buttons off their shirts with one breath."

Well, about a thousand of the lumberjacks met those requirements, and Paul hired them all. Then he built a gigantic logging camp with bunkhouses a mile long and bunks ten beds high. The camp's chow table was so long that it took a week to pass the salt and pepper from one end to the other. Paul dug a few ponds to provide drinking water for everyone. Today we call those ponds the Great Lakes.

Things went pretty well at the Big Onion Lumber Company until the Year of the Hard Winter. One day Shot Gunderson, the crew boss, complained to Paul, "Boss, it's so cold that the flames for all the lanterns are freezing. And, Boss, when I give orders to the woods crew, all my words freeze in the air and hang there stiff as icicles."

"Well, haul away your frozen words and store them somewhere next to the lantern flames," Paul advised. "They'll both thaw out in the spring."

Sure enough, they did. The only problem was that, come spring, the melting lantern flames started some mean little brush fires. And when Shot's frozen words thawed, old cries of "Timber!" and "Chow time!" started to echo throughout the woods, causing all sorts of confusion. But other than that, things ran pretty smoothly.

Well, there's stories and stories about Paul Bunyan. For many years, old loggers sat around potbellied stoves and told about the good old times with Paul. Those loggers are all gone now, but many of their stories still hang frozen in the cold forest air of the North Woods, waiting to be told. Come spring, when they start to thaw, some of them might just start telling themselves. It's been known to happen.

**Focus on Genre**

Stories and songs about John Henry have been around since the 1870s. He became famous as the steel driver who hammered faster than a machine. Did John Henry exist? No one knows for sure. But like Paul Bunyan, he stands for the deeds of many others.

# John Henry Races the Steam Drill

Retold by Paul Robert Walker

The Big Bend Tunnel was the longest tunnel in America — a mile and a quarter through the heart of the West Virginia mountains. The C & O Railroad started building it back around 1870. There was plenty of hard work for everyone, but the steel-driving men worked the hardest. And the hardest-working steel-driving man of them all was John Henry.

Now, John Henry was a powerful man — six feet tall and two hundred pounds of rippling muscle. He swung his nine-pound hammer from sunup to sundown, driving a steel drill into solid rock. Little Bill, the shaker, turned John Henry's drill between hammer blows and pulled it out when the hole was done. When there were enough holes, the demolition boys filled them with nitroglycerine and blew the rock to kingdom come. Then John Henry drove more steel — day after day in the heat and darkness and stale air of the tunnel.

John Henry always sang while he drove the steel — and at the end of every line he brought that nine-pound hammer down like a crash of thunder.

*This old hammer* (Bam!)
*Rings like silver* (Bam!)
*Shines like gold, boys,* (Bam!)
*Shines like gold.* (Bam!)

*Ain't no hammer* (Bam!)
*In these mountains* (Bam!)
*Rings like mine, boys,* (Bam!)
*Rings like mine.* (Bam!)

One day, Captain Tommy interrupted John Henry in the middle of his song. "John Henry," he said, "the company wants to test one of those new steam drills. They say a steam drill can do the work of three or four men. But I say a good man can beat the steam. And I say you are the best man I have."

John Henry rested his nine-pound hammer on his broad, muscular shoulder. "Captain Tommy," he said, "a man ain't nothin' but a man. Before I let that steam drill beat me down, I'll die with my hammer in my hand."

"Son," offered Captain Tommy, "if you beat that steam drill, I'll give you one hundred dollars and a new suit of clothes."

"That's mighty generous," said John Henry, "but don't you worry about that. Just go to town and buy me a twenty-pound hammer. This nine-pound maul is feeling light."

The news of the contest spread through the camp like a strong wind whipping down the mountain. The company men said John Henry was a poor working fool who didn't stand a chance against that mighty steam drill. Some of the working men thought the same. But the steel-driving men knew John Henry — and they believed in the power of a mighty man.

That night, John Henry told his wife, Polly Ann, about the contest. "Don't you strain yourself, honey," said Polly Ann. "'Course we could use that hundred dollars — and you need a new suit of clothes."

John Henry smiled and kissed Polly Ann. "I ain't worried about money or clothes," he said. "Don't y'see sugar — a man ain't nothin' but a man, and a man's got to beat the steam."

The next morning, the steel drivers crowded into the Big Bend Tunnel. It was hot and dusty, and the air was so foul that a man could hardly breathe. The only light was the flickering of lamps burning lard oil and blackstrap molasses.

The company man wheeled the steam drill into the tunnel and set it up against the rock. It was nothing but a machine — all shiny and modern and strange. Then John Henry walked in and stood beside it. He was nothing but a man — all black and fine and natural.

Captain Tommy handed John Henry a brand-new twenty-pound hammer. "There ain't another like it in West Virginia," he said. "Good luck, son."

John Henry held the hammer in his hand and felt its fine natural weight. In the flickering light of the tunnel, the head of that hammer shone like gold. "Gonna call this hammer Polly Ann," he said.

Little Bill sat on the rock, holding the six-foot drill in his hands. John Henry towered above the steel, just waiting to begin. It was so quiet in that tunnel, you could hear the soft breathing of the steel-driving men.

Captain Tommy blew his whistle. The company man turned on the steam drill. John Henry swung his twenty-pound hammer back and brought it down with a crash like thunder. As he swung it back again, he began to sing:

> *This old hammer* (Bam!)
> *Rings like silver* (Bam!)
> *Shines like gold, boys,* (Bam!)
> *Shines like gold.* (Bam!)

John Henry kept driving steel and the steam drill kept drilling. Pretty soon the whole mountain was rumbling and shaking. John Henry's muscles bulged and strained like they never bulged and strained before. Sweat cascaded down his powerful chest, and veins protruded from the sides of his handsome face.

"Are you all right, John Henry?" asked Captain Tommy.

"Don't you worry," said John Henry. "A man ain't nothin' but a man — and a man's got to beat the steam." Then he went on singing:

> *Ain't no hammer* (Bam!)
> *In these mountains* (Bam!)
> *Rings like mine, boys,* (Bam!)
> *Rings like mine.* (Bam!)

When they hit the end of the six-foot drill, Little Bill pulled it out and shoved in a longer drill — and then a longer one and a longer one still. John Henry swung his twenty-pound hammer and drove that steel. He swung and drove faster and harder, and faster and harder, until that Polly Ann hammer caught fire. The whole Big Bend Tunnel glowed with the blue flame of John Henry's hammer.

"Time!" shouted Captain Tommy.

"Time!" cried the company man, shutting off the steam drill.

"Time," gasped John Henry, leaning on his hammer. "I need a cool drink of water."

While John Henry drank his water, Captain Tommy and the company man measured the holes. The steam drill had done nine feet; John Henry had drilled fourteen.

"John Henry!" shouted the steel drivers. "John Henry beat the steam!"

"Congratulations, son," said Captain Tommy, slapping him on the back. "I don't care what you say — I'm gonna give you a hundred dollars and a new suit of clothes."

John Henry leaned heavily on his hammer and sucked in the stale air of the tunnel. "That's mighty generous, Captain Tommy. But you give that hundred dollars to Polly Ann. And you bury me in that suit of clothes." Then he slumped to the ground, clutching his hammer in his hand. "I beat the steam," he gasped, "but I broke inside."

As his eyes closed, John Henry lay back against the black earth and whispered, "A man ain't nothin' but a man."

The Tennessee frontiersman, Davy Crockett, was the real-life subject of many a tall tale. But there is no truth to the story that he had a wife named Sally Ann Thunder Ann Whirlwind. Good thing for Davy, because in her he would have met his match!

# Sally Ann Thunder Ann Whirlwind

Retold by Mary Pope Osborne

One early spring day, when the leaves of the white oaks were about as big as a mouse's ear, Davy Crockett set out alone through the forest to do some bear hunting. Suddenly it started raining real hard, and he felt obliged to stop for shelter under a tree. As he shook the rain out of his coonskin cap, he got sleepy, so he laid back into the crotch of the tree, and pretty soon he was snoring.

Davy slept so hard, he didn't wake up until nearly sundown. And when he did, he discovered that somehow or another in all that sleeping his head had gotten stuck in the crotch of the tree, and he couldn't get it out.

Well, Davy roared loud enough to make the tree lose all its little mouse-ear leaves. He twisted and turned and carried on for over an hour, but still that tree wouldn't let go. Just as he was about to give himself up for a goner, he heard a girl say, "What's the matter, stranger?"

Even from his awkward position, he could see that she was extraordinary — tall as a hickory sapling, with arms as big as a keelboat tiller's.

"My head's stuck, *sweetie*," he said. "And if you help me get it free, I'll give you a pretty little comb."

"Don't call me sweetie," she said. "And don't worry about giving me any pretty little comb, either. I'll free your old coconut, but just because I want to."

Then this extraordinary girl did something that made Davy's hair stand on end. She reached in a bag and took out a bunch of rattlesnakes. She tied all the wriggly critters together to make a long rope, and as she tied, she kept talking. "I'm not a shy little colt," she said. "And I'm not a little singing nightingale, either. I can tote a steamboat on my back, outscream a panther, and jump over my own shadow. I can double up crocodiles any day, and I like to wear a hornets' nest for my Sunday bonnet."

As the girl looped the ends of her snake rope to the top of the branch that was trapping Davy, she kept bragging: "I'm a streak of lightning set up edgeways and buttered with quicksilver. I can outgrin, outsnort, outrun, outlift, outsneeze, outsleep, outlie any varmint from Maine to Louisiana. Furthermore, sweetie, I can blow out the moonlight and sing a wolf to sleep." Then she pulled on the other end of the snake rope so hard, it seemed as if she might tear the world apart.

The right-hand fork of that big tree bent just about double. Then Davy slid his head out as easy as you please. For a minute he was so dizzy, he couldn't tell up from down. But when he got everything going straight again, he took a good look at that girl. "What's your name, ma'am?"

"Sally Ann Thunder Ann Whirlwind," she said. "But if you mind your manners, you can call me Sally."

From then on Davy Crockett was crazy in love with Sally Ann Thunder Ann Whirlwind. He asked everyone he knew about her, and everything he heard caused another one of Cupid's arrows to jab him in the gizzard.

"Oh, I know Sally!" the preacher said. "She can dance a rock to pieces and ride a panther bareback!"

"Sally's a good ole friend of mine," the blacksmith said. "Once I saw her crack a walnut with her front teeth."

"Sally's so very special," said the schoolmarm. "She likes to whip across the Salt River, using her apron for a sail and her left leg for a rudder!"

Sally Ann Thunder Ann Whirlwind had a reputation for being funny, too. Her best friend, Lucy, told Davy, "Sally can laugh the bark off a pine tree. She likes to whistle out one side of her mouth while she eats with the other side and grins with the middle!"

According to her friends, Sally could tame about anything in the world, too. They all told Davy about the time she was churning butter and heard something scratching outside. Suddenly the door swung open, and in walked the Great King Bear of the Mud Forest. He'd come to steal one of her smoked hams. Well, before the King Bear could say boo, Sally grabbed a warm dumpling from the pot and stuffed it in his mouth.

The dumpling tasted so good, the King Bear's eyes winked with tears. But then he started to think that Sally might taste pretty good, too. So opening and closing his big old mouth, he backed her right into a corner.

Sally was plenty scared, with her knees a-knocking and her heart a-hammering. But just as the King Bear blew his hot breath in her face, she gathered the courage to say, "Would you like to dance?"

As everybody knows, no bear can resist an invitation to a square dance, so of course the old fellow forgot all about eating Sally and said, "Love to."

Then he bowed real pretty, and the two got to kicking and whooping and swinging each other through the air, as Sally sang:

> *We are on our way to Baltimore,*
> *With two behind, and two before:*
> *Around, around, around we go,*
> *Where oats, peas, beans, and barley grow!*

And while she was singing, Sally tied a string from the bear's ankle to her butter churn, so that all the time the old feller was kicking up his legs and dancing around the room, he was also churning her butter!

And folks loved to tell the story about Sally's encounter with another stinky varmint — only this one was a *human* varmint. It seems that Mike Fink, the riverboat man, decided to scare the toenails off Sally because he was sick and tired of hearing Davy Crockett talk about how great she was.

One evening Mike crept into an old alligator skin and met Sally just as she was taking off to forage in the woods for berries. He spread open his gigantic mouth and made such a howl that he nearly scared himself to

death. But Sally paid no more attention to that fool than she would have to a barking puppy dog.

However, when Mike put out his claws to embrace her, her anger rose higher than a Mississippi flood. She threw a flash of eye lightning at him, turning the dark to daylight. Then she pulled out a little toothpick and with a single swing sent the alligator head flying fifty feet! And then to finish him off good, she rolled up her sleeves and knocked Mike Fink clear across the woods and into a muddy swamp.

When the fool came to, Davy Crockett was standing over him. "What in the world happened to you, Mikey?" he asked.

"Well, I — I think I must-a been hit by some kind of wild alligator!" Mike stammered, rubbing his sore head.

Davy smiled, knowing full well it was Sally Ann Thunder Ann Whirlwind just finished giving Mike Fink the only punishment he'd ever known.

That incident caused Cupid's final arrow to jab Davy's gizzard. "Sally's the whole steamboat," he said, meaning she was something great. The next day he put on his best raccoon hat and sallied forth to see her.

When he got within three miles of her cabin, he began to holler her name. His voice was so loud, it whirled through the woods like a hurricane.

Sally looked out and saw the wind a-blowing and the trees a-bending. She heard her name a-thundering through the woods, and her heart began to thump. By now she'd begun to feel that Davy Crockett was the whole steamboat, too. So she put on her best hat — an eagle's nest with a wild-cat's tail for a feather — and ran outside.

Just as she stepped out the door, Davy Crockett burst from the woods and jumped onto her porch as fast as a frog. "Sally, darlin'!" he cried. "I think my heart is bustin'! Want to be my wife?"

"Oh, my stars and possum dogs, why not?" she said.

From that day on, Davy Crockett had a hard time acting tough around Sally Ann Thunder Ann Whirlwind. His fightin' and hollerin' had no more effect on her than dropping feathers on a barn floor. At least that's what *she'd* tell you. *He* might say something else.

Sid Fleischman has created his own tall tale characters in his stories about farmer Josh McBroom. In this tale, the McBroom family has to cope with unpredictable weather and, as usual, neighbor Heck Jones.

# February

by Sid Fleischman

Illustrated by Walter Lorraine

It's not generally known, but I invented air conditioning. I read in the paper the idea has already spread to the big cities.

But, shucks, everyone is welcome to it. Folks around here call it McBroom's Natural Winter Extract & Relief for the Summer Dismals. You can make your own, same as us.

February is about the last month you can lay in a supply of prime Winter Extract.

Wait for an infernal cold day. When the mercury in the thermometer drops to the bottom — you're getting close. But the weather's still a mite too warm.

When the mercury busts the glass bulb and rolls over to the fireplace to get warm — that's Extract weather.

"Will*jill*hester*chester*peter*polly*tim*tom*mary*larry*andlittle*clarinda!*" I shouted to our young'uns. "Bulb's shattered. Fetch the ripsaws, the crosscut saws, and let's get to work!"

Cold? Mercy, it was so cold outside *the wind had frozen solid.*

Didn't we get busy! We began sawing up chunks of frozen wind.

Now, you got to do the thing right. Wind's got a grain, just like wood. So be positive to use the crosscut saw against the grain, and the ripsaw along with it.

It fell dark before we finished harvesting and hauling that Winter Extract to our icehouse. And there stood our neighbor Heck Jones. That skinflint is so mean and miserly he brands the horseflies over at his place for fear someone will rustle 'em.

"Are you hidin' my left sock, McBroom?" he asked.

"Of course not," I said.

"Someone stole it off the clothesline. My best black sock, too! It only had three holes in it. If I catch the thief, I'll have him in a court of law!"

He loped away, grumbling and snarling.

We finished packing sawdust around the chunks of wind to keep them frozen. "Good work, my lambs," I said. "We're all set for the Summer Dismals."

Well, Heck Jones walked around in one sock the rest of winter, and summer, too.

As soon as the days turned sizzle-hot, we'd set a chunk of Winter Extract in the parlor. In a second or three it would begin to thaw — just a cool breeze at first. But when that February wind really got whistling, it would lift the curtains!

One hot night I fetched in a nice chunk of frozen wind without bothering to scrape off the sawdust. A few minutes later I saw a black thing shoot across the room. Something had got frozen in our Winter Extract.

"Heck Jones's sock!" I declared. "I can smell his feet!"

He was sure to think we'd stolen it. He'd have us in a court of law! I made a grab for it, but the February wind was kicking up such a blow it shot the sock past the curtains and far out the window.

I could see Heck Jones asleep in his hammock, one sock on, the other foot bare. The left sock hoisted its tail like a kite in the air and started down.

I declare, if I didn't see it with my own eyes, I'd think I was scrambly-witted. That holey black sock had the instinct of a homing pigeon. It returned right to Heck Jones's left foot and pulled itself on. I think it navigated by scent.

What Heck Jones thought when he awoke and looked at both feet — I can't reckon.

# Think About the TALL TALES

1. Compare John Henry with Paul Bunyan. How are they alike and different as tall tale characters?

2. How are the exaggerations in "February" different from the exaggerations in the other three tall tales? How are they similar?

3. Which tall tale character do you admire the most? Why?

4. Do you think Sally needs to prove that she's stronger than a man? Why or why not?

5. If you could invent another exaggerated deed for one of the tall tale characters, what would it be?

**Internet**

## Send an E-Postcard

Send an e-postcard to a friend telling about a tall tale character you liked. Include a few details telling what made the character unusual. You'll find the postcard at Education Place. **www.eduplace.com/kids**

**Narrating**

# Write Your Own Tall Tale

Now that you've read a few tall tales, write one of your own.
Think of a heroic main character with amazing abilities.
Think of a problem that the character has to solve. Then write
a tall tale about how the character solves the problem. The
postcard images on this page might give you some ideas for
your tall tale.

**Tips**

- **Exaggerate qualities or features of your character, such as size or strength.**
- **Exaggerate features of the setting, such as the weather, landscape, or animals.**
- **Have your character change something in nature — for example, end a heat wave or create a river.**

# 2

# Give It All You've Got

"You never fail until you stop trying."

— *Florence Griffith Joyner*

# Give It All You've Got

## with Phyllis Reynolds Naylor

Dear Reader,

In this theme you will be reading about people who show courage in the face of a challenge, such as my character Doug Grillo in *The Fear Place*. There were times I was challenged in my own life.

I almost drowned when I was young. While playing in a lake, I stepped in a hole and went under. I watched bubbles rise up through the green water above me, until a cousin pulled me out. Gasping and choking, I crawled back to the bank.

Later, because of this scary experience, I was the last one in our crowd to learn to swim. At the ocean I was terrified of the waves that swept me under, turning me upside down. Finally I got up the nerve to crouch down when I saw a breaker coming and let the ocean roll over me. What a thrill to discover I could do this!

Sometimes it takes courage to do things that aren't physically frightening, but might embarrass us. It could be giving a speech, perhaps, or trying out for a play. When I was sixteen, I started writing stories for a church magazine. I received a few dollars for each one. Then I decided to write for other magazines.

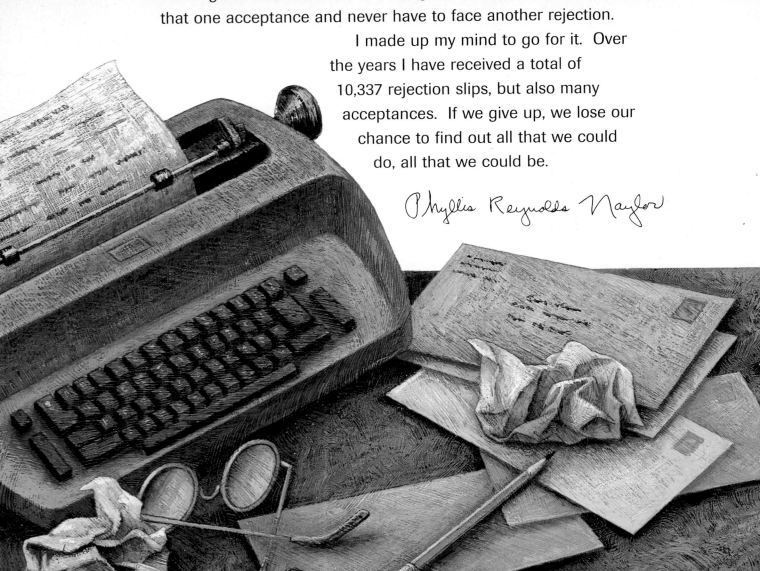

For two years I wrote stories and sent them out, but back they came. This was humiliating. I imagined how the editors must have laughed at what I wrote. I decided to burn all my writing, and asked the editors who were still holding stories of mine to return them.

All were sent back except one, and in its place came a check for sixty dollars. I had a decision to make: I could either risk sending out more stories and having them returned, or stop with that one acceptance and never have to face another rejection.

I made up my mind to go for it. Over the years I have received a total of 10,337 rejection slips, but also many acceptances. If we give up, we lose our chance to find out all that we could do, all that we could be.

*Phyllis Reynolds Naylor*

# Go for It!

Phyllis Reynolds Naylor overcame a fear of drowning and later persisted in trying to get her stories published. Think about fears you've conquered and goals you've achieved.

As you read the theme selections shown below, ask yourself what each selection tells you about "giving it all you've got." What hurdles need to be overcome before the main character achieves the goal — whether it's a gold medal performance or just surviving?

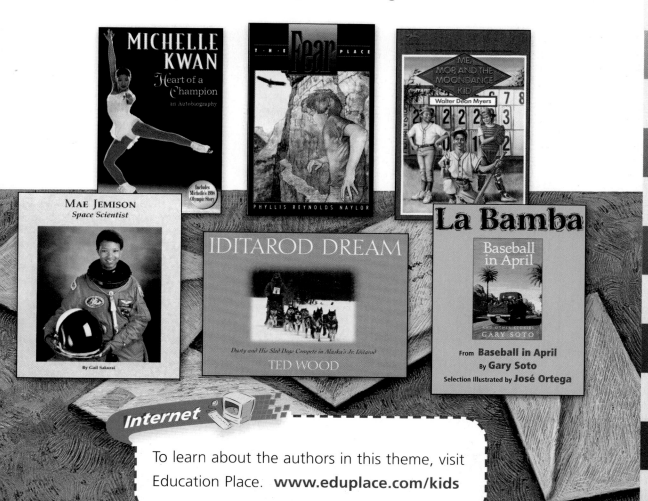

MICHELLE KWAN
Heart of a Champion
an Autobiography

Includes Michelle's 1998 Olympic Story

THE Fear PLACE

PHYLLIS REYNOLDS NAYLOR

ME, MOP, AND THE MOONDANCE KID
Walter Dean Myers

MAE JEMISON
Space Scientist

By Gail Sakurai

IDITAROD DREAM

Dusty and His Sled Dogs Compete in Alaska's Jr. Iditarod

TED WOOD

La Bamba

Baseball in April

GARY SOTO

From **Baseball in April**
By **Gary Soto**
Selection Illustrated by **José Ortega**

**Internet**

To learn about the authors in this theme, visit Education Place. **www.eduplace.com/kids**

## Background and Vocabulary

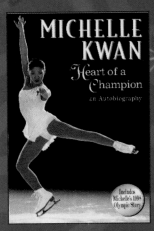

**Michelle Kwan**

**Genre** Autobiography

### Key Vocabulary

amateur
artistic
elements
judges
presentation
pressure
programs
required
technical

**Vocabulary Reader**

Skating to Fame
by Lee S. Justice

*e* • Glossary

# Figure Skating

In *Michelle Kwan: Heart of a Champion*, Michelle explains why figure skating isn't as simple as it looks. Senior ice skaters are under intense **pressure** to perform well, not only for themselves, but for the audience and the **judges**.

Skaters work long hours to practice their **presentations** . While skating, they need to balance both the **artistic** and **technical** sides of their performance. In other words, the feeling they bring to the music is as important as the number of spins they can turn in the air. ▶

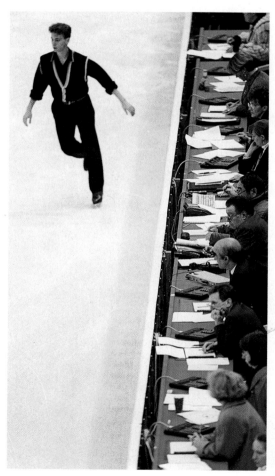

◀ Competitive skaters are expected to perform a **required** number of **elements** , or skills, in their **programs** . A panel of judges evaluates the skaters on their jumps, spins, and footwork.

After the judges fill out worksheets, they put their marks on scorecards and hand them to the referee. The scores are then put into a computer and flashed on the scoreboard. The highest score an **amateur** skater can receive is 6.0.▼

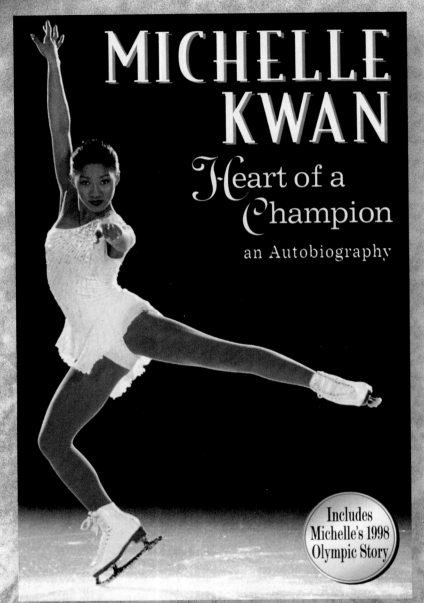

MICHELLE KWAN
Heart of a Champion
an Autobiography

Includes Michelle's 1998 Olympic Story

## Strategy Focus

This autobiographical selection is told by Michelle Kwan. As you read, **evaluate** how well you get to know her through her own words.

*The year was 1992. Twelve-year-old Michelle Kwan was feeling confident about her ice skating. She and her sister, Karen, had been practicing at Ice Castles, a private skating rink, with their new coach, Frank Carroll. Michelle thought she was ready to compete at the Junior Nationals that year. Anticipating perfection, she skated disastrously. After the Nationals, Michelle was determined to prove to herself, her coach, and the rest of the world how much better she could skate.*

Okay, so I learned a lot from my experience in Junior Nationals. But even after bombing there, I still believed in myself. *I* knew I was a much better skater than that. Not just a better Junior skater — I thought I was ready to become a Senior skater, at the age of twelve.

As usual, I was impatiently thinking ahead. It was nice that Karen and I were skating at the same level, but if I didn't take the test now so that I could qualify my way into the 1993 Senior Nationals, I'd never make it to the 1994 Olympics. Karen was working hard as a Junior and didn't feel ready to move up to the highest level yet. But I really did feel ready — even if I had to move up without her.

I had this burning desire to compete in the big time. To be out there with Lu Chen and Surya Bonaly and Nancy Kerrigan. To compete with Tonya Harding, the only American woman who could do a triple Axel. I knew myself, and I knew my skating. I didn't see why I couldn't do it.

Others did.  Frank, for one.  He said the thing to do was to wait.  If we worked hard all year, I'd have a good chance of winning the Junior Nationals in 1993.  Frank said the judges like to get to know a skater before they give them high scores at Seniors competitions.  They like to know you've paid your dues.

Frank went off to a coaches' conference in Canada for a week.  And I did something that I don't usually do:  I ignored the wisdom of somone who was older and wiser than me and I took the Senior test.  This is a good example of what I mean when I say I'm impatient.  I do have a mind of my own, and at that moment I felt like I knew me and my abilities better than anyone else.

Anyway, we went to Los Angeles to take the test.  All I had to do was skate my program for a panel of judges.  If I could do all the skills the USFSA required for Senior skaters in competitions, they move me on up.  Easy as pie.  I'd get my little pin, and go home as a *Lady* skater.  After that, I couldn't skate at the lower levels anymore.

I passed, no problem, like I expected.  But then came the hard part.  I had to tell Frank.

Frank is one of the greatest coaches in the world.  I already had a huge amount of respect for him.  At the same time, I couldn't resist a challenge.  When he came home, I explained to him that the challenge of becoming a top-level skater and maybe getting into the 1994 Olympics was irresistible to me.  I hoped he'd understand.

All the same, he flipped his lid.  He was furious.  For a few days he wouldn't talk to me.  He didn't think I was ready for the big leagues.  He thought I'd skate onto the ice in my first Senior competition, and the judges would say, "Who is this *kid*?"

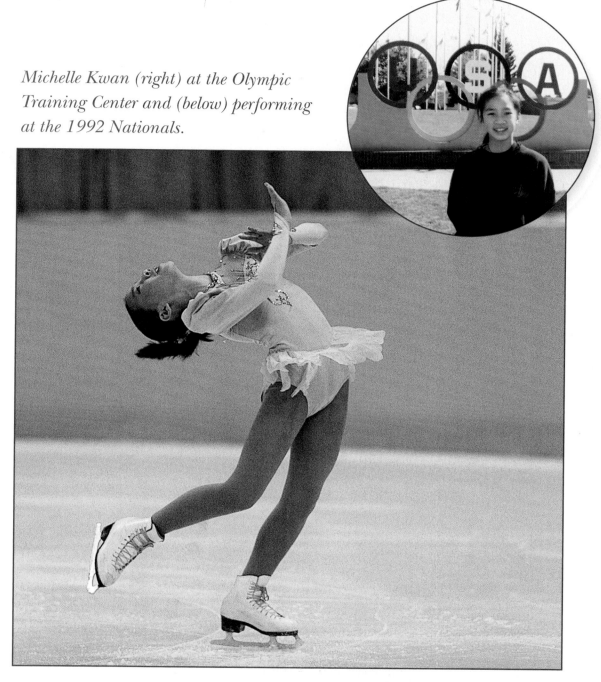

*Michelle Kwan (right) at the Olympic Training Center and (below) performing at the 1992 Nationals.*

Things were bad between us for a while. I apologized and apologized, and hoped he would calm down.

When he finally did, he sat me down and said, "Young lady, you have no idea what it means to be a Senior skater. You know next to nothing about the artistic side of skating. You need to understand how to *hear* the music. You are going to have to *transform* your skating."

I took it all in. Frank was right, of course. I was a good jumper, but my skating wasn't elegant or beautiful. And I hadn't thought that much about really *listening* to the music. I just got out there and jumped around.

Frank said I would have to be a perfectionist in every aspect of my presentation. My costumes, my hair, my face. My spirals, my edges, my footwork. He asked if I had any idea of the work I had ahead of me. I told him that *now* I did, and that I would do whatever I had to do . . . whatever he told me to do.

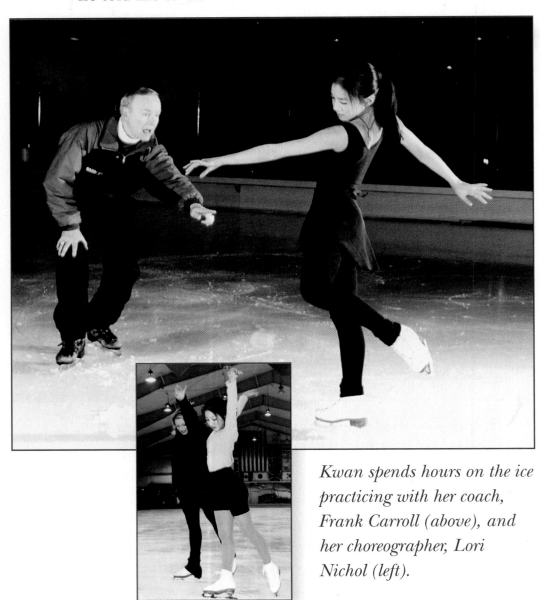

*Kwan spends hours on the ice practicing with her coach, Frank Carroll (above), and her choreographer, Lori Nichol (left).*

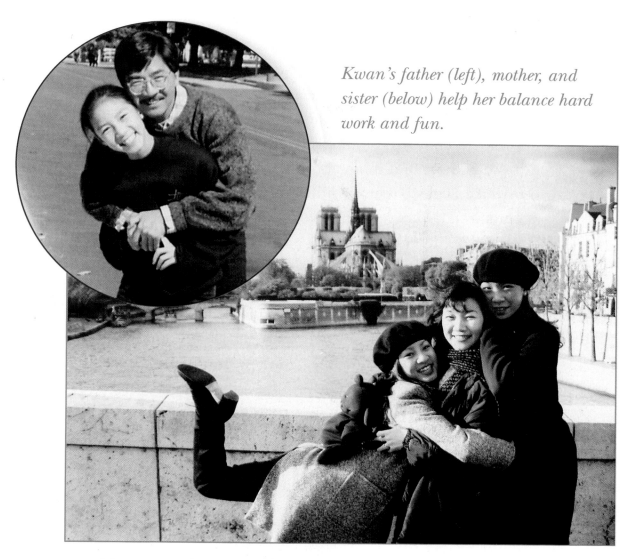

*Kwan's father (left), mother, and sister (below) help her balance hard work and fun.*

My parents listened to what Frank said, too. My mom was worried that I wasn't ready for this next big step. My dad reminded me of the thin line between discipline and pressure. Although they both wanted me to have discipline, they were afraid I was too young for the kind of pressure I'd face.

But my parents said that if I wanted it with all my heart, and if I was ready for the hard work ahead, they'd back me up like they always had. And they'd keep an eye on me to make sure I was still having fun and being myself.

I did want it, and I did feel ready. The judges gave me a pin that said I was a Senior skater. But I wouldn't really be one until I could make myself one. So that's what I set out to do. Like I said, I *love* a challenge.

Now that I'd made the leap to the Senior level, it wasn't enough anymore to be a talented kid. All of a sudden I would be compared to the best skaters in the world. I had to study them and think about the ones who came before me, like Peggy Fleming and Dorothy Hamill, Janet Lynn and Linda Fratianne.

I would need to take parts from all of them. Peggy Fleming's grace and artistry. Brian Boitano's heart. Dorothy Hamill's elegance.

Every skater has qualities that make him or her special. When I was little, my jumping made me stand out. I had good "spring," which means I could get up high in the air without seeming to make much effort. At a very young age I was able to do the triple jumps that most skaters don't get till they're older.

But my programs were simple. I was young and I looked it. I had a lot of work ahead of me to bring my programs up to the level of the elite skaters. In a great program, every movement should flow naturally into the next one. The music and skating should seem like they were meant for each other. The music should seem to *fill* the skater, just like it fills the arena.

Each skater has two programs for competitions. There's the "technical" or "short program," which is two minutes and thirty seconds long. And there's the "freeskate" or "long program," which is four minutes long for women (four and a half for men). The long program is by far the more important of the two. That's where "artistry" counts most.

The judges look for many required elements in a program. If the skater leaves any out, they deduct points from the score. You have to make sure the judges see those ele-

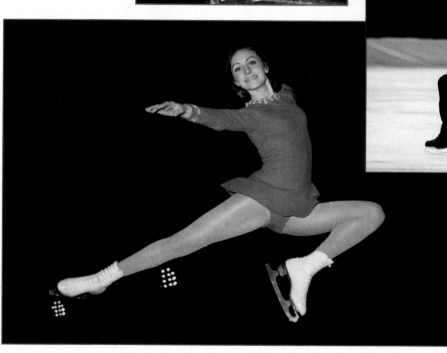

*Dorothy Hamill (left), Brian Boitano (below, right), and Peggy Fleming (below, left), have all inspired Kwan.*

ments, but you can't interrupt the flow of the program to point at yourself and say, *"Look at this!"*

Spirals and spread eagles, which are harder to do well than you might think, show off edges, balance, flexibility, and speed. But they have to seem effortless and smooth.

Spins can be more tiring than jumps. You have to use all your muscles to hold your body tight in order to get the most revolution and speed that you can while staying centered on one spot. You have to be able to step out of a spin and into the next part of your program as if it's the easiest thing in the world.

*Kwan needs to stay focused both before and during a competition.*

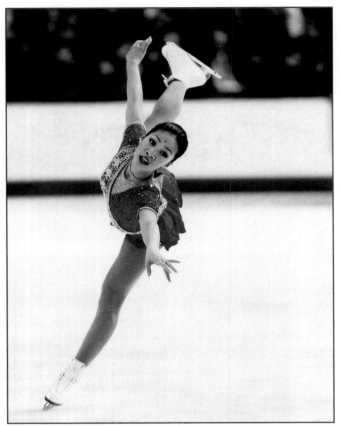

As with spins, the most difficult and athletic jumps take great strength. You have to have speed going into your jump and speed coming out of it. You need power in your legs to push yourself high into the air.

But a skater's mind has to be strong, too, and focused. It shouldn't look to the judges like this triple Lutz is any more difficult than anything else you've done. With combination jumps, the second one has to follow the first one smoothly.

Look at three-time world champion Elvis Stojko. He does quadruple/triple combinations. That's *seven revolutions,* total! It's amazingly difficult, but he makes it look simple.

When I started as a Senior, my programs were bumpy. The jumps and the steps and the spins weren't connected. I didn't let the music help me flow from one move to another. I didn't understand about *interpreting* the music. I rarely even smiled when I skated back then. To get to the level of great artists like Peggy, Dorothy, and Brian, you have to be *both* an athlete and an artist.

Most elite skaters have three forty-five-minute long practice sessions on the ice every day, usually with their coaches. They spend at least another hour in a gym making their muscles stronger and more flexible. On top of that, they work "on the floor" with their coaches, practicing jumps without the momentum and speed the ice gives them. They spend hours and hours with their choreographers developing new programs.

At the end of a day like this your body aches everywhere. Your back hurts from doing layback spins. Your bottom hurts from falling. Your shoulders, your legs — you just hurt all over. But there's still more to do.

Every month there's at least one major competition, plus exhibitions. The most important competitions come in the late winter and early spring. Nationals are in January or February and Worlds are in March. And in an Olympic year, the Olympics take place between Nationals and Worlds. So you can see, there's hardly any time between the competitions to take a breath!

There are costumes to be fitted and fixed — costumes are my mother's specialty (she works together with a designer on mine). But aside from practice clothes and gloves, the only piece of equipment a skater needs is her skates. (A warning about gloves: Skaters use them to wipe their noses, which run like crazy on an ice rink. Never borrow a skater's gloves!)

Most skaters use just one pair of skates all year long. They usually get a new pair at the beginning of the season, and it takes weeks and weeks to break them in. Sometimes it takes all season to get them just right. When I first start using new skates, it's agony. Most skaters have really ugly feet. You should see how swollen and gnarled my toes are when I take off my skates. On second thought, you don't want to!

I'd always worn used skates and didn't get an actual brand-new pair of skates until 1995 (they're expensive!). A skater has to pick out the right boot and then put the blade on with screws.

My father is good with skates. For years he cut the heels of my boots lower for me so that my weight wouldn't go too far forward. And he always has to fiddle with the blade, making sure it's placed properly.

Sometimes everything feels different in new skates. Your weight is distributed differently. Your balance feels strange. A jump that was no problem at all last year is suddenly impossible — until you figure out how to adjust yourself to new skates.

Adjustment is something young skaters have to deal with just about every day. Our bodies are always changing. Not only do we get taller all the time, but as we get older we find a pound or two in places we never even noticed before. Luckily the changes don't usually happen overnight. When we're on the ice every day, we can adjust to them gradually.

I *love* moving across the ice. So I didn't mind when I started to get a little bigger and stronger because I could put some real weight into my edges and increase my speed. I was able to really *cover* the surface of the ice. That's when I feel most like I'm flying.

Another change that happened when I became a Senior skater was that I had the chance to be noticed by the millions of people who watch skating on TV.

If you're an amateur and eligible to compete in all the major competitions, like the Olympics, that doesn't mean you can't do *any* professional work. There are professional competitions and exhibitions throughout the year that the USFSA allows eligible skaters to do, and some of them pay very well.

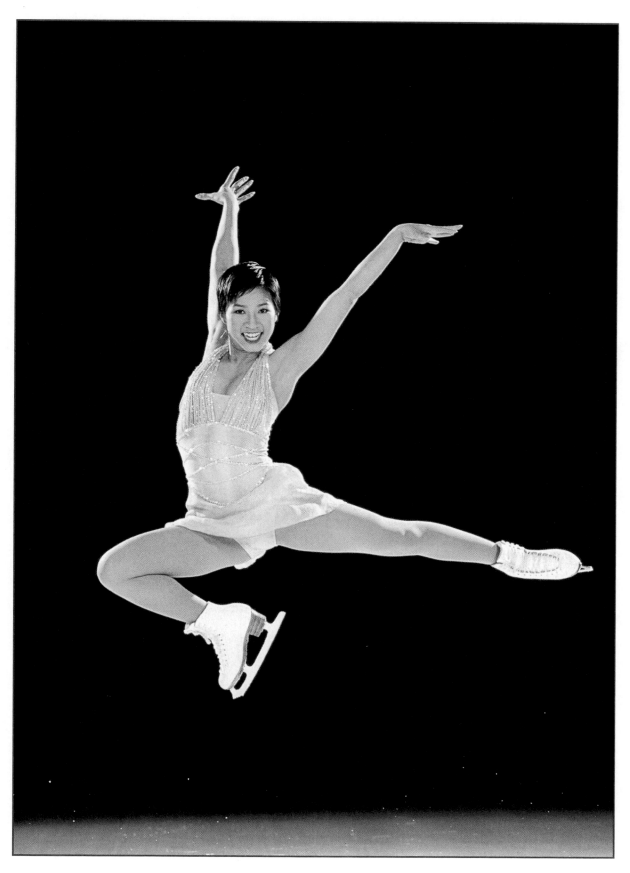

*Kwan's love of skating shows in this spectacular leap.*

Money wasn't in the picture for *me* yet, though. If anything, the cost of training went up then — by a lot. The scholarships that Karen and I received paid for our living expenses and ice-time at Ice Castle. The USFSA gave us some support, too. But we had to pay Frank and buy skates. We also each had to have three costumes a year. Plus it was expensive to travel to the competitions — which, now that I was a Senior, were all over the world!

The life of a top-level skater is intense. A lot of skaters get so overwhelmed by it that they can't even think about their schoolwork. Many drop out of school. But I'd never want to do that, and my parents would never let me.

While all of this new activity was going on, I also had to study. I went to a regular school until the eighth grade when I became a Senior skater and my schedule got crazy. Since then I've had a tutor, who comes to my house. But that doesn't mean I have it easy. I still have to take tests and do homework (lots of it!), just like everybody else.

One of the most difficult and important challenges of being a full-time skater at such a young age is remembering that skating isn't everything. You have to work hard to remember that you're just at the very *beginning* of your life. People may call you a "Lady" or a "woman skater" or a "Senior," but you can't forget that you're really still a kid. And you can never forget how important school is.

That's why I've always tried to carry two images of myself in my mind. There's the picture of the skater I dream of being. But skating is only a sport, after all, and you should only do it if you really love it. The bigger picture I keep in mind is of the *person* I want to be and the life I want to live. That's the real challenge.

# Meet the Author

## MICHELLE KWAN

**FACT FILE**

**Born:** July 7, 1980

**Birthplace:** Torrance, California

**Hometown:** Manhattan Beach, California

**Family:** Michelle Kwan is the youngest of three children. She has a brother, Ron, and a sister, Karen.

**First skating experience:** She first stepped onto the ice at age five, after watching her older brother play hockey.

**Early success:** Kwan won her first skating competition at the age of seven.

**Continued success:** In 2002, she won her sixth gold medal at the U.S. Figure Skating Championships.

**Records:** Kwan is the only multiple winner of the Skater of the Year Award from the U.S. Figure Skating Association. At the U.S. Nationals she received fifteen 6.0s (out of eighteen) for artistry, more than any other U.S. skater in history.

**Hobbies:** When she's not skating, Kwan enjoys swimming, bowling, bicycling, and spending time with friends.

**Skating philosophy:** "Work hard, be yourself, and have fun."

**Second book:** Kwan is also the author of *The Winning Attitude: What It Takes To Be a Champion.*

If you would like to learn more about Michelle Kwan, visit Education Place. **www.eduplace.com/kids**

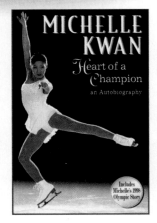

# Responding

## Think About the Selection

1. Do you think Michelle's decision to become a Senior skater is a good one? Why or why not?

2. Would you rather be the best member of a less-skilled group, or, like Michelle, a newcomer in a very talented group? Explain.

3. How do Michelle's parents support her desire to become a great skater? Give examples from the selection to support your answer.

4. Would you enjoy the challenges and hard work of a skater's life? Why or why not?

5. How does Michelle's opinion of herself change during the time period of the selection? What events help cause this change?

6. Michelle says she has two images of herself: as a great skater and as a good person. Why do you think these two images are important to her?

7. **Connecting/Comparing** Compare Michelle Kwan's determination with Warren Faidley's in *Eye of the Storm.* How are they alike? How are they different?

## Describing

## Write About a Performance

Write a newspaper article that describes a skating performance. Tell whether the skater performed well or not and why. What qualities or skills made the skater stand out?

 Tips

- Use active verbs and colorful, specific, descriptive words.
- Order the details in a way that makes sense. Consider chronological order or order of importance.

## Math

### Calculate Elapsed Time

Six skaters, two women and four men, each present a "long program" (described on page 144). There is a ten-minute break between skaters. How long will the performance for all skaters last? How much of the total time will be skating time, and how much will be waiting time?

**BONUS** **Make up your own math "riddle of the rink." Give it to a friend to answer.**

## Listening and Speaking

### Give a Pep Talk

A skating coach might give a pep talk to encourage a skater before a performance. Draft a pep talk Frank might give to Michelle just before she goes onto the ice at a big competition. Then, with a partner playing the role of Michelle, give your pep talk in front of the class.

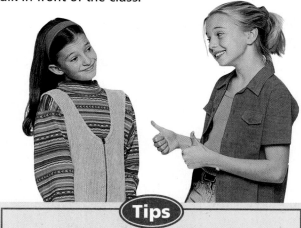

**Tips**
- **Use cheerful, encouraging language.**
- **Include a few last-minute pointers about the performance.**

*Internet*

## Complete a Web Crossword Puzzle

You've learned a lot about ice skating and Michelle Kwan. Test what you know by completing a crossword puzzle that can be printed from Education Place.

**www.eduplace.com/kids**

**Genre**

**Maps**

**Skill: How to Read a Map**

❶ Use **symbols** on a map to identify cities, roads, rivers, and so on. Refer to the **map key** to see what the symbols stand for.

❷ One inch on the map **scale** stands for a certain number of miles. Use a ruler to estimate the number of miles between two points.

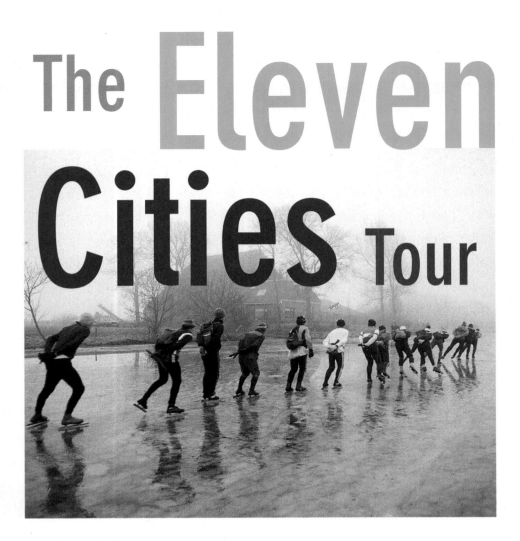

# The Eleven Cities Tour

Hundreds of miles of canals criss-cross the Netherlands, a flat, low-lying country on the western edge of Europe. For much of the year, boats use these canals to travel between Dutch towns and cities. But when the weather gets cold enough, the traffic on the canals changes as Dutch skaters by the millions hit the ice. Those long, straight stretches of frozen canals allow the Dutch to give full rein to their national passion: speed skating. ●●●●●●●●●●●●●●●●●●●●●●●●●

If figure skating is a little like dancing, speed skating is like running. And because the Netherlands is one of the few countries in the world where you can run from town to town on skates, the skating **tour** has become especially popular. In a tour, skaters follow a route that visits a certain number of cities. Tours may be skated as races, or just for the fun and challenge of completing them.

The Eleven Cities Tour, or *Elfstedentocht*, is probably the most famous of these tours. The idea behind it goes back to the 1700s, when individuals attempted to skate between all eleven towns of Friesland, a northern province of the Netherlands. Those who made it were considered to be very skilled skaters.

**Netherlands**

## *Elfsteden* route

**The 124-mile long Tour route winds through eleven towns in Friesland, one of the provinces of the Netherlands.**

**Key**
— tour route
● towns
— roads

0          5          10 miles
Scale: 1 inch equals 7 miles

Dokkum

finish

start          Leeuwarden

Harlingen          Franeker

Bolsward

Sneek

IJlst

Workum

Hindeloopen

Stavoren          Sloten

The first official Eleven Cities Tour race took place in 1909, but it has been held only fourteen times since then. In order for the Tour to take place, the ice must be frozen at least six inches thick all along the race route. Winters in the Netherlands don't usually get that cold, so many years may go by between one race and the next. There was no Eleven Cities Tour between 1963 and 1985, a gap of twenty-two years!

The winter of 1997 was an especially cold one, though, and on January 2, the board in charge of the Tour made an announcement: the race — the first since 1986 — would be held in two days. Skaters scrambled to make it to Leeuwarden, the city where the race begins and ends. Finally, at 5:30 in the morning on January 4, the starting gun sounded and over 16,000 racers were off and skating.

Competitors had until midnight to complete the 124-mile race, but they were skating in tough conditions. Bumps and holes in the ice made the going very difficult. A strong wind slowed down the racers and made an already cold day even colder — the wind-chill factor was –4 degrees Fahrenheit.

Despite the cold, half a million spectators lined the canals to cheer on the competitors. Another nine million, three-fifths of the Netherlands' population, watched on television. (By comparison, only a little more than two-fifths of American households watched the 1997 Super Bowl.)

The first racers crossed the finish line a little after noon. Other skaters continued to come in throughout the afternoon. By midnight, many were begging spectators to push them across the finish line so they could receive a medal for completing the race. Over 6,000 competitors weren't able to finish, dropping out because of exhaustion, frostbite, or other injuries.

Obstacles were nothing new for the Eleven Cities Tour. The winner of the 1929 race lost a toe to frostbite. And the 1963 race took place in a blizzard so severe that only 126 of the 9,862 participants were able to make it to the finish line.

Although there were several Olympic skaters in the field, the winner of the 1997 Tour was Henk Angenent, a Dutch Brussels-sprout farmer who completed the course in 6 hours, 49 minutes. The winner of the women's division, Klasina Seinstra, had a time of 7:49. Their prizes? No cash — just a medal and the honor of having their names placed on the winners' list of the Netherlands' greatest race.

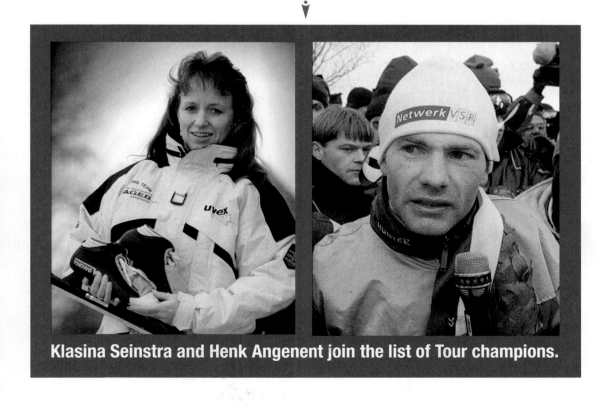

**Klasina Seinstra and Henk Angenent join the list of Tour champions.**

# A Personal Essay

A personal essay explains the writer's opinion on a topic and gives reasons to support the opinion. Use this student's writing as a model when you write a personal essay of your own.

# Becoming an Actor

> A **beginning** often states a goal.

My name is Johnny, and I am currently a fifth grader in California. There are many things I like to do such as drawing, swimming, or playing with my friends Colby, Matt, and Benji. When I grow up, I want to become an actor. My goal is to follow my dream and give it all I've got to become a professional stage and film actor.

> A personal essay states an **opinion** near the beginning.

I really think that if you want to be a well-rounded actor, it is important to learn how to be a great dancer. Right now I am taking a musical theater class in San Diego. Some people my age think that dancing is just for girls. In my opinion, jazz, ballet, and tap are fun to learn. Some of the greatest football players have learned ballet to help them with their form. I am taking dancing classes because I have always liked dancing, and I know in the long run it will help me with my acting.

Acting classes are getting me ready to become an actor. My dad drives me up to Los Angeles every Saturday for acting classes. I am learning how to read scripts, and I am also learning how to pull out emotions on the spot. It's not as easy as it looks to be on the stage or on television. I am learning that becoming an actor is a lot of hard work but a lot of fun at the same time.

My advice to anyone wanting to become an actor would be not to give up hope. There are so many people who want to become actors and so many good actors who work very hard, but many of them give up too fast and too soon. It is very easy to get discouraged if you are rejected at auditions.

I feel lucky to be starting so young. I know that if I learn from the best and I am dedicated to becoming a well-rounded actor, I will someday reach my goal of acting on the stage, television, or film.

It's important to stay with the **focus**.

Using **details** makes an essay come alive.

A good **ending** ties the essay together.

## Meet the Author

# Johnny U.
**Grade:** five
**State:** California
**Hobbies:** acting, drawing, and swimming
**What he wants to be when he grows up:** an actor

## Background and Vocabulary

Baseball in April

AND OTHER STORIES
GARY SOTO

*La Bamba*

**Genre** **Realistic Fiction**

### Key Vocabulary

applause
audience
forty-five record
limelight
pantomimes
talent

**Vocabulary Reader**

Fanfare for Food

*e* ● Glossary

# Talent

Have you ever been to a **talent** show? Most talent shows include several different kinds of acts. For example, the main character in "La Bamba" **pantomimes**, or acts out, the words to a **forty-five record**.

# Show!

Whether the talent show is competitive or just for fun, being on stage in front of an audience can be a little scary. But, if you really like being in the limelight, you'll forget all about your fears once you hear the applause!

Everyone has a talent. Yours might be playing an instrument, reciting a poem, acting in a skit, or telling jokes. What would you perform in a talent show?

## Meet the Author GARY SOTO

Gary Soto grew up in a Mexican American neighborhood in Fresno, California. Memories from his childhood inspire many of his short stories. His idea for "La Bamba" comes from a classmate who forgot the words to the song "Sugar Shack" during the school talent show.

Besides writing, Soto enjoys reading, Aztec dancing, traveling, and practicing karate. In 1999, he was honored with the Literature Award of the Hispanic Heritage Foundation. Soto's other books for young readers include *Boys at Work, The Pool Party, Off and Running, Local News,* and *Crazy Weekend.*

## Meet the Illustrator JOSÉ ORTEGA

Born in Guayaquil, Ecuador, José Ortega moved to the United States when he was five years old. He tells young people that "the most important thing is what gets you excited about working on something for hours. In the end, you are discovering yourself."

To find out more about Gary Soto and José Ortega, visit Education Place.

**www.eduplace.com/kids**

# La Bamba

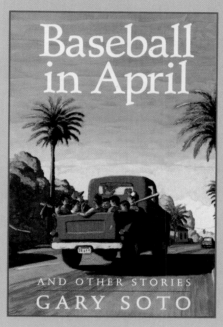

**From Baseball in April**

**By Gary Soto**

**Selection Illustrated by José Ortega**

## Strategy Focus

What will happen when Manuel enters his school's talent show? As you read the selection, **summarize** the problem and the events in your own words.

Manuel was the fourth of seven children and looked like a lot of kids in his neighborhood: black hair, brown face, and skinny legs scuffed from summer play. But summer was giving way to fall: the trees were turning red, the lawns brown, and the pomegranate trees were heavy with fruit. Manuel walked to school in the frosty morning, kicking leaves and thinking of tomorrow's talent show. He was still amazed that he had volunteered. He was going to pretend to sing Ritchie Valens's "La Bamba" before the entire school.

Why did I raise my hand? he asked himself, but in his heart he knew the answer. He yearned for the limelight. He wanted applause as loud as a thunderstorm, and to hear his friends say, "Man, that was bad!" And he wanted to impress the girls, especially Petra Lopez, the second-prettiest girl in his class. The prettiest was already taken by his friend Ernie. Manuel knew he should be reasonable, since he himself was not great-looking, just average.

Manuel kicked through the fresh-fallen leaves. When he got to school he realized he had forgotten his math workbook. If his teacher found out, he would have to stay after school and miss practice for the talent show. But fortunately for him, they did drills that morning.

During lunch Manuel hung around with Benny, who was also in the talent show. Benny was going to play the trumpet in spite of the fat lip he had gotten playing football.

"How do I look?" Manuel asked. He cleared his throat and started moving his lips in pantomime. No words came out, just a hiss that sounded like a snake. Manuel tried to look emotional, flailing his arms on the high notes and opening his eyes and mouth as wide as he could when he came to *"Para bailar la baaaaammmba."*

After Manuel finished, Benny said it looked all right, but suggested Manuel dance while he sang. Manuel thought for a moment and decided it was a good idea.

"Yeah, just think you're like some rock star," Benny suggested. "But don't get carried away."

During rehearsal, Mr. Roybal, nervous about his debut as the school's talent coordinator, muttered under his breath when the lever that controlled the speed on the record player jammed.

"Darn," he growled, trying to force the lever. "What's wrong with you?"

"Is it broken?" Manuel asked, bending over for a closer look. It looked all right to him.

Mr. Roybal assured Manuel that he would have a good record player at the talent show, even if it meant bringing his own stereo from home.

Manuel sat in a folding chair, twirling his record on his thumb. He watched a skit about personal hygiene, a mother-and-daughter violin duo, five first-grade girls jumping rope, a karate kid breaking boards, and a skit about the pilgrims. If the record player hadn't been broken, he would have gone after the karate kid, an easy act to follow, he told himself.

As he twirled his forty-five record, Manuel thought they had a great talent show. The entire school would be amazed. His mother and father would be proud, and his brothers and sisters would be jealous and pout. It would be a night to remember.

Benny walked onto the stage, raised his trumpet to his mouth, and waited for his cue. Mr. Roybal raised his hand like a symphony conductor and let it fall dramatically. Benny inhaled and blew so loud that Manuel dropped his record, which rolled across the cafeteria floor until it hit a wall. Manuel raced after it, picked it up, and wiped it clean.

"Boy, I'm glad it didn't break," he said with a sigh.

That night Manuel had to do the dishes and a lot of homework, so he could only practice in the shower. In bed he prayed that he wouldn't mess up. He prayed that it wouldn't be like when he was a first-grader. For Science Week he had wired together a C battery and a bulb, and told everyone he had discovered how a flashlight worked. He was so pleased with himself that he practiced for hours pressing the wire to the battery, making the bulb wink a dim, orangish light. He showed it to so many kids in his neighborhood that when it was time to show his class how a flashlight worked, the battery was dead. He pressed the wire to the battery, but the bulb didn't respond. He pressed until his thumb hurt and some kids in the back started snickering.

But Manuel fell asleep confident that nothing would go wrong this time.

The next morning his father and mother beamed at him. They were proud that he was going to be in the talent show.

"I wish you would tell us what you're doing," his mother said. His father, a pharmacist who wore a blue smock with his name on a plastic rectangle, looked up from the newspaper and sided with his wife. "Yes, what are you doing in the talent show?"

"You'll see," Manuel said with his mouth full of cereal.

The day whizzed by, and so did his afternoon chores and dinner. Suddenly he was dressed in his best clothes and standing next to Benny backstage, listening to the commotion as the cafeteria filled with school kids and parents. The lights dimmed, and Mr. Roybal, sweaty in a tight suit and a necktie with a large knot, wet his lips and parted the stage curtains.

"Good evening, everyone," the kids behind the curtain heard him say. "Good evening to you," some of the smart-alecky kids said back to him.

"Tonight we bring you the best John Burroughs Elementary has to offer, and I'm sure that you'll be both pleased and amazed that our little school houses so much talent. And now, without further ado, let's get on with the show." He turned and, with a swish of his hand, commanded, "Part the curtain." The curtains parted in jerks. A girl dressed as a toothbrush and a boy dressed as a dirty gray tooth walked onto the stage and sang:

*Brush, brush, brush*
*Floss, floss, floss*
*Gargle the germs away — hey! hey! hey!*

After they finished singing, they turned to Mr. Roybal, who dropped his hand. The toothbrush dashed around the stage after the dirty tooth, which was laughing and having a great time until it slipped and nearly rolled off the stage.

Mr. Roybal jumped out and caught it just in time. "Are you OK?"

The dirty tooth answered, "Ask my dentist," which drew laughter and applause from the audience.

The violin duo played next, and except for one time when the
girl got lost, they sounded fine.  People applauded, and some even
stood up.  Then the first-grade girls maneuvered onto the stage
while jumping rope.  They were all smiles and bouncing ponytails
as a hundred cameras flashed at once.  Mothers "awhed" and
fathers sat up proudly.

The karate kid was next.  He did a few kicks, yells, and chops,
and finally, when his father held up a board, punched it in two.
The audience clapped and looked at each other, wide-eyed with
respect.  The boy bowed to the audience, and father and son ran
off the stage.

Manuel remained behind the stage shivering with fear.  He
mouthed the words to "La Bamba" and swayed from left to right.
Why did he raise his hand and volunteer?  Why couldn't he have
just sat there like the rest of the kids and not said anything?
While the karate kid was on stage, Mr. Roybal, more sweaty than
before, took Manuel's forty-five record and placed it on a new
record player.

"You ready?" Mr. Roybal asked.

"Yeah . . ."

Mr. Roybal walked back on stage and announced that Manuel Gomez, a fifth-grader in Mrs. Knight's class, was going to pantomime Ritchie Valens's classic hit "La Bamba."

The cafeteria roared with applause. Manuel was nervous but loved the noisy crowd. He pictured his mother and father applauding loudly and his brothers and sisters also clapping, though not as energetically.

Manuel walked on stage and the song started immediately. Glassy-eyed from the shock of being in front of so many people, Manuel moved his lips and swayed in a made-up dance step. He couldn't see his parents, but he could see his brother Mario, who was a year younger, thumb-wrestling with a friend. Mario was wearing Manuel's favorite shirt; he would deal with Mario later. He saw some other kids get up and head for the drinking fountain, and a baby sitting in the middle of an aisle sucking her thumb and watching him intently.

What am I doing here? thought Manuel. This is no fun at all. Everyone was just sitting there. Some people were moving to the beat, but most were just watching him, like they would a monkey at the zoo.

But when Manuel did a fancy dance step, there was a burst of applause and some girls screamed. Manuel tried another dance step. He heard more applause and screams and started getting into the groove as he shivered and snaked around the stage. But the record got stuck, and he had to sing

*Para bailar la bamba*
*Para bailar la bamba*
*Para bailar la bamba*
*Para bailar la bamba*

again and again.

Manuel couldn't believe his bad luck. The audience began to laugh and stand up in their chairs. Manuel remembered how the forty-five record had dropped from his hand and rolled across the cafeteria floor.  It probably got scratched, he thought, and now it was stuck, and he was stuck dancing and moving his lips to the same words over and over.  He had never been so embarrassed.  He would have to ask his parents to move the family out of town.

  After Mr. Roybal ripped the needle across the record, Manuel slowed his dance steps to a halt.  He didn't know what to do except bow to the audience, which applauded wildly, and scoot off the stage, on the verge of tears.  This was worse than the homemade flashlight.  At least no one laughed then, they just snickered.

Manuel stood alone, trying hard to hold back the tears as Benny, center stage, played his trumpet. Manuel was jealous because he sounded great, then mad as he recalled that it was Benny's loud trumpet playing that made the forty-five record fly out of his hands. But when the entire cast lined up for a curtain call, Manuel received a burst of applause that was so loud it shook the walls of the cafeteria. Later, as he mingled with the kids and parents, everyone patted him on the shoulder and told him, "Way to go. You were really funny."

Funny? Manuel thought. Did he do something funny?

Funny. Crazy. Hilarious. These were the words people said to him. He was confused, but beyond caring. All he knew was that people were paying attention to him, and his brothers and sisters looked at him with a mixture of jealousy and awe. He was going to pull Mario aside and punch him in the arm for wearing his shirt, but he cooled it. He was enjoying the limelight. A teacher brought him cookies and punch, and the popular kids who had never before given him the time of day now clustered around him. Ricardo, the editor of the school bulletin, asked him how he made the needle stick.

"It just happened," Manuel said, crunching on a star-shaped cookie.

At home that night his father, eager to undo the buttons on his shirt and ease into his recliner, asked Manuel the same thing, how he managed to make the song stick on the words "*Para bailar la bamba.*"

Manuel thought quickly and reached for scientific jargon he had read in magazines. "Easy, Dad. I used laser tracking with high optics and low functional decibels per channel." His proud but confused father told him to be quiet and go to bed.

"Ah, *que niños tan truchas*," he said as he walked to the kitchen for a glass of milk. "I don't know how you kids nowadays get so smart."

Manuel, feeling happy, went to his bedroom, undressed, and slipped into his pajamas. He looked in the mirror and began to pantomime "La Bamba," but stopped because he was tired of the song. He crawled into bed. The sheets were as cold as the moon that stood over the peach tree in their backyard.

He was relieved that the day was over. Next year, when they asked for volunteers for the talent show, he wouldn't raise his hand. Probably.

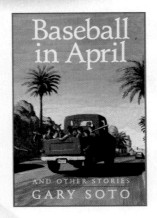

# Think About the Selection

**1.** Describe the different emotions Manuel feels at the beginning of the story. How would you have felt in his position?

**2.** How well do you think Manuel handles the unpleasant surprise of the scratched record? What else could he have done when the record started to skip?

**3.** Compare Manuel's experience with the flashlight and his experience with the record. Which one do you think was worse? Why?

**4.** What do you think Manuel learns about himself as a result of the talent show?

**5.** Think about the different talents of the students who perform in "La Bamba." If you could perform in a talent show, what would you do?

**6.** Why do you think the author ends the story with the word *Probably*?

**7.** **Connecting/Comparing** What advice about performing might Michelle Kwan give Manuel? What advice might he give to her?

**Narrating**

## Write a Sequel

Suppose that Manuel *does* volunteer for the next school talent show. What kind of act might he perform? Write a follow-up story about what Manuel does to get into the limelight once again.

**Tips**

- **List five words that describe Manuel.**
- **Keep these qualities in mind as you write your sequel.**
- **Be sure to include a problem and a solution.**

# List Sounds in a Sequence

Frequency is the number of sound waves made per second. A low sound, like a rumble, has a low frequency. A high sound, like a squeak, has a high frequency. List all of the sounds of the talent show in "La Bamba," including applause. Order them according to what you think their frequencies are, from lowest to highest.

**Bonus** Create a similar chart for the sound frequencies of your classroom.

# Make a Poster

Create a poster that advertises the talent show in "La Bamba," including the acts. Make the poster colorful and exciting so that people will want to come and see the show. You can cut out pictures from magazines or draw your own.

Internet

# E-mail a Friend

Send an e-mail message to a friend who might enjoy this story. Tell the friend a little bit about the story and why he or she might like it.

**Genre**

**Time Lines**

**Skill: How to Read a Time Line**

❶ Read the title to find out what events the time line shows.

❷ Locate the **first** and **last dates** to find out what time period is being shown.

❸ Read the **events** from left to right, or from earliest to latest event, depending on how the time line is arranged.

# History of Recorded Sound

**I**f you were to pantomime in a talent show, as Manuel did, you would probably play a cassette tape or a CD, not a vinyl record. The time line below shows how recording and listening to music has changed in just a few generations.

## 1870        1880

### 1877

Thomas Edison invents a phonograph with a tinfoil cylinder, making the first recording of a human voice ("Mary Had a Little Lamb").

**1887**

Emile Berliner patents the Gramophone, a new type of phonograph, by using a disc made of durable shellac.

**1927**

The electric "juke box" is invented to replace pianos that play when coins are inserted.

**1906**

The Victrola, a phonograph in an enclosed cabinet, is introduced.

**1890**        **1900**        **1910**        **1920**

**1898**

Valdemar Poulsen patents the first magnetic recorder, called the Telegraphone, using steel wire.

**1915**

The "record player" is invented; it allows records to be played at 78 revolutions per minute (rpm).

**1960s**
Music is recorded on plastic tape — either on 8-tracks, which are about the size of a standard paperback book, or on cassettes.

**1949**
The first extended play 45 rpm vinyl record is introduced.

**1935**
The Magnetophone, the first true magnetic tape recorder, is invented.

**1930**    **1940**    **1950**    **1960**

**1948**
The first 33$\frac{1}{3}$ rpm long-playing (LP) vinyl record is introduced. It can play up to 23 minutes on each side.

**1958**
Stereophonic or "stereo" sound is developed. Sound signals move through two separate channels, giving the effect of musicians being spread out on a stage.

## Twenty-First Century:
Enhanced CDs, recordable mini-discs (MDs), and Digital Compact Cassettes (DCCs) will become more widely available.

## 1983
Compact discs (CDs) and players, which use laser technology, are available for the first time in the U.S. Unlike vinyl records, CDs cannot be worn down.

## 1970s
Music is recorded digitally using laser beams.

**1970    1980    1990    2000    2010**

## 1988
CDs outsell record albums for the first time.

## 1979
The first portable audio cassette player with head-phones is introduced.

**The Fear Place**

 **Realistic Fiction**

### Key Vocabulary

adventure
excitement
frightened
terrified

**Vocabulary Reader**

**Everest Challenge**
by Ben Heath

*e* ▶ Glossary

# Facing Fear!

Everyone is afraid of *something*. The main character in *The Fear Place* is **terrified** of being on a high mountain ledge. Do you have a fear place?

It's a mystery why people are **frightened** by some things, but not other things. You might be scared of spiders, while your friend keeps one as a pet. Your friend might dislike roller coasters, while you get a feeling of **excitement** or **adventure** from them.

There are many ways to deal with fear. You could try to avoid the thing that scares you. Or, little by little, you could get used to something until one day it doesn't seem as scary as it did before. Sometime you may find yourself forced to face your fear. You just might surprise yourself by having more courage than you thought possible.

# Meet the Author **Phyllis Reynolds Naylor**

**Early writing:** In elementary school, Naylor began writing her own stories. She made booklets by stapling scrap paper together. After writing the story and drawing the pictures, she would glue an envelope to the inside cover. Placing an index card inside it made it look like a library book that her friends could check out. "I was the author, illustrator, printer, binder, and librarian, all in one."

**Favorite part of her job:** She says that "the best part about writing is the moment a character comes alive on paper, or when a place that existed only in my head becomes real."

**Accomplishments:** Naylor published her first story at age sixteen and since then has written over 100 books for children and adults, including the Newbery Award-winner *Shiloh*. She is also the author of *Saving Shiloh*, *Shiloh Season*, *The Grand Escape*, *The Healing of Texas Jake*, and *The Boys Start the War*.

# Meet the Illustrator **Paul Lee**

**Hobby:** "I yo-yo. Wherever I go, I always have at least one yo-yo on me, usually in a holster on my belt. It comes in handy when I have to wait in line for something."

**Career choice:** "I realized that I would not be happy unless I had a future in which I could draw all the time."

**Advice to artists:** "Practice. Practice. Practice."

For more about Phyllis Reynolds Naylor and Paul Lee, visit Education Place.

**www.eduplace.com/kids**

# T·H·E Fear PLACE

## PHYLLIS REYNOLDS NAYLOR

## Strategy Focus

Look at the title, introduction, and illustrations before you read the selection. What can you **infer** about Doug? What do you **predict** will happen?

**O**n vacation in Colorado, Doug Grillo is alone. His parents have left on an emergency. His brother Gordie has gone off by himself after a fight with Doug. (Their mom and *her* brother fought, too.) Doug has kept busy studying mammals for his Scout merit badge, even befriending a cougar he calls Charlie. But now he has set off to find Gordie. To reach him, Doug must find the same courage his dad found when he fled Cuba. Doug must get past his Fear Place: a narrow ledge six hundred feet above a canyon, which he had vowed never to face again.

What path there was led over scattered pitches of bedrock, across ramps
of boggy tundra, then climbed some more, becoming a narrow, zigzag-
ging passageway. Doug followed the steep-slanting boilerplate rock,
ledged with wildflowers, catching glimpses now and then of a
distant snowfield. At one point he could see a ridge far above where he
could just make out an elk cow leading her calf.

At times the journey seemed futile, for Doug would climb,
scrabbling and panting, up the rock face, around steep boulders, then
make his way, feet sliding, down another gully, losing all the altitude
he'd worked so hard to gain.

He was dismayed that he was thirsty again. At this rate, there
would be little left for Gordie, so he took the cap off his canteen and
drank only a swallow.

Every time he stopped, the fear inside him grew larger, however. At times it seemed to be the climb that frightened him most; other times it was worry about his brother. And then, as though that weren't worry enough, his parents. He plowed on, keeping his mind on other things, trying to remember the wildlife he'd seen so far. Elks — he could use those in his report; a snowshoe rabbit — he'd use that one, too. And a marten. He'd also seen two Steller's jays and a gray jay. Too bad he wasn't working on a merit badge in Bird Study while he was here.

Doug was nearing the first ridge. At nine thousand feet, he'd read, oxygen was about half of what it was at sea level. He had no idea how high he was. Stormy Peaks, to his left, was over twelve thousand feet. With each ascending step, the air seemed to change. A mountain has its own weather, Dad had told him. At high altitudes, a hiker could encounter sunshine, rain, sleet, ice pellets, wind, and snow, all in one afternoon, sometimes even in the space of an hour. The weather changed minute by minute, valley by valley, range by range.

It helped to keep his mind busy.

"This isn't so bad," he said aloud, wanting to hear a human voice, even his own. "You've climbed a lot worse than this."

Walking along the ridge crest, he followed a route through a long granite fin that stretched like a roofless tunnel before him. He remembered this tunnel from the first time he was up here, and was reassured he was on the right path. If only it went on like this all the way to where Gordon was camped, he'd have no problem. He had strength; stamina. A climb like this, no matter how rocky, he could do forever, as long as there were sides to enclose him.

When he came out again into open space, the winds buffeted him. A hawk he had startled from a nearby rock flew directly past, so close that Doug could hear the steady flap of its wings. He held tightly to a rock, not wanting to look down, but did. It didn't frighten him particularly, because there was plenty of room between him and the edge. Over the rocky hogbacks slabbed with quartz and sprinkled with muscovite, he could see a tongue of aspen crowding the narrow gorge below. It looked like the set for a model railroad.

It occurred to him that if he were more like the other members of his family, he would actually enjoy a hike like this. He would have set out that morning with a feeling of excitement. Then he thought of Gordon and how this wasn't the time for adventure. What would he find when he got up there? All the possibilities . . .

That was another word to remember, possibilities. Almost anything was possible, Mom had told him once. But not everything was probable. Which was more likely, that he'd find Gordon okay up there on the ridge, or that something awful had happened? That he'd find Gordon okay, he guessed.

Which was more likely, that he would get around the ledge just fine, or that his foot would slip and he'd fall six hundred feet to his death? He shakily sucked in his breath. That everyone else would be able to get around the ledge without trouble he had no doubt. That he, Doug Grillo, could do it, was a different story.

So he tried to think of the climb as something ordinary. When he stopped at the next level place on the trail, not even winded, he took time to look out between the trees. He could just make out Longs Peak from here — "old granitehead," they called it.

Weird, he was thinking now, that there were probably a hundred climbers on it right this minute, and Doug couldn't see any of them. Looking into the distance at Longs Peak, in the quiet of morning, it looked peaceful and unthreatening.

It didn't fool him for a minute. He knew the stories of the people who had died. He knew about the guy who . . . Doug pushed the thought out of his mind. Don't! he told himself as he set off again. Concentrate on rocks.

Okay. Rocks. Precambrian rock, his dad had told him. The rock that formed Longs Peak was here before there was anything else on the planet. Heat and pressure changed sediments to harder and harder rock, until sediments became schist and gneiss, quartz and feldspar. Mica. Layers of rock. Layers that had their beginnings in some huge disturbance inside the earth. He'd done a paper on it once for science.

Doug didn't know why, but he felt a vague sense of discomfort, like some unpleasant memory tapping at the side of his head. No, he thought fiercely. He was doing too well. No unpleasant thoughts now, thank you.

The muscles in Doug's legs carried him easily with each stride. He forced himself to think positively, concentrating on his strength. He didn't even bother to rest at the next place the ground leveled out, but moved on around the curve of the mountain, inching down steep, rocky troughs chiseled out by water, then making his way through a long maze of rocky outcrops.

Layers. It came back to him now. That was the word that seemed so unpleasant. Layers of rock, he'd been thinking, that had their beginnings in some huge . . . Layers of feelings, of grudges. Wasn't that how Mom had described it, with her and Uncle Lloyd? One thing piled on top of another, she had said. So many layers we never did get to the bottom of it.

Would Mom have climbed this mountain to rescue Lloyd? Well, Doug was doing it for Gordon, wasn't he? So no, what happened between her and Lloyd was not the same as him and Gordie at all. She was right.

There was a noise behind him and he stopped. It was like a rock falling, tumbling — rolling behind him down the trail, too far back for him to have caused it. He turned and waited, seeing nothing, hearing nothing more, then moved on again.

At this point there was a vertical face of rock on one side of him, boulders and scrub trees on the other. With each upward step he took, the small trees retreated from the landscape, but the wide expanse of boulders remained. He liked that — liked a wide span between him and the gorge below, a monstrous guardrail. If ever the fear that terrified him in high places convinced him to simply fling himself over the edge and get it over with, the boulders would be there to say no.

Suddenly he felt that familiar thump against his thigh.

"Man, Charlie!" he gasped, leaning against the rock wall. "You scared me half to death!"

The cougar came up around him, looked at Doug a moment, then moved on, checking once to see if he was coming.

"Hold your horses," he said, unsure of whether he wanted her with him or not.

Was it conceivable, he wondered, that the cougar had a den up here? That she spent most of the day among the rocks, coming home each morning, then going out to hunt around dusk?

That was another thing to think about now, one more thing to occupy his mind. But thinking about Charlie led to thinking about Gordon, and Doug decided it would have been better if the cat hadn't come.

The rocky path far up ahead suddenly fell into shadow, and Doug glanced at the sky. The clouds overhead were hard to read. Dark around the edges, with the sun gleaming behind them, and the wind trying to push them, unwanted, from this part of the sky.

The farther Doug climbed, the narrower the stretch of safety on his left. When he first started out, there was nothing at all but trees and meadow, then trees and rocks, then mostly boulders and a few scrubby trees. Each time he stepped, however, the span on his left grew smaller.

Now the low, twisted trees gave way to rock entirely, and the span had narrowed to the point that Doug could see the gorge below almost continuously. The hillside seemed to be receding, the edge coming closer to the trail. There were a few places, Doug was sure, where, if he were to lie down crosswise on the path, his feet against the cliff, his arms stretched above his head, his fingers would touch the drop-off.

He tried to redirect his thoughts.

"How you doin' up there, Charlie?" he called shakily to the cougar, who seemed to be waiting for him at the next rise. The cat stretched out her head toward the sun and panted, the closest thing yet to a smile.

But there was a drumbeat starting now in Doug's chest; he could feel it. Seemed almost to hear it. Like a foghorn out over a bay; the far-off whistle of a train. . . .

He thought of various guys in his troop — how they would be enjoying the trail about now, exclaiming every time there was a new view of the canyon below. He tried to imagine himself in their bodies, becoming Frank Jameson, for example, or Teddy Heinz. They were always the first ones to the top of any climb.

But it didn't work. He *wasn't* Teddy or Frank, he was Doug Grillo, who had come up this way with his family two years ago and had not been able to make it back without help. Now he was Doug Grillo here alone.

About two hundred yards more, he guessed, and he'd be at the spot. Snow-splattered ridges gleamed in the distance. He felt he could remember every rock, every root of the ledge. Should he stop awhile and get his nerve up? Catch his breath?

He kept going, making his way around the next bend. The wind was soundless, sweeping the sun-filled sky. And suddenly, there it was, sooner than he had thought. The span of safety on his left gave way entirely, and he was face-to-face with the Fear Place.

Even the cougar stopped, lifted her head, and sniffed the air. She looked down over the edge, then back, as if to see if Doug were coming.

I can't! A swell of fear engulfed him, and for a moment the trees far below seemed to come up to meet him. Clinging tightly to a scrubby bush growing out of the face of the rock, Doug stared without blinking at the ledge stretching before him, even narrower than he remembered. Was this possible? Could it have eroded to twenty inches in places?

There was nothing separating him from the edge of the cliff and a plunge downward. There were even places that the ledge tipped slightly toward the yawning gap, places where loose rocks and stones lay ready to trip him, make him skid.

He could smell the difference in the air here above the canyon, sharp and moist. It beckoned him downward, and each breeze seemed to punch him in the stomach, shoot upward, socking him again beneath the chin.

Far below him, the rocky floor of the canyon waited. He could see the tops of the trees, a meandering stream, boulders. He wondered how long it would take his body to reach the bottom. How it would feel to . . . *no!*

Immobile, Doug swallowed and tried to get a grip on his fear. His mouth felt as though it were lined with dust. He attempted to measure the length of the ledge with his eyes — the length of the place where his heart stopped pumping and his legs wouldn't move. *That* place. About nine yards to the curve, and a few yards more after that, if he remembered right. It didn't seem so long when he thought about it, but looking out there now, it seemed impossible.

Maybe there were times it paid to be cautious. Maybe there were places that only fools would tread. Hadn't his mother said something like that once, or was it "Where angels fear to tread?" If there was such a place, this was it.

Would he ever make Eagle Scout if he couldn't try something like this? Would he even *live* to make Eagle Scout if he did? One slip of the foot and . . .

Stop it. His other self. As though he never took any other kinds of risks — riding his bike at top speed around corners, for example.

Look at the ledge, he told himself, and see if you could make it without falling off if it was drawn on the sidewalk with chalk.

Sure, no problem.

Could he do it if it were only half as wide, drawn with chalk on the sidewalk?

Of course. A fourth as wide, even. Give him a path on the sidewalk five inches wide, marked with chalk, and he could go for a mile, never stepping outside the boundaries once.

Okay, then. He had twenty inches, minimum. Do it, he told himself. It was the cougar who showed him how.

The cat simply walked out on the ledge, hugging the side of the mountain, but not too closely. Not leaning inward, as Doug tended to do. As he followed, and as he thought about it, Doug realized that were his body at an angle and he slipped, his feet would be pointing toward the edge of the cliff. He needed to keep upright. He would remember that chalk line on the sidewalk.

It wasn't so bad at first. The ledge varied in width between three and three and a half feet.

Three feet is a yardstick, he told himself. Three feet is the width of a kitchen table, the width of a cot. Probably wider here than his sleeping bag. Yet he lay on top of it on hot summer nights and never rolled off, not even in his sleep. He could do this. Piece of cake. He swallowed.

Ahead, the cougar's left hind foot seemed to displace a small stone at the side of the path, and it rolled over the edge. Doug heard it hit a rock below, then another. The cougar glanced toward the gorge and kept going, ears up.

197

The path was narrowing now, and somewhere ahead was the curve where it was narrowest of all, where he couldn't see what he was getting to. Somewhere, right on the bend, was the place he had flattened himself against the rock. *I can't.* The words seemed to be building up already in his throat.

He felt the needle pricks in the palms of his hands again, and in the soles of his feet. Felt the tightening of his body, the rigidity of his chest, as though, if he tensed himself enough, he might be too stiff or too hard or too impenetrable to topple.

Ahead, the cougar's body swayed with every motion, limbs sleek and relaxed. She took the curves as easily as a tire rolling along on its own momentum. She didn't walk carelessly, but in a deliberate, rhythmical manner, joints loose, paws secure.

As he approached the curve, Doug took a deep, shaky breath and let it out. Then another. He looked down at his feet and blew upward, to fan his face.

His right bootlace was untied, the ends dangling.

He would not try to tie it here. Bend over here and he might lose his balance altogether. He would have to go around the bend dragging that lace.

Hollow-eyed with terror, his mouth dry, he began to maneuver himself around the narrow curve, watching each step to see where his foot would go next, scanning the wall of rock to see what his hand could clutch.

He would not allow himself to look down at the canyon. Would not let himself even glance at the large birds that were circling, soaring, just off in the huge space to his left. The cougar had gone on, probably so far ahead Doug would find it sitting beside Gordie's tent.

"Remember Dad on the raft," he said aloud, his voice trembling. He tried to remember the day Dad had told him about, when he was sure the sun would kill them all, broil them there in the open sea. They had seen a rowboat and paddled toward it, and when they got there it had four men in it, all refugees like themselves, and all of them dead. Was this as bad as that?

Then, answering his own question, he said aloud, "No."

He lied. It was worse.

He was still moving forward. Had decided not to face the wall and walk sideways for fear his repositioning himself might be more dangerous than walking straight. But just as he rounded the narrowest spot on the ledge, he came face-to-face with the cougar.

His strength almost gave way.

Was this it, then? He had come all this way to face a cougar who wanted to turn around and go back? Who would nudge him backward, step over step, possibly pushing between him and the cliff wall, sending him over the edge?

Their eyes were on each other — fixed solidly on each other for the first time.

"Ch-Charlie," Doug said. "I can't get by. You've got to move."

The cat came on, so close her muzzle was almost against Doug's hipbone. Nudged him. And then the animal backed off. It seemed to Doug that her long body must be moving backward in sections, like a caterpillar. He couldn't see the rest of her, only that tawny head, the amber eyes, moving slowly away from him, leading still. She had not wanted to go back, perhaps; only wanted to see how Doug was doing.

Any minute Doug expected to hear the clawing, scratching sounds of a cougar falling over the edge. Things happened, even to the most expert of animals. And then Charlie disappeared silently from view. But when Doug took the last few steps along the ledge, he saw the cougar's tail ahead of him, Charlie having turned herself around again.

The path was widening here — on ahead, wider still. And finally there were scrub bushes to the left, making a safety rail between him and the canyon below.

He'd made it. Done it.

## Think About the Selection

**1.** Of all the obstacles Doug faces, which one is the most difficult for him to overcome? How do you know this?

**2.** What does Doug do to keep his mind off the danger he is in? Do you think his strategy works?

**3.** What do you think happened before at Doug's "fear place"? Find clues in the story that suggest what might have occurred.

**4.** Doug says that his scout troop would have enjoyed the hike. Would you enjoy it? Explain why or why not.

**5.** Do you think Doug would have succeeded if the cougar hadn't been there? Give reasons for your answer.

**6.** What do you think will happen next in this story? Why?

**7.** **Connecting/Comparing** Compare Doug's act of courage in *The Fear Place* with Manuel's act of courage in "La Bamba." How are the boys' actions alike? How are they different?

## Write About an Experience

Write a few paragraphs about a time when you had to overcome an obstacle to reach an important goal.

- First, list the most important details of the experience.
- Check your verbs to be sure they are all in the right tense.

# Study the Geography of a Region

Find details in the story that give information about the terrain where Doug is hiking. These may include details about rock types, landforms, and wildlife. Use this information to write an entry for a guide book about the Rocky Mountains.

**Bonus** Read more about the geography and wildlife of the Rocky Mountains. Then write a description of the region.

# Describe an Illustration

Choose an illustration from the selection that you think best represents the "fear place." Then write a paragraph that tells why you chose that illustration.

## Post a Review

Would you recommend *The Fear Place* to a friend? Why or why not? Write a review of *The Fear Place* and post your review on Education Place.

www.eduplace.com/kids

204

# Blind to Limitations

By Brent H. Weber

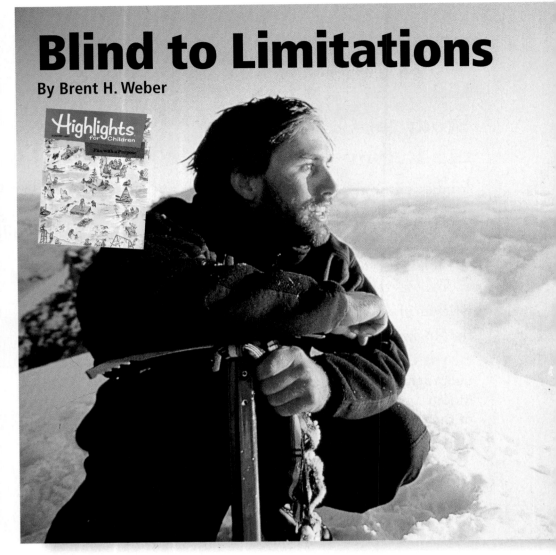

**With the wind howling at their backs, the five climbers cautiously made their way up the unforgiving stretch of mountain. The icy trail was only two feet wide, with a drop of 9,000 feet on one side and 2,000 feet on the other.**

And Erik Weihenmayer could not see a thing.

"I was just so tired and dizzy, my head was spinning," says Weihenmayer, who is blind. "I took this giant step up, and the guy in front of me said, 'Congratulations, you're on top of North America.'"

Erik Weihenmayer climbed North America's highest peak despite being unable to see.

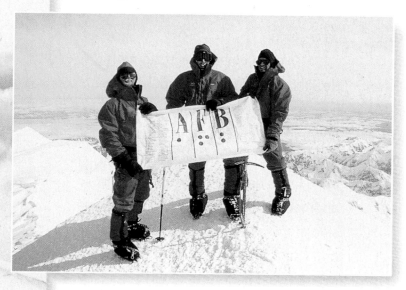

**From left, Jeff Evans, Erik Weihenmayer, and Sam Epstein display the American Foundation for the Blind flag at the top of Mount McKinley.**

With that giant step, Erik had reached the top of Alaska's Mount McKinley, the highest peak in North America.

Erik is a modern-day adventurer. The fifth-grade teacher has quite a list of accomplishments for someone who lost his sight at age thirteen because of an eye disease. He hiked the Inca Trail in Peru, trekked the Boltera Glacier in Pakistan, and crossed jungles in New Guinea. He has been scuba-diving and skydiving.

Erik knew that a blind woman named Joni Phelps had climbed the 20,320-foot Mount McKinley in 1993. He decided to try to become the first blind man to do it. He knew it would be his most ambitious adventure yet. He hoped the climb would help raise money for the American Foundation for the Blind.

But Erik was not completely prepared for what he would face. Even in midsummer, with its daylong sunshine, temperatures on Mount McKinley can drop to forty degrees below zero. Huge crevasses, unexpected snowstorms, and even an occasional avalanche can present perilous conditions for any climber.

After they were about a third of the way up the mountain, one of the other climbers said to Erik, "I want you to point to the summit."

"I was standing at seven thousand feet," Erik recalls. "I pointed up to where I thought the summit would be. He said, 'Nope.' And I kept pointing higher and higher until I pointed where I honestly thought the sun would be. He said, 'There it is.' I was just blown away, and thought, 'Am I going to be able to do this?'"

Sighted people often wonder if Erik's experiences are incomplete because he is not able to see.

"I use my other senses to gain pleasure from what I do, so even though I can't see what's around me, I experience it in a different way," he says. "I have the sense of feeling the snow and hearing the wind, and I even have a sense of space around me."

Erik's family have supported his many adventures. They even rented a small plane and flew over Erik as he neared the top of Mount McKinley.

"We heard this buzz coming through the air; they had timed it perfectly," Erik says. "We all waved our ski poles. It was just an incredible feeling. That was probably my proudest moment, to know that my whole family was up there watching me."

Two days later, Erik had another surprise as the climbers made their way back down the mountain toward their base camp.

"We were near the bottom of Heartbreak Hill, and I heard 'Hip-hip-hooray!' It was my family. They had flown to our base camp and were standing in a big chorus, cheering us on." Erik's brothers ran to him as he approached. "One brother grabbed one side of my pack, the other grabbed the other side, and I was kind of floating over the last half of that hill."

"When I got to the base camp, my girlfriend, Ellen Reeve, was waiting with chocolate milk and Oreo cookies."

Erik is looking forward to his next challenge.

"People can do extraordinary things," he says. "Although mountain climbing has nothing to do with blindness, I told myself that it would be an awful tragedy if blindness had to change and limit the enjoyment I get out of life. I can get to the top of most of the things I set my mind to. I just have to get there differently."

"If you ask the kids in my class if there is anything that holds them back, almost everyone will say something," Erik says, referring to his students at Phoenix Country Day School in Arizona. "So, in a way, the climb up Mount McKinley was to say that whatever your obstacles in life, you can get around them."

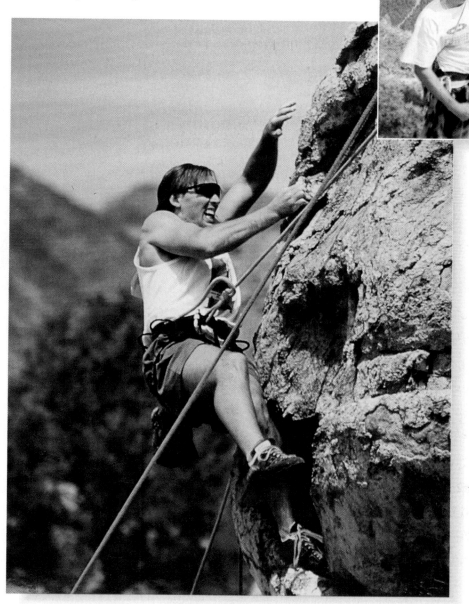

"I can get to the top of most of the things I set my mind to. I just have to get there differently."

**Erik does some rock climbing in Arizona.**

## Background and Vocabulary

MAE JEMISON
*Space Scientist*

By Gail Sakurai

**Mae Jemison:
Space Scientist**

**Genre** **Biography**

### Key Vocabulary

astronaut
launches
mission specialist
orbit
reusable spacecraft
satellite
space shuttle

**Vocabulary Reader**

Preparing for
Lift-Off
By Carlynn Trout

*e* **Glossary**

# Exploring Space

**W**hen the Soviet Union launched the first artificial **satellite** in the 1950s, the space race between the Russians and the Americans began. Since then, there have been many historic space events, including the first mission to have an African American female **astronaut** aboard, described in *Mae Jemison: Space Scientist.*

### 1957
The Soviet Union **launches** the first artificial satellite, *Sputnik 1.*

### 1961
The first human in space is Russian cosmonaut Yuri Gagarin aboard *Vostok 1.* The first American in space is Alan Shepard (left) aboard *Freedom 7.*

### 1962
John Glenn aboard *Friendship 7* is the first American to **orbit** the Earth.

### 1963
Russian Valentina Tereshkova is the first woman in space.

## 1999
Eileen Collins is the first female commander of a shuttle mission.

## 1995
Cosmonaut Valery Polyakov completes a record 488 days in space aboard the Russian space station *Mir*.

## 1992
**Mission specialist** Mae Jemison (left) is the first African American woman in space.

## 1983
Sally Ride is the first American woman in space.

## 1981
The first **reusable spacecraft**, the **space shuttle** *Columbia*, is launched.

## 1969
Americans Neil Armstrong and Edwin "Buzz" Aldrin (right) walk on the moon during the *Apollo 11* mission.

# MAE JEMISON
## *Space Scientist*

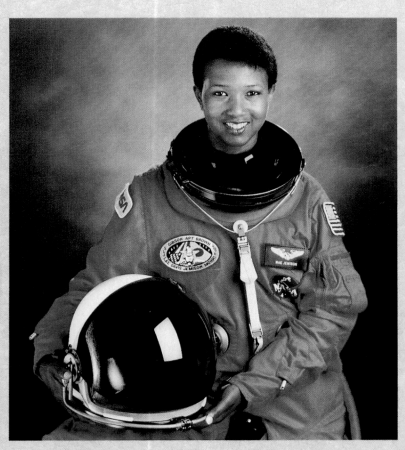

By Gail Sakurai

## Strategy Focus

As you read about space missions in this selection, **monitor** your understanding. If you do not understand something, reread or read ahead to **clarify**.

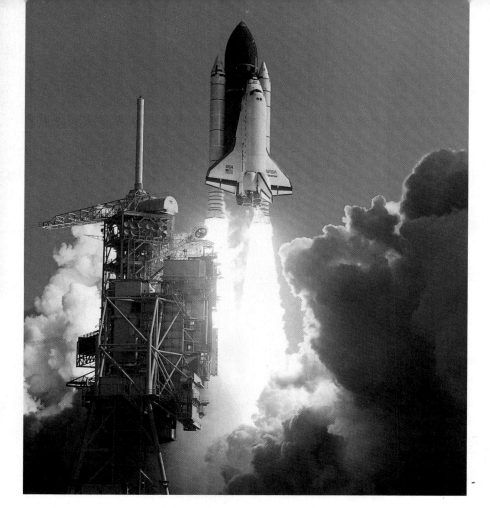

# THREE . . .
## TWO . . .
### One . . .
#### Liftoff!

The space shuttle *Endeavour* thundered into the morning sky above Kennedy Space Center. Higher and higher it soared over the Atlantic Ocean. A few minutes later, *Endeavour* was in orbit around Earth.

Aboard the spacecraft, astronaut Mae Jemison could feel her heart pounding with excitement. A wide, happy grin split her face. She had just made history. She was the first African-American woman in space. The date was September 12, 1992.

But Mae wasn't thinking about dates in history books. Her thoughts were of the wonder and adventure of space travel. "I'm closer to the stars — somewhere I've always dreamed to be," Mae said during a live television broadcast from space.

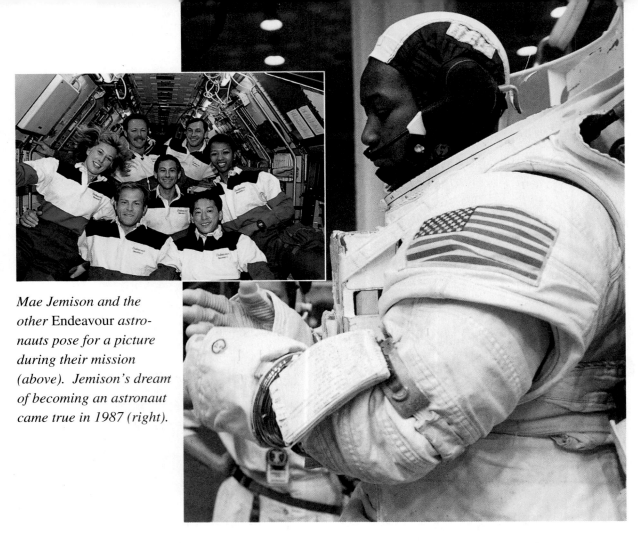

*Mae Jemison and the other* Endeavour *astronauts pose for a picture during their mission (above).* **Jemison's dream of becoming an astronaut came true in 1987 (right).**

Mae's dream didn't come true overnight. It happened only after many long years of hard work, training, and preparation. Her success story began nearly thirty-six years earlier, in a small town in Alabama.

Mae Carol Jemison was born on October 17, 1956, in Decatur, Alabama. While she was still a toddler, Mae and her family moved to the big city of Chicago, Illinois. Mae considers Chicago her hometown because she grew up there.

Mae was the youngest child in her family. She had an older brother, Charles, and an older sister, Ada. Her parents, Charlie and Dorothy Jemison, were helpful and supportive of all of Mae's interests. "They put up with all kinds of stuff, like science projects, dance classes, and art lessons," Mae said. "They encouraged me to do it, and they would find the money, time, and energy to help me be involved."

Other adults were not as encouraging as Mae's parents. When Mae told her kindergarten teacher that she wanted to be a scientist, the teacher said, "Don't you mean a nurse?" In those days, very few African-Americans or women were scientists. Many people, like Mae's teacher, couldn't imagine a little black girl growing up to become a scientist. But Mae refused to let other people's limited imaginations stop her from following her dreams.

Mae loved to work on school science projects. She spent many hours at the public library, reading books about science and space. On summer nights, she liked to lie outside, look up at the stars, and dream of traveling in space. Mae was fascinated by the real-life space flights and moon landings that she watched on television. Mae Jemison knew that she wanted to be an astronaut. Although all the astronauts at that time were white and male, Mae wasn't discouraged.

Science and space were not young Mae's only interests. She also loved to dance. Mae started taking lessons in jazz and African dance at the age of nine. By the time she was in high school, Mae was an accomplished dancer, and she frequently performed on stage. She was also skilled at choreography, the art of creating a dance.

In 1973, Mae graduated from Chicago's Morgan Park High School, where she was an honor-roll student and excelled in science and math. That fall, Mae entered Stanford University in California. At Stanford, she specialized in African and Afro-American studies, and chemical engineering. Mae continued her dancing and choreography. She also became involved with student organizations, and she was elected president of the Black Student Union.

After receiving her Bachelor of Science degree from Stanford, Mae enrolled at Cornell University Medical College in New York. She had decided to become a doctor. Medical school was demanding, but Mae still found time to participate in student organizations. She served as president of both the Cornell Medical Student Executive Council and the Cornell chapter of the National Student Medical Association.

Mae traveled to several countries as part of her medical training. She studied medicine in Cuba. She helped provide basic medical care for people in rural Kenya and at a Cambodian refugee camp in Thailand.

Mae received her Doctor of Medicine degree from Cornell University in 1981. Like all new doctors, she served an internship, a period of practicing under experienced doctors. Mae completed her internship at the Los Angeles County/University of Southern California Medical Center. Then she started working as a doctor in Los Angeles.

Although she had settled into a career as a doctor, Mae wasn't finished traveling yet. She remembered the trips she had taken during medical school, and she still wanted to help people in other parts of the world. Mae decided to join the Peace Corps, an organization of volunteers who work to improve conditions in developing nations.

*Before NASA chose Jemison for the space program, she was working as a doctor in Los Angeles.*

*Jemison at the Johnson Space Center in Houston, Texas.*

Mae spent more than two years in West Africa. She was the Area Peace Corps Medical Officer for Sierra Leone and Liberia. She was in charge of health care for all Peace Corps volunteers and U.S. embassy employees in those two countries. It was an important responsibility for someone who was only twenty-six years old.

"I learned a lot from that experience," Mae said. "I was one of the youngest doctors over there, and I had to learn to deal with how people reacted to my age, while asserting myself as a physician."

When her tour of duty in the Peace Corps was over, Mae returned to Los Angeles and resumed her medical practice. She also started taking advanced engineering classes.

*Jemison learns wilderness and water survival skills as part of her NASA training sessions.*

Mae had not forgotten her dream of traveling in space. Now that she had the necessary education and experience, Mae decided to try and become an astronaut. She applied to the National Aeronautics and Space Administration (NASA), which is responsible for U.S. space exploration. After undergoing background checks, physical exams, medical tests, and interviews, Dr. Mae Jemison was accepted into the astronaut program in June, 1987. She was one of only fifteen people chosen from nearly two thousand qualified applicants!

Mae didn't let success go to her head. "I'm very aware of the fact that I'm not the first African-American woman who had the skills, the talent, the desire to be an astronaut," she said. "I happen to be the first one that NASA selected."

Mae moved to Houston, Texas, where she began a year of intensive training at NASA's Johnson Space Center. She studied space shuttle equipment and operations. To learn how to handle emergencies and deal with difficult situations, Mae practiced wilderness and water survival skills. Survival training also helps teach cooperation and teamwork. These are important abilities for astronauts who must live and work together for long periods in a cramped space shuttle.

Mae took lessons on how to move her body and operate tools in a weightless environment. On Earth, the force of gravity keeps us from floating off the ground. But in space, there is less gravity, so people and objects drift about. Since there is no "up" or "down" in space, astronauts don't need to lie down to sleep. They can sleep in any position. To keep from drifting while asleep, they zip themselves into special sleeping bags attached to the shuttle's walls.

During training, Mae got a preview of weightlessness. She flew in a special training jet that simulates zero gravity. The jet climbs nearly straight up, then loops into a steep dive. This is similar to the loop-the-loops on many roller coasters. For thirty seconds at the top of the loop, trainees feel weightless. Their feet leave the floor and they can fly around inside the padded cabin.

At the end of her training year, Mae officially became a mission specialist astronaut. "We're the ones people often call the scientist astronauts," Mae explained. "Our responsibilities are to be familiar with the shuttle and how it operates, to do the experiments once you get into orbit, to help launch the payloads or satellites, and also do extravehicular activities, which are the space walks."

*Jemison and astronaut Jan Davis experience weightlessness in NASA's zero-gravity training jet.*

In the 1970s, NASA designed the space shuttle as the first reusable spacecraft. A shuttle launches like a rocket, but it returns to Earth and lands on a runway like an airplane. A space shuttle has many uses. It carries both equipment and people into space. Astronauts aboard a shuttle can capture, repair, and launch satellites. Shuttles are often used as orbiting laboratories, where space scientists conduct experiments in a zero-gravity environment. In the future, space shuttles might transport supplies and workers for building space stations.

Although Mae was a full-fledged astronaut, she still had to wait four more years before she went into space. While she waited, Mae worked with the scientists who were developing experiments for her mission. She also trained with her fellow crew members. In her spare time, Mae liked to read, travel, ski, garden, dance, and exercise. She also enjoyed taking care of Sneeze, her white, gray, and silver African wildcat.

On September 12, 1992, the long wait was over. Space shuttle *Endeavour* perched on the launch pad like a great white bird waiting to take flight. Everything was ready for the liftoff.

Mae awoke early to shower and dress. She ate breakfast with the other astronauts. Then, Mae and the crew put on their orange space suits and boarded a van for the short drive to the launch pad. For two-and-a-half hours until liftoff, they lay on their backs, strapped into their seats, as the countdown progressed. At 10:23 A.M., precisely on time, *Endeavour* lifted off on its historic space journey.

Dr. Mae Jemison earned her place in the history books as the first African-American woman in space. Mae said, "My participation in the space shuttle mission helps to say that all peoples of the world have astronomers, physicists, and explorers."

*Endeavour*'s mission was devoted to scientific research. Mae was responsible for several key experiments. She had

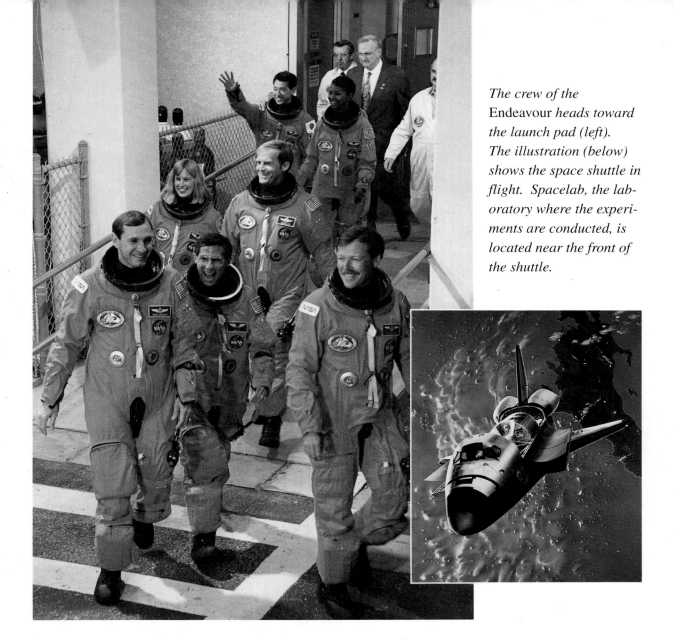

*The crew of the* Endeavour *heads toward the launch pad (left). The illustration (below) shows the space shuttle in flight. Spacelab, the laboratory where the experiments are conducted, is located near the front of the shuttle.*

helped design an experiment to study the loss of bone cells in space. Astronauts lose bone cells in weightlessness, and the longer they stay in space, the more they lose. If too many cells are lost, bones become weak and can break easily. Scientists hope to find a way to prevent this loss. Mae explained, "The real issue is how to keep people healthy while they're in space."

Mae investigated a new way of controlling space motion sickness. Half of all astronauts experience space sickness during their first few days in space. They often feel dizzy and nauseated. Astronauts can take medicine to control space sickness, but the medicine can make them tired.

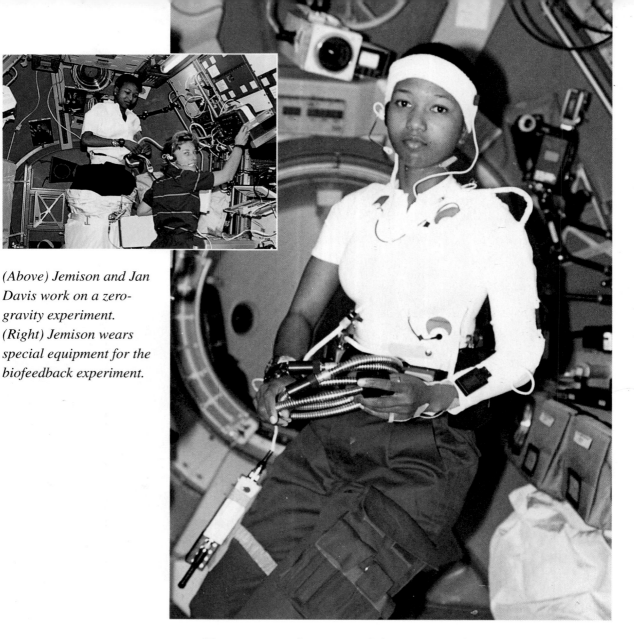

*(Above) Jemison and Jan Davis work on a zero-gravity experiment. (Right) Jemison wears special equipment for the biofeedback experiment.*

To carry out the space-sickness experiment, Mae had been trained in the use of "biofeedback" techniques. Biofeedback uses meditation and relaxation to control the body's functions. Mae wore special monitoring equipment to record her heart rate, breathing, temperature, and other body functions. If she started to feel ill, she would meditate. She concentrated intensely on bringing her body back to normal. The purpose of the experiment was to see if Mae could avoid space sickness without taking medication. The results of the experiment were not conclusive, but space researchers still hope to use biofeedback in the future.

Mae was also in charge of the frog experiment. Early in the flight, she fertilized eggs from female South African frogs. A few days later, tadpoles hatched. She then watched the tadpoles carefully. Her goal was to find out if the tadpoles would develop normally in the near-zero gravity of space. "What we've seen is that the eggs were fertilized and the tadpoles looked pretty good," said Mae. "It was exciting because that's a question that we didn't have any information on before."

On September 20, 1992, at 8:53 A.M., *Endeavour* landed at Kennedy Space Center. The crew had spent more than 190 hours (almost eight days) in space. They had traveled 3.3 million miles and had completed 127 orbits of Earth!

After her space mission, Mae returned home to Chicago. Her hometown welcomed her with six days of parades, speeches, and celebrations. Then she went to Hollywood to accept the American Black Achievement Awards' Trailblazer Award for being the first African-American woman in space. In 1993, Mae was inducted into the National Women's Hall of Fame in Seneca Falls, New York.

Mae Jemison had made her childhood dream come true. She was ready for new challenges. A few months after her space flight, Mae took a leave of absence from NASA to teach and to do research at Dartmouth College in New Hampshire. Then, on March 8, 1993, she permanently resigned from the astronaut corps.

*The* Endeavour *touches down at the Kennedy Space Center.*

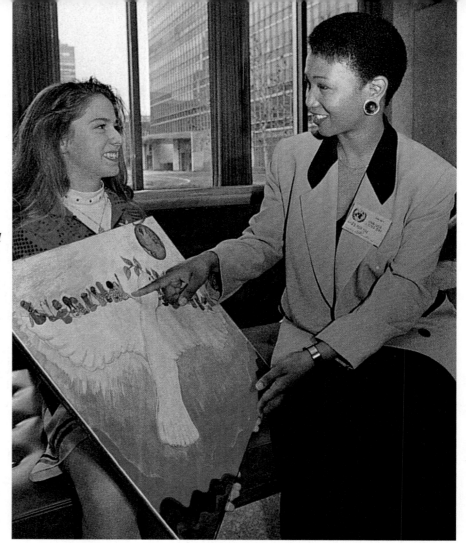

*Jemison congratulates Jill Giovanelli, age thirteen, winner of the International Peace Poster Contest.*

Mae formed her own company called The Jemison Group, Inc. The Jemison Group's goal is to develop ways of using science and technology to improve the quality of life. Mae's company makes a special effort to improve conditions in poor and developing countries.

The company's first project used satellite communications to provide better health care for people in West Africa. Mae also established an international summer science camp for young people.

Besides her work with The Jemison Group, Mae spends much of her time traveling around the country, giving speeches, and encouraging young people to follow their dreams. Mae Jemison believes in the motto:

"Don't be limited by others' limited imaginations."

# Meet the Author

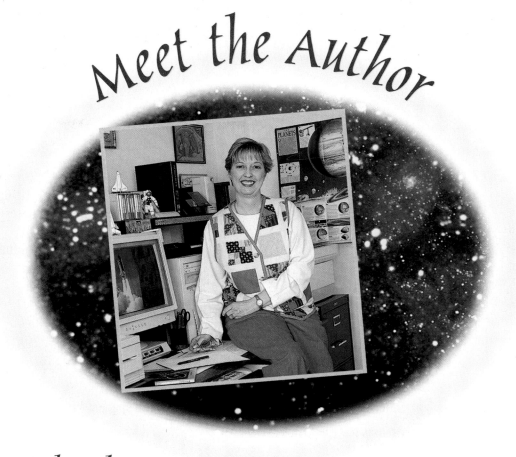

**Gail Sakurai** first decided to become a writer as a child. She had hoped to have her first book published by the time she was a teenager, but her plan did not quite work out. Sakurai says, "My childhood dream came true with the publication of my first book in 1994 — only twenty-nine years later than originally planned."

Her first book, *Peach Boy: A Japanese Legend*, is a retelling of a Japanese folktale that her husband used to tell to their sons at bedtime. She has continued to write nonfiction books and retellings of folktales.

She says that the two most difficult parts of her job are having enough time to write and starting. Once she does begin, she writes quickly because she has already planned the words in her mind.

Sakurai has written several other books for young people, including *The Liberty Bell, Stephen Hawking, Paul Revere's Ride,* and *The Jamestown Colony.*

If you would like to read more about Gail Sakurai, visit Education Place. **www.eduplace.com/kids**

# Responding

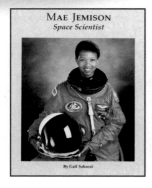

MAE JEMISON
Space Scientist

By Gail Sakurai

## Think About the Selection

**1.** What obstacles did Mae Jemison have to overcome to achieve success in her life?

**2.** How did Mae show that she had many talents even before she graduated from high school? Use examples from the selection to support your answer.

**3.** What do Mae's career changes tell you about her?

**4.** Think about the Jemison Group's goals. In what way do these goals represent a mix of Mae's talents and lifelong interests?

**5.** Since childhood Mae dreamed of traveling in space. What are some of your dreams for the future?

**6.** Which one of Mae's accomplishments impressed you most? Why?

**7. Connecting/Comparing** Why do you think the stories of Mae Jemison, Michelle Kwan, Doug Grillo, and Manuel Gomez all belong in a theme titled *Give It All You've Got*? What qualities do they share?

## Informing

## Write an Interview Script

Write the script that you would use if you could interview Mae Jemison. What questions might you ask her about her life and work?

### Tips

- **Brainstorm what you're most interested in finding out about Mae Jemison.**
- **Use the correct end marks for statements and questions.**

## Create a Fact Sheet

With a partner, create a fact sheet about what it is like to travel in the space shuttle. Include information about how to train for a space mission. Use information from the selection and from other sources. You might use the fact sheet to give an oral presentation.

Space Travel
I. Getting Ready

## Present a TV Broadcast

Mae Jemison made a live TV broadcast from *Endeavour*. Present your own version of this broadcast. Tell viewers all about *Endeavour*'s mission.

### Tips

- Write a broadcast script, or note your important points on index cards. Put the cards in order.
- Speak slowly and clearly.

*Internet*

## Complete a Web Word Find

You've learned a lot of vocabulary related to space missions in this selection. Try finding those words in a puzzle that can be printed from Education Place.

**www.eduplace.com/kids**

**Science Article**

**Skill: How to Use Text Organization**

Headings, **paragraphs,** and **captions** can help you see how the information in a nonfiction article is organized.

❶ First, read the **headings.** They identify the topic or main point covered in each section of an article.

❷ Look for new **paragraphs.** Each new paragraph signals a new main idea.

❸ Read the **captions** to find out what the photographs or diagrams show.

# Into the Deep

## Explorers in new underwater vehicles hope to unlock the secrets of the oceans' depths.

Sea explorer Graham Hawkes is ready to take a historic plunge. In the next few months, he will venture deep into the Pacific Ocean in an awesome new vessel. Most ocean-exploring vehicles drop straight down through the water. Some creep slowly along the ocean floor gathering samples and information. But *Deep Flight I,* which Hawkes helped design, zips around like a fighter plane.

Steering with joysticks, Hawkes can make the vessel roll, turn, dive and shoot for the surface. He'll get a close-up view of the wondrous life and landscape of the dark, silent world under the sea. "These vehicles are so small and light, you can send them anywhere," says Hawkes.

For years people have said the last unexplored frontier is outer space. But we really don't have to leave our planet to boldly go where no one has gone before. About 75 percent of the earth's surface is covered by the sea, and we haven't come close to seeing it all. "We know more about Mars than we do about the ocean," says Sylvia Earle, a marine biologist who helped create *Deep Flight I.*

DEEP FLIGHT I
Able to dive to 3,300 ft.
14 ft. long

# What's Down There?

With *Deep Flight I* and a fleet of other new vessels and robot craft, explorers hope to discover all sorts of riches in the sea. Among these riches are unusual living creatures. Some may prove useful as sources of medicine, food and chemicals.

The deep ocean is home to some of earth's oddest creatures. The anglerfish, the gulper eel and other deep dwellers have crushproof bodies that allow them to survive the ocean pressures 5,000 feet down. Some have body parts that can glow in the dark to attract prey.

At even greater depths, researchers have found bizarre eight-inch-long tube worms, and clams that are the size of dinner plates. They live in the boiling-hot waters near ocean vents. The vents are cracks where seawater seeps into the earth's crust and then shoots back up like a geyser. With temperatures reaching 750°F, it's amazing that anything lives nearby!

The vents constantly spew out valuable minerals like iron, copper, nickel, cobalt and manganese. The material hardens into chimneys known as "black smokers." (One of the biggest is nicknamed Godzilla.) Parts of the Pacific sea floor are littered with potato-size nuggets of these minerals. Mining companies are eager to scoop them up.

# The Very, Very Bottom

The ocean floor is not flat. Valleys, canyons, mountains and even volcanoes shape the underwater world. The deepest known point is the Mariana Trench near the Pacific island of Guam. In 1960 two scientists in a research vessel traveled 35,800 feet down — about seven miles — to explore it. A Japanese vessel went nearly that deep again last year.

Japan has a good reason to explore the ocean bottom. Southern Japan sits on a shaky part of the sea floor where three pieces of the earth's crust meet. Those pieces, called tectonic plates, shift slightly each year. The shifting can trigger earthquakes like the one that killed 5,500 people in Kobe, Japan, in 1995. Scientists say studying the plates may help them predict earthquakes.

# A Costly Quest

It costs millions of dollars to explore the deep sea. Not everyone agrees on how to do it. Some explorers say we should focus on the part of the ocean that is 20,000 feet deep or less. That's about 97 percent of the ocean. Exploring the deepest 3 percent requires more expensive equipment and is more dangerous.

But other scientists say exploring the very deepest part of the ocean will be worth the risk and cost. Greg Stone, a marine biologist in Boston, Massachusetts, says we can count on finding new animals and other discoveries we can't even imagine. "We won't know what it holds until we've been there," he says.

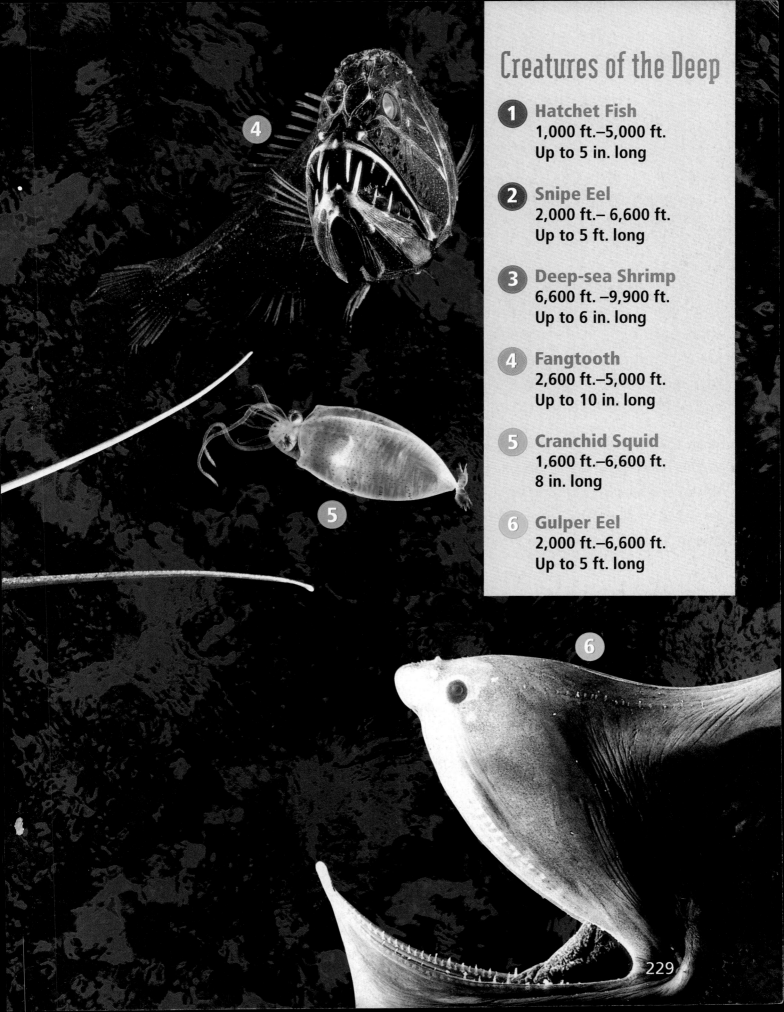

## Creatures of the Deep

**1** **Hatchet Fish**
1,000 ft.–5,000 ft.
Up to 5 in. long

**2** **Snipe Eel**
2,000 ft.– 6,600 ft.
Up to 5 ft. long

**3** **Deep-sea Shrimp**
6,600 ft. –9,900 ft.
Up to 6 in. long

**4** **Fangtooth**
2,600 ft.–5,000 ft.
Up to 10 in. long

**5** **Cranchid Squid**
1,600 ft.–6,600 ft.
8 in. long

**6** **Gulper Eel**
2,000 ft.–6,600 ft.
Up to 5 ft. long

# Check Your Progress

You have met four characters who face challenges and push themselves to new limits. Bring those ideas with you as you read and compare two new selections and polish your test-taking skills.

First, take a fresh look at the letter from Phyllis Reynolds Naylor on pages 132–134. When she writes, "I made up my mind to go for it," what other characters and events from the theme do you think of?

Now read about two more challenges: competing in a race and playing baseball. As you read, think about how the main characters face their challenges, and what part their attitude plays in what they do.

# Read and Compare

**Nonfiction**

Follow Dusty and his team of sled dogs in the 158-mile Junior Iditarod race in Alaska.

**Try these strategies:**
Question
Summarize

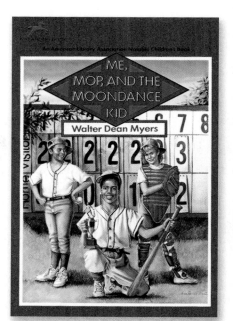

**Realistic Fiction**

If the Elks want to make the play-offs, T.J. and Moondance will first have to solve some big problems.

**Try these strategies:**
Predict and Infer
Evaluate

**Strategies in Action**  *Look for ways to use all your reading strategies as you read the selections.*

230 **A**

# IDITAROD DREAM

## BY TED WOOD

**Dusty Whittemore, age 15, is competing in his second Junior Iditarod. This two-day sled dog race, a shorter version of the Iditarod Trail race, is for mushers aged fourteen to seventeen. It starts and ends in Wasilla, Alaska, and follows a loop of 158 miles past road crossings, along rivers, and across frozen lakes. Last year, Dusty lost his way and came in fourth. This year he has his best dog team ever and hopes to outrace his friends Andy and Noah.**

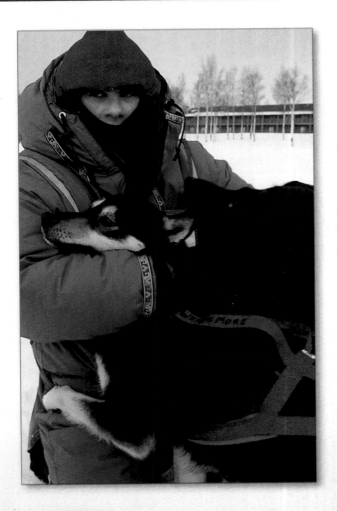

Ten minutes before his start, Dusty, his father, and three friends working as handlers hook the dogs up to the sled. Each dog looks small but is tremendously powerful. Dusty has to walk each dog from the truck, lifting its front legs off the snow. With all four legs down, a sled dog would pull Dusty off his feet. Even hooked up, the dogs are so excited by the other teams it takes every hand to hold them in place.

Dusty's team moves to the starting line, straining against the handlers. His mother rides the sled with him, stepping on the brakes to help control the sled. She's nervous, remembering how Dusty got lost last time. But she's also very proud, and she kisses him good-bye before hopping off the sled.

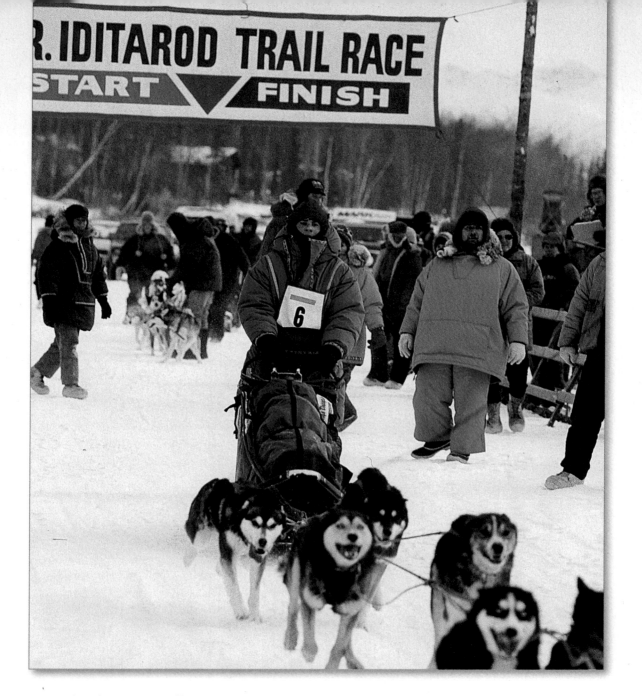

The dogs are pulling so hard now that five people can barely hold them back. Then the announcer yells, "Go!" The handlers step away and Dusty flies from the start.

They cross the lake safely, following the red plastic cones marking the route. But as they enter the woods Dusty is on edge. He's never done this part of the trail, and it's crowded with obstacles. Snowmobiles roar along the same trail, and within ten miles he has to cross four roads. Sometimes the roads are so slick the dogs fall, or they get confused by the cars and spectators. Dusty knows he just needs to survive this part until he hits the main Iditarod trail.

At the first road, the team roars over the pavement and around a sharp turn coming off the road. But they're going too fast, and the sled skids sideways, crashing into a tree. Dusty stops dead and can't believe he didn't break the sled. I'm out of control, he says to himself. I'd better slow the team down.

Back on the trail, he uses his track brake to slow the dogs. He gets them into a strong, steady pace and is able to pass two racers only five miles from the start. He crosses the next road and quickly overtakes another racer. Right before the final road crossing, ten miles out, Dusty passes the last racer. He knows he's in the lead now, that his team is running well, but he can't think about that. He just wants to get through this part and onto the main Iditarod Trail, which he knows from last year's race.

Finally, eleven miles out, Dusty hits the familiar trail leading into the thick Alaskan forest. The team is running perfectly now, strong and fast, as they head into the hilly section of the race. Dusty is in a rhythm, too. He runs beside the sled up hills to lighten the load for his team. Around tight corners he jumps from left runner to right runner, digging in the edges to steer the sled through the curves.

The trail is only a few feet wide in the woods, and coming around a blind corner the dogs run smack into two snowmobiles stopped in the path. Unable to pass, the dogs spin and run in circles, tangling their lines before Dusty can get to them. It takes him five minutes to straighten them out and get under way. As he goes around the next curve and down a hill, he spots another snowmobile roaring full speed toward him. The machine almost hits Annie and QT in the lead, but it flies off the trail to avoid the collision. The two lead dogs stop dead, but the others can't. They pile into each other, making a huge tangle of dogs and line.

Dusty can't believe it. Two tangles in less than five minutes. He frantically unknots his team, sure that another racer will catch up to him because of the delays. A tangle is a musher's second-worst nightmare. The dogs can injure their feet in the lines, or strangle when they wrap around each other.

Finally under way, Dusty and the dogs are on edge and can't settle into a pace. Please don't see another snowmobile, he says to himself. Then he spots moose tracks on the trail, and his fears mushroom. Running into a moose is a musher's worst nightmare. Because dogs look like wolves to a moose, a moose may attack a team and can kill several dogs before a musher can frighten it off. There's no going around a moose. If Dusty sees one, all he can do is wait for it to move and hope it doesn't charge.

But the team carries him safely out of the forest and onto a wide, open meadow. Dusty passes a small wooden sign that says "Nome 1,049 miles" and knows from the year before that he can relax for a while through these barren flats. The flats lead to frozen Flathorn Lake, three and a half hours from the start. Here, on the edge of the lake, Dusty takes his first break. He tosses all the dogs fish snacks, big chunks of frozen salmon that will keep their energy up. He says hi to each as well, checking their feet for injuries. QT and Blacky have splits in the webs between their toes, so Dusty puts booties on their feet to protect them as they run.

He takes only five minutes, still expecting to see another racer coming close behind. Trails cross in every direction at the lake, and it's here that Dusty got lost last year. Today, he chooses the right path and speeds out onto the huge snowy lake. It's like running on an ocean of white; Dusty feels relaxed and at home. Out on the lake he suddenly realizes how big his lead is. He can see five miles behind him and there's not one racer in sight. He can't believe it. Where are Andy and Noah? he asks himself.

From the lake Dusty turns on to the Susitna River. It looks like a winding snow highway disappearing into the wilderness. Here, he stops at the one checkpoint in the race, and while an official examines his sled and required cargo, Dusty checks the dogs. He decides to take Annie off the lead. She's been looking back while running and seems nervous. She must not have recovered from the encounter with the snowmobile, Dusty thinks.

Dusty moves young Jazz to lead with QT. But Jazz proves too inexperienced, and three miles from the checkpoint Dusty switches Jazz for Bettie. Now the team is running well again, and they move quickly, silently, up a tributary of the Susitna called Yentna River. There's no need to yell orders here. They know the way to Yentna Station, but Dusty still calls their names to keep them happy.

Just after five P.M. — seven hours after he started — Dusty arrives at Yentna station, the halfway point and overnight stop. The station is a little log house that can only be reached by plane, snowmobile, or dog sled. Visitors can stay in the house, but racers can't. By the rules, they have to stay with the dogs.

Dusty feels great. He knows he's had a fast race — but, more important, the dogs look fresh and are still eager to run. He smiles to himself, knowing that his training has paid off.

But there's no time to relax. He has hours of dog chores to do. Each racer gets one bale of straw for bedding; after Dusty ties the sled off to a small tree, he spreads the straw around the dogs. It will protect them from the cold snow as they sleep.

Next, he fires up his stove to melt snow for water. While it heats, he fills a cooler with twenty pounds of hamburger and dry food. He pours the heated water into the cooler, letting the frozen meat soak up the warm liquid. Twenty hungry eyes watch as Dusty finally dishes up the warm meal.

After dinner, Dusty checks the dogs' feet for web cracks, putting on ointment where needed. Then he hears other dogs and looks up. He'd forgotten about the other racers. It's Noah, the second racer to arrive at Yentna — thirty-eight minutes behind Dusty. Andy arrives next, eight minutes after Noah. Over the next four hours the remaining racers straggle in. Everyone is required to stay at Yentna ten hours. Dusty arrived so early that his departure time is three-thirty the next morning. He decides not to sleep and helps the other racers build a big fire in the snow. They all help each other; that's the rule of the wilderness.

Before his three-thirty start, Dusty melts more water for the dogs, feeds everyone, packs his sled, and finally makes sure his head-lamp batteries work for the trip back.

It's snowing lightly as he leaves Yentna, and there's no moon. The only light comes from Dusty's headlamp. The dogs are excited to run, but Dusty doesn't like the night. He can't see the trail markers or nearby moose. The dogs are his only eyes, so he chooses Bettie and QT to lead him out. They did the trail once, Dusty figures, so they can do it again.

Once again the dogs are gobbling up the miles. They run the Yentna River and Flathorn Lake in the dark; at first light, Dusty stops at the Nome sign. As he gives the dogs fish snacks, he finally lets himself believe that if nothing bad happens he can expect to win. Dusty and his team move through the hills easily and take all four road crossings smoothly.

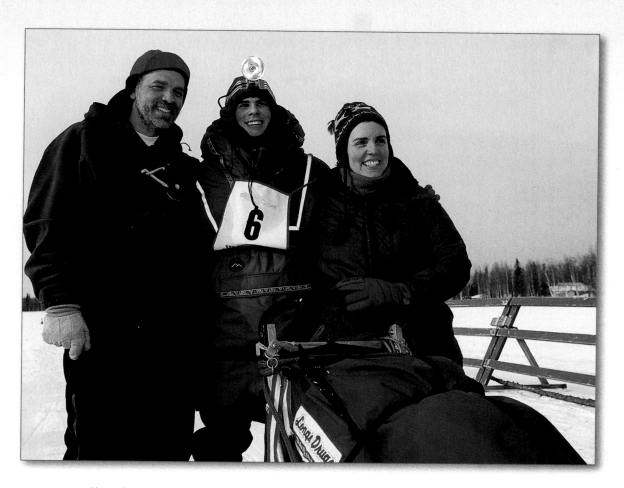

Finally, the lake appears, like a welcome mat, and Dusty begins to smile as he heads for the finish. He's running so fast that the spectators and most of the racers' families haven't arrived yet. But he spots his mother and father cheering him on, and when he crosses the finish line his mother showers him with hugs and kisses. His father's proud smile is so big it almost looks frozen with happiness.

TV and radio announcers swarm Dusty. "How does it feel to win, Dusty?" they ask.

"I would have had a big smile even if I'd come in last," he says. "But it feels great to win."

Because he ran so fast, rumors are flying that Dusty has mistreated his dogs, pushing them too hard. But now, looking at them, everyone knows this isn't true. The dogs are still strong, barking, jumping, and eager to run farther. Dusty has treated them just right. He knows they are his trusted partners — and they're champions.

# Me, Mop, and the Moondance Kid

## by Walter Dean Myers    illustrated by Stephen Fuller

T.J., his brother Moondance, and their friend Mop are trying to make the play-offs with their baseball team, the Elks. The team's supporters include Marla, the Elks' coach, a neighbor named Peaches, and Sister Carmelita from the orphanage where the brothers lived before they were adopted. But the boys' father, who was once a professional ball player, is discouraged. The Elks are playing the tough Pumas and T.J. is in right field. Now the Pumas' best hitter has just taken a big swing. . . .

I could hear the crack of the bat and saw the ball coming right out to me. It looked like it was growing bigger as it came.

I went running in for it. I knew I was going to catch it. It came down and down. I was banging my glove with my fist. I was all ready to catch it.

It was a little higher than I thought.

I went back two steps and reached up as far as I could. The ball flew just over my glove. It bounced over the fence for an automatic double.

Everybody in the infield was throwing their gloves down and looking at me. Everybody.

Even from where I was standing, way in the outfield, all by myself, I could see Dad shaking his head. I knew what he was thinking. He was wondering how come he had such a lousy kid playing ball.

They scored one more run and then we got up. When I went in, I saw Marla talking to everybody. Then when I got to the bench they all said things like "Nice try" and "You almost had it." But nobody looked at me and I knew that Marla had told them to say that.

We didn't score that inning, but neither did the Pumas during the top of the sixth.

I got up in the last of the sixth. There were two outs and I missed the first two pitches. Then I bunted at the next ball and hit it but it went foul. Then the umpire called me out because of a rule about a foul bunt on the third strike being an out.

The Pumas won, 17 to 3.

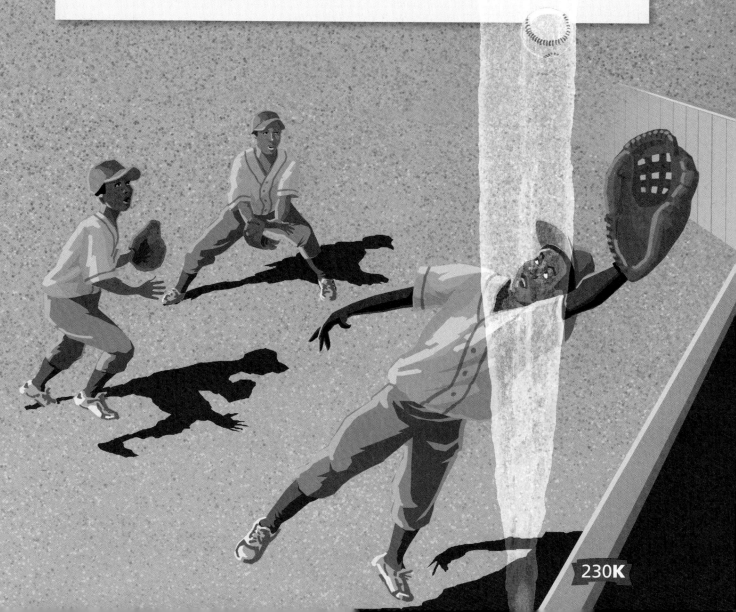

After the game I didn't even want to go near Dad. He came over to where me and Jennifer were packing up the bases in the old blue duffel bag that we carried our stuff in and went up to Marla.

"Tough loss," he said.

"They're all tough losses, Mr. Williams," Marla said.

"Titi said that you might actually make the play-offs." Dad shifted his weight from one foot to the other. "I can't see how you're going to win."

I pushed home plate as hard as I could down to the bottom of the bag.

"I don't know who this Titi is," Marla said. "But he might have also told you that we scored some runs against this team. If we had another pitcher besides Brian, if Moondance could throw the ball over the plate, for example, we would have a chance of at least being respectable."

"Why don't you let Titi help?" Dad said. "She used to be the best pitcher in our league."

"In the first place, I don't know this Titi," Marla said. "And I think it's a little late with the play-offs starting next week."

"You don't know Sister Carmelita?" Dad asked.

"Sister Carmelita?"

"Yeah, way back before she was a nun she used to play Little League ball right here in Lincoln Park," Dad said. "We used to call her Titi then. And she could pitch!"

Okay, so Sister Carmelita used to be a pitcher. But do you know who really helped Moondance turn out to be a good pitcher? Peaches! Okay, Peaches and Sister Carmelita.

Marla talked to Sister Carmelita and asked if she could help Moondance. Sister Carmelita said that she didn't know, but she would try. So we all went out to the playground the next day and Dad put the Sunday comics on the ground for the plate. Moondance started pitching to Mop.

Zip! Zip! Zip!

He could throw that ball over the plate so fast it wasn't even funny.

Zip! Zip! Zip!

Marla shook her head.

"Let's see how you hold the ball, Moondance." Sister Carmelita looked at how Moondance held the ball in his hand.

"Like this," Moondance said, holding the ball up.

Sister Carmelita held his hand still and moved the ball a little. "Try it that way," she said. "Don't let it touch your palm. It's a little trickier, but I think you can do it."

The first ball that Moondance threw went right over Mop's head.

"Follow through!" Sister Carmelita called out. "Bring your arm all the way down."

Zip! Whack!

That's the way the ball went. It went even faster than it did the first time he was throwing.

Zip! Whack!

The next ball went over Mop's head, but after that the ball was going right into the glove.

Zip! Whack!

Zip! Whack!

"T.J., stand at the plate." Marla handed me a bat.

No way I wanted to stand there with the bat. I looked at Marla to see if she really meant for me to stand there, but she had already gone over to sit on one of the benches. Dad was leaning against the backstop and Sister Carmelita was standing near Moondance out at the mound. It was as if they were watching a show or something.

I looked at Moondance and he looked at me. He had his tongue out and was wiping off his pitching hand. Mop got down on her knees and put one hand behind her back.

"Throw it past him, Moondance!" she yelled. "He can't hit!"

"Don't swing, T.J.," Marla called out. "I just want to see his control."

Zip!

The ball went outside and against the backstop. Dad looked at Moondance and one eyebrow went up. Mop got the ball and threw it back to Moondance. Sister Carmelita was talking to him, but I couldn't hear what she was saying.

You know how I felt? A little nervous. Even though I didn't have to swing at the ball, you get a little nervous when Moondance throws it with all of his might.

Zip!

The ball went outside and past Mop's glove again.

"Give him a target, Mop!"

"I am giving him a target!" Mop yelled back as she picked the ball up again.

"C'mon, Son." Dad made a fist and held it up toward Moondance. "Bring it high and tight."

I didn't know what that meant, but I saw the next ball go flying outside again.

"Stand on the other side, T.J."

That's what Marla said.

"No!" That's what I said. Moondance was throwing the balls just where she wanted me to stand.

"You're not scared of the ball, are you?" Dad asked.

"No," I said.

I went to the other side. I wasn't scared of the ball. I mean, if the ball and me were in a dark room together, I wouldn't be nervous or anything. I was afraid of being hit by the ball.

Moondance wound up and threw the ball. I dropped the bat and got ready to duck in case it came toward me, but it didn't. It went on the other side.

"Moondance, are you afraid of hitting him?" Marla got off the bench and started toward us.

"I don't want to hit anybody," Moondance said.

"Don't worry about it, just throw the ball to Hop," Dad said.

"That's Mop, M-O-P." Mop gave Dad a look.

"If you just aim for Mop's glove, you won't be that close to him," Marla said. "You can almost do it with your eyes closed."

I got away from the plate. He wasn't throwing the ball at me with his eyes closed.

"Just keep your eye on the glove," Sister Carmelita said. "Take your time."

Moondance looked at Mop's glove and kept his eyes right on it. He wound up and threw the ball again.

Zip!

Fast as anything, but outside. I think they were right. He didn't want to hit me.

Then Dad caught and Mop got up to bat. Same thing. Moondance didn't want to throw the ball near anybody.

Dad said he would talk to him and I saw Moondance look a little sad. Sometimes Dad says things that sound good, or at least okay, but deep down you know they're not. He said he would talk to Moondance, that everything would be okay. But you could tell by the way he said it that he wasn't happy with the way Moondance pitched. I could tell it and Moondance could tell it too.

It's bad when you mess up and people aren't happy with you. Like when I missed the fly ball and everybody on the team threw their gloves down. But I think it's even worse when you do something good, like Moondance did, and somebody isn't happy with you because you didn't do it good enough. Especially when that somebody is your dad.

Still, Sister Carmelita had helped Moondance a little, and we didn't even know that Peaches was going to help too.

When we got home, Dad got out all these pictures of him playing baseball. He looked great. I imagined myself doing some of the things he did.

WILLIAMS' HOMER SPURS ASU WIN!

"That's when we won the national championship," Dad said. "We made every paper in the state of Arizona every day that week!"

"That's where I first met him," Mom said. "All he ever talked about then was playing baseball. All he ever did was play baseball too. I think he married me because I could keep score."

Then he showed us the pictures of himself when he played for Kansas City.

"It must be hard to be a great baseball player," I said.

"Sometimes," Dad said. "It's even harder not to be a great ballplayer."

# Think and Compare

1. Compare the challenge Dusty faces with the one Moondance faces. How are the challenges different? How are they alike?

2. Compare a challenge you have faced with that of a character in this theme. Include the work that went into meeting the challenge and how you and the character felt.

3. Which character in the theme would have the best advice for the members of the Elks baseball team? What would that advice be?

4. How do different characters in the theme rely on the help of others to achieve their victories?

5. Every victory follows a low point. What are the low points of some characters in the theme? Compare how the characters react to their problems.

**Strategies in Action** How did you use one or more reading strategies for help during this theme?

# Write an Editorial

Think about how the characters worked to meet their goals. Then write a brief editorial that encourages others to work at an important activity in their lives.

**Tips**

- Choose an activity to write about, such as a sport or homework.
- List things a person can do to succeed in the activity.
- Explain why your advice is important.

# Filling in the Blank

Some test items ask you to complete a sentence. You must decide what is the best answer from several choices. A test about *Iditarod Dream* might include this sentence.

> Read the sentence with each ending. Fill in the circle in the answer row for the answer that best completes the sentence.
>
> **1.** A musher's worst nightmare is _____.
>
> **A** getting tangled
>
> **B** getting lost
>
> **C** running into a moose
>
> **D** crashing into a tree
>
> ANSWER ROW 1   Ⓐ Ⓑ ● Ⓓ

 **Understand the sentence.**

Find the key words in the sentence. Use them to understand what you need to do.

> I think the key words are *musher* and *worst*. I need to choose the worst thing that can happen to a musher in a race.

## ② Look back at the selection.

Think about where to find the answer. You may need to look in more than one place. Skim the selection, using the key words.

> I can probably find this information where something bad happens, or almost happens, to Dusty.

## ③ Narrow the choices. Then choose the best answer.

Read the sentence, trying each answer choice in the blank. Find the choices that are clearly wrong. Have a good reason for choosing an answer. Guess only if you have to.

> When Dusty gets tangled, I read that a tangle is a musher's second-worst nightmare. So **A** is wrong. When Dusty sees moose tracks, I read that running into a moose is a musher's *worst* nightmare. The answer is **C**.

# Poetry

*"If there were a recipe for a poem, these would be the ingredients: word sounds, rhythms, description, feeling, memory, rhyme and imagination. They can be put together a thousand different ways, a thousand, thousand . . . more."*

*— Karla Kuskin*

A poem can be about almost anything: a spider, a pair of sneakers, even your nose. It uses words carefully, describing or telling a story with exact **sounds**, **images**, and **rhythms**. As a poem grows, familiar things may begin to look remarkable. By the end of the poem you may feel you are seeing the world in a brand new way.

# Contents

# Places and Seasons

## Árbol de limón

Si te subes a un árbol de limón
siente la corteza
con tus rodillas y pies,
huele sus flores blancas,
talla las hojas
entre tus manos.
Recuerda,
el árbol es mayor que tú
y tal vez encuentres cuentos
entre sus ramas.

— *Jennifer Clement*

## Lemon Tree

If you climb a lemon tree
feel the bark
under your knees and feet,
smell the white flowers,
rub the leaves
in your hands.
Remember,
the tree is older than you are
and you might find stories
in its branches.

— *Jennifer Clement*

*Translated by
Consuelo de Aerenlund*

# Travel

The railroad track is miles away,
    And the day is loud with voices speaking,
Yet there isn't a train goes by all day
    But I hear its whistle shrieking.

All night there isn't a train goes by,
    Though the night is still for sleep and dreaming,
But I see its cinders red on the sky,
    And hear its engine steaming.

My heart is warm with the friends I make,
    And better friends I'll not be knowing;
Yet there isn't a train I wouldn't take,
    No matter where it's going.

— *Edna St. Vincent Millay*

# knoxville, tennessee

I always like summer
best
you can eat fresh corn
from daddy's garden
and okra
and greens
and cabbage
and lots of
barbecue
and buttermilk
and homemade ice-cream
at the church picnic
and listen to
gospel music
outside
at the church
homecoming
and go to the mountains with
your grandmother
and go barefooted
and be warm
all the time
not only when you go to bed
and sleep
          — *nikki giovanni*

# A Patch of Old Snow

There's a patch of old snow in a corner
 That I should have guessed
Was a blow-away paper the rain
 Had brought to rest.

It is speckled with grime as if
 Small print overspread it,
The news of a day I've forgotten —
 If I ever read it.

     — *Robert Frost*

# Early Spring

In the early spring, the snowfall is light
upon the mesa.
It does not stick to the ground very long.
I walk through this patchwork of snow and earth,
watching the ground for early signs.
Signs of growth.  Signs of rebirth.

Larkspur and wild onions are still
within the warmth of the earth.
I hear cries of crows off in the distance.
A rabbit bounds off into the sagebrush flat.
A shadow of a hawk disturbs the landscape momentarily.
It sees food and life abundant below that I cannot see.
The cycle of life continues.

Even as I stand here shivering in the afternoon chill,
just below me, young seedlings start
their upward journey.
Insects begin to stir.
Rodents and snakes are comfortable in their burrows.
Maybe to them we also disappear with the cold.
Not to be seen until spring.

For this generation, and many more to come,
this land is beautiful and filled with mysteries.
They reveal themselves and their stories —
if you look very carefully, and listen . . .

— *Shonto Begay*

239

# Civilization

I've stood here lately, looking at the path
Where deer once came to watch the sun go down,
Standing with their ears pricked for the sound
Of cars along the street.

I've longed to hear coyotes call again
Across the valley, howling from the hill,
Baying when the night stands black and still
Where sky and mountain meet.

I've watched for the raccoons, who crept
Along the rocks and over fallen wood,
Begging near our windows for some food,
Staring with black-ringed eyes.

Lizards, rabbits, snakes and moles.  They came,
Chewing the poppies, digging up the lawn,
Burrowing homes and holes.  But they have gone.
The mournful owls remember.  So do I.

— *Myra Cohn Livingston*

## Animals

# Dinner Together

Sitting by the barbecue
waiting for sausages and hot dogs
blue-gray smoke the same color
of the sky
I see a tiny spider
walking down from the sky with tiny six-
footed steps
down
down
in a perfectly straight
line
all the way
down
to the floor
then back up
the same line
rising from one cloud
up to another,
a silver speck
glistening
at its mouth,
climbing the invisible ladder.

— *Diana Rivera*

# Whirligig Beetles

| | |
|---|---|
| We're whirligig beetles | |
| we're swimming in circles, | We're whirligig beetles |
| black backs by the hundred. | we're swimming in circles, |
| | black backs by the hundred. |
| | We're spinning and swerving |
| We're spinning and swerving | as if we were on a |
| as if we were on a | mad merry-go-round. |
| mad merry-go-round. | |
| We never get dizzy | |
| from whirling and weaving | We never get dizzy |
| and wheeling and swirling. | from whirling and weaving |
| | and wheeling and swirling. |
| | The same goes for turning, |
| The same goes for turning, | revolving and curving, |
| revolving and curving, | gyrating and twirling. |
| gyrating and twirling. | |
| The crows fly directly, | |
| but we prefer spirals, | The crows fly directly, |
| arcs, ovals, and loops. | but we prefer spirals, |
| | arcs, ovals, and loops. |
| | We're fond of the phrase |
| "As the whirligig swims" | "As the whirligig swims" |
| | meaning traveling by |
| | the most circular |

circular
roundabout
backtracking
indirect
serpentine
tortuous
twisty,
best possible
route.

roundabout
backtracking
indirect
serpentine
tortuous
twisty and
turny,
best possible
route.

— *Paul Fleischman*

# The Shark

My sweet, let me tell you about the shark.
Though his eyes are bright, his thought is dark.
He's quiet — that speaks well of him.
So does the fact that he can swim.
But though he swims without a sound,
Wherever he swims he looks around
With those two bright eyes and that one
      dark thought.
He has only one, but he thinks it a lot.
And the thought he thinks but can never complete
Is his long dark thought of something to eat.
Most anything does, and I have to add
That when he eats his manners are bad.
He's a gulper, a ripper, a snatcher, a grabber.
Yes, his manners are drab.  But his thought
      is drabber.
That one dark thought he can never complete
Of something — anything — somehow to eat.

Be careful where you swim, my sweet.

— *John Ciardi*

# It's All the Same to the Clam

You may leave the clam on the ocean's floor,
It's all the same to the clam.
For a hundred thousand years or more,
It's all the same to the clam.
You may bury him deep in mud and muck
Or carry him 'round to bring you luck,
Or use him for a hockey puck,
It's all the same to the clam.

You may call him Jim or Frank or Nell,
It's all the same to the clam.
Or make an ashtray from his shell,
It's all the same to the clam.
You may take him riding on the train
Or leave him sitting in the rain.
You'll never hear the clam complain,
It's all the same to the clam.

Yes, the world may stop or the world may spin,
It's all the same to the clam.
And the sky may come a-fallin' in,
It's all the same to the clam.
And man may sing his endless songs
Of wronging rights and righting wrongs.
The clam just sets — and gets along,
It's all the same to the clam.

— *Shel Silverstein*

244

# THE BAT

By day the bat is cousin to the mouse.
He likes the attic of an aging house.

His fingers make a hat about his head.
His pulse beat is so slow we think him dead.

He loops in crazy figures half the night
Among the trees that face the corner light.

But when he brushes up against a screen,
We are afraid of what our eyes have seen:

For something is amiss or out of place
When mice with wings can wear a human face.

— *Theodore Roethke*

People

# CAMPFIRE

Just think —
when Mother was my age,
she could build a fire
with sparks from rocks,
catch a bunch of
grasshoppers and
roast them whole
for a summer
night's snack!

"Get me a good stick,"
she says, "thin but strong,"
and I bring her one
from the woods
behind our tent.
On the way back
I see a brown bag
by her feet —
could it be?

When the fire is spitting ready,
she reaches
in the bag, rustling,
and hands me
one big, fat, luscious
marshmallow.

— *Janet Wong*

# Be Glad Your Nose Is on Your Face

Be glad your nose is on your face,
not pasted on some other place,
for if it were where it is not,
you might dislike your nose a lot.

Imagine if your precious nose
were sandwiched in between your toes,
that clearly would not be a treat,
for you'd be forced to smell your feet.

Your nose would be a source of dread
were it attached atop your head,
it soon would drive you to despair,
forever tickled by your hair.

Within your ear, your nose would be
an absolute catastrophe,
for when you were obliged to sneeze,
your brain would rattle from the breeze.

Your nose, instead, through thick and thin,
remains between your eyes and chin,
not pasted on some other place —
be glad your nose is on your face!

— *Jack Prelutsky*

# Reggie

It's summertime
And Reggie doesn't live here anymore
He lives across the street
Spends his time with the round ball
Jump, turn, shoot
Through the hoop
Spends his time with arguments
        and sweaty friends
And not with us
He's moved away
Comes here just to eat and sleep
        and sometimes pat my head
Then goes back home
To run and dribble and jump and stretch
And stretch
And shoot
Thinks he's Kareem
And not my brother

— *Eloise Greenfield*

# WHAT ARE POCKETS FOR?

What are pockets for?
An old piece of sash cord,
a knob from a door;
a small U magnet,
if you can find it;
a sprung clock spring,
with the key to wind it;
oodles of marbles,
a twist of copper wire;
a baseball calendar,
a flint for fire;
one soiled jack of hearts
or the five of spades;
that unshown copy of
your last month's grades;
two colored pebbles,
one hickory nut;
a shell, some fish line
with three feet of gut;
a cog out of something
which never did run;
a cellophane of candy —
I'll give you one;

your first circus ticket stub,
the snap you took
of the clown on the slack
wire before it shook;
a flashlight bulb,
a dirty green stamp;
the long-missing part of
your bicycle lamp;
one thin pair of pliers
to ply or to nip;
one old zipper fastener
with nothing to zip;
that half-busted harness-
bell you found inside
the barn on the farm,
and the buckle too wide
for its three-inch strap;
and a whole lot more
of stuff. Did you say,
What are pockets for?

— *David McCord*

# Ode to
# Pablo's Tennis Shoes

They wait under Pablo's bed,
Rain-beaten, sun-beaten,
A scuff of green
At their tips
From when he fell
In the school yard.
He fell leaping for a football
That sailed his way.
But Pablo fell and got up,
Green on his shoes,
With the football
Out of reach.

Now it's night.
Pablo is in bed listening
To his mother laughing
To the Mexican *novelas* on TV.
His shoes, twin pets
That snuggle his toes,
Are under his bed.
He should have bathed,
But he didn't.
(Dirt rolls from his palm,
Blades of grass
Tumble from his hair.)

He wants to be
Like his shoes,
A little dirty
From the road,
A little worn
From racing to the drinking fountain
A hundred times in one day.
It takes water
To make him go,
And his shoes to get him
There.  He loves his shoes,
Cloth like a sail,
Rubber like
A lifeboat on rough sea.
Pablo is tired,
Sinking into the mattress.
His eyes sting from
Grass and long words in books.
He needs eight hours
Of sleep
To cool his shoes,
The tongues hanging
Out, exhausted.

— *Gary Soto*

# *Dream* Variation

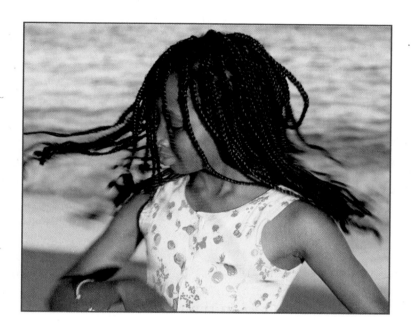

To fling my arms wide
In some place of the sun,
To whirl and to dance
Till the white day is done.
Then rest at cool evening
Beneath a tall tree
While night comes on gently,
    Dark like me —
That is my dream!

To fling my arms wide
In the face of the sun,
Dance! Whirl! Whirl!
Till the quick day is done.
Rest at a pale evening. . . .
A tall, slim tree. . . .
Night coming tenderly
    Black like me.

— *Langston Hughes*

# Think About the
# POETRY

1. Compare the purpose of a tall tale with the purpose of a poem. How are they different? Could they be alike? How?

2. Why do you think the poet who wrote "Travel" chose to use rhyme while the poet who wrote "knoxville, tennessee" chose not to?

3. Compare the different poems in the "Animals" section. Which was funniest? Which was the most surprising? Which created the most vivid picture? Explain your choices.

4. How do the poems in the "People" section use details and actions to make the person in the poem stand out?

5. Which poems showed you how a poem can do things that no other kind of writing can do? Explain.

## Take an Online Poll

What kinds of poems are your favorite? Poems about people? Poems about places? Funny poems? Poems that describe nature? Take our online poll and add your choice. Visit Education Place. **www.eduplace.com/kids**

# Write a Poem

Write a poem that begins with the words "I wish" or "I see" or "I remember." Repeat the opening phrase on every line or on alternating lines. Be as free and imaginative as you like. Do not try to make the poem rhyme.

**Variation:** Choose another phrase of your own to begin the poem.

> ### Tips
>
> - **If you need help getting started, work with a partner. Take turns adding lines.**
> - **Try adding a color, a place name, or an animal to each line of the poem.**
> - **Wait to correct your spelling and punctuation until after the poem is finished.**

# Voices
## of the
# Revolution

"We always had governed ourselves,
and we always meant to."

— *farmer at the Battle of Lexington, April 1775*

"The flame is kindled and like lightning
it catches from Soul to Soul."

— *Abigail Adams*

"I know not what course others
may take, but as for me, give me
liberty or give me death!"

— *Patrick Henry*

# Voices
## of the
# Revolution

## with Walter Dean Myers

**Dear Reader,**

The American Revolution created a new country, the United States of America. It also created a fascinating set of symbols that we have learned to love, and that represents our country and values.

### The Declaration of Independence

The Declaration of Independence is the document that announced to the world that the United States was a free nation. The day it was adopted, the Fourth of July, became a day symbolizing freedom, and the nation's birthday.

### First American Flag

The thirteen stripes of the first American flag represent the thirteen colonies that had broken away from England. The colonies together formed a new constellation, represented by the thirteen white stars.

### The Great Seal of the United States

We carry an image of the Great Seal in our wallets on the one dollar bill. On the front of the seal, a bald eagle holds the arrows of war in one talon and an olive branch of peace in the other. In its beak there is a ribbon bearing the motto *E Pluribus Unum* (Out of Many, One).

### The Bald Eagle

In June, 1782, the American bald eagle became our national emblem. The eagle was chosen for its long life, great strength, and majestic appearance. Benjamin Franklin, however, did not like the bald eagle. He preferred to have the wild turkey as our national bird.

### The Liberty Bell

The Liberty Bell was made in 1753 and was used to signal important events. It rang on July 8, 1776, when the Declaration of Independence was first read. The bell weighs 2080 pounds.

During the difficult days of the Revolutionary War, a war in which the colonists often found that they had to live under the hostile eyes of the British army, the symbols of the new country brought comfort and inspiration. For me, the Stars and Stripes of the American flag, the American bald eagle, and the Declaration of Independence have always been stirring symbols of what makes me proud to be an American.

*Walter Dean Myers*

**George Washington Crossing the Delaware, by Emmanuel Leutze (1816-1868)**

# Discover America

What thoughts or feelings do you have about the American symbols that Walter Dean Myers chose to write about?  Are there other American images that you would have chosen to stand for this nation?

Take a moment to review the theme selections shown below.  When you read them, remember the patriotism, or love of one's country, that is behind those symbols.  Think about how those same feelings inspire the characters to act the way they do.

Internet

To learn about the authors in this theme, visit Education Place.  **www.eduplace.com/kids**

**And Then What Happened, Paul Revere?**

Genre **Biography**

### Key Vocabulary

colonies
express
oppose
Patriot
revolution
taxes

**Vocabulary Reader**

e ● **Glossary**

# On the Brink of War

Between 1765 and 1770, people in the thirteen American colonies grew tired of being ruled by England. When the English king ordered more taxes , the colonists found ways to oppose him. *And Then What Happened, Paul Revere?* shows how one American Patriot helped begin a revolution to end English rule.

◀ The colonists showed their hatred of unfair taxes wherever possible — even on teapots!

▲

King George III sent soldiers to make the colonists obey his laws. In protest, Paul Revere created this picture of English ships arriving in Boston Harbor in 1768.

New England farmers prepared to fight the British on a moment's notice. That moment arrived on April 19, 1775, when the first shots of the American Revolution were fired in Lexington, Massachusetts.

◄ The Patriots came from many backgrounds and professions. Paul Revere, shown in this portrait by John Singleton Copley, was a silversmith and an **express** rider, spreading news of Patriot and British activities.

AND THEN WHAT HAPPENED,
PAUL REVERE?

by JEAN FRITZ

PICTURES BY MARGOT TOMES

⭐ **Strategy Focus**

As you read, **evaluate** the way Jean Fritz describes
Paul Revere.  How well do you think she tells the
story of his life?

In 1735 there were in Boston 42 streets, 36 lanes, 22 alleys, 4,000 houses, 12 churches, 4 schools, 418 horses (at the last count), and so many dogs that a law was passed prohibiting people from having dogs that were more than 10 inches high. But it was difficult to keep dogs from growing more than 10 inches, and few people cared to part with their 11- and 12-inch dogs, so they paid little attention to the law. In any case there were too many dogs to count.

Along with the horses, streets, and alleys, there were, of course, people in Boston — about 15,000. Four of them lived in a small wooden house on North Street near Love Lane. They were Mr. Revere, a gold and silversmith; his wife, Deborah; their daughter, Deborah; and their young son, Paul Revere, born the first day of the new year.

Of all the busy people in Boston, Paul Revere would turn out to be one of the busiest. All his life he found that there was more to do, more to make, more to see, more to hear, more to say, more places to go, more to learn than there were hours in the day.

In Boston there was always plenty to see. Ships were constantly coming and going, unloading everything from turtles to chandeliers. Street vendors were constantly crying their wares — everything from fever pills to hair oil to oysters. From time to time there were traveling acrobats, performing monkeys, parades, firework displays, and fistfights.

Once there was a pickled pirate's head on exhibit; once there was a polar bear.

And there was plenty for Paul to do. When he was a teenager, his father died, and Paul took over the silversmithing business. He made beads, rings, lockets, bracelets, buttons, medals, pitchers, teapots, spoons, sugar baskets, cups, ewers, porringers, shoe buckles, and candlesticks.

Once he made a silver collar for a man's pet squirrel.

To make extra money, he took a job ringing the bells in Christ Church. In Boston, church bells were rung not just on Sundays but three times a day on weekdays, at special hours on holidays and anniversaries, for fires and emergencies, whenever a member of the congregation died, and whenever there was especially good news or especially bad news to announce. Sometimes at a moment's notice word would come that the bells were to be rung, and off Paul would run, his hat clapped to his head, his coattails flying.

Busy as he was, Paul liked to do new things. If there was excitement around, he liked to find it. In the spring of 1756, when Paul was twenty-one years old, there was, as it happened, a war close by, and Paul didn't want to miss it. French soldiers, along with Indians, were attacking the borders of the colonies. So Paul grabbed his rifle, buckled on his sword, clapped his hat to his head, and off he went — coattails flying — to defend Fort William Henry on Lake George.

And what happened?

Paul spent the summer sitting around, cleaning his rifle and polishing his sword. And swatting flies. There were thousands of flies at Lake George that summer. But there were no French or Indians.

In November the Massachusetts men were sent home. Paul went back to Boston, married Sarah Orne, and began filling up his house with children. There were Deborah, Paul, Sarah, Mary, Frances, and Elizabeth (in addition to two babies who died young). Then Sarah died, and Paul married Rachel Walker, and along came Joshua, Joseph, Harriet, Maria, and John (in addition to three more babies who died young).

Paul kept putting up new chairs at the kitchen table, and now in addition to making buckles, spoons, cups, and all the other silver items, Paul had to find new ways to make money. So he engraved portraits, produced bookplates, sold pictures, made picture frames, brought out hymnbooks, and became a dentist. "Artificial Teeth. Paul Revere," he advertised. "He fixes them in such a Manner that they are not only an Ornament, but of real Use in Speaking and Eating."

You would think that with all Paul Revere did, he would make mistakes. But he always remembered to put spouts on his teapots and handles on his cups.

The false teeth that he whittled out of hippopotamus tusk looked just fine.

Generally when he did arithmetic in his Day Book, he got the right answers.

Of course, sometimes there were so many different things to do that he forgot what he was doing. In the beginning of a new Day Book, he wrote, "This is my book for me to —", but he never finished the sentence.

Sometimes he was in such a hurry that his writing looked sloppy. At the end of a letter he would write, "Pray excuse my scrawl."

Sometimes he was late for his work. There was a hymnbook, for instance, that didn't come out until eighteen months after he promised it.

Once he built a barn and by mistake put part of it on a neighbor's property.

Still, Paul Revere wasn't always at work. Occasionally he just dreamed. There was one page in his Day Book that he used simply for doodling.

But beginning in 1765, there was no time for doodling. The French had stopped bothering America, but now the English were causing trouble, telling the colonies they couldn't do this and couldn't do that, slapping on taxes, one after another. First there was a tax on printed matter — newspapers, diplomas, marriage licenses. When this was withdrawn, there was a tax on tea, glass, printers' colors, and paper. The one tax England would never give up was the tax on tea.

And what did Paul Revere do about it?

He became a leader of the Sons of Liberty, a secret club that found interesting ways to oppose the English.

One of Paul's busiest nights was December 16, 1773. He prepared for it by smearing his face with red paint and lampblack, pulling a tight stockinglike covering over his head, and draping a ragged blanket over his shoulders. Then he picked up his ax and joined other Sons of Liberty, all pretending to be Indians, all carrying axes.

And what were they up to?

They were going to make sure that no one in Boston would pay taxes on the three shiploads of tea that had just arrived from England. So they marched on board the ships, hauled the chests of tea onto the decks, broke them open with their axes, and dumped the tea — 10,000 pounds of it — into Boston Harbor. It was all done in an orderly fashion. No one was hurt; no other cargo was touched; the ships were unharmed. (There was only one minor incident when a man, found stuffing tea into the lining of his coat, had to be punished.)

When the Sons of Liberty finished, they marched home, washed their faces, and went to bed.

But not Paul Revere. Someone had to ride to New York and Philadelphia and spread the news. And Paul was picked to do it.

So off he galloped, his hat clapped to his head, his coattails flying. From Boston to Cambridge to Watertown to Worcester to Hartford *(watch out, dogs on the road! watch out, chickens!)* to New York to Philadelphia he went. And back. 63 miles a day. (This was not swatting flies!)

He was back in Boston on the eleventh day, long before anyone expected him.

Paul Revere became Massachusetts' Number One express rider between Boston and Philadelphia. He also became a secret agent. In the winter of 1774 it looked more and more as if the English soldiers in Boston meant to make war on America, and Paul's job was to try to find out the English plans.

He was far too busy now to write in his Day Book. He was too busy to make many silver teapots or to whittle many teeth. Instead, he patrolled the streets at night, delivered messages to Philadelphia, and kept himself ready at all times to warn the countryside.

Sometimes on his missions things went just right. He got past the sentries, got through the snow, kept his horse on the road, and kept himself on his horse.

Sometimes things went poorly. Once the English found him in a rowboat snooping around Castle Island in Boston Harbor. So they stopped him, questioned him, and locked him up. He stayed locked up for two days and three nights.

But all his rides, Paul knew, were small compared to the Big Ride that lay ahead. Nothing should go wrong with this one. In the spring, everyone agreed, the English would march into the countryside and really start fighting. And when they did, Paul Revere would have to be ahead of them.

On Saturday, April 15, spring, it seemed, had arrived. Boats for moving troops had been seen on the Charles River. English scouts had been observed on the road to Lexington and Concord. A stableboy had overheard two officers making plans.

At about 10 o'clock on Tuesday night, April 18, Dr. Joseph Warren, who was directing Patriot activities in Boston, sent for Paul Revere. Other messengers had been dispatched for Lexington and Concord by longer routes. Paul was to go, as planned, the same way the English were going — across the Charles River. He was to alarm the citizens so they could arm themselves, and he was to inform John Hancock and Samuel Adams, Boston's two Patriot leaders who were staying in Lexington. And Paul was to leave now.

He had already arranged a quick way of warning the people of Charlestown across the river. Two lanterns were to be hung in the steeple of the North Church if the English were coming by water; one lantern if they were coming by land.

So Paul asked a friend to rush to the North Church. "Two lanterns," he told him. "Now."

Then he ran home, flung open the door, pulled on his boots, grabbed his coat, kissed his wife, told the children to be good, and off he went — his hat clapped to his head, his coattails flying. He was in such a hurry that he left the door open, and his dog got out.

On the way to the river Paul picked up two friends, who had promised to row him to the other side. Then all three ran to a dock near the Charlestown ferry where Paul had kept a boat hidden during the winter. Paul's dog ran with them.

The night was pleasant, and the moon was bright. Too bright. In the path of moonlight across the river lay an armed English transport. Paul and his friends would have to row past it.

Then Paul realized his first mistake. He had meant to bring cloth to wrap around the oars so the sound would be muffled. He had left the cloth at home.

That wasn't all he had left behind. Paul Revere had started out for his Big Ride without his spurs.

What could be done?

Luckily, one of Paul's friends knew a lady who lived nearby. He ran to her house, called at her window, and asked for some cloth. This lady was not a time waster. She stepped out of the flannel petticoat she was wearing and threw it out the window.

Then for the spurs. Luckily, Paul's dog was there, and luckily, he was well trained. Paul wrote a note to his wife, tied it around the dog's neck, and told the dog to go home. By the time Paul and his friends had ripped the petticoat in two, wrapped each half around an oar, and launched the boat the dog was back with Paul's spurs around his neck.

Paul and his two friends rowed softly across the Charles River, they slipped carefully past the English transport with its 64 guns, and they landed in the shadows on the other side. Safely. There a group of men from Charlestown who had seen the signal in the church steeple had a horse waiting for Paul.

And off Paul Revere rode on his Big Ride.

He kept his horse on the road and himself on his horse, and all went well until suddenly he saw two men on horseback under a tree. They were English officers. One officer sprang out and tried to get ahead of Paul. The other tried to overtake him from behind, but Paul turned his horse quickly and galloped across country, past a muddy pond, toward another road to Lexington.

And what happened to the officers?

One of them galloped straight into the mud and got stuck; the other gave up the chase.

Paul continued to Lexington, beating on doors as he went, arousing the citizens. At Lexington he woke up John Hancock and Samuel Adams and advised them to leave town. He had a quick bite to eat, and then, in the company of two other riders, he continued to Concord, warning farmers along the way.

For a while all went well. And then suddenly from out of the shadows appeared six English officers. They rode up with their pistols in their hands and ordered Paul to stop. But Paul didn't stop immediately.

"Stop!" one of the officers shouted. "If you go an inch farther, you are a dead man."

Paul and his companions tried to ride through the group, but they were surrounded and ordered into a pasture at one side of the road.

In the pasture six other officers appeared with pistols in their hands.

One of them spoke like a gentleman. He took Paul's horse by the reins and asked Paul where he came from.

Paul told him, "Boston."

The officer asked what time he had left Boston.

Paul told him.

The officer said, "Sir, may I crave your name?"

Paul answered that his name was Revere.

"What! *Paul* Revere?"

Paul said, "Yes."

Now the English officers certainly did not want to let Paul Revere loose, so they put him, along with other prisoners, at the center of their group, and they rode off toward Lexington. As they approached town, they heard a volley of gunfire.

"What was that?" the officer said.

Paul said it was a signal to alarm the countryside.

With this piece of news, the English decided they'd like to get back to their own troops in a hurry. Indeed, they were in such a hurry that they no longer wanted to be bothered with prisoners. So after relieving the prisoners of their horses, they set them free.

And then what happened?

Paul Revere felt bad, of course, to be on his Big Ride without a horse. He felt uneasy to be on a moonlit road on foot. So he struck out through the country, across stone walls, through pastures, over graveyards, back into Lexington to see if John Hancock and Samuel Adams were still there.

They were. They were just preparing to leave town in John Hancock's carriage. Paul and Hancock's clerk, John Lowell, went with them.

All went well. They rode about two miles into the countryside, and then suddenly John Hancock remembered that he had left a trunk full of important papers in a Lexington tavern. This was a mistake. He didn't want the English to find those papers.

So what happened?

Paul Revere and John Lowell got out of the carriage and walked back to Lexington.

It was morning now. From all over the area farmers were gathering on Lexington Green. As Paul crossed the green to the tavern, there were between 50 and 60 armed men preparing to take a stand against the English. The troops were said to be near.

Paul went into the tavern, had a bite to eat, found the trunk, and carried it out, holding one end while John Lowell held the other. As they stepped on the green, the troops appeared.

And then what happened?

274

Paul and John held onto the trunk. They walked right through the American lines, holding onto the trunk. They were still holding on when a gun was fired. Then there were two guns, then a succession of guns firing back and forth. Paul did not pay any attention to who was firing or who fired first. He did not stop to think that this might be the first battle of a war. His job was to move a trunk to safety, and that's what he did.

The battles of Lexington and Concord did, of course, begin the Revolutionary War. And they were victories for the Americans who have talked ever since about Paul Revere's ride. Some things went well on Paul's ride, some things went poorly, but people have always agreed that the ride was a success.

But now that the war had started, what did Paul Revere do?

Naturally, he kept busy. He rode express for the Committee of Safety, for which he was paid 4 shillings a day. (He had asked for 5.) He printed paper money for the colony, engraved its official seal, supervised the setting up of a powder mill, learned how to make brass and iron cannon, and took part in two military engagements — one in Rhode Island, one in Maine. And as a lieutenant colonel in the Massachusetts militia, he was put in command of the fort at Castle Island.

Some things went well for Paul during the war. Some things went poorly — the same as always.

At the end of the war Paul was 48 years old. He went back to silver-smithing, but this wasn't enough to keep him occupied. So he opened a hardware store. In addition to hardware, he sold sandpaper, playing cards, woolen cloth, sealing wax, fish lines, wallpaper, pumice stones, pencils, and spectacles. (Once he sold Samuel Adams two dozen sleigh bells.)

Later he set up a foundry and made stoves, anvils, forge hammers, bolts, cogs, braces and pumps.

Then he began to make church bells. He made 398 bells, most of them weighing at least 500 pounds. He charged 42 cents a pound for them and often had trouble collecting his bills. (75 of his bells still ring in New England steeples.)

Still later he learned how to roll sheet copper, set up a rolling mill, and made copper sheathing for ships. And when the dome of Boston's new Statehouse was built, Paul gave it a shiny copper covering.

But Paul Revere was not always at work. Sometimes he just dreamed. Sometimes he would go back in his mind to the days when he was Massachusetts' Number One express rider. Then, if anyone were around, Paul would talk about his Big Ride. He even wrote out the story of his ride — in a hurry, of course, for the writing looked sloppy.

Boston was not the same as it had been when Paul was a young man.

*Taken, in Part, from an Engraving by Paul Revere*

No one bothered now to count the streets and the alleys, the horses and houses. They were too busy putting up new buildings, tearing down hills, filling in ponds, building bridges, and making the city bigger. They still did count the people, however. In 1810, when Paul was 75 years old, there were 33,787 people in Boston. Nineteen of these were Paul's grandchildren. He also had great-grandchildren, but no one bothered to keep a record of them. But it was the great-grandchildren, more than anyone else, who liked being around when Paul told his story. If he paused or if he appeared to be reaching an end, they would urge him to keep on.

"And then what happened?" they would ask.
"And *then* what happened?"

## Meet the Author

# Jean Fritz

**Home:** Dobbs Ferry, New York

**Accomplishments:** Fritz has written more than forty-four books for children and adults.

**Childhood:** Fritz was born in China where her parents were missionaries. She came to the United States at age thirteen and found her American roots by reading about American heroes.

**Reasons for writing about history:** Fritz likes to show the human side of famous people. She believes that truth is often funnier than fiction.

**Sampler of her books:** *Where Was Patrick Henry on the 29th of May?, What's the Big Idea, Ben Franklin?, Won't You Sign Here, John Hancock?*

## Meet the Illustrator

# Margot Tomes

**Accomplishments:** Before her death in 1991, Tomes illustrated more than sixty-six books, four of them by Jean Fritz.

**Childhood:** Tomes was born in 1917 in Yonkers, New York. She loved old books and fairy tales, even though her fascination with monsters kept her awake at night.

**Reasons for becoming an illustrator:** Tomes called herself a "pre-television person." She preferred to spend her time reading and looking at book illustrations.

Find out more about Jean Fritz and Margot Tomes at Education Place.

**www.eduplace.com/kids**

# Responding

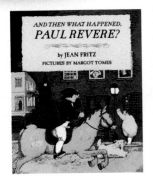

## Think About the Selection

**1.** Which word best describes Paul Revere for you: *smart, ambitious, busy, lucky, energetic, accomplished,* or some other word? Explain your choice.

**2.** Find examples in the selection to prove or disprove this statement: Paul Revere could not have carried out his famous midnight ride without help from others.

**3.** Jean Fritz writes that Paul Revere sometimes was forgetful, daydreamed, and made mistakes. Why do you think she included this information?

**4.** If Paul Revere were alive today, what would he be interested in? What kind of job do you think he might have? Explain your answer.

**5.** Compare Paul Revere's busy schedule with your own. Do you like to do many different things? Do you prefer to have just a few activities? Why?

**6.** Paul Revere used to tell his grandchildren stories about his life. If you were one of his grandchildren, what questions would you want to ask him?

**7.** **Connecting/Comparing** Of all Paul Revere's contributions to the American Revolution, which do you think is his most valuable one and why?

## Write a Message

Paul Revere carried news of the Boston Tea Party to New York and Philadelphia. Write a message that he might have carried, giving details about the event and explaining its importance.

 **Tips**

- **Begin the message with the most important facts.**
- **Include details that tell who, what, when, where, why, and how.**

## Math

# Compute Revere's Earnings

On p. 276, Jean Fritz tells us that Paul Revere made church bells. If each bell weighed 500 pounds, how much money did he earn making bells? If everyone paid their bills, how much did he earn from the bells that are still ringing in New England?

**PAUL REVERE & SON,**
*No. 13, Lynn Street, North End, BOSTON,*

## Science

# Compare Metals

Paul Revere made objects from many different metals: silver, copper, brass, and iron. Review the text to see how Revere used these metals. Choose one of the metals and explain how that metal is used today.

**Bonus** Find out more about one of the metals listed above. Report your findings to the class.

# Go on a Web Field Trip

Connect to Education Place and learn more about colonial America.

**www.eduplace.com/kids**

**Genre**

## Song Lyrics

**Skill: How to Read Song Lyrics**

**❶** Look for these parts of a song:

**Lyrics:** all the words of a song.

**Chorus:** part that is repeated.

**Stanzas:** two or more lines of verse.

**❷** Read the **lyrics** above or below the lines of musical notes. Notice the rhythm of the words.

**❸** Read the remaining **stanzas**. Repeat the **chorus** at the end of each stanza.

# Yankee Doodle

by Jerry Silverman

The surest way to popularize an idea in song is to set new words to a familiar melody. As early as 1767, there was mention in Philadelphia of a comic song called "Yankee Doodle."

When the word "yankee" first appeared in print, people were not quite sure what it meant. To this day there is some confusion about its origin. Some people believe it comes from an Indian word; others think it is based on a French word. The strongest possibility is that it comes from the Dutch name for the English colonists: "Jan Kaas," or "Jan Kees." Jan (yan) is Dutch for John; kees means cheese. "John Cheese" was not meant as a compliment. Neither was "Doodle," which means a fool.

"Yankee Doodle" first appeared in print in a London broadside in 1775. Its subtitle was "The Lexington March." The British band played it on the march to Lexington. In those days, European armies played loud music on the way into battle. It cheered up the soldiers and gave them courage. In this case, the strains of the music let the Minutemen know exactly where the British were.

The Minutemen also realized that the British were trying to make fun of them by calling them "Yankee Doodles." In the true spirit of the times, the familiar melody was taken up by the Americans (with new words by a Harvard College student, Edward Bangs) and sung right back at them. It is this version of "Yankee Doodle" that has gone down in American history.

In verse one, a boy visits a rebel, or patriot, camp with his father. The entire song is a light-hearted description of his impressions of the soldiers, captains, and arms. "Hasty pudding" was a quickly prepared cornmeal mush.

> *Yankee Doodle went to town*
> *Riding on a pony;*
> *Stuck a feather in his cap*
> *And called it macaroni.*

This well-known verse doesn't seem to have anything to do with the rest of the song. Most people who sing it probably assume that it is just a bit of Revolutionary War nonsense. Not at all!

This verse was sung by the British to taunt the patriots. In eighteenth-century England, a "macaroni" was a gentleman who wore overly fancy clothes in what he thought was the "Italian style," to try and make himself look more important than he really was. In other words, a macaroni was a dandy.

And just what was Yankee Doodle trying to do? He was, from the British point of view, getting "all dressed up" and "putting on airs." Yankee Doodle, in this verse, represents the colonies and their foolish desire to be free of Great Britain.

General Washington in military uniform on a white horse, painted around 1835.

# Yankee Doodle

1. Fath'r and I went down to camp, A - long with Cap - tain Good - ing, And there we saw the men and boys As thick as ha - sty pud - ding.

*Chorus*

Yan - kee Doo - dle keep it up, Yan - kee Doo - dle dan - dy; Mind the mu - sic and the step, And with the girls be han - dy.

2. And there we see a thousand men
   As rich as Squire David,
   And what they wasted every day,
   I wish it could be saved. *Chorus*

3. I see a little barrel, too,
   The heads were made of leather,
   They knocked upon with little clubs,
   And called the folks together. *Chorus*

4. And there was Captain Washington,
   And gentle folks about him;
   They say he's grown so tarnal proud
   He will not ride without them. *Chorus*

5. He got him on his meeting-clothes,
   Upon a slapping stallion,
   He set the world along in rows,
   In hundreds and in millions. *Chorus*

# Fighting with Fife and Drum

Songs like "Yankee Doodle" were made popular by boys who signed up with the colonial army to play the drum or the fife, a wind instrument that looks like a flute.

Army leaders depended on the young fifers and drummers to give commands to the troops during a battle. Each drumbeat or tune had a different meaning. The drum's loud rattle could be heard over the roar of muskets and cannons. The fife's shrill notes could carry a long distance.

After a battle, the fifers and drummers helped to gather the scattered company together. On the way back to camp, they kept up the soldiers' spirits with lively marching tunes. In camp, they signaled when it was time to eat or to take a break.

The musicians often wore a different uniform from the soldiers so that officers could locate them quickly. But the different uniforms enabled the enemy to locate them also. Because of their important role, the boys were key targets, and many did not survive to see the outcome of the war.

*The Spirit of '76,* **from the painting by Archibald Willard**

# A Story

A story is a narrative made up by the author. Use this student's writing as a model when you write a story of your own.

# The Boston Tea Party

> A good story has a clear **plot** with a **problem**.

My father, James Codder, was going to throw tea off the boat. "Dad, please don't go to Boston Harbor. You might get arrested," I begged him.

He simply said, "No, Drew, the taxes are way too high. I have to stand up for what I think is right. You'll understand when you're older."

> It's important to introduce the **characters** and the **setting** right away.

"I don't think I will," I told him. He didn't listen to me. "One more day," I said to myself while I was getting into my bed.

The day came when my dad was going to Boston Harbor. "Drew," he said, "You're coming. We need a lookout." I didn't even want to argue because I'd have to go anyway. I kept saying to myself, "I'm too young to go to jail. I'm too young to go to jail." I was living in fear practically the whole day!

When we were eating dinner, my father and I were dressed in black, and my father said with pride, "Tonight's the night!" I got my coat and my scarf, and went outside shaking with fear.

"It's going to be about an hour's walk," he told me. I almost fainted. I hated the thought of my dad going to Boston Harbor in the first place, and now I had to walk three miles with him to get there. It just wasn't fair. I didn't want to argue, or I'd be grounded forever. We talked about what we would do when we got to Boston Harbor. We were going to meet the other people at a boat called the *Beaver*, which was filled with tea from England. I was exhausted, but my father was marching with pride.

After about ten minutes, I asked, "Are we there yet?" When I heard that it would be about ten more minutes, I felt relieved; at that point, I couldn't even feel my legs. We got there in time so I didn't collapse. We got to the boat, and everyone else was already there.

**Dialogue** makes the story real for the reader.

**Details** create mental pictures for the reader.

"This is my son Drew," my father said as he introduced me to his friends.

They looked at the boat and stared at it for a long time. Then someone said, "Let's do it! Let's throw this tea into the harbor!"

When everyone was getting into the boat, my father said, "You'll have to stay here." I nodded my head, and then I sat on a bench. It was freezing near the harbor. The men put on Native American clothing. I thought it was odd, but then my dad explained to me that they didn't want to get caught. I couldn't help thinking that this wasn't really fair. I hoped no one would get caught or be blamed.

I sat on the bench, terrified. After about ten minutes, I called up to my father, "Can we go? I'm cold and scared!" My father didn't hear me, so I just closed my eyes. I wondered if we were going to get caught. I tried to forget about it. I looked at my father. He looked back at me and smiled. I looked at the boxes, and there were only ten boxes left! I was so relieved!

> A good story often has suspense.

I went up to the boat and asked my dad, "Can I throw the last box off the boat?" He nodded his head. I climbed aboard and took the box from my dad's hands, and threw it as hard as I could. It made a big splash. I felt very important.

Everyone got out of their disguises and got off the boat. We were about to walk home, but one of my dad's friends said, "Need a ride?" My dad delightedly nodded his head. We got into the carriage and rode into the night.

A good ending **resolves** the story's problem.

## Meet the Author

# Drew W.

**Grade:** five
**State:** Massachusetts
**Hobbies:** skateboarding
**What he wants to be when he grows up:** a skateboarder

**Katie's Trunk**

 **Historical Fiction**

## Key Vocabulary

arming
drilling
just
rebels

Vocabulary Reader

e ● Glossary

# Who Were the Tories?

At the time of the American Revolution, nearly one third of all colonists were Tories, or Loyalists, who remained loyal to the king of England and believed that English laws were fair and just. They opposed the rebels who were arming and drilling to prepare for war. The story of *Katie's Trunk* shows how neighbor turned against neighbor in the growing trouble with England.

*George III became king of England in 1760, shortly before he posed for this portrait by the English painter Allan Ramsay.*

Even some famous Patriot families included Tories. Benjamin Franklin's son, William, the governor of colonial New Jersey, sided with the British.

**Benjamin Franklin**

**William Franklin**

The American Revolution caused between 75,000 and 100,000 Loyalists to leave the colonies. Most fled to Canada. This sketch shows a Tory family camping on its way up the St. Lawrence River in 1784.

## Meet the Author
# Ann Turner

When she writes historical fiction, Ann Turner tries to imagine herself as a child, alive in a particular time and place. She asks herself, "What would I do then? How would I feel and react?"

The story for *Katie's Trunk* came from a conversation between Turner and her aunt about an old trunk that used to be in her grandmother's basement. "'One of our ancestors hid in it when the Revolutionary soldiers came,' she told me one day. I was astonished. 'You mean we were *Tories*?' I had to write a story about it, and the character of Katie came to mind — a rebellious, spirited girl (as I was) who would have wanted to protect her family's things from the rebels." Turner's other books include *Dakota Dugout, Dust for Dinner, Red Flower Goes West,* and *Mississippi Mud: Three Prairie Journals.*

## Meet the Illustrator
# Ron Himler

As a child in Cleveland, Ohio, Ron Himler spent many hours each week drawing at his grandmother's house. Since then, in a career that spans three decades, he has illustrated more than eighty books.

Himler lives in the American Southwest, where his special interest is researching and painting the ceremonies of Native Americans.

To find out more about Ann Turner and Ron Himler, visit Education Place. **www.eduplace.com/kids**

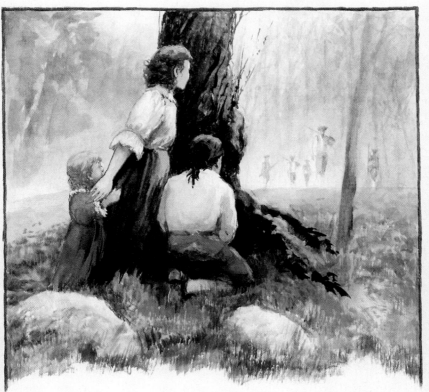

# KATIE'S TRUNK
## by Ann Turner

illustrations by Ron Himler

### Strategy Focus

What would it be like to be a Tory if your neighbors were Patriots? When you read, **summarize** the conflict between Katie's family and their neighbors.

When I'd been bad all day long,
hiding Hattie's doll under the sofa
and never telling where it went,
Mama sighed and said, "I should sit you down
to sew long seams all day
and get the goodness straight inside,
Katie.  What is wrong with you?"

I couldn't tell it with a name,
though I felt it inside,
the way a horse knows a storm is near.
I could feel the itchiness in the air,
the wind bringing cold,
the clouds tumbling over the trees
bringing rain — a sour rain.

"Must be," Mama sighed and sat down to tea,
"must be all this trouble and fighting.
Why, it makes me skittish as a newborn calf,
all this marching and talking,
these letters your Papa speaks of,
that tea they dumped in the harbor."

Mama's hand shook.

"Tea! In the harbor! Wasting God's good food."

Brother Walter said, "That's not the least of it.

It will get worse."

She peered at him.

"How could it be worse, Walter?"

Then she shut her lips on the words.

Already we had lost friends, neighbors,

families we had played with on the green

and helped with building their new barns.

Celia Warren no longer spoke to me.
Her brother, Ralph, no longer spoke to Walter.
Sometimes I heard that word hissed, "Tory!"
like a snake about to bite.
The rebels were arming, brother told me,
marching and drilling beyond the meadows.

I'll never forget the day they came.
The sun was hot on the mill pond
and Walter, Hattie, and I watched the dragonflies
peel their skins off on the long grass
and fly away.
Something like smoke rose over the road
and out of it Papa came running. "Get your mother!
Hide in the woods. The rebels are coming!"

We ran to the house,
Mama's face like a white handkerchief.
She shoved a piece of pork pie in our hands
and ran us out to the thick woods
where we could hide.
Crouched in the underbrush,
I felt like an animal in a trap.  And suddenly
I was so mad I could not still myself.

I raced for the house,
Mama's fierce whisper trying to call me back.
I would not let John Warren and Reuben Otis
hurt our house and things.  It was not right,
it was not just, it was not fair.

Inside our parlor, I touched each thing
I loved:  Mama's pineapple teapot,
the silver tray, shining like a moon,
the pictures of all our kin
ranged across the wall — home.

Then I heard voices by the door,
Reuben Otis, John Warren, Harold Smith
and others, not our neighbors.
"This'll be fine pickings!"
They paused on the front step
and ripped the knocker off the wood.

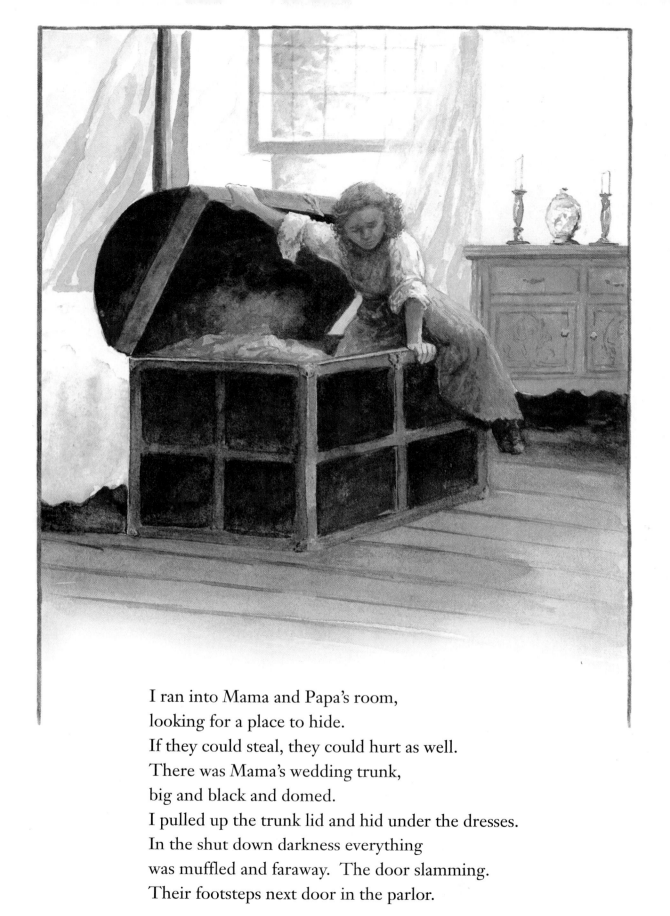

I ran into Mama and Papa's room,
looking for a place to hide.
If they could steal, they could hurt as well.
There was Mama's wedding trunk,
big and black and domed.
I pulled up the trunk lid and hid under the dresses.
In the shut down darkness everything
was muffled and faraway. The door slamming.
Their footsteps next door in the parlor.

"English goods!" someone spat
and something hit the floor and broke.
My breath stuck in my throat.
I heard Reuben say,
"Mr. Gray has money here.  Look hard for it."
John Warren spoke of arms they would buy.
The air closed around my mouth
like a black cloth.

I bit my hand and prayed,
though I was never much good at that.
I thought my words might go up to God
like bubbles in a pond to the silver top
where they would burst.  "Please, God,
don't let them find me, don't let them hurt us,
let me breathe."
The footsteps came closer, someone leaned against
the trunk.  My breath got caught somewhere midst
my stomach and chest, and I could not
get it back.  There wasn't enough air.
John Warren said, "Fine dresses and silver here."
He pulled up the lid and the sweet air rushed in.
I sucked in a breath as a dress was snatched out.
The rustlings drowned their words,
another dress went, and a hand touched me.
I wanted to bite it, to make him jump and shout,
but I stilled myself.  Maybe he didn't know.
Suddenly, he shouted, "Out!  The Tories
are coming.  Back to the road!  Hurry!"
He did not close the lid, and footsteps sounded
out the door.

Sudden quiet.  My heart beat loud
as the horses galloping down the road.
Quiet as quiet, I crept
to the window and looked out.  No one.
Puffs of smoke far down on the green.

A horse thudding past, riderless;
someone's hat blowing by in the gusty wind.
Would I ever play with Celia again?
Would I always wear this name, Tory, as if
it were written on my chest?

I sat down, hugged my knees
and began to cry.
Walter ran inside and hugged
me so tight
my nose stuck to his shirt.
Mama, Papa, and Hattie came next,
white as the moon and as silent.
Only Mama scolded, "Katie! Leaving us
that way . . ." Her voice broke
and she sat beside me and stroked my hair.
Papa looked out the window. "It's not bad,
dear ones, just a skirmish.
No one's hurt that I can see."

Walter's mouth snapped open and then
shut tight. I wiped my eyes on his sleeve.
A sudden thread like a song
ran through my head. When Mama asked me
to sew straight seams to get the goodness straight
I knew I couldn't do it.
But John Warren had. When I hid
in the black stuffy trunk,
when my breath got lost in Mama's dresses,
he left the trunk lid up to let me breathe
and called the others away.

He'd left one seam of goodness there,
and we were all tied to it:
Papa, Mama, Walter, Hattie
and me.

# Responding

**KATIE'S TRUNK**
by Ann Turner

illustrations by Ron Himler

## Think About the Selection

1. What is it like for Katie to be a member of a Tory family living among rebel neighbors? How does the conflict make her feel?

2. If you were Katie's friend Celia Warren, would you stop speaking to Katie? Explain what you would do and why.

3. Katie says "It was not fair" for rebels to break into her house. Do you agree with her? Why or why not?

4. Do you think Katie was right or wrong to run back to her house? Explain your answer. Find evidence from the selection that supports your opinion.

5. What causes John Warren to leave the trunk lid open and call the other rebels away? What effect does his action have on Katie?

6. Katie says that John Warren left a "seam of goodness there, and we were all tied to it" on page 303. What does she mean? What effect might that "seam of goodness" have on her family?

7. **Connecting/Comparing** Both Katie and Paul Revere face challenges caused by the conflict with England. What do you think is the biggest challenge each one faces? How does each respond to that challenge?

## Creating

## Write a Scene for a Screenplay

Assume that *Katie's Trunk* is going to be made into a movie. Write a screenplay for one scene. For example, you might choose the scene in which Katie hides after hearing the rebels at the door.

> **Tips**
> - Write each character's name before his or her lines.
> - Write instructions telling the actors where to move and how to say their lines.

## Art

# Make a Mobile

On p. 298, Katie notices things that represent home for her. Create a mobile using cardboard, magazine photographs, drawings, or foil to show things that represent home for you. Thread string through your creations and tie them to a hanger.

**Bonus** Write a poem about your family to hang from your mobile.

## Listening and Speaking

# Hold a Debate

Reread what Katie's mother says about the Boston Tea Party and other conflicts. Do you agree with her? With a partner or small group, make a list of reasons supporting the Patriot or Tory point of view. Invite another group to take the opposite point of view. Present your opinions to the class in a debate.

### Tips

- Be sure each group has equal time to speak.
- Support your opinion with strong reasons.
- Give a summary at the end of the debate.

## Internet

# Write a Review

Write your own review of *Katie's Trunk*. What did you like? What didn't you like? Explain why. Then post your review on Education Place.

**www.eduplace.com/kids**

**Genre**

**Primary Sources**

**Skill: How to Read Primary Sources**

*Before you read . . .*

Ask yourself: What **event** or issue does this document tell about? Who wrote it?

*While you read . . .*

❶ Use a dictionary to look up meanings of **unfamiliar** words.

❷ Ask yourself: What is the writer's point of view?

❸ Summarize the **main idea** of the passage.

# In Their Own Words

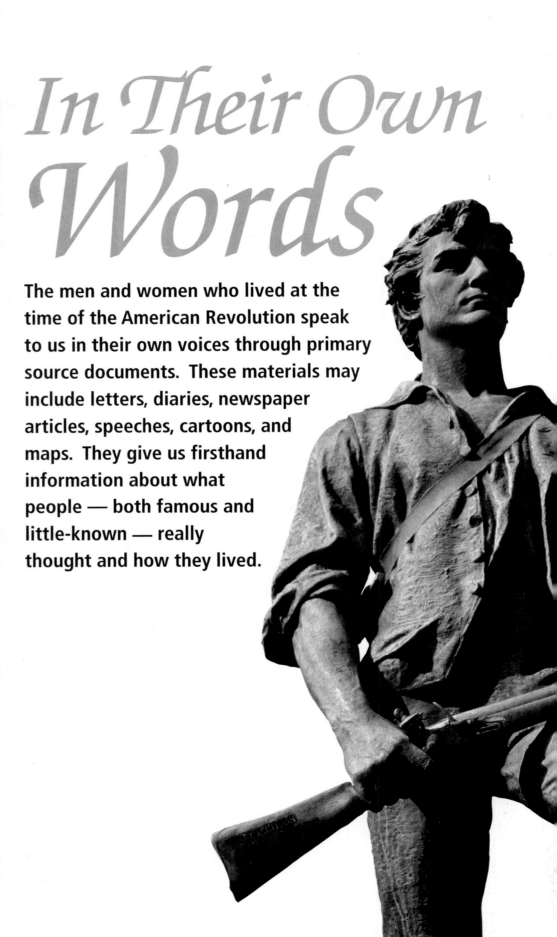

The men and women who lived at the time of the American Revolution speak to us in their own voices through primary source documents. These materials may include letters, diaries, newspaper articles, speeches, cartoons, and maps. They give us firsthand information about what people — both famous and little-known — really thought and how they lived.

When war began, the American army urgently needed soldiers. Notices like this one were posted to persuade men to enlist.

---

Cambridge, April 28, 1775
*To: The Massachusetts Committee of Safety*
*An Appeal for Help*
*Gentlemen:*

*The barbarous murders committed on our innocent brethren on Wednesday the 19th . . . have made it absolutely necessary that we immediately raise an army to defend our wives and children from the butchering hands of an inhuman soldiery. . . . [They] will, without doubt, take the first opportunity in their power to ravage this devoted country with fire and sword.*

*Death and devastation are the certain consequences of delay. . . . Hasten and encourage, by all possible means, the enlistment of men to form the army, and send them forward to headquarters at Cambridge.*

---

◀ This statue at Lexington, Massachusetts, honors the farmers who stood their ground against the British in April of 1775.

After the clash between the colonists and the British on April 19, 1775, a British officer wrote this letter to his father. What is his opinion of the Yankees?

Boston, April 23, 1775

*My Dear Sir,*

*It is impossible [for you not to] hear an account, and probably a most exaggerated one, of the little fracas that happened here a few days ago between us and the Yankee scoundrels. Our bickerings and heart-burnings, as might naturally be expected, came at length to blows, and both sides have lost some men . . . The rebels, you know, have [for] a long time been making preparations as if to frighten us . . . Though they are the most absolute cowards on the face of the earth, yet they are just now worked up to such a degree of enthusiasm and madness that they are easily persuaded . . . that they must be invincible.*

*from the Memoir and Letters of Captain Evelyn*

▲

Most Revolutionary soldiers carried powder horns, which held gunpowder for firing rifles. Made from animal horn and wood, some powder horns were elaborately carved, like this one made by James Pike of New Hampshire. "Regulars" were British soldiers; the Liberty Tree was a popular symbol of the rebellion; and "Provincials" were American soldiers.

An encampment of Loyalists on the banks of the St. Lawrence River in Ontario, Canada. ▶

The Ingraham family, like thousands of other Loyalists, fled to Canada after the American Revolution. Years later, Hannah Ingraham described her family's move from Albany, New York, to the province of New Brunswick, Canada, in the autumn of 1783, when she was eleven years old.

It was a sad, sick time after we landed in Saint John. We had to live in tents. The government gave them to us and rations, too. It was just at the first snow then, and the melting snow and the rain would soak up into our beds as we lay. Mother got so chilled and developed rheumatism and was never well afterwards.

[Later we went] up the river in a schooner and were nine days getting to St. Anne's. . . . We lived in a tent at St. Anne's until Father got a house ready.

One morning when we awoke, we found the snow lying deep on the ground all around us. Then Father came wading through it and told us the house was ready and not to stop to light a fire and not to mind the weather, but follow his tracks through the trees. . . . It was snowing fast and oh, so cold. Father carried a chest and we all took something and followed him up the hill.

There was no floor laid, no windows, no chimney, no door, but we had a roof. . . . We toasted bread [around a small fire] and all sat around and ate our breakfast that morning. Mother said . . . "This is the sweetest meal I ever tasted for many a day."

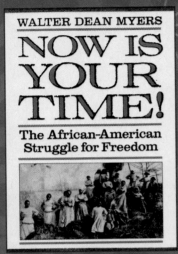

WALTER DEAN MYERS

# NOW IS YOUR TIME!

The African-American
Struggle for Freedom

**James Forten**

## Key Vocabulary

abolitionists
assisted
conflict
influential
privateer

**Vocabulary Reader**

Nero Hawley's
Fight for Freedom

*e* **Glossary**

# Fighting for Freedom

Many African Americans played important roles in the American Revolution. Some, like James Forten, a sail-maker from Philadelphia, fought at sea. Others served as soldiers or spies, or smuggled food through British lines. In all, more than 5000 black soldiers, both free and enslaved men, risked their lives for America's independence. Many fought to gain their own freedom as well.

This painting is widely ▶ believed to be a portrait of James Forten (1766–1842). After the Revolution, Forten was **influential** in the fight to free slaves.

◀ This Philadelphia school, which James Forten attended, was founded by Quakers, who were **abolitionists** . They wanted to get rid of slavery and **assisted** African Americans in getting an education and finding good jobs.

Hundreds of African American men served in the Continental navy. The sailor in this 1779 portrait may have been on the crew of a **privateer**, a private ship used in naval **conflict**. James Forten also served on a privateer.

By 1778, Rhode Island and Massachusetts each had an African American army unit. The Patriot leader John Hancock presented this flag to the Massachusetts troop in honor of its bravery. ▼

## Meet the Author Walter Dean Myers

Growing up in New York City, Walter Dean Myers read and wrote constantly, filling one notebook after another with stories and poems. In his twenties, Myers entered a contest for picture book writers. He won. Today, he has published more than thirty-five books for children and young adults. *Now Is Your Time* describes the important roles that African Americans played in our nation's history. "History has made me an African American," says Myers. "What we understand of our history is what we understand of ourselves."

Myers's novels about young people include *Me, Mop, and the Moondance Kid,* and *Mop, Moondance, and the Nagasaki Knights.*

## Meet the Illustrator

# Leonard Jenkins

Leonard Jenkins was born in Chicago, Illinois. By the time he was in high school, he was exhibiting his paintings and selling them to admirers.

Jenkins believes that talent and hard work are essential for an artist. But he adds, "Your art must go beyond how well you can paint. It has to go to the soul."

Find out more about Walter Dean Myers and Leonard Jenkins at Education Place. **www.eduplace.com/kids**

# JAMES FORTEN

From *Now Is Your Time*

WALTER DEAN MYERS

## NOW IS YOUR TIME!

The African-American Struggle for Freedom

By Walter Dean Myers

Selection illustrated by Leonard Jenkins

## ⭐ Strategy Focus

James Forten served on a ship during the Revolution. As you read, think of **questions** to discuss with classmates about his experiences.

It was early morning on Tuesday, September 2, 1766, in the city of Philadelphia. The roads into the city were already filling with farmers bringing in produce to sell. Windows in the city were coming alive with the glow of lamplight. Small factory owners trudged through the winding streets to small shops. Printers, shoemakers, blacksmiths, candle makers, bakers — all began the business of the day. For Philadelphia was indeed a city of business.

As day broke over the harbor, the masts of the ships loomed against the gray skies. The ships rocked at their moorings as if they, too, were ready for the new day.

Hundreds of free men of African descent lived in Philadelphia. The city was the home of a number of noted abolitionists — people who wanted to abolish, or do away with, the practice of slavery — including the Quakers, a powerful and influential religious group. More important was the fact that Africans could find work in Philadelphia.

Many of the Africans worked the docks, loading and unloading the ships that brought products to the colonies from all over the world. Others were tradesmen and seamstresses, cooks, barbers, and common laborers. All along the eastern seaboard, from Baltimore to New England, free Africans worked on boats, hauling loads, carrying passengers, and fishing. Many opened restaurants. Others bought their own boats and tried their luck on the brisk waterfronts.

Thomas Forten, a free African, was employed by Robert Bridges, a sail-maker in Philadelphia. Sail making was a profitable but difficult job. Sewing the coarse cloth was brutal on the hands. The heavy thread had to be waxed and handled with dexterity. A person trying to break the thread with his hands could see it cut through his flesh like a knife. But Forten appreciated his job. It paid reasonably well and the work was steady.

Forten helped in all aspects of sail making and assisted in installing the sails on the ships the firm serviced. With the income from his work he had purchased his wife's freedom. Now, on this early Tuesday morning, a new baby was due. The baby, born later that day, was James Forten.

Young James Forten's early life was not that different from that of other poor children living in Philadelphia. He played marbles and blindman's bluff, and he raced in the streets. When he was old enough, he would go down to the docks to see the ships.

Sometimes James went to the shop where his father worked and did odd jobs. Bridges liked him and let him work as much as he could, but he also encouraged Thomas Forten to make sure that his son learned to read and write.

The Fortens sent their son to the small school that had been created for African children by a Quaker, Anthony Benezet. He believed that the only way the Africans would ever take a meaningful place in the colonies would be through education.

Thomas Forten was working on a ship when he fell to his death. James Forten was only seven at the time. His mother was devastated, but still insisted that her son continue school. He did so for two more years, after which he took a job working in a small store.

What James wanted to do was to go to sea. He was fourteen in 1781 when his mother finally relented and gave her permission. America was fighting for its freedom, and James Forten would be fighting, too.

He knew about the difficulties between the British and the American colonists. He had seen first British soldiers and then American soldiers marching through the streets of Philadelphia. Among the American soldiers were men of color.

A black child in Philadelphia in the 1700's had to be careful. There were stories of free Africans being kidnapped and sold into slavery. He had seen the captives on the ships. They looked like him: the same dark skin, the same wide nose; but there was a sadness about them that both touched his heart and frightened him. He had seen Africans in chains being marched through the streets, on their way to the South. He never forgot the sight of his people in bondage, or accepted it as natural that black people should be slaves.

But the black soldiers Forten saw were something special. Marching with muskets on their shoulders, they seemed taller and blacker than any men he had ever seen. And there were African sailors, too. He knew some of these men. They had been fishermen and haulers before the conflict with Great Britain; now they worked on privateers and navy ships. Sometimes he heard talk about naval battles, and he tried to imagine what they must have been like.

In the summer of 1781, James Forten signed on to the privateer *Royal Louis,* commanded by Stephen Decatur, Sr. The colonies had few ships of their own to fight against the powerful British navy and issued "letters of marque" to private parties. These allowed the ships, under the flag of the United States, to attack British ships and to profit from the sale of any vessel captured.

The *Royal Louis* sailed out of Philadelphia in August and was quickly engaged by the British vessel *Active,* a heavy armed brig sent from England to protect its trade ships.

The *Royal Louis*'s guns were loaded with gunpowder that was tamped down by an assistant gunner. Then the cannonball was put into the barrel and pushed against the powder. Then the powder would be ignited. The powder had to be kept belowdecks in case of a hit by an enemy ship.

Forten's job was to carry the powder from below to the guns. Up and down the stairs he raced with the powder as shots from the British ship whistled overhead. There were large holes in the sails and men screaming as they were hit with grapeshot that splintered the sides of the ship. The smell of gunpowder filled the air as Captain Decatur turned his ship to keep his broadside guns trained on the *Active.* Sailors all about Forten were falling, some dying even as others cried for more powder.

Again he went belowdecks, knowing that if a shot ripped through to the powder kegs, or if any of the burning planks fell down into the hold, he would be killed instantly in the explosion. Up he came again with as much powder as he could carry.

After what must have seemed forever with the two ships tacking about each other like angry cats, the *Active* lowered its flag. It had surrendered!

Decatur brought his ship into Philadelphia, its guns still trained on the limping *Active.*

The crowd on the dock cheered wildly as they recognized the American flag on the *Royal Louis.* On board the victorious ship James Forten had mixed feelings as he saw so many of his comrades wounded, some mortally.

The *Royal Louis* turned its prisoners over to military authorities. On the 27th of September, the *Active* was sold; the proceeds were split among the owners of the *Royal Louis* and the crew.

320

The sailors with the worst wounds were sent off to be cared for. The others, their own wounds treated, were soon about the business of repairing the ship. Forten must have been excited. Once the fear of the battle had subsided and the wounded were taken off, it was easy to think about the dangerous encounter in terms of adventure. And they had won.

The missing crew was replaced. The ship was checked carefully by its captain and found to be in fine fighting condition. The crew carried more ammunition aboard, more powder, and fresh provisions. Once more they sailed for open waters.

On the 16th of October, 1781, they sighted a ship, recognized it as British, and made for it instantly. As they neared, a second ship was spotted, and then a third. Decatur turned to escape the trap, but it was already too late. The three British ships, the *Amphyon,* the *Nymph,* and the sloop *Pomona,* closed in. It was soon clear that the *Royal Louis* had two choices: to surrender or to be sunk.

The *Royal Louis* lowered its flag. It had surrendered, and its crew were now prisoners. Forten was terrified. He had heard the stories of the British sending captured Africans to the West Indies to be sold into slavery. He knew the *Pomona* had sailed back and forth from the colonies to the island of Barbados, where many Africans already languished in bondage. It was a time for dread.

James was taken aboard the *Amphyon* with others from his crew. On board the British ship Captain Beasley inspected the prisoners. There were several boys among the American crew, and he separated them from the older men.

Captain Beasley's son looked over the boys who had been captured. Many of them were younger than he was. Although still prisoners, the boys were given more freedom than the men, and Beasley's son saw the Americans playing marbles. He joined in the game, and it was during this playing that he befriended Forten.

The result of this tentative friendship was that Captain Beasley did not, as he might have done, send Forten to a ship bound for the West Indies and slavery. Instead he was treated as a regular prisoner of war and sent to the prison ship the *Jersey*.

Dark and forbidding, the *Jersey* was a sixty-gunner anchored off Long Island, in New York. It had been too old to use in the war and had been refitted first as a hospital ship and then as a ship for prisoners. The portholes had been sealed and twenty-inch squares carved into her sides. Across these squares iron bars were placed.

The captain of the *Jersey* greeted the prisoners with a sneer. All were searched under the watchful eyes of British marines. The wounded were unattended, the sick ignored. The pitiful cries of other prisoners came from belowdecks. A few pale, sickly prisoners, covered with sores, were huddled around a water cask. Then came the cry that some would hear for months, others for years.

"Down, Rebels, down!"

They were rebels against the king, to be despised, perhaps to be hanged. Traitors, they were being called, not soldiers of America. James was pushed into a line on deck. The line shuffled toward the water cask, where each man could fill a canteen with a pint of water. Then they were pushed roughly belowdecks.

The hold of the ship was dark. What little light there was came from the small squares along the hull. The air was dank as men relieved themselves where they lay. Some of the prisoners were moaning. Others manned pumps to remove the water from the bottom of the boat.

Sleep was hard coming, and James wasn't sure if he wouldn't still be sold into slavery. Beasley's son had liked him, he remembered, and the boy had offered to persuade his father to take James to England. It would have been better than the hold of the *Jersey*.

In the morning the first thing the crew did was to check to see how many prisoners had died during the night. Many of the prisoners were sick with yellow fever. For these death would be just a matter of time.

Forten later claimed that the game of marbles with Beasley's son had saved him from a life of slavery in the West Indies. But on November 1, two weeks after the capture of the *Royal Louis,* the news reached New York that Brigadier General Charles Cornwallis, commander of the British army in Virginia, had surrendered to George Washington. Washington had strongly protested the British practice of sending prisoners to the West Indies. It was probably the news of his victory, more than the game of marbles, that saved the young sailor.

James Forten was not a hero. He did not single-handedly defeat the British, or sink a ship. But he fought, like so many other Africans, for the freedom of America, and he fought well. He was only one of thousands of Africans who helped to create the country known as the United States of America.

In Philadelphia, after the war, James Forten became an apprentice to the man his father had worked for, Robert Bridges. Like his father, James was a hard worker. Eventually he would run the business for Robert Bridges, and by 1798 he owned it. At its height the business employed forty workers, both black and white. Forten became one of the wealthiest men in Philadelphia. He married and raised a family, passing on to them the values of hard work he had learned from his father. Forten made several major contributions to the sail-making business, among them a method of handling the huge sails in a shop, which allowed sails to be repaired much faster and saved precious time for ship owners. In the coming years he would use his great wealth to support both antislavery groups and the right of women to vote — at a time when over 90 percent of all Africans in America were still in a state of enslavement.

James Forten became one of the most influential of the African abolitionists. He spent much of his life pleading for the freedom of his people in the country his people had helped to create.

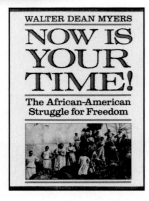

# Think About the Selection

1. We remember James Forten more for his life after the American Revolution than for his role during the war. Use the selection to discuss whether this statement is true or false.

2. Do you think James Forten was treated fairly when he was a prisoner? How do you think prisoners of war should be treated?

3. After the British ship, the *Active,* surrendered, James Forten had "mixed feelings" about the victory. Why? Describe the feelings he may have had.

4. James Forten and Captain Beasley's son shared an interest in playing marbles. What interests do you have that might help build a friendship?

5. Choose one of the events that helped shape James Forten's life. What do you think he learned from this experience?

6. Walter Dean Myers writes that James Forten was "not a hero." Do you agree or disagree? Explain why. What do you think it means to be a hero?

7. **Connecting/Comparing** Many people, both Patriots and Tories, risked their lives during the American Revolution. Compare the dangers that Paul Revere, Katie Gray, and James Forten each faced during the war.

Persuading

# Write a Dialogue

What do you think James Forten said to persuade his mother to let him go to sea? What might she have said in reply? Write a dialogue between Forten and his mother that shows how each feels.

**Tips**

- Be sure that each character states his or her opinion clearly and backs it up with strong reasons.
- Use correct punctuation and capitalization.

# Create a Pamphlet

Based on what you have read about Philadelphia in this selection, create a pamphlet that tells about the city's strong points in 1781. Try to persuade people to move to the city.

# Write a Caption

Look back at the illustrations in the selection. Choose one that you find interesting or exciting. Then write a caption that provides a short explanation of what is happening in the illustration.

Internet

# Take an Online Quiz

In this theme, *Voices of the Revolution,* you read about people who helped create the United States. Take our online quiz at Education Place to see what you remember. **www.eduplace.com/kids**

**Genre**

**Directions**

**Skill: How to Follow Directions**

❶ Read through the directions, noting **materials** needed and the sequence of steps. Pay special attention to **order words** such as *first, next, then, after,* or *finally.* Study pictures or diagrams, if provided.

❷ **Gather** the materials. **Reread** the steps, one at a time, and **follow** each in sequence.

❸ If you don't understand a step, **reread** the directions. **Check** diagrams again.

# Games of Young America

**When James Forten and Captain Beasley's son played marbles on the deck of the British ship *Amphyon*, they were taking part in a game that has been popular for more than 2000 years.**

Many games from the time of the American Revolution are still with us, such as tag, leap frog, and hide-and-seek. Other games have changed only slightly. Jackstraws, quoits, and the game battledore and shuttle-cock are known today as pick-up sticks, horseshoes, and badminton.

Most colonial games relied on simple objects found at home. One of the most popular games of the revolutionary period, hoop-rolling, used the wood or metal hoops that held barrels together.

The games described here would look very familiar to James Forten and his friends. When you play them you will be keeping alive traditions that are hundreds of years old.

# Marbles, or "Ring Taw"

As you will discover, hitting the marbles in the circle requires practice and skill!

**Players:** 2 to 5
**Materials:** 6 marbles or cranberries per player
**Object of the Game:** To win marbles belonging to other players

## How to Play

**1** Draw a circle, three feet in diameter, on a level surface.

**2** Draw another circle, one foot in diameter, in the center of the first circle.

**3** Place marbles inside the smaller circle, five marbles for each player. Save the sixth marble as the "shooter."

**4** To choose the first player, take turns shooting from the outside circle. To shoot, cradle the marble in one hand and release it with a fast flick of the thumb. The player whose shooter lands closest to the inside circle has the first turn.

**5** Take turns trying to shoot marbles out of the inside circle. Players keep all the marbles they shoot out. A turn ends when a player misses.

**6** Play until all the marbles have been shot from the circle. The player with the most marbles is the winner.

# Snail

In the 1700s, children often scratched the pattern for this game in the dirt with a stick.

**Players:** 2 to 4

**Materials:** Number cube; up to four different kinds of markers (beans or buttons); a game board, as shown.

**Object of the Game:** To be the first player to arrive at the center of the spiral.

## How to Play

1. Choose markers — a different marker for each player.
2. Take turns rolling a number cube. The highest number goes first.
3. The first player rolls a number cube and moves the number of spaces shown. The next player rolls and moves. Take turns to the left around the circle.
4. No player may land in an occupied space. If a player rolls a three and that space is occupied, he or she must give up that turn.
5. The winner is the first to land on the last spot in the center of the spiral. A player close to the last spot cannot move if he or she rolls a number higher than the remaining spaces.

332

# Eleven Men's Morris

This game may remind you of tic-tac-toe.

**Players:** 2

**Materials:** Two different kinds of markers such as beans or pennies; eleven markers for each player. A game board, as shown, copied on paper or poster board.

**Object of the Game:** To make the most rows of three markers in a line and remove opponent's markers from the board.

## How to Play

**1** Choose markers. Decide who goes first.

**2** Take turns putting down one marker at a time, always placing markers at a point where lines cross or meet. Markers can be placed horizontally, vertically, or diagonally. Three markers in a straight line make a row. When a player makes a row, he or she can remove the opponent's marker if it is not already part of a row.

**3** When all the markers have been placed on the board, continue to try to make rows by moving a marker in any direction to the next vacant point.

**4** The game ends when one player has only two markers left, or when no one can make another move. The player with more markers left on the board wins.

# Check Your Progress

This theme has shown you both real and fictional events from America's Revolutionary War. Think about that period of history as you read and compare two new selections and practice a new kind of test.

Before you begin reading, go back to the letter from Walter Dean Myers on pages 256–258. Think about how the power of symbols he writes about is related to the beliefs of Paul Revere, Katie, and James Forten.

Now meet more young people of the Revolution in the following selections. As you read, compare and contrast the work they do. See how that work connects with the actions of other characters in the theme.

# Read and Compare

**Historical Fiction**

Ellen Toliver, a shy girl of ten, must help deliver a secret message to George Washington.

Try these strategies:
Predict and Infer
Question

**Nonfiction**

Learn about three young people who really were spies during the Revolution.

Try these strategies:
Monitor and Clarify
Summarize

**Strategies in Action** *Call on all your reading strategies for help as you read.*

# Toliver's Secret

by Esther Wood Brady
illustrated by Joel Spector

*It is 1776. Ten-year-old Ellen Toliver has discovered that her grand-father is a spy for the Patriots. Grandfather has hidden a secret message for General Washington in a loaf of bread. The message may help bring a much-needed victory to the Patriot army, where Ellen's brother Ezra is fighting. But Grandfather has badly sprained his ankle. He is asking Ellen to deliver the message for him!*

"Can you understand what I have been telling you?"

"I think so."

Ellen could see that Grandfather was very serious about the need to send his message. She, too, had been worried about all the news of lost battles and retreats, especially since Ezra was with that army. She remembered how joyous everyone had been last July when they heard about the Declaration of Independence. There had been bonfires on the village green and singing and dancing in the streets. And then the British army came to New York and there had been three months of defeat.

"If you understand how important it is to take the message, Ellen, I'll tell you how it can be done. And then you are to decide."

Ellen listened and didn't say a word.

"You walk down to the docks near the Market-house and get on a farmer's boat — or an oysterman's. They come over early every morning and they go back to Elizabeth-town at eleven o'clock. Elizabeth is a very small town. When you get off the boat, you'll find the Jolly Fox Tavern without any trouble. My good friend Mr. Shannon runs the tavern, and you give the loaf of bread to him. That's all there is for you to do, Ellen. The Shannons will welcome you and take good care of you."

Sailing across the Bay didn't seem so hard. It was finding a boat here in New York and asking a stranger for a ride that worried her.

"How could I find the right boat to take me?" she asked. She didn't intend to go, but she thought she'd ask anyway.

"The docks are right near Front Street where we walked on Sunday afternoon. The farmers and the oystermen tie up their boats near the Market-house. They are friendly people and they often take passengers back to Elizabeth-town since the ferryboat stopped running. I'll give you money to pay."

"And how would I get home again — if I should decide to go?" she said in a very low voice.

"Oh, the Shannons will put you on a boat early in the morning. You'll be back here by ten o'clock."

"Does Mr. Shannon take the bread to General Washington?" she asked.

"No, he takes it to a courier who will ride part of the way. Then he'll give it to another courier who will ride through the night with it. And finally a third man will carry it to the General in Pennsylvania."

Ellen thought about the messengers riding alone through the countryside to carry the secret message. She wondered how it felt to be all alone among the British soldiers.

Mother interrupted. "It's too much to ask of her, Father. She's only ten."

Her father reached out and squeezed her hand. "Abby, dear," he said, "I know you are distressed because of all that has happened this fall. But don't make the child timid. We all have to learn to do things that seem hard at first. A child can't start too early to learn that."

Ellen knew her grandfather wouldn't send her if he thought she couldn't do it. Now that she thought it over she knew that if she walked carefully she could remember the way to Front Street. And she would have money to pay for the boat. She had liked sailing across the East River when she and Mother had taken the ferryboat from Brooklyn to New York last November. Perhaps it wouldn't be too hard. "But what would I do if I got lost?"

"If you lose your way, just speak up and ask someone for directions," said Grandfather.

"You're sure there is no one else to take it for you, Grandfather?"

"With this bad ankle I can't walk around New York to find one of my friends — and I wouldn't know where to send you or your mother to look. Besides, there isn't time. I need your help, Ellen."

Ellen was quiet for a long time.

"Very well," she said finally. "I'll do it — if you are really sure I can."

"I know you can, Ellen. And Abby," he said, "this is nothing too hard for a child of ten. The Shannons will take good care of her, you may be sure of that. In that chest in the kitchen are clothes that Ezra left here years ago. Go out and see what you find, Ellen."

Now that she had decided to go, Ellen ran quickly to the kitchen and poked around among the blankets and old clothes in the chest that sat near the fireplace. She was eager to see what was there. "Here's a striped cap," she exclaimed. "And here's that old blue jacket with the holes in the elbows. I remember these brass buttons." Grandfather had bought Ezra all new clothes when he had come to New York to visit several years ago.

Ellen put on a red knitted shirt that was too small and the blue wool jacket that was too big. The brass buttons made her think of Ezra's grin. She put on heavy gray stockings before she pulled up the short breeches. The leather breeches were so old and stiff they could almost stand alone. She kicked up her legs to make them soften up.

Not since she was a small child had she known what fun it was to kick her legs as high as she could. She tried to kick the skillet that hung beside the fireplace.

"These will be better for walking than petticoats," she said as she pranced about the kitchen. "Why can't girls wear these, too?"

"Ellen Toliver," said her mother primly. "It would be unseemly."

After trying on Ezra's boots, which were too big for her, she decided she would wear her own leather shoes to make walking easier. Certainly it would be easier to jump out of the way of horses and wheelbarrows and it would be better for climbing on the boat.

She ran into the shop to show her grandfather how she looked. For the first time since he fell on the ice, Grandfather laughed. "You look like a ragged little urchin all right," he said, "with those holes in your elbows. But all the better. No one will even notice you. And now we must cut your hair."

Mother picked up the scissors and stroked Ellen's long brown hair. "Couldn't we just tuck her hair under the cap?" she asked.

"No," said Ellen firmly. "I might forget and take it off! That would be dreadful. Besides, it might look bunchy beneath a cap." Better to have it short and not worry about it. She remembered her friend

Lucinda who had short hair with a band of ribbon around her head. Lucinda looked very pretty with short hair. "Cut it off!" she said impatiently.

Grandfather smiled from his couch. "You'll do right well, Ellen," he said. "Tie a pigtail in back with a cord and then just snip off the part that is too long."

Ellen could feel her mother's hands tremble as she tied back the hair and snipped at the long pigtail.

"It will grow back," Ellen said to her. "How do I look?" Jumping up from the chair she stepped over the hair on the floor and stared at herself in the mirror.

"Why, I favor my father with my hair tied back!" she exclaimed. Her brown eyes were just like her father's eyes although not stern like his. Her face was thin like his, too. She stared at herself. Suddenly the person staring back at her didn't look like Ellen Toliver, and for a minute it frightened her to look so changed. Glancing sideways she could see her grandfather smiling his old cheerful smile.

Mother had given him the loaf of bread which he was wrapping in a blue kerchief and tying with a good strong knot.

"Where shall I hide the bread?" Ellen asked him.

"Don't hide it," he told her. "Don't think of hiding it. Just go along swinging this blue bundle as if it were nothing at all. There is only one thing to be careful about, Ellen. Be sure you give the bread to no one but Mr. Shannon."

His eyes grew as hard as they had been earlier that morning, when she surprised him in the kitchen. "No one but Mr. Shannon. He and I might hang if we were caught."

"Hang!" cried Ellen. "You mean on a gallows tree?"

Ellen's hands trembled so that she could hardly button the brass buttons on her jacket. No one had mentioned hanging before. If she had known her grandfather might hang she never would have agreed to do it. It wasn't fair. She gulped and at last the words came out. "I can't do it, Grandfather. I just can't. I'm too scared and I might make a mistake."

"You can do it, Ellen. Better than anyone else. No one in the world will suspect a loaf of bread in the hands of a child. If, perchance, someone found the message in the bread, just act surprised and say you don't know a thing about it!" He smiled at her to encourage her. "Just hang onto the bread good and tight until you see Mr. Shannon. That won't be hard to do, now will it?"

"But don't talk to any strangers, Ellie," Mother pleaded.

"Now, Abby. She has common sense."

"You're sure I won't make a mistake, Grandfather?"

"I can't see where you could go wrong, Ellen. The boatmen are kindly and they take people every day. And at the other end of the trip are my good friends the Shannons."

"Well, then," she said. "I think I am all ready now."

"Good!" cried Grandfather. "When you hand the bread to Mr. Shannon say this to him, 'I have brought you a present for your birthday.' He will understand what it means."

Mother slipped two corncakes into her pocket. "You'll get hungry before you get there, I'm sure." She was trying hard to sound cheerful. "I've always heard about Mistress Shannon's good potpies, and now you can eat one."

Grandfather slipped some coins into her pocket. Then he squeezed her hand until it hurt.

"God bless you, Ellen. I'm proud of you."

Mother pulled the red and white striped cap down around her ears and gave her a pair of mittens as well as a hug that almost smothered her. Then she stepped to the door and opened it. "I think you are a brave girl, Ellen."

Ellen stood at the top of the steps and looked up and down the street. She took a deep breath. Mother had said she was brave and Grandfather had said he was proud of her — well, she hoped they were right.

# Mary Redmond, John Darragh, and Dicey Langston: SPIES

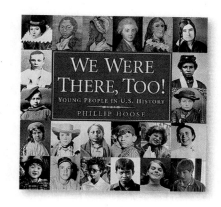

WE WERE THERE, TOO!
YOUNG PEOPLE IN U.S. HISTORY
PHILLIP HOOSE

by Phillip Hoose • illustrated by C.B. Mordan

**Young people made excellent spies during the American Revolution. Often over-looked by adults, they heard and saw plenty. Secrets were everywhere, encoded even in the way laundry was hung on the line to dry. Patriots and loyalists lived together and spoke the same language. Sometimes you couldn't help but overhear.**

In 1777, British troops invaded Philadelphia and took over the city. Many colonists fled, but some stubbornly stayed in their homes, even when British soldiers moved in. With enemies living just walls apart, Philadelphia became a city of secrets. The British didn't know whom they could trust. Armed redcoats patrolled the streets and set up guard posts around the town. Colonists had to show passes and state their business before they could even go to the marketplace.

The city was honeycombed with spies, many of them children. Some worked in teams. One girl named Mary Redmond worked with a boy who carried messages into Philadelphia from Continental soldiers camped in the surrounding countryside. The messages were stitched into the back of his coat. The public market was the handoff place.

Mary's job was to watch the British soldiers closely as the boy approached the market. If it ever looked as if the British were on to him, she was supposed to flash a signal to nearby contacts. One morning, though, there was no time to signal. Mary saw two British soldiers eyeing her partner as he neared the market. Both men started toward him. With no time to signal for help, Mary took off running across the square as fast as she could and, pretending to be playing, drove her shoulder hard into the boy's legs in a flying tackle. He went down in a heap. As they rolled in the dust she threw her shawl over his back, ripped the message from his coat back, and stuffed it in her dress. Then, laughing, she skipped away from both the boy and the puzzled soldiers and went on to deliver the message. Later she liked to recall that her loyalist relatives enjoyed chuckling over "our little black-eyed rebel." She doesn't say if they ever found out that their little rebel was a spy.

Elsewhere in Philadelphia, a group of British officers took over a large room in the home of Lydia Darragh, a pleasant Quaker woman. Normally, Quakers stayed out of wars, but Lydia's son Charles had enlisted in the Continental army and was now a lieutenant. The British tenants used the room as a "council chamber," to make war plans. As they schemed, Mr. and Mrs. Darragh and their fourteen-year-old son, John, lay flat on the floor above them, ears pressed hard against a crack between two boards. Whenever they heard important information, Mr. Darragh wrote it down in code on small scraps of paper. Mrs. Darragh sewed the messages inside large cloth-covered buttons and fastened them to John's coat.

Then it was all up to John. If the British caught him delivering military secrets, he could be jailed or even executed. Looking as casual as he could, he would wander out the door, through the city, and to the road that led from town, presenting his pass to British soldiers at each checkpoint. Sometimes they questioned him roughly and shook him down, but they never thought to inspect his coat buttons. Once past the guard, he would fade into the trees at the edge of the city and go to meet his brother, who would cut off his buttons and send them straight to George Washington.

Farther south, fifteen-year-old Dicey Langston lived in peril. The southern colonies had more loyalists than those up north. Many country people resented the wealthy planters along the coast and didn't mind a bit if the British put them in their place. Dicey lived among loyalists near Spartanburg, South Carolina, but her father and her brothers were patriots. Neighbors distrusted her, and with good reason. They knew her brothers were militia-men, scattered in secret places in the woods nearby.

As she did her chores, Dicey often overheard her neighbors and loyalist uncles talking about troop movements. Whenever she heard anything of interest, she hiked off to inform her brother's militia unit, camped across the Enoree River. But one night she stayed away too long and returned to face a group of men shining lanterns in her eyes and asking pointed questions about where she had been. After that, her father made Dicey promise to stop sneaking away. She did, until she overheard one secret she couldn't keep. A company of loyalist soldiers called the Bloody Scout knew exactly where her brother's militia was headquartered. They were planning to wipe it out.

With no time to lose, Dicey slipped into the woods after dark and ran until she came to the edge of the Tyger River. Heavy rains had raised the angry water almost to the banks and washed out the footbridges. Dicey steeled herself and plunged in. In an instant the water was up to her neck and the current was carrying her rapidly away. She was far downstream by the time she struggled to the opposite bank. Shivering, she retraced her steps and found her brother's camp.

After that, life became terrifying for the Langston family. One night armed soldiers rode up to their house with orders to kill every Langston man. Only Dicey's father, Solomon Langston, frail and elderly, was still there. A soldier dismounted from his horse, took out a pistol, and shoved the barrel against the old man's chest. Dicey sprang between her father and the gun. The soldier threatened to kill her father if she didn't move, but she stood her ground and said he'd have to kill her first. The soldier hesitated, then reholstered his pistol and ordered his men to depart.

### What Happened to Dicey Langston?

She lived to be an old woman in South Carolina. At the time of her death she liked to boast that she had thirty-two sons and grandsons willing to bear arms for their country.

# Think and Compare

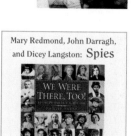

by Phillip Hoose

1. How is Ellen Toliver like Mary Redmond or Dicey Langston? How is she different from them? What advice would they have for her?

2. Compare what you learn about fictional characters in the theme (Ellen and Katie) with what you learn about real historical characters. Who do you know better and why?

3. All the main characters in the theme show courage. Choose two characters and compare their deeds. Is there one you are more impressed with? Explain why.

4. Do you think Dicey Langston would be understanding toward Katie and her Loyalist family? Why or why not?

5. Do you think it was right that the characters in the theme took the risks they did? Explain.

**Strategies in Action** Explain how you used reading strategies to help you understand one of the selections.

KATIE'S TRUNK
by Ann Turner

illustrations by Ron Himler

## Write a Letter

Write a letter that Dicey Langston might have written to one of her grandchildren, telling about her adventures as a spy. Be sure to include the date, greeting, closing, and signature.

### Tips

- **Reread the part about Dicey Langston.**
- **Write brief notes telling how she felt and what she did.**
- **Think about the tone Dicey might use. Would she brag? Would she create suspense?**

# ✓ Writing a Personal Response

Some test items ask you to write a personal response to a topic, based on your ideas and experience. Here is a sample test topic about *Toliver's Secret.*

---

**Write your response to this question.**

Do you think it was right for Ellen's grandfather to ask her to go on the mission? Explain your answer in one or two paragraphs. Use information from the selection and your own experience.

---

## ① Understand the question.

Find the key words. Use them to understand what you need to do. Decide what to write about.

## ② Get ready to write.

Look back at the selection. List details that help answer the question. Think about yourself. List thoughts or experiences that help answer the question.

Here are two sample lists.

| Selection | Experience |
|-----------|-----------|
| The Patriots needed help. | I have helped my parents. |
| Grandfather could not ask anyone else. | Kids are able to do a lot. |
| Ellen was able to help. | It's fair to ask a kid to help if no one else can help. |

## ③ Write your answer.

Use details from both of your lists. Write a clear and complete answer.

Here is a good answer to the test question.

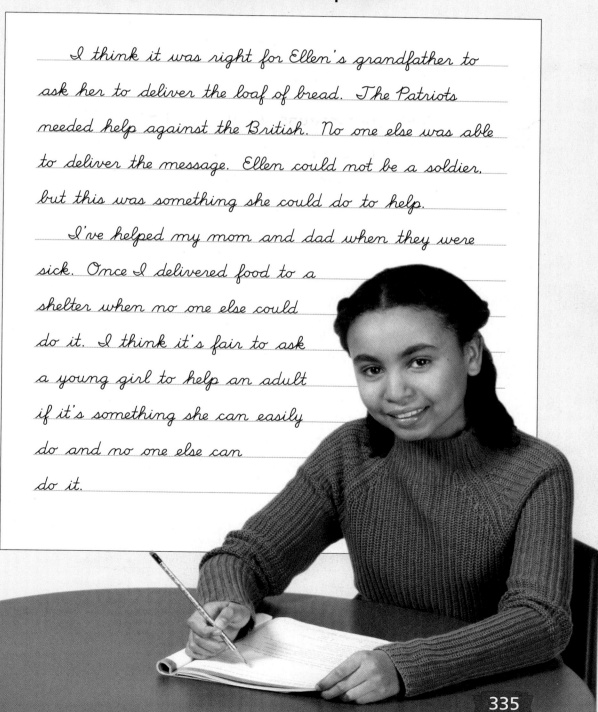

I think it was right for Ellen's grandfather to ask her to deliver the loaf of bread. The Patriots needed help against the British. No one else was able to deliver the message. Ellen could not be a soldier, but this was something she could do to help.

I've helped my mom and dad when they were sick. Once I delivered food to a shelter when no one else could do it. I think it's fair to ask a young girl to help an adult if it's something she can easily do and no one else can do it.

# Person to Person

*Cuando ayudamos a otro,
ambos nos fortalecemos.*

When one helps another,
both gain in strength.

— *Ecuadorian proverb*

# Person to Person

## with Lensey Namioka

Dear Reader,

In this theme you will read about how people help each other and complicate each other's lives. This is true of the characters in my book, *Yang the Second and Her Secret Admirers*. It was also true in my family.

After I arrived in America from China at the age of eight, my brothers and sisters and I quickly began learning English. My father became worried that we might forget our Chinese. He insisted that we speak only Chinese at home. Father enforced his rule very strictly. If we sneaked an English word into a Chinese sentence, he would make us pay a fine. It was a penny for each

English word. We had to put the coins into a big bowl in the dining room. The sight of the bowl served as a reminder to keep English words out of our mouths during dinner.

Money was short in those days, and my allowance was ten cents a month. So a fine of a penny really hurt.

Our first winter in America was hard. We were living in Connecticut, and storms sometimes dumped a foot of snow overnight. To keep us warm while we walked to school, Mother bought us long, woolen pants worn by skiers.

At breakfast one morning, I asked my sister whether she was going to wear her ski pants. I was speaking in Chinese, but I used the English words *ski pants*.

Father pounced. "That's a fine of two pennies for *ski* and *pants*!"

Chinese children obeyed their parents, but this time I rebelled. "How do you say *ski pants* in Chinese?" I demanded.

For once Father was stumped. Skiing was not known in China at that time, and there was no word for the sport. "How about *hua xue kuzi*?" suggested my eldest sister. It literally meant "pants for sliding around in the snow."

The picture of our family sliding around in the snow made us all laugh. Father had to admit defeat, and I got away scot-free with my two English words.

From that time on, whenever we couldn't avoid using an English expression, we'd refer to it as "ski pants." This was baffling to outsiders. They wondered why, in a conversation about politics, for instance, we'd start talking about pants and skiing.

Father eventually mellowed. Even he could find no elegant Chinese translation for *cheeseburger*.

As you will see in *Person to Person*, people often change people.

Best,

*Lenny Namioka*

# People Meeting People

Think about Lensey Namioka's family story. Maybe it brings to mind a time when members of your family made a difference in each other's lives.

Now take a look ahead at the selections shown below. As you read them, think about how each one fits into a theme about people connecting. You may find that the characters remind you of someone you know — including yourself.

To learn about the authors in this theme, visit Education Place. **www.eduplace.com/kids**

# Volunteering

**Mariah Keeps Cool**

**Key Vocabulary**

amazingly
celebration
compete
decorate
volunteer

Vocabulary Reader

Help Is on the Way
by Lee S. Justice

*e* ● Glossary

To **volunteer** is to give your time and energy freely, not because you have to, but because you want to.

In *Mariah Keeps Cool*, one of the characters volunteers her time at a shelter for the homeless. Other characters organize a party to benefit the shelter.

Have you ever volunteered to do something? What did you do? How did you feel while you were helping?

Maybe you've been part of a team of volunteers. People can be **amazingly** productive when they're all working together, whether it's to perform in a play, clean up litter on a beach, or **decorate** a wall with a mural.

Members of a team of volunteers don't **compete** with each other. They're working together for a common goal: to finish a job, to create something, to help people. And at the end, there's often a **celebration** to say: We did it!

**These students in St. Paul, Minnesota, are helping to clean up their neighborhood.**

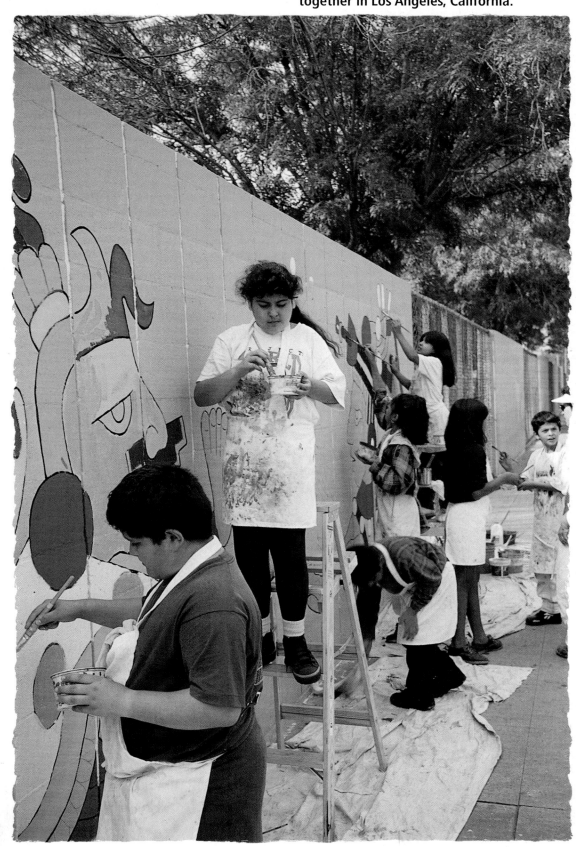

Creating a mural brings student artists together in Los Angeles, California.

# Mildred Pitts Walter

**Born:** Sweetville, Louisiana, 1922

**Home:** Denver, Colorado

**Work:** Shipwright helper during World War II; elementary school teacher; children's book writer since 1969

**How her writing career began:** Looking for books by and about African Americans for her students, Walter was challenged by a publisher to write one herself. The result was her first book, *Lillie of Watts: A Birthday Discovery*.

**Family:** "I think family is everything within the lives of human beings. Not just the nuclear family, but the extended family — grandmothers, uncles, cousins, friends, community, city, country."

**Booklist:** *Justin and the Best Biscuits in the World*; *Kwanzaa: A Family Affair*; *Have a Happy*; *Mississippi Challenge*; *The Suitcase*

# Nneka Bennett

**Born:** New Jersey, 1972

**Favorite art materials:** Watercolor paints and colored pencil

**Illustrators she especially admires:** Leo and Diane Dillon

**To young artists:** "You can take my mom's advice: Follow your heart and don't let anyone sway you away from your dreams."

Internet

To find out more about Mildred Pitts Walter and Nneka Bennett, visit Education Place. **www.eduplace.com/kids**

# MARIAH KEEPS COOL

by Mildred Pitts Walter

## Strategy Focus

Read the selection title and the introduction. What do you **infer** about Mariah? How do you **predict** her plans will turn out?

*Mariah and her pals — the Friendly Five — are getting ready for a big swim meet, with the help of their classmate and coach, Brandon. Meanwhile, Mariah is planning a surprise birthday party for her sister Lynn, with guests bringing donations for the homeless shelter where Lynn volunteers. Organizing the party has also brought Mariah closer to her half sister, Denise.*

Only four days before Lynn's birthday and nine days before the swim meet. Mariah felt there were not enough hours in the day for all she had to do. Lynn's party took time, but the hardest work continued to be getting ready for the meet. Each step she took as she walked down the street was measured to the approach on the springboard. She often thought about Lorobeth and wondered if all this work was worth it. Maybe she could never compete and win.

Besides now having to spend four hours a day swimming, instead of two, she had to spend time on the party. Each afternoon she worked with Brandon, members of the Friendly Five, and Denise at Brandon's house getting everything ready. Denise was more helpful than Mariah had imagined. Today she was going to show the Friendly Five how to make paper flowers to decorate their yard for the party.

Everything seemed under control except Lynn. Mariah felt that Lynn suspected something unusual was going on when Lynn sometimes suggested that Denise do things with her. Whenever Denise begged off, Lynn, sometimes offended, wanted to know just what Denise was up to.

Mariah was grateful that Mama often stepped in and insisted that Lynn do things with, or for, her.

That afternoon when Mariah was leaving for Brandon's she called, "See you later, Denise."

"Where y'all going?" Lynn wanted to know.

Realizing she had made a mistake, Mariah quickly said, "I'm going to Brandon's to swim."

"So where will you see Denise later?"

"At home.  Same time I'll see you.  When I get back."

As soon as Mariah reached Brandon's she called and asked her mama to please call home and send Lynn on an errand so Denise could more easily join them at Brandon's.

Finally Denise arrived.  In Brandon's room they all got busy cutting colorful paper flower petals and clipping thin wire, wrapping it with strips of green paper to make flower stems.  Mariah was surprised at how quickly Denise shaped the petals and stems into beautiful flowers. Soon all the girls were turning out flowers while Brandon worked on signs and banners.

"I think Lynn suspects something," Denise said.

"She better not know. This has to be a surprise," Cynthia said.

Just then Brandon's mother rushed to the door. "Hurry, get out to the pool. Lynn is coming."

They all started up. "Not you, Denise," Mariah commanded. "You hide in here."

"Oh, we don't have on our suits," Trina whispered as they all raced through the house.

"Take off your shoes," Mariah demanded. "Sit on the edge of the pool. Splash your feet."

Mariah listened as Brandon's mama talked to detain Lynn, and when Lynn entered the backyard Mariah called out as if surprised, "Lynn, what you doing here?"

"I was on an errand this way and thought I'd stop to see how you guys are doing with your strokes for the meet. You're not swimming today?"

"I'm letting them rest for a little while," Brandon said. "They'll be at it pretty soon."

"Please, Brandon, give us the day off," Nikki suggested.

"No way. We gotta work. And Lynn, you had better go."

"Let me see them for a little while. Just once," Lynn pleaded.

"No spectators when we work. Rules. Suit up, girls," Brandon ordered.

"Bye, Lynn," they all sang as they marched inside.

When Lynn had gone they rushed back to Brandon's room. "Whew!" Mariah exclaimed. "Brandon, you saved the day."

"Something's up," Trina said.

"Yeah. But who could've told?" Jerri asked.

"I really don't think she knows," Denise said. "I think maybe she suspects something."

"We better hurry and finish all this stuff," Mariah said. "This is getting to be hard on the nerves."

At dinner on the day before her birthday Lynn announced, "I just want to do nothing on my birthday but rest in bed all day."

Oh, no, Mariah thought as she glanced at Mama and then at Denise. Did Lynn know? Was she going to make it impossible for them to pull the party off as a surprise? Lynn really could be a pain.

"Fine," Denise agreed with Lynn. "Mariah and I will make breakfast and serve you in bed."

"You and Riah make breakfast?" Lynn laughed.

"Sure. We can fix fruit and cold cereal, huh, Riah?"

"You can make your specialty, Denise," Mariah suggested.

"She wouldn't want corn muffins for breakfast." Denise laughed. That was the only thing Denise made successfully since she had started to learn to cook.

"Yours are so good, Denise, maybe," Lynn said.

"We'll give you millet cereal for sure," Mariah said, and they all laughed.

Mariah went to bed worried. How would they ever get ready for the party? If only her sister were not so weird!

Early the next morning Mariah and Denise took a tray to Lynn's room, followed by Mama and Daddy. They sang "Happy Birthday" and as they were leaving Lynn to eat alone, Mama asked, "Lynn, are you sure you want to stay in bed all day?"

"I'm sure."

"Aw, Lynn . . ."

Mama quickly raised a hand. "Riah, we must honor that."

In the kitchen Mariah argued. "She can't be here. We'll never get things done. Do something, Mama. Take off from work and get her out of here."

"I had planned to take half a day off," Mama said.

"Hey, remember, Lynn said she wanted some books," Denise reminded them.

"She'd never refuse to shop for books," Mariah said. "And take her to lunch and to a movie, Mama."

"What if she won't go?" Denise suggested.

"She will," Mama said. "She'd better."

Mariah joined her friends at the rec center. They all wanted to know what time to come to get ready for the party.

"Might not be a party." Mariah told them about Lynn's decision to stay in bed all day.

"Somebody talked and she's being cool, huh?" Trina suggested.

"She makes me sick even if she is my sister," Mariah fumed.

"We told you. She's weird," Jerri said.

"I can say that, but you can't, okay?"

Mariah returned home just before noon and Lynn was still in her room. "I don't think she's gonna get up," Mariah said to Denise.

Denise responded quickly, "If she wants to act that way, I don't care. There'll be no surprise. We'll have to tell her."

Just then Mama came home. She went to Lynn's room. Mariah heard her say, "Lynn, I know you don't want a celebration, but I took off so you and I can do something."

"I don't want anything special."

"This isn't special. We'll go to the bookstore. How about that?"

"If we go maybe Riah and Denise would like to come, too."

Mariah wanted to shout *No!* but Mama said it for her, "No, no. We said no big thing. Just me and you. Get up and get ready."

As soon as they were out of the house, Mariah rushed to the phone. "Lynn's left the house. The surprise is on."

By three o'clock that afternoon Daddy had picked up all the things from Brandon's and everyone was there ready to work. Brandon's mother and Cynthia's grandmother came to help, too.

Mariah liked the way Denise had mixed and matched the colorful paper that covered the boxes. Only Denise and Lynn would dare mix those colors, she thought. The boxes were amazingly attractive.

Brandon put his handmade signs on the boxes: MEN'S AND BOYS' CLOTHING; WOMEN'S AND GIRLS' CLOTHING; and there was a box with the sign: CLOTHING FOR SMALL CHILDREN. Then he helped Mariah's daddy string the big banners across the yard so that they could not be seen from the street.

"Where's the music?" Brandon asked.

"Oh, I forgot the music," Mariah shouted.

"What's a party without music?" Trina asked.

"Don't worry," Daddy said. "I'll call Brandon's dad. He'll rig it up." Brandon's father supplied equipment for concerts and big parties.

Soon everything was ready. The yard looked festive as people began to arrive. The Friendly Five worked collecting food to put in boxes marked: CANNED GOODS and STAPLES AND DRIED FOODS. Denise worked with Brandon's mother and Cynthia's grandmother separating clothing and filling boxes.

Mariah looked around. The yard looked like a magic garden with the flowers and colorful boxes, the lights and banners. People stood together talking softly, waiting. Where was Lynn? Mariah worried. Had something happened?

Brandon's father set up the musical equipment and went to help Mariah's daddy get the grill ready for the hot dogs and bring out the tub of ice for the soft drinks. The cake, hot dog buns, chips, and all the relishes were on the table. Why didn't Mama bring Lynn?

Finally, Mariah heard the car in the driveway. She became so excited she could hardly say softly with force, "Quiet, everybody. She's here."

Lynn entered the backyard and they all shouted, *"SURPRISE!"*

Lynn's eyes widened, her mouth opened, she quickly covered it to stifle the sound and then spun around and tried to escape. Mama held her there until she came to herself.

Mariah beamed. She rushed to Lynn and threw her arms around her. "We did it," she cried. Lynn looked stunned, truly surprised. Mariah watched as Lynn looked at the banners: HAPPY BIRTHDAY, LYNN, WE LOVE YOU and SHARING IS CARING. Then Lynn saw the boxes filled with food and clothing for St. Martin's Shelter. Mariah knew she was fighting back tears when she said, "I didn't want a party, but I'm so glad all of you are here. I know my friends at St. Martin's will be happy to know that you care." She looked at Mariah, "Why didn't I think of this? I bet this was your idea, Riah."

"She's guilty!" a member of the Friendly Five shouted.

"And my friends and our sister, Denise, made it happen," Mariah said proudly. "Give them a hand." After everyone applauded, Mariah shouted, "Let's party."

Brandon picked a record, with some help from the Friendly Five. The music and the smell of hot dogs roasting filled the air. Mariah moved about making sure everyone was getting enough to eat and was having a good time.

Soon she had nothing to do. She stood with her friends watching Lynn and all of her friends dancing. No one asked her or the other Friendly Five members to dance.

"Go ask Brandon to come and dance with us," Jerri suggested.

"Not me," they all cried.

"I'll ask him," Mariah volunteered.

She came back without him. "His excuse is that he's playing the music."

"And Lynn's friends all think we're too young," Trina complained.

"We don't need them. Let's dance together, or by ourselves," Mariah said.

Later everyone sang "Happy Birthday" and shared Lynn's birthday cake and ice cream. After that, the crowd stayed on, reluctant to leave.

After midnight, when all the guests were gone, Mariah, still happy, did not even notice how tired she felt. The Friendly Five huddled with Brandon. "Now on to the meet," Mariah cried. With joined hands raised they shouted, "One down and one to go!"

"We did it once," Mariah said, "and we'll do it again."

357

by Mildred Pitts Walter

# Think About the Selection

1. Why do you think Mariah chooses the gift she does for Lynn? Do you think it was the right choice? Why or why not?

2. Would you like to receive, or give, the kind of gift Lynn received? Why or why not?

3. When Jerri says that Lynn is weird, Mariah replies, "I can say that but you can't, okay?" Why does Mariah say this?

4. Is Lynn surprised by the party, or did she know that something was up? Find details in the story that support your answer.

5. How would you describe Mariah? Would you like to have a friend like her? Explain.

6. How do the Friendly Five show that they are good problem solvers?

7. **Comparing/Contrasting** How do you think this selection fits the theme *Person to Person*? What do people do for each other?

# Write an Invitation

In planning Lynn's party, Mariah might have sent invitations to the guests. Write an invitation Mariah might have sent. Give all the important information a party guest would need to know, including the surprise.

## Tips

- Tell when and where the party is, and for whom.
- Include details about what to bring and why.
- Capitalize proper nouns and check for correct punctuation.

## Health

# Plan a Healthy Diet

With a partner, review the categories of food that Lynn's guests collected for the homeless shelter on page 354. Note that *staples* means "important basic foods," such as flour or rice. Under each category, make a list of foods that you think would contribute to a healthy diet.

**Bonus** Plan a meal using the foods in your list.

## Viewing

# Review an Illustration

Choose one of the illustrations in *Mariah Keeps Cool*. With a partner, discuss your thoughts about it. How does it fit with the words on the page? Is it a scene you would have chosen to illustrate? Why do you think the illustrator made the choices she did? If you wish, review more illustrations.

# Take an Online Poll

In a group, brainstorm a list of ways you could help people in your community. Then take an online poll at Education Place to find out how other students your age have helped out in their communities. **www.eduplace.com/kids**

**Genre**

**Newspaper
Article**

**Skill: How to Read
a News Article**

*Before You Read . . .*

Read the title or head-
line. Try to figure out
the topic of the article.

*As You Read . . .*

Look for answers to
these questions:

- **Who** or **what** is the
  news article about?

- **When** and **where**
  are the events
  taking place?

- **Why** are the events
  taking place: what
  has caused them?

- **How** are the events
  unfolding: what are
  the steps?

# One Pair
of Shoes
### and a lot of good souls!

*by Ms. Ginsberg's fifth grade class
at the Ramaz School in New York City, New York*

Many people in the world are less fortunate
than you or me. They don't have shoes or even
a house. My school decided to do something to
help.

— *Samantha Springer, age 11*

# How it all started

One day on Zev Alpert's way to school, he saw a homeless man walking on the street without shoes. Zev didn't like the fact that it was close to winter and people who didn't have shoes would freeze their feet, so when he got to school he asked Ms. Ginsberg (our teacher) if he could start a shoe drive. She asked "Why?" Zev explained how he saw a man without shoes and Ms. Ginsberg said, "We're already doing City Harvest. Sorry, I don't think we can do it with everything else we have to do." Ms. Ginsberg thought about what Zev told her and started to regret the answer that she gave to him, so she went over to Zev and said "You know what? We will do the shoe drive and I regret what I said to you." That is how it got started.

— *Jonathan Robin*

# How it all works

We get the shoes by giving out flyers to different people in the school building. Shoes come in from parents and kids. When we get to the school in the morning we always hang up our coat and books. But there's one thing different: We know that when we finish, if we have time left, we will polish and tie shoes. We buy different kinds of polish and make old shoes new again. It seems as though there's no end to them!

— *Jacob Savage*

To make the shoe drive successful we made posters and hung up advertisements.

— *Eric Rechschaffen, age 11*

Every Friday I go to the shoe stores to pick up shoes. I tell people every 2 pairs of shoes they bring in they get 15% off. This way it will help the shoe stores get more customers and help us get more shoes.

— *Hannah Zimet, age 11*

## What we do with the shoes

A call came in from a drop-in shelter named Peter's Place on 23rd St. and 7th Ave. Our class delivered the shoes to Peter's Place. We had gotten 136 pairs of women's shoes and 62 pairs of men's shoes. We delivered the shoes and stayed for about two hours. In those two hours we played with the people, who were mostly seniors, watched television, and played ping-pong, chess, and checkers.

When we got back to school, we made plans to return. We decided to go have lunch at Peter's Place. We also decided to bring some gifts to the people at the shelter. Another class had an even greater task. They had to collect children's shoes and give them to a shelter for the children.

— *Jess Mermelstein, age 10*

The word *mitzvah* means a good deed in Hebrew. The project of giving shoes to those who need them is a big mitzvah.

— **Samuel Jesselson**

Every morning when I go to school, I always see a lot of people working with the shoes. They wash the shoes, polish them, and tie them, and much more. This has been going on since November and I still don't get bored helping and watching the shoes in motion. It's just amazing that so many kids get involved and want to help.

— **David Pollack, age 11**

So far we have collected about 800 pairs of shoes and we hope to reach at least 1,500!

— **Samantha Springer, age 11**

# A Personal Narrative

A personal narrative gives a first-person account of a true experience. Use this student's writing as a model when you write a personal narrative of your own.

# Grand Slam!

A good **beginning** catches the reader's interest.

"Smack!" It looks like it's going all the way past the pale silver fence, 135 yards away from the plate.

"Oh man," I said, as the ball plopped down on the ground just before the fence. "Nick almost had a homer!"

Then I heard coach John say, "Shepard, you're up!"

Nervous and dripping with sweat, I got up to the plate. There were two outs and three men on: Ron, Nick, and Mike.

**Dialogue** makes a personal narrative come alive.

"Strike one!" called the ump. "Ball one! . . . Ball two!" Then again, "Strike two!"

The pressure was on as my teammates cheered, "Let's go, Tim. Let's go!" The pitch was there. It was a big, fat meat ball. I swung as hard as I could.

"Crack!" I hit the microscopic ball. As I ran to first, I saw my first base coach signaling me to go to second. As I touched second, I saw the ball glide over the fence. Then I heard a bang. "Beep! Boop! Boop! Beep! Beep! Boop! Beep! Boop!" I had hit a car, but I was still happy. It was a grand slam. I slowed down to a trot.

As I touched the dirty home plate, my team crowded around me. They were screaming and cheering. I tried desperately to run from them, but they kept chasing me around the field. I gave up the chase and they dog-piled me. I was so happy that my cheeks felt bright red.

Then I noticed something. My grand slam had just won us, the Vipers, the championship game! We had won 9 to 8. WE WERE THE CHAMPS!

> **Details** help the reader follow the narrative.

> A good **ending** ties the narrative together.

## Meet the Author

**Tim S.**
**Grade:** five
**State:** Florida
**Hobbies:** sports, reading, and writing
**What he'd like to be when he grows up:** a lawyer

**Mom's Best Friend**

Genre **Nonfiction**

### Key Vocabulary

dog guide
instinct
mastered
memorizing
obedience training
obstacles

**Vocabulary Reader**

A Team
of Two

*e* **Glossary**

# A Special Relationship

*Mom's Best Friend* describes the special attachment between Sally Hobart Alexander and her **dog guide**, Ursula.

**Visiting dogs help cheer up people in hospitals.**

Dogs were probably the first animals to be tamed and trained by people. Their original role may have been to help people hunt. Since then dogs have **mastered** such jobs as guiding blind and hearing-impaired people, rescuing accident victims, and visiting and cheering up hospital patients.

German shepherds and Labrador retrievers are popular dog guides for the blind.

Hearing dogs act as ears for the hearing-impaired.

You will read about the **obedience training** Ursula goes through to learn her job. But **memorizing** routines and learning to avoid **obstacles** is only half of that special relationship between dog and human. The other half is a dog's **instinct** for being a pal.

When both halves of the relationship fit together — the learning and the love — something nice happens. The trained helper becomes a best friend.

Many dogs are specially trained for finding and rescuing people.

## Meet the Author
# Sally Hobart Alexander

Sally Hobart Alexander grew up in rural Pennsylvania where she hiked, swam, and acted out stories with her friends. Alexander was in her twenties, teaching third grade in California, when she lost her eyesight to a rare disease. The next year, she was teaching again, at a center for the blind in Pittsburgh. Making up stories for her two children led Alexander to a career as a children's book author. Her first book, *Mom Can't See Me*, was also illustrated by photographer George Ancona.

## Meet the Photographer
# George Ancona

George Ancona grew up near Coney Island in Brooklyn, New York. He learned photography from his father, and began to draw by copying photographs. After traveling in Mexico, his parents' birthplace, Ancona studied in art school and worked as a designer for magazines and television. Since then he has kept busy as a photographer and author of children's books.

To find out more about Sally Hobart Alexander and George Ancona, visit Education Place. **www.eduplace.com/kids**

# Mom's Best Friend

Sally Hobart Alexander

Photographs by George Ancona

**Strategy Focus**

As you read about Mom and her dog guide, Ursula, **monitor** your understanding of Ursula's training. If necessary, reread and use the photographs to **clarify**.

369

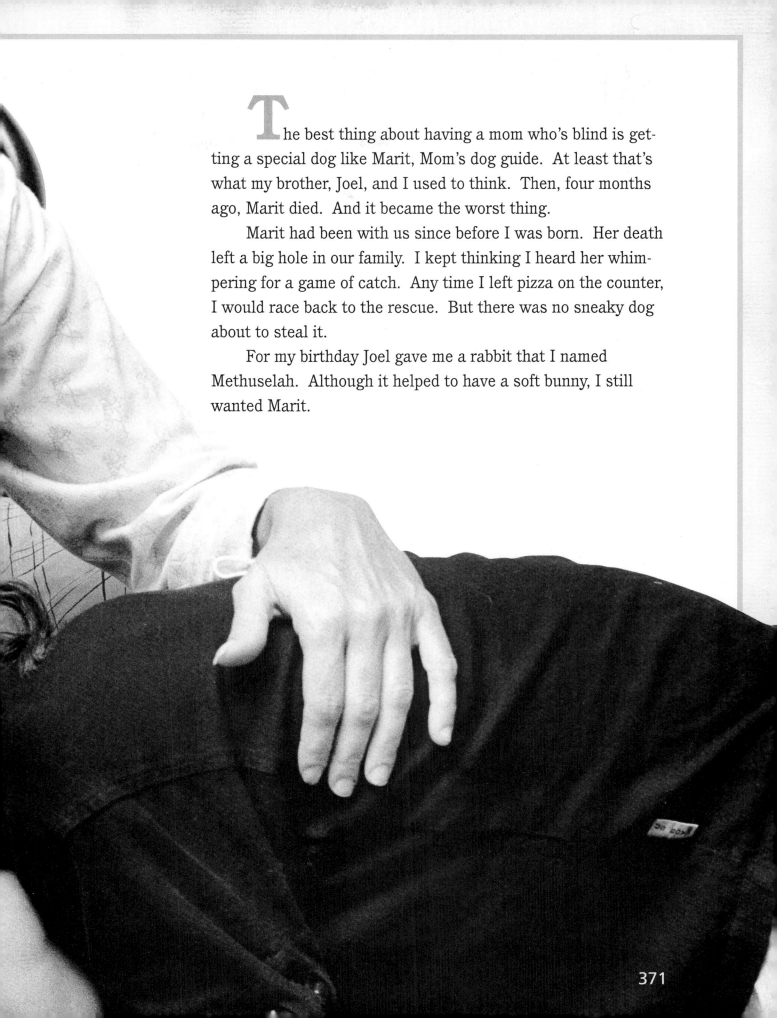

The best thing about having a mom who's blind is getting a special dog like Marit, Mom's dog guide. At least that's what my brother, Joel, and I used to think. Then, four months ago, Marit died. And it became the worst thing.

Marit had been with us since before I was born. Her death left a big hole in our family. I kept thinking I heard her whimpering for a game of catch. Any time I left pizza on the counter, I would race back to the rescue. But there was no sneaky dog about to steal it.

For my birthday Joel gave me a rabbit that I named Methuselah. Although it helped to have a soft bunny, I still wanted Marit.

**M**om missed her even more. She didn't lose just a sweet, furry pet. She lost her favorite way of traveling, too. She had to use her cane again, and crept along the sidewalk like a snail. Once, when she crossed the street, she missed the opposite curb and kept walking toward the traffic. I had to holler to get her onto the sidewalk.

After that, I worried about her running errands by herself. I asked her to "go sighted guide," holding Dad's, Joel's, or my arm. Sometimes she did. But mostly she used the cane. She didn't want to depend on us — or on anybody.

A lot of blind people do fine with a cane. It's like a real long arm to help them feel what's around: walkways, hedges, mailboxes.

With a dog guide, blind people use their hearing more than touch. Mom has trained her ears. It's amazing: she can tell when something, like a movie marquee, is above her head, and when she passes a lamppost. She knows from the change in the sound of her footsteps.

**I**n spite of Mom's special hearing, I worried. I was relieved when she decided to go back to The Seeing Eye for a new dog guide.

Before Mom left, I told her I wouldn't be able to love the new dog as much as Marit. Mom hugged me and said, "The night before you were born, I wondered how I could love a second child as much as your brother. Then you came, and like magic, I was just as crazy about you."

The Seeing Eye, in Morristown, New Jersey, was the first dog guide school in the United States. (Now there are nine others.) It trains German shepherds and Labrador and golden retrievers for three months. Then, for about a month, it teaches blind people to use the dogs.

When Mom arrived at The Seeing Eye, she was met by her instructor, Pete Jackson.

I missed Mom as much as I missed Marit, but at least Mom called every night. She also wrote letters and sent pictures.

Mom's first day was a cinch. She'd gone to Seeing Eye twelve years before to get Marit, and still remembered her way around. Usually when she's in a new place she has to move from room to room with her cane, memorizing the layout.

In the morning Mom walked with Pete Jackson so that he could check her pace. He wanted to choose the dog that would suit her best. Then she was free to play the piano, exercise . . . and worry. Would she get along with the new dog? Would they work well together?

The next day she got Ursula. What a strange name! The staff at Seeing Eye's breeding station had named Ursula when she was born. (Ursula's brothers and sisters were also given names starting with *U*.) Dog guides need a name right away so that Seeing Eye can keep track of the four hundred or so pups born each year. At two months of age, the pups go to Seeing Eye puppy-raising families to learn how to live with people. At fifteen months, they are mature enough to return to Seeing Eye for the three-month training program.

Dad said that Ursula means "bear." But in the pictures Mom sent, Ursula looked too pipsqueaky to be called bear. Mom explained that Seeing

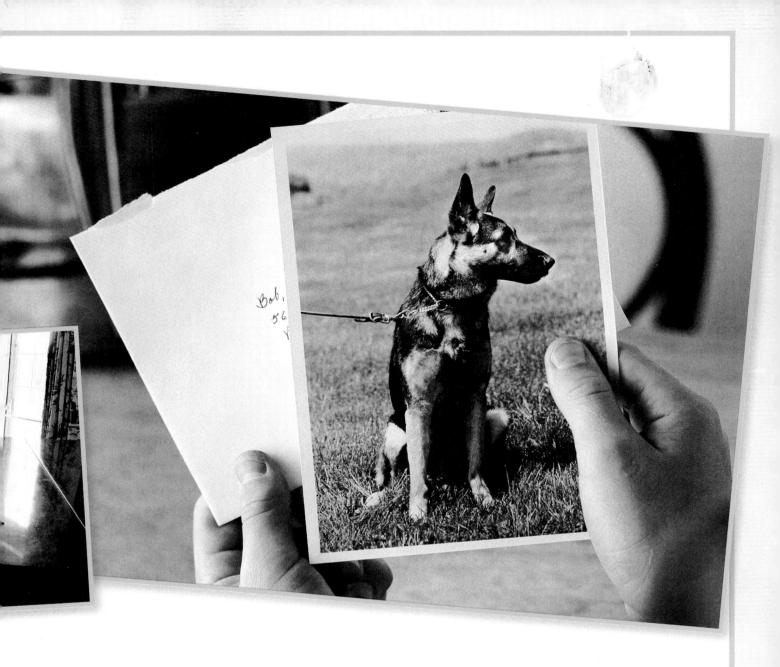

Eye is now breeding some smaller dogs. They are easier to handle and fit better on buses and in cars.

My friends thought dog guides were little machines that zoomed blind people around. Until Mom went away, even I didn't understand all the things these dogs were taught.

But on Mom's first lesson in Morristown, Ursula seemed to forget her training. She veered on a street crossing and brushed Mom into a bush. Mom had to make her correct herself by backing up and walking around the bush. Then Mom praised her.

After ten practice runs with Pete, Mom and Ursula soloed. Ursula didn't stop at a curb, so Mom had to scold her and snap her leash, calling, "Pfui." Later Ursula crashed Mom into a low-hanging branch. "Ursula will have to start thinking tall," Mom said that night, "or I'll have to carry hedge clippers in my purse."

Even though Ursula had walked in Morristown a lot with Pete, she was nervous when Mom's hand was on the harness. Mom talked and walked differently. And Mom was nervous, too. Ursula moved so much faster than old Marit had, and Mom didn't trust her.

Every day Mom and Ursula made two trips. Every week they mastered new routes. Each route got longer and more complicated, and Mom had less time to learn it. Every night Mom gave Ursula obedience training: "Come. Sit down. Rest. Fetch." I thought she should try obedience training on Joel.

While Mom worked hard, Dad, Joel, and I went on with our normal lives — school, homework, soccer, piano, spending time with friends. We divided Mom's chores: Dad did the cooking, Joel, the vacuuming and laundry, and I did the dishes, dusting, weeding. The first two weeks were easy.

In a phone call Mom said that things were getting easier for her, too. "Remember how tough curb ramps have been for me?" she asked. "They feel like any other slope in the sidewalk, so I can't always tell that I've reached the street. Well, Ursula stopped perfectly at every ramp. And she guided me around, not under, a ladder and right past a huge parking lot without angling into it. But best of all, she actually saved my life. A jackhammer was making so much noise that I couldn't hear whether the light was green or red. When I told Ursula, 'Forward!' she refused to move and kept me from stepping in front of a car. (Of course, Pete would have saved me if Ursula hadn't.)"

**M**om barely asked about us. It was all Ursula, Ursula, Ursula! She seemed to be forgetting Marit, too. When a letter came a few days later, I was sure she didn't miss anyone.

Dear Bob, Joel, and Leslie,

Today Ursula and I faced several disasters! She tried hard to ignore a boxer dog who wanted to play. A few minutes later, a great Dane lunged out from nowhere, jumped all over her, and loped off. Ursula's instinct is to chase dogs, but she didn't move a paw after that one. As if the dogs weren't enough trouble, fire engine sirens went off. Ursula just strolled down the sidewalk.

Mostly, life is smooth here. Seeing Eye is a vacation — no cooking, no cleaning, lots of time to talk to new friends, like Dr. Holle, the veterinarian. And since I don't have many blind friends, it's a treat to be with my roommate and the twenty other students. We laugh about the same things, like the great enemy of the blind — trash collection day! Every twenty feet there's a garbage can reeking of pizza, hoagies, old cheese. Usually Ursula snakes me around these smelly obstacles. But sometimes the temptation to her nose wins out, and I have to correct her, all the while holding my own nose.

Some trainees really inspire me, like Julie Hensley, who became blind from diabetes at twenty-two. Even though she's been blind for twelve years, she still teaches horses to do stunts. She judges her location from a radio playing music in the center of the pen, and gallops around as fast as she ever did when she could see.

Bob Pacheco used to race motorcycles and hunt. Then, two years ago, when he was twenty-nine, he developed optic atrophy and became blind two months later. He took up fishing, swimming, even trapping. But something was missing. He couldn't get around quickly enough. After the first trip with his dog guide, he was overjoyed. "Sally!" He grabbed my hand. "I don't feel blind any more."

The dogs are wonderful, and the people here are very special. So are you.

Love, Mom

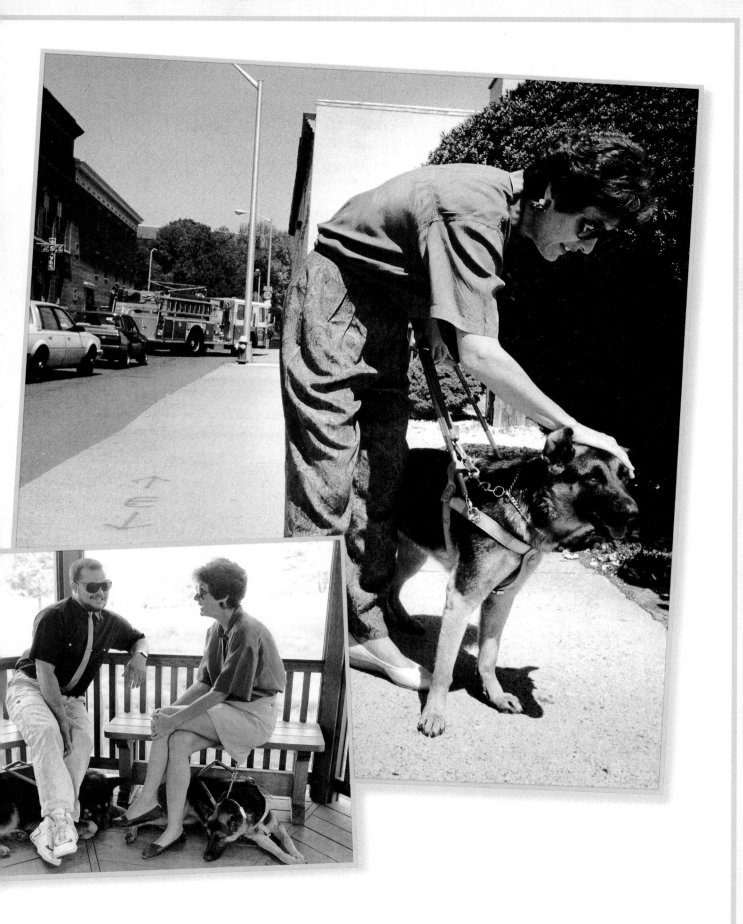

**W**ell, life at home wasn't very wonderful or special. Dad ran out of the casseroles Mom had frozen ahead of time, and although his meals were okay, I missed Mom's cooking. Worse, the dishes kept piling up. I never knew Joel ate so much.

Then things got really bad. While Dad was teaching his American literature night class, Joel and I faced a disaster Mom and Ursula couldn't have dreamed of: the toilet bowl overflowed! We wiped the floor with towels. As Joel took the towels down to the washing machine, he found water dripping through the ceiling — all over the dining room table, all over the carpet. He ran for more towels, and I ran for the furniture polish and rug shampoo. When Dad got home, everything looked perfect. But I wrote a braille letter.

Dear Mom,
Come home soon. The house misses you.
Love,
Exhausted in Pittsburgh

Mom wrote back.
Dear Exhausted,
Hang on. We'll be home to "hound" you Thursday. Be prepared. When you see me, I will have grown four more feet.
Mom

I couldn't laugh. I was too tired and worried. What if I couldn't love Ursula? Marit was the best dog ever.

Soon they arrived. Ursula yanked at her leash and sprang up on me. She pawed my shoulders, stomach, and arms just the way Marit used to, nearly knocking me over. She leaped onto Joel, licking him all over. As she bounded up onto me again, I realized Mom was right. Like magic, I was crazy about this shrimpy new dog.

But by the end of the day, I had a new worry. Was *Ursula* going to love *me*? She seemed friendly enough, but keyed up, even lost in our house.

Mom explained that Ursula had already given her heart away three times: first to her mother, then to the Seeing Eye puppy-raising family, and finally to Pete. Mom said we had to be patient.

"Remember how Marit loved you, Leslie? When you were little, she let you stand on her back to see out the window. Ursula will be just as nuts about you. Love is the whole reason this dog guide business works."

So I tried to be patient and watched Mom work hard. First she showed one route in our neighborhood to Ursula and walked it over and over. Then she taught her a new route, repeated that, and reviewed the old one. Every day she took Ursula on two trips, walking two or three miles. She fed her, groomed her, gave her obedience training. Twice a week Mom cleaned Ursula's ears and brushed her teeth.

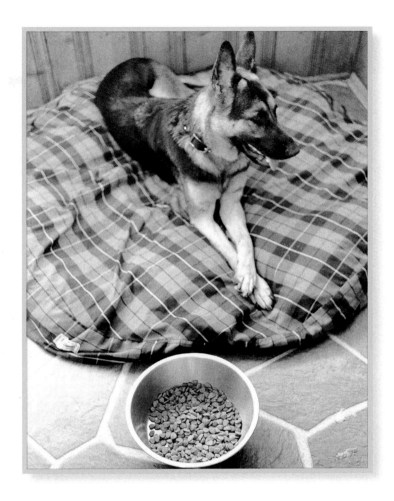

"I'm as busy as I was when you and Joel were little!" she said.

Mom and Ursula played for forty-five minutes each day. Joel, Dad, and I were only allowed to watch. Ursula needed to form her biggest attachment to Mom.

Mom made Ursula her shadow. When she showered or slept, Ursula was right there.

Still, Ursula didn't eat well — only half the amount she'd been eating at Seeing Eye. And she tested Mom, pulling her into branches, stepping off curbs. Once she tried to take a shortcut home. Another time, because she was nervous, she crossed a new street diagonally.

Crossing streets is tricky. Ursula doesn't know when the light is green. Mom knows. If she hears the cars moving beside her in the direction in which she's walking, the light is green. If they're moving right and left in front of her, it's red.

I worried about Ursula's mistakes, but Mom said they were normal. She kept in touch with her classmates and knew that their dog guides were goofing, too. One kept eating grass, grazing like a cow. Another chased squirrels, pigeons, and cats. Still another always stopped in the middle of the street, ten feet from the curb. Once in a while her friends got lost, just like Mom, and had to ask for help.

Mom said it takes four to six months for the dogs to settle down. But no matter how long she and Ursula are teamed up together, Ursula will need some correcting. For instance, Ursula might act so cute that a passerby will reach out to pet her. Then Mom will have to scold Ursula and ask the person not to pet a dog guide. If people give Ursula attention while she's working, she forgets to do her job.

After a month at home, Ursula emptied her food bowl every time. She knew all the routes, and Mom could zip around as easily as she had with Marit.

"Now it's time to start the loneliness training," Mom said. She left Ursula alone in the house, at first for a short time while she went jogging with Dad. Ursula will never be able to take Mom jogging because she can't guide at high speeds.

Each week Mom increased the amount of time Ursula was alone. I felt sorry for our pooch, but she did well: no barking, no chewing on furniture.

Then Mom said Joel and I could introduce Ursula to our friends, one at a time. They could pet her when she was out of harness.

Every morning Ursula woke Joel and me. Every night she sneaked into my bed for a snooze.

Finally Mom allowed Joel and me to play with Ursula, and I knew: shrimpy little Ursula had fallen for us, and we were even crazier about her.

But we haven't forgotten Marit. Joel says that Ursula is the best dog alive. And I always say she's the best dog in this world.

## Think About the Selection

1. What can you tell about the family in *Mom's Best Friend* from the way the family members manage while Mom is away?

2. What are other relationships in *Mom's Best Friend* besides the one between Mom and Ursula? Review the selection and report what you find.

3. What traits does a person need to be a good trainer of dog guides? Tell why you would or would not be good at this job.

4. Why do you think Ursula needs to form her strongest attachment to Mom?

5. Why do you think it takes so long for Ursula to settle down after moving to her new home?

6. Explain what Mom means when she says on page 381, "Love is the whole reason this dog guide business works."

7. **Connecting/Comparing** Compare the family described in this selection with Mariah's family in *Mariah Keeps Cool*. Think about how the members work together, and what is important to each family.

## Write an Audiotape Message

Suppose the family sent audiotape messages back and forth to stay in touch. Write the text of an audio greeting Mom might have sent, or write a message her family might have sent to her. Tell what the sender's day-to-day life is like. If you like, tape-record your message.

**Tips**

- Use language and a tone you might use in everyday speech.
- Add humor or emotion.

386

## Science

# Compare How Sounds Are Absorbed

Reread the description of Mom's hearing on page 372. What does it tell about how objects absorb, or muffle, sounds? Make a list of the different places Mom goes in the selection and note how sounds might be absorbed, or not, by her surroundings. Which places might be louder? Which might be quieter? Why?

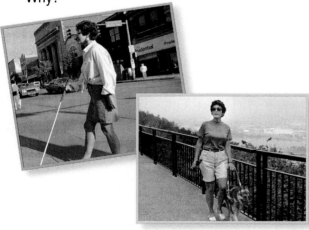

## Math

# Map a Route

Make a map of a two-mile route Mom and Ursula could take to practice Ursula's dog guide skills. Draw your route to scale. Use a formula in which one inch equals a fraction of a mile. Find information in the selection to help you figure out what obstacles to include, such as low branches and traffic lights.

**Bonus** Number each obstacle. Below the map, write what Ursula should do when she encounters each obstacle.

# Post a Review

What would you like to tell others about *Mom's Best Friend*? What did you learn while reading it? Post your review at Education Place. **www.eduplace.com/kids**

## Science Article

**Skill: How to Outline**

*Before you read . . .*

Think about the parts of an outline:

**Title:** what the selection is about

**I. Main topic:** tells a main idea
   A. **Subtopic:** gives key details about the main topic

*As you read . . .*

- Make an outline by turning each heading into a main topic.

- Look for key details to list as subtopics.

# Monkeys with

**Well-trained monkeys shine at helping human friends overcome limits.**

A man is thirsty and wants a drink of water, but he can't get it for himself. The man, George Boyle of Cleveland, Alabama, can't move his arms or legs because his neck was broken in a car accident. So his good friend Gizmo gets the drink for him.

Gizmo is a helpful, playful monkey. Here Gizmo gets ready to place a water bottle in a holder, open it, and insert a straw. Gizmo does other tasks for Boyle, who gets around using a wheelchair.

# a Mission

by Suzanne Wilson

Gizmo, 14, is a capuchin (kuh-PYOO-shun) monkey. She comes from Helping Hands, an organization in Boston, Massachusetts, that trains capuchins to help people with disabilities. In South America capuchins live in the wild. But the monkeys from Helping Hands are born at a special breeding facility near Boston. Intelligent and small, capuchins easily form relationships with people.

## Family First

"She's like my sister," says Elizabeth Ford, 13, about Sadie. The capuchin has lived with Elizabeth's family in Norton, Massachusetts, for three years. Sadie will spend another two or three years there, getting used to living with people. Then she'll be trained to help a person with a disability.

Like Elizabeth, Sadie enjoys eating snacks. Unlike Elizabeth, though, her favorite hangout is on the roof (right). Elizabeth will be sad when Sadie leaves to start her training, but says, "I know she'll be helping somebody."

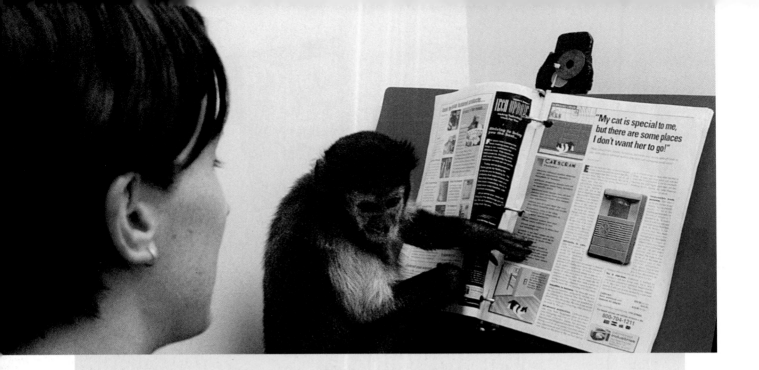

# Learning to Help

Training follows the family stay. At Helping Hands, a monkey called Patty learns to turn the pages of a magazine (above). "The monkeys are so curious, and they love doing the tasks," says trainer Sue Costa.

Using a laser pointer, Costa indicates objects a monkey must work with or fetch. First the monkeys learn the basics — getting food and drinks or retrieving dropped objects. Then they learn special tasks, such as loading a computer disk, putting a cassette into a VCR, or punching telephone buttons. After about 18 months, most monkeys are ready for work. Then Helping Hands carefully matches humans to monkeys, based on personality.

Living 30 to 40 years, a capuchin is a long-term companion. People don't have to pay for their capuchin helpers. But training and caring for the monkeys is costly. Helping Hands can afford to place only six to ten monkeys a year.

**Lunch is served when Kimba opens a sandwich holder.**

**A red laser light shows Patty which switch to flip.**

# Working

Gizmo finished her training. Now she doesn't monkey around when she's busy at work. She knows she'll earn a reward when she positions the magazine Boyle wants to read (right). Boyle blows through a straw to dispense fruit juice treats to Gizmo. While he reads, Gizmo watches traffic from the window, plays, or sits in the sun. She likes musical toys and watching TV commercials. At night she sleeps in a big cage with her stuffed animals and a blanket.

Every morning a health-care worker helps Boyle bathe and dress. Then Boyle and Gizmo spend the day together. "She's a lot like a child," says Boyle. He gives Gizmo presents on her birthday and knows when she's happy by the way she chirps. Gizmo often knows what Boyle wants before he asks her. Friends for five years, they will be together for many more.

**Gizmo comes to the rescue when Boyle asks her to scratch his nose.**

**Yang the Second and Her Secret Admirers**

Genre **Realistic Fiction**

## Key Vocabulary

heritage
opera
traditions

Vocabulary Reader

**Two Traditions of Dance**

*e* ● Glossary

# Honoring Your Heritage

What is a **heritage** ? Where does it come from? Why is it important?

A heritage is a collection of **traditions** passed down through many generations. It includes the special customs and values that children learn from their parents and grandparents.

In *Yang the Second and Her Secret Admirers*, one character deeply values her Chinese heritage. Eating *dim sum*, listening to Chinese **opera** , wearing Chinese clothes — these traditions are all part of her heritage.

In the Chinese meal called *dim sum*, diners are served a wide variety of small dishes, one after the other.

Think about the culture of your grandparents — or of their grandparents. What traditions have you learned from them? Perhaps there is a dish from a family recipe, an old song you sing, or a dance that you perform on holidays.

Sometimes many cultures may contribute to your heritage. Think about the sports you play, the foods you eat, the music you listen to, and the languages you speak. How many different cultures are part of who *you* are?

The Chinese characters *Chuán Tŏng* mean "heritage."

传统

Chinese opera presents plays based on Chinese history and folklore.

Traditional Chinese instruments include the *erhu*, a stringed instrument related to the violin.

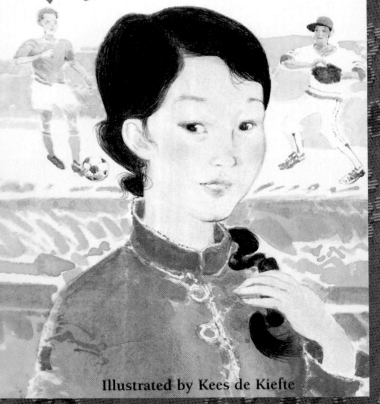

Lensey Namioka

Yang the Second
and
Her Secret Admirers

Illustrated by Kees de Kiefte

## Strategy Focus

Who is Yang the Second? Who secretly admires her? As you read the selection, use what you discover about characters and events to create more **questions** that you can ask your classmates.

*As the oldest daughter in her family, Second Sister clings to her Chinese heritage and refuses to make any friends. But her younger brother and sister have a plan, which they have practiced at the home of their friend, Kim O'Meara. What if Second Sister overhears them saying that Paul Eng, her classmate, likes her? And what if Paul overhears them saying that Second Sister likes him? Who knows what might happen next?*

By the next day I was beginning to have second thoughts about our plot. It could turn out to be really embarrassing for Second Sister.

She looked so unhappy sometimes that I thought it might be mean to play a trick on her. Once, Second Sister, Third Sister, and I were at a shopping mall, and we went into a restaurant for refreshments. Third Sister saw some of her friends there, and she went over to their table. Soon we heard them talking and laughing.

Second Sister sat with her head down, sipping her drink, and she suddenly looked very forlorn. In China she had lots of friends, and she would be sitting with them, talking and laughing. She could have made friends here, too, but she preferred to stay home like a grouch.

But Second Sister isn't always a grouch, and I remembered the times when she was kind to me. Like the days when my family still wanted me to play the violin, for instance. Father, Mother, and Eldest Brother had all thought that I played so badly because I wasn't trying hard enough. Second Sister wasn't like the rest of them. She thought that I had it in me to be a good musician, but that I gave up playing so that my friend Matthew could play in our family string quartet. We all knew that Matthew had real musical talent. Second Sister thought I was being noble and letting Matthew take my place because of our friendship. It was just the kind of thing she would do for her own friends. She simply refused to believe that a member of the Yang family would have a terrible ear. It wasn't in our genes.

*I* wanted to get Third Sister alone and discuss whether we should go on with our trick. But I didn't get a chance. Third Sister came home just before dinner, and we all sat down around the dinner table. Mother had cooked my favorite dish: pork stewed with yellow turnips. Normally I eat so much of this dish that I get scolded for hogging it (can you hog a dish of pork?).

But I was too busy with my thoughts to eat much. I jumped when Mother said, "What's the matter, Yingtao? Aren't you feeling well? You aren't eating your favorite."

"I'm fine," I muttered. Hurriedly, I took a big helping.

Eldest Brother began to ask Second Sister about the demonstration she had given that day in school. Her class was studying different types of entertainment in countries all over the world, and she had offered to talk about Chinese opera.

To demonstrate background music in opera, Second Sister brought in an *erhu*, a kind of Chinese violin with two strings, and played it to her class. She usually played a viola, but she jumped at this chance to show how a traditional Chinese instrument sounded.

Father beamed. "I'm glad you did it. We concentrate so hard on playing Western music that sometimes we forget there is a long tradition of music in China."

"Did the class enjoy your demonstration?" asked Eldest Brother.

"A few of the kids made faces when I hit the high notes on the *erhu*," said Second Sister. "But most were very interested. Afterward some of them came up and wanted to try it."

Then she frowned. "You know that boy Paul Eng? He told me he had never seen or heard the instrument before!"

I had to defend Paul. "What's so strange about that? I bet very few people in this country have seen one!"

Second Sister's lips curled scornfully. "Maybe that's true of your average American. But you'd think somebody like Paul Eng would care more about his Chinese heritage!"

Lately Second Sister has been using the word *heritage* a lot. I'm not quite sure what she means by our Chinese heritage. Does she mean being as Chinese as possible? But her own instrument is a viola, a Western instrument. Or does she mean clothes? Is that why she likes to wear her cloth jacket with the high collar and buttons down the front? Maybe she means eating Chinese food with chopsticks. But Paul ate Chinese food — the whole Eng family had been eating *dim sum* in Chinatown just the other day.

Listening to the scornful way Second Sister talked about Paul, I decided it would be a great joke after all to get the two of them together, like that couple in the movie. My eyes met Third Sister's, and we nodded to each other.

*I*n our family Third Sister and I do the dishes, while Second Sister and Eldest Brother help Mother with some of the cooking. As Third Sister scraped the garbage into the disposal, I filled a big pan with hot, sudsy water and began putting the dishes in.

The chopsticks I washed by rubbing them against one another: You hold a bunch of them and roll them between your two hands, making a *burrrr* sound. The rubbing makes the chopsticks really clean.

Once I even did it in time to music. Eldest Brother was practicing a piece, and I added a rhythmic part with the chopsticks. I have a terrible ear for pitch — that is, I'm no good at telling high from low. But I've got pretty good rhythm. Eldest Brother enjoyed my chopsticks accompaniment. It was the only time he ever said anything good about my music making.

"Shh! Not so loud with the chopsticks," whispered Third Sister. "I think Second Sister is finished in the pantry. Let's start when she goes up the stairs."

I dropped the chopsticks into the pan, and after a minute Third Sister winked at me in a signal to begin our act.

"Isn't it touching," said Third Sister in a loud whisper, "the way Paul Eng went up to Second Sister after her demonstration?"

This wasn't the opening line we had planned, but it was a good one. I did my best to play up to it. "Yeah, he must have been really hurt when she didn't say anything friendly back to him."

We paused and listened. Second Sister's steps paused at the foot of the stairs. Instead of going up to her room to practice, she was stopping to hear more.

"Are you sure he likes her?" asked Third Sister. Now we were using the lines we had rehearsed. "After all, she hasn't been nice to him at all. In fact she's been awfully mean every time his name comes up."

There was no sound from Second Sister. She must have been listening intently. I risked a short pause, and washed a few plates. Then I sighed heavily. "Poor Paul. I asked him once about his batting stance. He was very nice to me and explained everything patiently." I paused to wash a couple of rice bowls before continuing. "Then he looked at me sort of anxiously. He asked me whether Second Sister ever went out with boys — you know, on dates."

"So that *proves* he likes her!" exclaimed Third Sister. "What did you tell him?"

"I had to tell him the truth," I said, and sighed again. "I told him Second Sister wouldn't look at a boy who didn't speak Chinese."

"Poor Paul!" Third Sister said. The two of us were beginning to repeat ourselves, so we didn't say anything more and went on washing dishes. Besides, we had said enough.

Our ears were eagerly cocked, and sure enough, we could hear Second Sister's steps going slowly up the stairs. They sounded thoughtful.

*A*rranging for Paul to overhear Kim and Third Sister wasn't easy. The trouble was that neither our family nor the O'Mearas knew the Engs outside of school. Besides, Third Sister, Kim, and I went to elementary school, while Paul went to the same high school as Eldest Brother and Second Sister. Except at school concerts or baseball games, we just didn't run into the Engs much.

Days passed, and I almost gave up hope. I noticed that Second Sister sometimes had on a peculiar expression. Her face would be screwed up, like she was trying to get a piece of gristle out from between her teeth. She must have been chewing over our remarks she had overheard.

That meant the first part of our scheme was working. But what good did it do if we couldn't carry out the second part?

Our chance came at last. It was our spring vacation, and as a treat Mrs. O'Meara took Kim, Third Sister, and me to visit the Pacific Science Center.

Mrs. O'Meara said she was sick and tired of having kids underfoot all the time. "Jason is acting really strange," she said. "He goes around mooning and bumping into things!" So she chased him out of the house with orders to practice soccer with his friends. It was the first time she ever had to order him to practice.

Mrs. O'Meara offered to drop Kim and Third Sister at the Science Center. I had hoped to play with my friend Matthew, but he had to go to the dentist. He protested that it was totally unfair for someone to see a dentist during vacation. "Life *is* totally unfair," said his mother as she dragged him off.

So Mrs. O'Meara took me along with Kim and Third Sister, who didn't mind me tagging along. It turned out to be a good thing we went together.

*T*he Science Center is a big museum with lots of buttons to push. Things go squirting and squeaking and beeping and gurgling. We're supposed to learn important scientific facts from all this. In spite of that, it's loads of fun.

While Kim and Third Sister played with machines that speeded up their voices and made them sound like Donald Duck, I went over to look at a box containing poisonous spiders. Next to that was a tall glass case with a section of a beehive in it. I was just about to go over when I saw Paul Eng standing behind the case, looking at the bees.

I rushed over to Third Sister and grabbed her arm. "I saw Paul over there!" I whispered. "Come on! This is our chance to carry out our plan!"

Third Sister and I hurried over to the case of bees, and she began her speech. Then she stopped. Kim had to be in the act, too, and she was still back at the sound machine, making like Donald Duck!

We ran back and got Kim over, but by then Paul had already gone.

Looking around frantically, we spotted him going into the dinosaur exhibit room. He stopped and peered at a tyrannosaurus, which roared menacingly.

We quickly positioned ourselves behind the dinosaur. Third Sister and Kim opened their mouths and tried to start our script.

*ROAR*, went the tyrannosaurus. The three of us looked at one another and shook our heads. This wasn't going to work.

I waited until I saw Paul reach one of the quiet dinosaurs, an armored stegosaurus. There was no time to be lost. "Come on!" I hissed to the other two.

Again we got ourselves into position, and Kim cleared her throat. "So what makes you think your sister likes Paul Eng?" she asked.

"Well, she was impressed by the way he played in that ball game," said Third Sister, "and she isn't usually interested in American sports."

I came in with my lines. "And I thought she didn't like him! I thought she only liked boys who spoke Chinese."

"That's what I thought, too," said Third Sister. "Second Sister told me what really changed her mind was how good he is in math. He's in her math class, you know."

As I listened to our act, the lines suddenly sounded really stiff and unnatural. How could anyone believe something as lame as this?

Maybe Kim and Third Sister felt that way, too. Their voices petered out and stopped. Then without another word, we began to shuffle off. I didn't dare to look behind me at Paul to see how he had taken our words.

*W*e went to the food court, where we were supposed to wait for Mrs. O'Meara to pick us up. For a while the three of us sipped our drinks without saying anything. I broke the silence and got the last drop of my drink with a loud slurp. "Do you think he fell for the act?"

"I don't know," muttered Kim. "It was okay when we were practicing the other day, but it sounded awfully phony just now."

Third Sister and I nodded. We both knew what she meant. In a way, I was almost relieved.

Suddenly Third Sister grabbed my arm. "Isn't that him over there?" she hissed.

She was right. Paul was standing at the pie counter, buying some refreshments. He was also buying something for his companion, the girl standing next to him.

It seemed that we had been wasting our time: Paul already had a girlfriend!

I felt a kick on my leg from Third Sister. She had seen Paul's girlfriend, too. I nodded and pointed out the couple to Kim.

The three of us sighed in unison. "I'm sorry," I said. "I should have found out whether Paul already had a girlfriend before we started all this."

We sat around glumly and thought about all the time and energy we had wasted. Then I heard a step behind me, and a soft cough.

"Hello," said Paul Eng's voice.

I spun around and stared. Paul and his girlfriend were standing by our table.

"Hi, Paul," I said weakly. Then I said the first thing that came into my head, "I'd give anything to hit a home run!"

Third Sister had better manners. "Hi, I don't know if you remember me. I'm Mary, and this is my friend Kim."

Paul looked embarrassed. That wasn't surprising, after the conversation he had overheard. In his place, I would have avoided the Yang family like chicken pox.

But for some strange reason, Paul didn't go away. He just stood there. Three months seemed to go by as we all waited and squirmed.

Finally the girl with Paul poked him. He cleared his throat, swallowed, and said, "This is my sister, Melanie. You met her at the *dim sum* restaurant, didn't you?"

Now I realized that the girl looked familiar. She wasn't his girlfriend at all. She was his sister! There was still hope our trick might work.

Melanie poked her brother again, and again Paul cleared his throat. "You have another sister, don't you? Her name is Yinglan, right?" His voice sort of died off.

Third Sister and I nodded solemnly. "That's right," I acknowledged. "I do have another sister, called Yinglan."

There was a pause. The five of us stared at one another some more, and three more months passed.

*I*t's hard for Americans to remember Chinese names. Unlike Third Sister, Second Sister refused to give herself an English name. I thought it was a good sign that Paul knew Second Sister's name, since that meant he had really paid attention to her — even before we played our trick.

Melanie poked Paul for the third time, and for the third time he cleared his throat. A family of frogs must have set up housekeeping with his tonsils. "Er . . . I noticed Yinglan in my math class," he began. "But she's only a sophomore, isn't she?"

"She got put a year ahead," admitted Third Sister. Then she added quickly, "It's not that she's a math genius, or anything. It's just that Chinese schools are more advanced in math."

"Very good, very good . . . ," said Paul absently. Then he must have realized that he sounded foolish, and his voice faded. Suddenly he took a deep breath and said in a rush, "Does your sister ever go out with boys, you know, on dates?"

We did it! Our trick had worked. I caught Third Sister's eye, and we both smothered an urge to laugh. Paul's words were almost exactly the same as the ones Second Sister had overheard while we were doing dishes!

Paul must have seen the laughter in our eyes. He turned red as a sunset. Dragging Melanie after him, he rushed out of the food court. He almost crashed into Mrs. O'Meara, who had come to pick us up.

"Who was that?" asked Mrs. O'Meara, staring after the Engs. "Friends of yours?"

"I hope so," Third Sister said slowly. She looked at me and then at Kim. The three of us beamed at one another and silently congratulated ourselves on our success.

# MEET THE AUTHOR
# Lensey Namioka

**Chinese Heritage:** Born in Beijing, China, Namioka moved to the United States at the age of nine. She started school before she could speak English.

**Like Author, Like Character:** Namioka, like Second Sister, excelled at math in school. She went on to teach math at Cornell University.

**Hobby:** Music. She says: "[I] prefer to make it myself badly than to hear it performed superbly."

**Bylines:** Namioka began her literary career by writing humorous articles for a newspaper. She then turned to children's books. Read her other books about the Yang family: *Yang the Youngest and His Terrible Ear*; *Yang the Third and Her Impossible Family*; and *Yang the Eldest and His Odd Jobs*.

# MEET THE ILLUSTRATOR
# Kees de Kiefte

**Dutch Heritage:** "I was born in a small medieval town alongside a river in Holland a long time ago."

**Advice:** "Sit down in a city center and observe people, sometimes making note-like drawings and adding word-like notes. . . . Doing this you LOOK as well as REMEMBER."

**On Himself:** "I am a clumsy dreamer coming to life while drawing."

Internet

To find out more about Lensey Namioka and Kees de Kiefte, visit Education Place. **www.eduplace.com/kids**

# Responding

## Think About the Selection

1. If you moved to a new country, like Second Sister, what reminders of your heritage would you hold on to? What traditions would you miss?

2. What advice would you give Second Sister to help her feel more comfortable with life in the United States?

3. Compare and contrast the way Second Sister and Paul Eng react after they hear the false rumor.

4. Do you think Yingtao and his sister should have tricked Second Sister and Paul as they did? Explain.

5. On page 405, the author writes: "The five of us stared at one another some more, and three more months passed." Explain this silence.

6. What do you think will happen next in the story? Why?

7. **Connecting/Comparing** Yingtao plays a trick on Second Sister. Mariah misleads Lynn in *Mariah Keeps Cool*. How are these two kinds of trickery alike and different?

## Summarizing

### Write a Personal Introduction

It is your job to introduce Paul Eng to Second Sister. Write an introduction of one or two paragraphs, telling one of the characters what the other is like.

### Tips

- Begin by listing the characters' interests and talents.
- Decide which features should get the most emphasis.
- Be sure your introduction includes each character's name, grade, and age.

## Social Studies

## Learn About Traditions

Second Sister plays an *erhu*, a Chinese violin with two strings. Look through the story to find other details about Chinese traditions. With a partner, do research to learn more about these traditions. Then write and illustrate a report sharing what you learned.

## Listening and Speaking

## Act It Out

With five classmates, act out the end of the selection, beginning with the scene at the Science Center. Decide who will play the parts of Yingtao, Third Sister, Kim, Paul, Melanie, and Mrs. O'Meara. Look for clues in the story to help you figure out what each character says or does.

Internet

## E-mail a Friend

Would you recommend *Yang the Second and Her Secret Admirers* to a friend? Send an e-mail to a friend telling what you liked or didn't like about it.

# Art

## Link

**Magazine Article**

**Skill: How to Read a Magazine Article**

*Before you read . . .*

- Read the title and, if available, the introduction, **headings**, and **captions**.

- Think about the **topic** of the article, and predict what you will learn about it.

*As you read . . .*

- Look for the main ideas in each section.

- The **headings** can help you figure out the main ideas.

- Think about how the main ideas fit together.

# Hands&

The orange crane Lauren is holding takes her about 15 minutes to fold. It's worth the effort, though, says Lauren. According to her grandmother, cranes bring good luck!

410

# Hearts

*By Candace Purdom*

**Read about three girls and their grandmothers who, like Yinglan, keep alive skills that are part of their heritage.**

## Folds & Creases

Lauren Okada can turn a piece of paper into a duck! She does it through *origami* (or-uh-GAH-mee), the Japanese art of paper folding. Two years ago, Lauren's grandmother Mary began teaching Lauren how to fold, tuck, and crease colorful paper to make an origami box. "At first it was pretty hard," says the ten-year-old from Ohio. "If you don't fold it evenly, it comes out pretty bad!" But Lauren loved making the shapes appear as if by magic. So she spent many more hours with her grandmother, learning to fold stars, birds, balloons, and other intricate shapes.

Lauren's grandmother learned origami from *her* mother, who brought the art with her from Japan. As a girl, Mary often gave her friends the paper objects she made. Now Lauren does the same thing! For one birthday party, Lauren folded each guest a box that she filled with candy. She and her grandmother also made origami ornaments to hang on their Christmas tree. They have a colorful collection that they add to each year. It's a tradition Lauren and her grandmother love to share.

411

Grandy Jean, Morgan, and a fellow quilter, Louise Carter, add stitches to a Double Wedding Ring quilt, a design often made for new brides.

# Bits & Pieces

More than a century ago, Morgan Friday's great-great-grandmother stitched together pieces of fabric to make colorful patchwork quilts. Today, Morgan and her grandmother, Grandy Jean, carry on the tradition at old-fashioned quilting bees in their Texas town.

When Morgan, 12, first joined the quilters, she helped out by threading needles and organizing the quilting supply cabinet. But soon the women invited her to sew. In the beginning, Morgan was nervous. She remembers asking, "What if I mess up?" The women answered, "Just take out the stitches and start again!"

During bees, Morgan helps connect the top, middle, and bottom layers of the quilt with tiny stitches. Sewing around every piece on the top layer can take the group 20 to 24 hours! But Morgan loves sitting and listening to the stories the women share as they stitch.

Morgan's grandmother has a saying: "When you give somebody a quilt, tell them to count the stitches and they'll know how much you love them." Morgan agrees; "It means a lot because you put a lot of work into it!"

# Twists & Coils

Cynthia Burns, 10, loves going to the Charleston Market with her grandmother. That's where they make and sell sweetgrass baskets, a craft that's been in her family for centuries. Cynthia's ancestors came to South Carolina from Africa as slaves. They brought with them the special basket-making technique that her family still uses today.

Sweetgrass grows in nearby marshes and is known for its sweet smell. Cynthia began twisting the grass into baskets when she was seven. Her Grandma Helen starts each one by tying a bundle of long pine needles in a knot — needles that she and Cynthia rake up together in the forest. Cynthia then twists bunches of sweetgrass and bulrushes. She connects the coils of twisted grass, one row on top of the other, using skinny palm leaves.

Most baskets take Cynthia a few weeks to complete. She signs the bottom of each one she makes. Cynthia is proud of her talent and her family tradition. "My grandma always tells me to pass it down," she says, "and to someday tell my daughter to pass it down, too!"

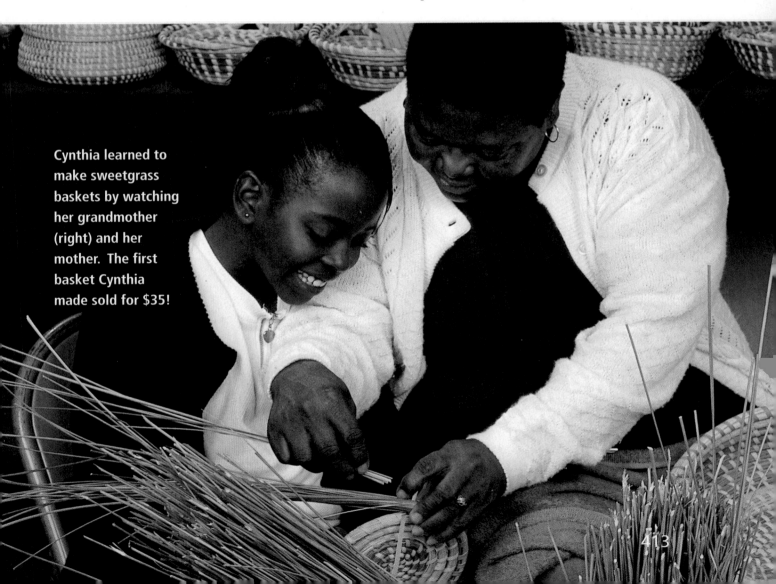

Cynthia learned to make sweetgrass baskets by watching her grandmother (right) and her mother. The first basket Cynthia made sold for $35!

413

# Background and Vocabulary

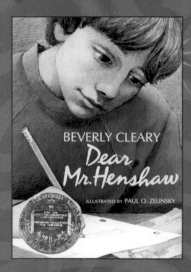

*Dear Mr. Henshaw*

**Genre** **Realistic Fiction**

## Key Vocabulary

diary
description
difference
experience
prose

**Vocabulary Reader**

**Making a Magazine**
by Gary Miller
illustrated by Chiho Perkins

*e* • **Glossary**

414

# A World of Writing

Writing plays a big part in the life of Leigh Botts, the main character in *Dear Mr. Henshaw*. Consider the kinds of writing you do, at home or at school. Then ask yourself how writing makes a **difference** in your life.

Do you keep a **diary** or journal? If so, how is it valuable to you? Maybe you use it to record your deepest thoughts and feelings. Maybe you use a journal to keep a record of your travels or other **experiences**. Writers also jot down ideas in journals and notebooks, and develop those ideas later. Does that sound like you?

Letter writing can be a good way to appreciate the events of your life. Writing a **description** of something you did or saw can make old memories and feelings fresh again. The person who receives your letter will enjoy reading it, too.

Have you written a story, or some other kind of creative **prose** or poetry? Leigh Botts tries writing different stories — first a fantasy, then a mystery — before he finds a kind of writing that he feels comfortable with. Think about the stories *you* have to tell.

415

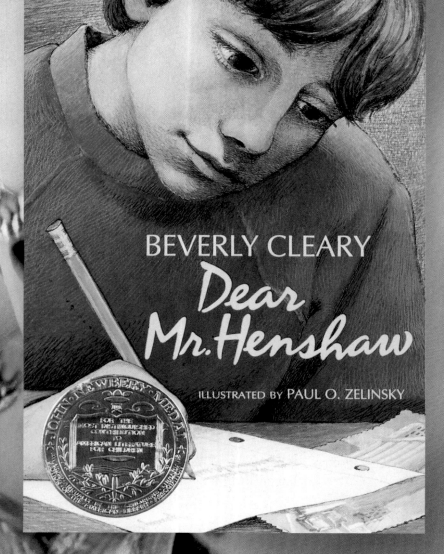

BEVERLY CLEARY

Dear Mr. Henshaw

ILLUSTRATED BY PAUL O. ZELINSKY

## Strategy Focus

The author has chosen to show the main character only through his diary entries and a letter. As you read, **evaluate** how well this format works in telling Leigh's story.

*S*ince the second grade, Leigh Botts has been writing to Boyd Henshaw, a children's book author. First in those letters, and now in his diary, Leigh has been describing his life in a house beside a gas station in Pacific Grove, California, a town known mainly for the monarch butterflies who spend the winter there. Leigh's parents are divorced and he seldom sees his dad, a long-distance truck driver. When they spoke on the phone recently, his dad was about to go out for pizza with a lady and her son, and Leigh is worried that his dad might get married again. At school, Leigh has had to cope with an unknown thief who was stealing from his lunchbox. But he has made his first friend, Barry. And there's a writing contest Leigh is thinking about entering: the winners get to have lunch with a famous children's book author.

# Saturday, March 17

Today is Saturday, so this morning I walked to the butterfly trees again. The grove was quiet and peaceful, and because the sun was shining, I stood there a long time, looking at the orange butterflies floating through the gray and green leaves and listening to the sound of the ocean on the rocks. There aren't as many butterflies now. Maybe they are starting to go north for the summer. I thought I might write about them in prose instead of poetry, but on the way home I got to thinking about Dad and one time when he took me along when he was hauling grapes and what a great day it had been.

# Tuesday, March 20

Yesterday Miss Neely, the librarian, asked if I had written anything for the Young Writers' Yearbook, because all writing had to be turned in by tomorrow. When I told her I hadn't, she said I still had twenty-four hours and why didn't I get busy? So I did, because I really would like to meet a Famous Author. My story about the ten-foot wax man went into the wastebasket. Next I tried to start a story called *The Great Lunchbox Mystery*, but I couldn't seem to turn my lunchbox experience into a story because I don't know who the thief (thieves) was (were), and I don't want to know.

Finally I dashed off a description of the time I rode with my father when he was trucking the load of grapes down Highway 152 through Pacheco Pass. I put in things like the signs that said STEEP GRADE, TRUCKS USE LOW GEAR and how Dad down-shifted and how skillful he was handling a long, heavy load on the curves. I put in about the hawks on the telephone wires and about that high peak where Black Bart's lookout used to watch for travelers coming through the pass so he could signal to Black Bart to rob them, and how the leaves on the trees along the stream at the bottom of the pass were turning yellow and how good tons of grapes smelled in the sun. Then I copied the whole thing over in case neatness counts and gave it to Miss Neely.

## Saturday, March 24

Mom said I had to invite Barry over to our house for supper because I have been going to his house after school so often. We had been working on a burglar alarm for his room which we finally got to work with some help from a library book.

I wasn't sure Barry would like to come to our house which is so small compared to his, but he accepted when I invited him.

Mom cooked a casserole full of good things like ground beef, chilies, tortillas, tomatoes and cheese. Barry said he really liked eating at our house because he got tired of eating with a bunch of little sisters waving spoons and drumsticks. That made me happy. It helps to have a friend.

Barry says his burglar alarm still works. The trouble is, his little sisters think it's fun to open his door to set it off. Then they giggle and hide. This was driving his mother crazy, so he finally had to disconnect it. We all laughed about this. Barry and I felt good about making something that worked even if he can't use it.

Barry saw the sign on my door that said KEEP OUT MOM THAT MEANS YOU. He asked if my Mom really stays out of my room. I said, "Sure, if I keep things picked up." Mom is not a snoop.

Barry said he wished he could have a room nobody ever went into. I was glad Barry didn't ask to use the bathroom. Maybe I'll start scrubbing off the mildew after all.

# Sunday, March 25

I keep thinking about Dad and how lonely he sounded and wondering what happened to the pizza boy. I don't like to think about Dad being lonesome, but I don't like to think about the pizza boy cheering him up either.

Tonight at supper (beans and franks) I got up my courage to ask Mom if she thought Dad would get married again. She thought awhile and then said, "I don't see how he could afford to. He has big payments to make on the truck, and the price of diesel oil goes up all the time, and when people can't afford to build houses or buy cars, he won't be hauling lumber or cars."

I thought this over. I know that a license for a truck like his costs over a thousand dollars a year. "But he always sends my support payments," I said, "even if he is late sometimes."

"Yes, he does that," agreed my mother. "Your father isn't a bad man by any means."

Suddenly I was mad and disgusted with the whole thing. "Then why don't you two get married again?" I guess I wasn't very nice about the way I said it.

Mom looked me straight in the eye. "Because your father will never grow up," she said. I knew that was all she would ever say about it.

Tomorrow they give out the Young Writers' Yearbook! Maybe I will be lucky and get to go have lunch with the Famous Author.

# Monday, March 26

Today wasn't the greatest day of my life. When our class went to the library, I saw a stack of Yearbooks and could hardly wait for Miss Neely to hand them out. When I finally got mine and opened it to the first page, there was a monster story, and I saw I hadn't won first prize.

I kept turning. I didn't win second prize which went to a poem, and I didn't win third or fourth prize, either. Then I turned another page and saw Honorable Mention and under it:

## A Day on Dad's Rig
*by*
*Leigh M. Botts*

There was my title with my name under it in print, even if it was mimeographed print. I can't say I wasn't disappointed because I hadn't won a prize, I was. I was really disappointed about not getting to meet the mysterious Famous Author, but I liked seeing my name in print. Some kids were mad because they didn't win or even get something printed. They said they wouldn't ever try to write again which I think is pretty dumb. I have heard that real authors sometimes have their books turned down. I figure you win some, you lose some.

Then Miss Neely announced that the Famous Author the winners would get to have lunch with was Angela Badger. The girls were more excited than the boys because Angela Badger writes mostly about girls with problems like big feet or pimples or something. I would still like to meet her because she is, as they say, a real live author, and I've never met a real live author. I am glad Mr. Henshaw isn't the author because then I would *really* be disappointed that I didn't get to meet him.

## Friday, March 30

Today turned out to be exciting. In the middle of second period Miss Neely called me out of class and asked if I would like to go have lunch with Angela Badger. I said, "Sure, how come?"

Miss Neely explained that the teachers discovered that the winning poem had been copied out of a book and wasn't original so the girl who submitted it would not be allowed to go and would I like to go in her place? Would I!

Miss Neely telephoned Mom at work for permission and I gave my lunch to Barry because my lunches are better than his. The other winners were all dressed up, but I didn't care. I have noticed that authors like Mr. Henshaw usually wear old plaid shirts in the pictures on the back of their books. My shirt is just as old as his, so I knew it was OK.

Miss Neely drove us in her own car to the hotel, where some other librarians and their winners were waiting in the lobby. Then Angela Badger arrived with Mr. Badger, and we were all led into the dining room which was pretty crowded. One of the librarians who was a sort of Super Librarian told the winners to sit at a long table with a sign that said Reserved. Angela Badger sat in the middle and some of the girls pushed to sit beside her. I sat across from her. Super

Librarian explained that we could choose our lunch from the salad bar. Then all the librarians went off and sat at a table with Mr. Badger.

There I was face to face with a real live author who seemed like a nice lady, plump with wild hair, and I couldn't think of a thing to say because I hadn't read her books. Some girls told her how much they loved her books, but some of the boys and girls were too shy to say anything. Nothing seemed to happen until Mrs. Badger said, "Why don't we all go help ourselves to lunch at the salad bar?"

What a mess!  Some people didn't understand about salad bars, but Mrs. Badger led the way and we helped ourselves to lettuce and bean salad and potato salad and all the usual stuff they lay out on salad bars.  A few of the younger kids were too short to reach anything but the bowls on the first rows.  They weren't doing too well until Mrs. Badger helped them out.

Getting lunch took a long time, longer than in a school cafeteria, and when we carried our plates back to our table, people at other tables ducked and dodged as if they expected us to dump our lunches on their heads. All one boy had on his plate was a piece of lettuce and a slice of tomato because he thought he was going to get to go back for roast beef and fried chicken. We had to straighten him out and explain that all we got was salad. He turned red and went back for more salad.

I was still trying to think of something interesting to say to Mrs. Badger while I chased garbanzo beans around my plate with a fork. A couple of girls did all the talking, telling Mrs. Badger how they wanted to write books exactly like hers. The other librarians were busy talking and laughing with Mr. Badger who seemed to be a lot of fun.

Mrs. Badger tried to get some of the shy people to say something without much luck, and I still couldn't think of anything to say to a lady who wrote books about girls with big feet or pimples. Finally Mrs. Badger looked straight at me and asked, "What did you write for the Yearbook?"

I felt myself turn red and answered, "Just something about a ride on a truck."

"Oh!" said Mrs. Badger. "So you're the author of 'A Day on Dad's Rig!'"

Everyone was quiet. None of us had known the real live author would have read what we had written, but she had and she remembered my title.

"I just got honorable mention," I said, but I was thinking, She called me an author. *A real live author called me an author.*

"What difference does that make?" asked Mrs. Badger. "Judges never agree. I happened to like 'A Day on Dad's Rig' because it was written by a boy who wrote honestly about something he knew and had strong feelings about. You made me feel what it was like to ride down a steep grade with tons of grapes behind me."

"But I couldn't make it into a story," I said, feeling a whole lot braver.

"Who cares?" said Mrs. Badger with a wave of her hand. She's the kind of person who wears rings on her forefingers. "What do you expect? The ability to write stories comes later, when you have lived longer and have more understanding. 'A Day on Dad's Rig' was splendid work for a boy your age. You wrote like *you*, and you did not try to imitate someone else. This is one mark of a good writer. Keep it up."

I noticed a couple of girls who had been saying they wanted to write books exactly like Angela Badger exchange embarrassed looks.

"Gee, thanks," was all I could say. The waitress began to plunk down dishes of ice cream. Everyone got over being shy and began to ask Mrs. Badger if she wrote in pencil or on the typewriter and did she ever have books rejected and were her characters real people and did she ever have pimples when she was a girl like the girl in her book and what did it feel like to be a famous author?

I didn't think answers to those questions were very important, but I did have one question I wanted to ask which I finally managed to get in at the last minute when Mrs. Badger was autographing some books people had brought.

"Mrs. Badger," I said, "did you ever meet Boyd Henshaw?"

"Why, yes," she said, scribbling away in someone's book. "I once met him at a meeting of librarians where we were on the same program."

"What's he like?" I asked over the head of a girl crowding up with her book.

"He's a very nice young man with a wicked twinkle in his eye," she answered. I think I have known that since the time he answered my questions when Miss Martinez made us write to an author.

On the ride home everybody was chattering about Mrs. Badger this, and Mrs. Badger that. I didn't want to talk. I just wanted to think. A real live author had called *me* an author. A real live author had told me to keep it up. Mom was proud of me when I told her.

The gas station stopped pinging a long time ago, but I wanted to write all this down while I remembered. I'm glad tomorrow is Saturday. If I had to go to school I would yawn. I wish Dad was here so I could tell him all about today.

March 31

Dear Mr. Henshaw,

I'll keep this short to save you time reading it. I had to tell you something. You were right. I wasn't ready to write an imaginary story. But guess what! I wrote a true story which won Honorable Mention in the Yearbook. Maybe next year I'll write something that will win first or second place. Maybe by then I will be able to write an imaginary story.

I just thought you would like to know. Thank you for your help. If it hadn't been for you, I might have handed in that dumb story about the melting wax trucker.

Your friend, the author,
Leigh Botts

P.S. I still write in the diary you started me on.

## MEET THE AUTHOR *Beverly Cleary*

Beverly Cleary took up writing because, like Mildred Pitts Walter, she couldn't find enough books about the kids she knew — "plain, ordinary boys and girls," as she called them. Since 1950 Cleary has introduced dozens of extraordinary characters to readers, including Henry Huggins, Ramona Quimby, and Leigh Botts. Cleary's mother once started a lending library in Oregon, and Cleary went on to become a librarian herself, in Yakima, Washington. Telling stories and thinking about characters led directly to her first book, *Henry Huggins*.

*Dear Mr. Henshaw* was a change for Cleary to a more serious character, and critics approved. The book won the Newbery Medal in 1984. You can read more about Leigh Botts in Cleary's book *Strider*.

## MEET THE ILLUSTRATOR *Nancy Carpenter*

Nancy Carpenter grew up in Philadelphia, Pennsylvania. She says that she learned how to draw princesses and ballerinas before she learned how to talk.

In elementary school, Carpenter's mother was her art teacher, and she often felt that her mom was hard to impress. It turns out that her mom had always liked Carpenter's artwork, but hadn't wanted to appear to be playing favorites in class!

To find out more about Beverly Cleary and Nancy Carpenter, visit Education Place. **www.eduplace.com/kids**

# Think About the Selection

**1.** Why do you think Leigh decides to write "A Day on Dad's Rig" instead of using his other story ideas?

**2.** Writing is important to Leigh. In what ways do you think writing helps him?

**3.** On page 420, Leigh says: "It helps to have a friend." Helps how? Describe a time when having a friend has helped you.

**4.** What kind of person is Angela Badger? Name some story details that help reveal her personality.

**5.** How would you sum up the advice Angela Badger gives Leigh about writing stories?

**6.** What does Leigh's behavior at the luncheon tell you about him?

**7.** **Connecting/Comparing** Leigh Botts uses his writing to connect with people. How do Mariah, Mom, and Yingtao make connections with people?

**Expressing**

## Write a Letter

Like Leigh, write a letter to the author of your favorite book. Tell why you liked the book and describe what you like to write about.

**Tips**

- Use details from the book to tell what you liked.
- Begin a new paragraph for each new subject.
- Be sure to use correct letter form when you write your letter.

# Design a Book Jacket

What if Leigh's story, "A Day on Dad's Rig," were made into a book? Design a book jacket for it. Include the title, the author's name, and illustrations. View some real book jackets before you begin to find out what information to include on the front, back, and spine.

**Bonus** Write a description of the book and a brief author biography for the two side flaps.

# Perform a Radio Show

Picture Angela Badger hosting a radio show in which young writers call her for advice. In a group, prepare a script for the show. Create questions and answers for Mrs. Badger. Write an introduction that an announcer might say at the beginning. Then perform the radio show.

**Internet**

# Send an E-Postcard

What books have you been reading during this theme? Which ones would you recommend? Send an electronic postcard to a friend. You'll find one at Education Place. **www.eduplace.com/kids**

**Genre**

### Poetry

### Skill: How to Read a Poem

*As you read . . .*

- Pause at the end of each line, but pay attention to punctuation. Ask yourself how the lines fit together.

- Enjoy the rhythm and sound of the poem. What do you "hear" in your mind?

- Ask yourself: What is the poem about? How does the poem make me feel? What pictures does the poem create in my mind? With these ideas, read the poem again.

# More Young Writers

Write honestly about what you know and feel strongly about, says Mrs. Badger in *Dear Mr. Henshaw*. Here are five students who have done just that.

## Los ojos de mi gente

Los ojos de mi gente son brillantes
Cuando están tristes o felices
Los ojos de mi gente son las estrellas
De la media noche en el firmamento

## The Eyes of My People

The eyes of my people are bright
They are sad, they are glad
The eyes of my people are stars
In the arch of the midnight sky
— *DaMonique Domínguez, 11, California*

## To Mother

I remember those days at the old house
the house where my life began
You would weed the small garden
of blue-starry forget-me-nots and violets
tending those delicate dahlias
you so loved
I frolicked on the grass, in the sprinkler
running in and out of the junipers
both of us building —
me building forts and imaginary worlds
you building reality, building the garden
building me

— *Aaron Wells, 11, Oregon*

## Problems

As my life comes to a mountain
I climb it
As my life comes to a river
I swim across it
As my life comes to an obstacle
I overcome it
And as my life comes to a stop sign
I rest a while

— *Kevin A. Zuniga, 12, Texas*

## Swish

My basketball springs
like a tumbleweed jumping up and down
in the dusty afternoon
the ball goes up and up
till it encircles
the rim like a
hurricane or a tornado
beginning
the net tickles its side
as it swishes through
another three-pointer makes the day

— *Chance Yellowhair, Arizona*

# Maputo Saturday Craft Market

It's Friday afternoon,
nearly evening.
The whir of my bike is comforting in the silence.
One or two late workers hurrying home.
I stop my bike,
breathing in the cool evening air.
The plaza.
Today it is a barren stone circle
Patches of grass and a tree or two
is all it has to offer.
But for me, the plaza is special
My heart leaps in anticipation
of Saturday morning
when the plaza comes alive.

At first, just a vendor.
Then two,
then three.
Mostly young boys and men
Cloths are spread out on the sidewalk
Gentle hands unwrap intricate wooden carvings,
handsome wooden chests,
and hand-painted toys.
Red wooden cars, green airplanes, and multi-colored motorcycles
Most are small enough to fit in the palm of your hand.
Batiks are unfurled and carefully examined
Young boys push their way through the crowd
displaying the vividly dyed cloths.
Sellers hawk their merchandise in loud persistent voices
to buyers who argue in equally loud persistent tones
each trying to get the best price.

The market bustles with activity
enveloping me.
I become a part of it,
bargaining with vendors,
admiring the finely carved masks and jewelry,
Beaded necklaces, bracelets and earrings.
Comparing and choosing until midday.

I can't wait until tomorrow!
The plaza will come alive again,
with me swept up along into it.
I pedal off into the glowing darkness
thinking of and anticipating
the Saturday morning craft market.
— *Rebecca Beatriz Chavez, 11, Virginia*
*Rebecca was living in Maputo, Mozambique,*
*in Africa, when she wrote this poem.*

437

# Check Your Progress

In this theme you have read about different ways people connect with each other, both in person and through their writing. Now read and compare two new selections about people, and add to your test-taking knowledge.

Start by looking back at the letter from Lensey Namioka on pages 338–340. Think about how her "ski pants" story is a good opening for a theme about people getting involved in each other's lives.

In the selections that follow, you'll meet sets of characters who achieve a goal together. Compare their experiences. How are those experiences like or unlike that of other characters in the theme?

# Read and Compare

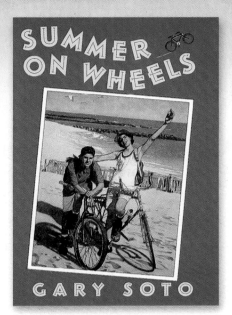

**Realistic Fiction**

Hector and Mando are two best friends who finish a journey with a splash.

**Try these strategies:**
Predict and Infer
Evaluate

**Nonfiction**

On a windy day in 1903, Wilbur and Orville Wright work together to change American history.

**Try these strategies:**
Question
Monitor and Clarify

**Strategies in Action**  *Remember to use all your reading strategies while you read.*

# SUMMER ON WHEELS

by Gary Soto    illustrated by Melanie Mitchell

For eight days, Hector and Mando have been bicycling across the city of Los Angeles, from East L.A. to the beach at Santa Monica. Along the way, they've been staying with Hector's relatives, including Uncle Isaac, whose job is to chauffeur his employer's super-competitive daughter, Sarah. Now their latest host, Hector's Aunt Teresa, is giving them a lift to their journey's end: the Pacific Ocean!

•••••••••••••••••••••••••••••••••••••••••••••••••••••

Aunt Teresa pulled the van to the side of the road and warned the boys that if they drowned she would be really mad at them.

"Don't forget," she warned. "Watch out for the *tiburones*, those sharks."

Hector blew his aunt a kiss and said, "Don't worry. We'll be cool." When he jumped out of the van, he hit his head again on the door frame, another lump to remember his vacation by.

"I'll be back in three hours," she told the boys and pulled away, her battered van rumbling and popping as it cut in front of a Mercedes-Benz.

The boys waved, turned, and raced to the beach, which was crowded but not so crowded that they had to step over people. They were happy. They had journeyed for over a week and now they were churning over the heavy sand. Out of breath, they slowed to a walk and then slowed to a complete stop when they heard in the sea breeze, "Hey, you *vatos*."

Hector looked around. He asked Mando, "Did you hear something?"

"Yeah," he said. They looked around but didn't see anyone. There was just a seagull squawking at them.

"Hey, you dumb boys."

Now they knew the words were directed at them. They looked at the seagull, which was rubbing its beak under the fold of its wing.

"Man," Hector whined, "someone is playing with us, Mando."

"I'm going to push their faces in the sand." Mando looked around, stern-faced and his hands rolled into hammers of anger. He hiked up his hands and stuck out his chest.

"Especially, you, Mando," the voice came again. "You skinny-legged dude."

"Who said that?" Mando screamed over the crashing waves.

Hector jerked his chin at Mando, indicating that the voice was coming from behind a striped umbrella. They tiptoed toward the umbrella and when they peeked around it, it was a shock that brought them to their knees.

"Hey, *vatos,*" Sarah taunted. "I've been waiting for you since ten this morning."

"Sarah, what are you doing here?" Hector asked, his face sliced up into a pumpkin smile.

"Waiting," she said. She capped her bottle of nail polish and held up her feet, wiggling her toes in the breeze. "You told me you were going to be here."

Hector remembered crowing that he and Mando were planning to go to Santa Monica. He didn't dream that she would follow them.

"You dudes hungry?" she asked. She pointed to a large wicker picnic basket with cheeses, crackers, fruit, gourmet peanuts, and club sandwiches lanced with toothpicks.

The boys looked at the food, big-eyed and with the buds of their tongues showing from their mouths. If they hadn't eaten the burritos earlier, they would have thrown their faces into this rich-person's grub.

"Nah," Hector growled. "We ate earlier."

"Good," Sarah said, closing the lid of the basket. "Because we're going surfing. You're not going to leave until I beat you and you're belly up on the beach!" She stood up with a leap, kicking a spray of sand into Hector's face.

This is Sarah all right, Hector thought as he rose to his feet, turned, and bumped into his Uncle Isaac, who was wearing orange swimming trunks identical to his own. A small nest of hair lay matted on Uncle's chest and goosebumps marched around his pale belly. He was cold and shivering without getting wet.

"Hello, Hector. Mando," he said with a nod, slightly embarrassed. "Chauffeuring has taken me to the beach, it appears."

"You look cool, Unc," Hector said. "We look like twins."

Mando hovered over the surfboards laid out on the sand. He turned to Hector and remarked, "Homes, this is gonna be hard."

"*Chale*," Sarah said. "You guys are top dogs. You can do anything."

Hector and Mando picked up their surfboards, not wanting to argue with Sarah, and dragged them toward the water. Uncle Isaac, tugging up his swim trunks, followed the boys and Sarah. They walked across the hot sand toward the roped-off surfing area. They stood at the edge of the crashing waves that came to meet them.

"It's too cold!" Hector screamed.

"Come on, dude," Sarah shouted and flopped her board into the foamy water.

Hector shrugged his shoulders, walked into the ocean, and flopped his board on the surface of the water. He looked back to the shore, where the lifeguard was eating a candy bar and looking at a magazine. The lifeguard didn't seem to care, and the wave that slapped Hector when his back was turned didn't seem to care either.

"Here goes," Hector said. He jumped onto his board and began to paddle out to where the waves mounted, tipped, and curled into white water. A line of surfers all in wet suits, hair matted to their scalps, waited there. Hector thought they seemed to know what they were doing. One was standing up on his board, gliding along the push of a wave.

"Come on," Hector yelled to Mando and his uncle, who were still hovering around the shore, splashing each other.

"Come on," Sarah yelled in return to Hector.

Hector paddled out to the deeper water, his body chilled and his feet kicking through the sea kelp. Hector and Sarah hugged their boards, waiting for a big wave. The sun looked like a gold coin behind a haze of fog and cloud.

"So how you guys been?" Sarah asked, her eyes facing the sea.

"Pretty good. We've been painting a mural in West Hollywood," he began to explain. "It's a mural of —"

"Here's one," Sarah interrupted. She started paddling, and Hector followed suit, his arms crawling as his hands scooped water. Soon the force of the wave was upon them.

When Hector saw Sarah stand up, he did the same. His body wobbled left, then right, but his arms balanced him as he rode to the shore, yelling that he was free and that he could fly. And that's what he did: he flew right off his board into the white water where he turned over and over. He came up spitting a mouthful of salt water, a disgusting taste that stayed on his tongue.

"That's pretty good," Sarah congratulated.

"Yeah, I guess so," he agreed. "Let's try it again."

Hector and Sarah were joined by Mando and Uncle Isaac, both shivering like dogs. They waded far out where seagulls circled above and a chilly wind raked the water. They waited for another wave. When it came rising like a hand, they paddled, jumped into standing positions, and rode awkwardly. Uncle Isaac was knocked off the board first, then Mando, and then Hector. Sarah glided effortlessly toward the beach, queen of the surfers.

Mando came up spitting water and Uncle Isaac surfaced with a crown of seaweed on his head. They both smiled and said, "*Órale*, let's do it again."

Lying on their boards, chin up and maneuvering over the rise and fall of waves, they paddled out again into the deep water. They waited in silence as they straddled the boards. When a monster wave arose, Sarah shouted, "Last one to the beach is a *sapo*."

"*Simón*," Hector yelled over the roar of the wave. He paddled fiercely and got to his feet, but in the confusion of trying to keep upright, he saw that he was riding backwards.

"The other way, dude," Mando yelled.

"*¡Chihuahua!*" Hector screamed. But he stayed calm. He dug his toes over the edge of the board and rode out the wave, the backwards champion of all time.

All afternoon they surfed and by the end of the day they were red-eyed from the salt water and ready to challenge the bigger boys and men. For Hector, this was the end of their vacation, one last spill in the source of all life — the ocean. He wanted to make the most of it, to live through every muscle in his thirteen-year-old body. He rode the waves over and over until Aunt Teresa arrived, kicking through the heavy beach sand and yelling that it was time to go home.

# The Wright Brothers
## How They Invented the Airplane

### by Russell Freedman

In 1899, Wilbur and Orville Wright, a pair of bicycle mechanics from Dayton, Ohio, wrote to the Smithsonian Institution to learn about experiments in flight. Now it is December of 1903. On a windy beach in Kitty Hawk, North Carolina, with a lifesaving crew, two boys, and a dog as witnesses, the brothers are trying to be the first to fly a motor-powered airplane, their hand-built "Flyer."

They started the motor. The propellers turned over, paddling loudly. The transmission chains clattered. The motor popped and coughed, and the whole machine seemed to shudder and shake. The two small boys took one look, backed away, and went racing across the sand dunes with the dog at their heels.

Wilbur and Orville tossed a coin to decide who should try first. Wilbur won. He lay down on the lower wing, sliding his hips into the padded wing-warping cradle. Orville took a position at one of the wings to help balance the machine as it roared down the starting track. Then Wilbur loosened the restraining rope that held the Flyer in place. The machine shot down the track with such speed that Orville was left behind, gasping for breath.

**Wilbur Wright in the Flyer after the first flight attempt**

**The crew of the U.S. Life Saving Station near the Wrights' camp**

After a 35- to 40-foot run, the Flyer lifted up from the rail. Once in the air, Wilbur tried to point the machine up at too steep an angle. It climbed a few feet, stalled, settled backward, and smashed into the sand on its left wing. Orville's stopwatch showed that the Flyer had flown for just 3½ seconds.

Wilbur wasn't hurt, but it took two days to repair the damage to the Flyer. They were ready to try again on Thursday, December 17, 1903.

They woke up that morning to freezing temperatures and a blustery 27-mile-an-hour wind. Puddles of rainwater in the sand hollows around their camp were crusted with ice. They spent the early part of the morning indoors, hoping the wind would die down a little. At 10 o'clock, with the wind as brisk as ever, they decided to attempt a flight. "The conditions were very unfavorable," wrote Wilbur. "Nevertheless, as we had set our minds on being home by Christmas, we determined to go ahead."

They hoisted the signal flag to summon the lifesavers. Then, in the biting wind, they laid down all four sections of the starting track on a level stretch of sand just below their camp. They had to go inside frequently to warm their hands by the carbide-can stove.

By the time the starting track was in place, five witnesses had shown up — four men from the lifesaving station and a teenage boy from the nearby village of Nags Head. They helped haul the Flyer over to the launching site.

Now it was Orville's turn at the controls. First he set up his big box camera, focused on a point near the end of the track, and inserted a glass-plate negative. Then he placed the rubber bulb that tripped the shutter in the big hand of John Daniels, one of the lifesaving men, and asked him to squeeze the bulb just as the Flyer took off.

The brothers shook hands. "We couldn't help but notice how they held onto each other's hand," one of the lifesavers recalled, "sort of like two folks parting who weren't sure they'd ever see one another again."

Orville took the pilot's position, his hips in the wing-warping cradle, the toes of his shoes hooked over a small supporting rack behind him. Like his brother, he was wearing a dark suit, a stiff collar, a necktie, and a cap. Wilbur turned to the lifesaving men and told them "not to look so sad, but to . . . laugh and holler and clap . . . and try to cheer Orville up when he started."

"After running the motor a few minutes to heat it up," Orville recalled, "I released the wire that held the machine to the track, and the machine started forward into the wind. Wilbur ran at the side of the machine, holding the wing to balance it on the track. Unlike the start

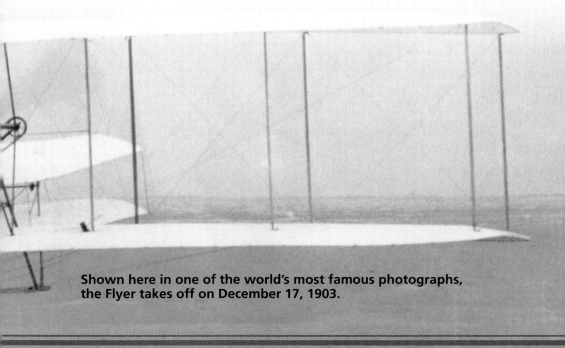

**Shown here in one of the world's most famous photographs, the Flyer takes off on December 17, 1903.**

on the 14th, made in a calm, the machine, facing a 27-mile-per-hour wind, started very slowly. Wilbur was able to stay with it till it lifted from the track after a forty-foot run. [John] snapped the camera for us, taking a picture just as the machine had reached the end of the track and had risen to a height of about two feet."

Wilbur had just let go of the wing when John Daniels tripped the shutter. The lifesavers broke into a ragged cheer. The Flyer was flying!

Orville couldn't hear them. He hung on to the control lever and stared straight ahead as the icy wind whistled past his ears and the motor clattered beside him. Buffeted by gusts, the Flyer lurched forward like a drunken bird. "The course of the flight up and down was exceedingly erratic," wrote Orville, "partly due to the irregularity of the air, and partly to lack of experience in handling this machine. . . . As a result the machine would rise suddenly to about ten feet, and then as suddenly dart for the ground. A sudden dart when a little over a hundred feet from the end of the track, or a little over 120 feet from the point at which it rose into the air, ended the flight. . . .

"This flight lasted only 12 seconds, but it was nevertheless the first in the history of the world in which a machine carrying a man had raised itself by its own power into the air in full flight, had sailed forward without reduction of speed, and had finally landed at a point as high as that from which it had started."

It had happened so quickly. A boy could have thrown a ball as far as the Flyer had flown. But the Wright brothers were elated. Seven years after Otto Lilienthal's fatal crash, four and a half years after Wilbur's letter to the Smithsonian Institution, they had launched a flying machine that could actually fly.

**Wilbur (left) and Orville Wright**

# Think and Compare

1. How is the friendship between Hector and Mando like the Wright brothers' partnership? How are the two relationships different?

2. The Wright brothers are trying to achieve a goal. Compare their goal with the goal of another character in the theme. Compare the way the characters go after their goals.

3. In each selection, the characters rely on others for help. Compare the help that Mrs. Badger gives Leigh Botts with the help that the lifesavers give the Wright brothers.

4. Sarah plays a trick on Hector and Mando, just as Yinglan's brother and sister play a trick on Yinglan. Which trick do you think is funnier or meaner? Why?

5. What do you think the Wright brothers and Mom in *Mom's Best Friend* might tell each other about problem-solving?

**Strategies in Action** When did you find reading strategies especially helpful during this theme? How did they help?

# Write an Essay

Write a few paragraphs about a time when you and a friend, like Hector and Mando, tried a new activity together.

### Tips

- Tell what you did in the order the events happened.
- Tell how you and your friend felt before, during, and after the activity.
- Include important details.

# ✔ Vocabulary Items

Some tests ask you to decide the meaning of a word in a sentence. A test about *Summer on Wheels* might have the following question.

---

**Read the question. Choose the best definition and fill in the circle in the answer row.**

1. Read this sentence from *Summer on Wheels*: "Mando came up spitting water and Uncle Isaac surfaced with a crown of seaweed on his head." What does *surfaced* mean?

   **A** swam quickly

   **B** came up from underwater

   **C** walked like a king

   **D** dived deep

   | ANSWER ROW 1 | Ⓐ ● Ⓒ Ⓓ |
   |---|---|

---

① **Understand the question.**

Find the word that the question asks about. Is it shown in context? Decide what you need to do.

> The question asks what *surfaced* means. I need to read the sentence for context and then choose the best meaning.

## 2 Think about what the word means.

Think about the word's parts. Look for the base word and a prefix or suffix. How is the word used in the context?

> The word ends with *ed*, so what Uncle Isaac did was in the past. He was probably under the water because he has seaweed on his head.

## 3 Narrow the choices. Then choose the best answer.

Try each choice in the context. Which choices are clearly wrong? Have a reason for choosing the best answer. Only guess if you have to.

> Uncle Isaac isn't walking, and the seaweed would fall if he dived, so **C** and **D** are wrong. **A** could be right, but I choose **B**. Uncle Isaac came up from underwater just as Mando did.

PLAYS

# Plays

## A play can appear on a stage or on the page.

Whether serious or funny, its job is the same. It tells a story through the words and actions of its characters.

The play's story unfolds in sections called **scenes**. The characters speak in lines of **dialogue**. **Stage directions** tell how a character feels or moves.

Here is a play you can read on the page and perform on stage.

## CURTAIN UP!

### CONTENTS

# The Case of the Runaway Appetite

## A JOE GILES MYSTERY

*by Rob Hale*

### Main Characters

**Joe Giles:** Head and sole employee of Finders Keepers Detective Agency, age eleven

**Veronica:** Princess of the Grand Duchy of Isselburg, age eleven

**Mrs. Bibby:** Veronica's chaperone, in her forties

### Secondary Characters

Voice on the phone
TV Anchor Kathy Keen
TV Reporter Mike Macintosh
Leo the Limo Driver
Mario
Celia
Sheriff McGrew

Deputy Fisk
Child
Babysitter
Girl
Moviegoer 1
Moviegoer 2
Veronica's Appetite
Newspaper Reporters

### Setting

The little town of Riverton, present day

## SCENE 1

*(Joe Giles's office, which is really the family kitchen. Joe is sitting at a kitchen table, partly in the shadows, addressing the audience in a confiding way, as if he's telling a story.)*

**Joe:** My name is Giles. Joe Giles. Maybe you've heard of me. I've got my ads up on bulletin boards all over town: Finders Keepers Detective Agency. You lose it — we find it. "We" means me. I've got this talent for finding things. Lost socks. Lost glasses. Lost car keys. . . .

*(Telephone rings.)*

**Joe:** Excuse me. . . . *(He picks up the phone.)* Finders Keepers, Joe speaking.
**Voice:** Is this the guy who finds lost things?
**Joe** *(Cautiously)*: Yes. . . .
**Voice:** Great! I just lost a game of tic-tac-toe! Do you think you can find it??
*(Voice laughs and hangs up.)*

**Joe:** *(He hangs up and resumes talking to the audience.)* I get a lot of that. The fact is, it's been a while since my last case. Mostly I've been hanging around my office — actually it's my mom and dad's kitchen — waiting for a client. Sometimes when the phone's no help, I turn on the TV and try the news.

(Joe *turns on TV. The following scene can be performed on video, live, or with puppets and backdrops.*)

**TV Anchor:** Next — Royalty in Riverton! Princess Veronica comes to town. News 4's Mike Macintosh is live at the Riverton Inn. . . .

**Joe** *(Getting interested)***:** Oh, that's right — Princess Veronica of some Grand Duchy or other is in town to dedicate a museum. Actually, this is a big deal. We almost never get celebrities in Riverton.

**Mike Macintosh:** This is Mike Macintosh at the Riverton Inn where Princess Veronica has just arrived with her entourage. I'll see if I can ask her a few questions. Princess Veronica!

**Veronica:** *(She speaks with a slight accent.)* Yes. How do you do?

**Mike Macintosh:** Princess, how are you enjoying your visit to our country so far? How do you like our customs? Our music? Our shopping malls? What do you think of American food?

**Veronica:** Well, I am enjoying my visit, but I have been kept very busy attending to my duties as my country's representative.

**Joe:** She needs to get out more.

**Veronica:** As for American food, I am sorry to say I have — what is the phrase? — "lost my appetite." But I hope I find it soon, so that I can enjoy your delicious hot dog and apple pie! Thank you. *(She leaves.)*

**Mike Macintosh:** Well, she may have lost her appetite, but she hasn't lost her charm. Back to you, Kathy.

**Joe:** I turn off the TV. *(He does so.)* I stand up. Suddenly I know what I have to do. It will be the greatest challenge of my career. I, Joe Giles, Riverton's smartest detective, will find Princess Veronica's appetite!

444

## SCENE 2

*(The lobby of the Riverton Inn. Reporters are taking pictures of Veronica.)*

**Joe:** I'm in luck. When I arrive at the Riverton Inn, there's the Princess sitting in the lobby surrounded by photographers. I make my move and present my card. Unfortunately, this lady gets in the way.

**Mrs. Bibby** *(Taking his card)*: I'll take that.

**Veronica:** Is it another reporter, Mrs. Bibby?

**Mrs. Bibby:** I can't tell. *(to* Joe*)* What's "Finders Keepers"?

**Joe:** Just what it says, ma'am. You lose, we find. Well, actually, I do. My name's Joe Giles. And I understand you've lost something very important, Princess.

**Veronica:** I have?

**Joe:**  Yes, I believe you said you've lost your appetite.  And I would consider it an honor and a privilege to find it for you.  At no cost, of course.

*(Long silence.  Then* Veronica *bursts out laughing.)*

**Mrs. Bibby:**  Young man, either you have no manners at all or a very bad sense of humor.  In any case, Princess Veronica has a dinner to get ready for in two hours.

**Veronica** *(Sobering up at the thought)*:  Dinner?  Oh, dear.  I wish I were a bit hungrier.

**Joe:**  Aha!  You see?  This is serious!  We can't waste any time!  Princess, please tell me, if you can.  Where were you when you lost your appetite?

**Mrs. Bibby:**  Of all the ridiculous . . .

**Veronica:**  No, I can tell you exactly where I was.  I was in the limousine coming in from the airport.  I happened to glance out the window and see a billboard.  It said: "Have you had your mush today?"  I have always had a great disliking for mush.  It was then that I lost my appetite.

**Joe:**  I know that billboard!  Princess, I'll need your help!  Would you be willing to go on a little expedition?

**Mrs. Bibby:**  All right, young man, this has gone far enough.  As Princess Veronica's chaperone, I must insist —

**Veronica:**  Actually, I *would* enjoy seeing a bit more of America, Mrs. Bibby.  And we do have a few hours.  And of course you'll come, too.

**Joe:**  There you go.

**Mrs. Bibby:**  Hm.  *(She thinks a while.)*  Well, I suppose the fresh air might do you good.  You *are* looking a little pale.  Very well.  But two hours, young man!  Not a second longer!

**Veronica:**  Lead the way, Mr. Giles.

**Joe:**  "Mr. Giles."  *(He looks pleased.)*  I could get used to that.  *(He leads the way offstage.)*

## SCENE 3

*(Inside Veronica's limousine, with Leo the Limo Driver behind the wheel)*

**Joe:** So here we are, me and the Princess and Mrs. B, riding along in the Princess's limo. I've never been in a limo before. It's amazing.

**Mrs. Bibby:** Who on earth are you talking to?

**Joe:** Nobody. It's just something detectives do. Say, Princess, would you happen to have a sheet of paper and a pen?

**Veronica:** Yes. In the writing desk. First drawer on the right.

*(Joe opens a drawer.)*

**Joe:** Wow, gold markers, embossed stationery. . . . Here you go, Princess. (*He hands her markers and paper.*) I want you to draw a picture of your appetite.

**Veronica:** Excuse me?

**Mrs. Bibby:** (*She shakes her head.*) Now I know he's balmy.

**Joe:** Don't think about it. Just draw what you think your appetite looks like, real quickly.

(Veronica *draws a quick sketch, using different colored markers.*)

**Mrs. Bibby** (*To both of them*)**:** It's just an expression! "To lose your appetite!" It's a figure of speech!

**Joe:** I know. (*He takes completed sketch from* Veronica.) Interesting. Green hair?

(Veronica *nods.*)

**Leo the Limo Driver:** Here we are, kids. Corner of Washington and Fourteenth.

**Joe:** Let's just hope the trail hasn't gone cold. Leo, meet us here in two hours.

**Leo:** You got it, chief.

(*They get out of limo; it drives off.*)

**Joe:** Okay, here's the billboard where you lost your appetite, Princess. Better not look up. Now the first thing to do is ask ourselves: Where would I go if I were a runaway appetite?

**Mrs. Bibby** (*Dryly*)**:** Somewhere delicious, I suppose.

**Joe:** Exactly! Like for instance that place right over there. The Napoli Pizza Palace.

**Veronica** (*Innocently*)**:** Is pizza delicious?

**Joe:** You're kidding me. You've never eaten a pizza?

**Veronica:** Not to my knowledge.

(Joe *looks disapprovingly at* Mrs. Bibby.)

**Mrs. Bibby:** Don't blame me. I don't make up the menus.

**Joe:** (*He shakes his head, sighs.*) Follow me.

SCENE 4

*(Napoli Pizza Palace. Music is playing in the background.)*

**Celia:** Hey, Mario, look who's back!

**Mario:** Who? *(He looks at* Veronica.*)* No way, that's not her.

**Celia:** Sure it's her. So, sugar, did you make up your mind? What'll it be, the pepperoni or the black olive?

*(Joe, Veronica, and* Mrs. Bibby *look at each other, baffled.)*

**Veronica:** Are you talking to me?

**Celia:** Well, of course, sugar.

**Veronica:** I believe you've confused me with someone else.

**Mario:** See, I told you. This one looks entirely different. Different hair, different clothes.

**Celia:** And I'm telling you that I never forget a face.

**Joe:** Wait a minute! (Joe *takes the sketch of* Veronica's Appetite *and hands it to* Mario.) Is this the person you saw?

**Mario:** Yeah, that's her. You've definitely captured the green hair and orange beret. (*Looks at* Veronica.) Now that you mention it, you do look alike.

**Celia:** I've got it. She was your twin sister, right?

**Veronica:** I believe I . . . need to sit down.

**Joe:** Quick! A glass of water!

(Mario *gets* Veronica *a glass of water.*)

**Mrs. Bibby:** (*She fans* Veronica *with a paper plate while turning to* Joe.) Listen to me, boy wonder. If this is a practical joke, you'll be running around trying to find your *head*!

**Joe** (*To* Mario *and* Celia): This other girl you saw — how did she act? Do you have any idea where she went?

**Mario:** Well, for the longest time she was just standing in the door, sniffing the aromas. Then she started turning all her pockets inside out, looking for change, I guess.

**Celia:** Poor kid. I was going to *give* her a slice of pizza, but she just kind of growled and took off. That way. (*She points.*) Toward the mall.

**Joe:** The mall?!

**Veronica** (*Reviving a bit*): Is that bad?

**Joe:** I don't know. So far she's kept herself under control. I'm not sure what a runaway appetite will do when she's in a food court surrounded by a dozen restaurants.

**Veronica:** We'd better hurry! Mrs. Bibby, let's go!

**Mrs. Bibby:** Will someone kindly explain to me what's going on?

(*They exit.*)

**Celia:** You know, for a day when we haven't had any customers, it's been pretty busy.

**Mario:** Yeah.

*(Outside the Riverton Mall)*

**Veronica:** But how could this happen? I've never heard of an appetite getting up and walking away before.

**Joe:** Hey, you're a princess. I'm a detective. Weird stuff always happens to people like us.

*(Sound of sirens and car doors slamming. Enter* Sheriff McGrew *and* Deputy Fisk.*)*

**Mrs. Bibby:** *Now* what?

**McGrew:** Well, look who it is! Mr. Finders Keepers himself! How's it going, kid? Find any lost kitty-cats lately?

**Joe:** No, sir. Are you out on a call?

**McGrew** *(Chuckles)*: A regular Junior Crimestopper, isn't he? Yeah, we're answering a Code 12: Disturbing the Peace.

**Joe:** Sounds dangerous.

**McGrew:** Not really. Seems as though someone's been bothering people in the food court.

**Fisk:** *(He takes out his pad and reads aloud.)* "Running around, sniffing people's plates . . . making funny yum-yum noises . . . loudest stomach grumbling I ever heard." Then someone offered her a french fry and she took off.

**Veronica:** Oh, the poor thing.

**McGrew:** Don't worry, miss. We'll — *(He looks at her and* Mrs. Bibby *closely.)* Say, it's the Princess and her chaperone, isn't it? *(He frowns.)* Giles, I don't recall anyone appointing *you* tour guide.

**Joe** *(At a sudden loss for words)*: Uh, well . . .

**Mrs. Bibby** *(Taking pity on* Joe*)*: Not to worry, Sheriff. It was my decision. I wanted to find someone who can offer the Princess a young person's point of view.

**McGrew** (*Smiling again*): I see. Well, that's okay then. Fine young man, our Joe here. He'll make a crackerjack detective some day.

**Joe:** Thank you, sir.

(*Exit* McGrew *and* Fisk.)

**Joe:** I owe you one, Mrs. B.

**Mrs. Bibby** (*Tartly*): Never mind that. We've got to find the Princess's appetite before she disturbs someone else's peace!

**Joe:** Maybe she's still in the mall. Come on! (*He starts to exit stage right.*)

**Veronica:** Wait.

(Joe *stops, turns.*)

**Veronica:** She's my appetite. *I'll* lead the way. *This* way. (*They exit stage left.*)

## SCENE 6

*(Inside the Riverton Mall, beside a fountain)*

**Joe:** What makes you so sure she went this way?

**Veronica:** I can't explain it. I just know.

*(Babysitter and Child are arguing beside fountain.)*

**Child:** I want to go swimming! I want to go swimming!

**Babysitter:** I already told you: you can't go in the fountain!

**Child:** No fair! That girl got to go in!

**Babysitter:** That was a no-no. Remember how the security man ran after her?

**Joe:** It sounds like your Appetite was here, all right. Maybe she was trying to cool off a little. Now where?

**Mrs. Bibby:** That's easy. Follow the wet sneakerprints.

*(Veronica runs off, stage left, unnoticed by Joe.)*

**Joe:** Hey, you're right, she did leave tracks. *(He looks around.)* Where did the Princess go?

**Mrs. Bibby:** She's way ahead of you. *(She points off-stage.)* Halfway up the escalator.

*(They exit stage left.)*

## SCENE 7

*(Riverton Mall, one floor up)*

**Joe** *(Looking around)*:  Oh, great.  Now we've lost the Princess *and* her Appetite.

**Mrs. Bibby:**  Maybe that young lady saw her.

**Joe** *(to Girl)*:  Excuse me, did you happen to notice a girl who looked sort of like a princess who was chasing after a girl with spiky green hair and an orange beret, only if you looked closely they each had the same face?

*(Girl calmly points to stage left.)*

**Joe:**  Thanks!  *(He stops.)*  Oh, no.  I was afraid of that.

**Mrs. Bibby:**  What's wrong?

**Joe:**  There's only one place in that direction.  The Multiplex.
The Princess and her Appetite could be in any one of six different movies!

**Mrs. Bibby:**  Well, Mr. Giles, you're the detective.  Which movie do *you* think they went to?

**Joe:**  Let's see.  *(He reads off the marquee.)*  *The Search for Delicious, Willy Wonka and the Chocolate Factory, Jaws* . . .

**Mrs. Bibby:**  *James and the Giant Peach, The Apple Dumpling Gang,* and *The Creature That Ate Philadelphia.*  They all sound like they'd appeal to an appetite.

*(Scream off-stage.  Mrs. Bibby and Joe look at each other.)*

**Joe:**  I think it came from *The Creature That Ate Philadelphia*!

*(They exit stage left.)*

## SCENE 8

*(Inside the movie theater of Cinema 8)*

**Moviegoer 1:** She tried to eat my popcorn!

**Moviegoer 2:** She tried to eat mine, too! It was awful!

**Moviegoer 1:** What, the popcorn?

**Moviegoer 2:** No, the Creature! She's the one who eats Philadelphia, right?

**Moviegoer 1:** I don't know. But these are amazing special effects!

**Moviegoer 2:** Look! There she is again! She's up on the stage by the movie screen!

*(Veronica's Appetite, wearing a green wig, an orange beret, and other colorful clothes, is standing against the movie screen, looking baffled.)*

*(Enter Sheriff McGrew and Deputy Fisk.)*

**McGrew** *(Speaking through a bullhorn)***:** All right, everybody. The situation is under control. I repeat — the situation — is —

**Fisk** *(Yelling)***:** UNDER CONTROL!

**McGrew** *(He gives Fisk a "Do you mind?" look. Then, to Appetite)***:** Come on down off the stage now. No one is going to hurt you.

**Appetite** *(Growls)***:** Hungry!

**McGrew:** I understand that. But you can't just help yourself to other people's food, can you? Now I'm going to ask you one more time, real nicely, to come on down off the stage.

**Appetite** *(Growls louder)***:** Hungry!!

**Veronica** *(Entering from stage left)***:** Can't you see you're scaring her? *(She's holding a giant tub of popcorn.)*

**Mrs. Bibby:** Veronica!

**McGrew:** Princess, I'm going to have to ask you to stay out of this —

**Joe:** Um, actually, Sheriff, the princess and that girl are sort of related to each other. Isn't that right, Mrs. Bibby?

**Mrs. Bibby:** Yes! They *are* extremely close, Sheriff. Don't worry, I'm sure the Princess can deal with this situation.

(McGrew *looks at her, hesitates, then backs off.*)

**Veronica** (*Coaxing*): See? I've got a big tub of popcorn. We can share it.

(*She gets up on the stage with the* Appetite, *who backs off a little.*)

**Veronica:** Don't be afraid. It's delicious. It's got real butter. And it's hot, too. Try some.

(*She takes a handful for herself and hands the popcorn to the* Appetite. *The* Appetite *eats some. She smiles, and says* "Mmm." *Then* Veronica *and the* Appetite *walk off-stage together, sharing the tub of popcorn and making* Mmm *sounds together.*)

(Moviegoers, Fisk, Joe, *and* Mrs. Bibby *applaud, as at the end of a movie.*)

**McGrew** (*Moved, but hiding it under a gruff show*): Okay, folks. The excitement's over. Get your refunds at the box office.

(*Exit* Moviegoers.)

(Veronica *returns alone, tossing up popcorn and catching it in her mouth.*)

**McGrew:** Nice job, Princess. You'd make a first-class negotiator. Now, where's your friend?

**Veronica:** (*She smiles.*) It's okay. She's safe and sound. I sent her home.

**McGrew** (*Pausing in disbelief*): You did *what*?? But that's interfering with police procedure, Princess! Your cousin violated a Code 12, a Code 28, and possibly a Code 81! Fisk, search the mall. Princess, I'm afraid I'm going to have to —

(Deputy Fisk *whispers in* McGrew's *ear.*)

**McGrew** (*Listening*): What? Oh, right. International incident. Highly embarrassing. The Mayor will not be pleased. (*He smiles.*) Well, we don't want to spoil the relations between our two countries, do we? (*He pauses.*) Just make sure your friend has a nice hot meal, okay, Princess?

**Veronica:** Okay, Sheriff. *(She gives the tub of popcorn to McGrew.)* Here. I'd better not spoil my appetite, now that I've got it back.

**McGrew:** Oh, sure, whatever you say. Can I give you folks a ride?

**Mrs. Bibby** *(Taking McGrew's arm)*: We'll settle for a police escort, Sheriff McGrew.

*(Exit McGrew, Mrs. Bibby, and Fisk.)*

**Veronica:** Thanks for finding my appetite, Mr. Giles.

**Joe:** That's Joe, Princess. And you're really the one who found her. I just found the trail.

**Veronica:** That's Veronica, Joe. Let's just call it a team effort. *(They exchange high fives.)* Will you be my guest at the museum dinner?

**Joe:** Glad to, Veronica. I just have to do one more thing. *(He moves upstage to address the audience.)* Well, I guess that closes the book on the Case of the Runaway Appetite. It had a little of everything. Movies, pizza, royalty. . . . And for Finders Keepers, it was a double success. Not only did I find an appetite, I found a friend.

**Veronica** *(Pulling him by the arm)*: Let's go, Joe. I'm starved!

**Joe:** Okay!

*(Exit Veronica and Joe.)*

●◖◗◖◗◖◗◖◗◖◗◖◗◖◗ CURTAIN ◖◗◖◗◖◗◖◗◖◗◖◗◖◗◖◗●

# *Think About the* PLAY

1. What does a play have in common with a story? How are the two genres different?

2. If *The Case of the Runaway Appetite* were a story instead of a play, what would you lose? What would you gain? Explain.

3. Think about each scene in *The Case of the Runaway Appetite*. How do you think each scene moves the events forward?

4. The play takes place in different settings — from Joe's house to a movie theater. How does each setting help the play?

5. How is each character important to the events in the play?

**Internet**

## Complete a Web Crossword Puzzle

What do you remember about the parts and features of a play? Test your knowledge by completing a crossword puzzle that can be printed from Education Place. **www.eduplace.com/kids**

**Narrating**

# Write the Opening Scene for a Play

Now that you've read *The Case of the Runaway Appetite*, write the opening scene for your own play. That scene might even lead you to write the whole play. If you wish, work with a partner.

Remember that a play has the same elements a story has: characters, a setting, a problem and solution, and events. But in a play, you show events only through the dialogue of the characters and stage directions.

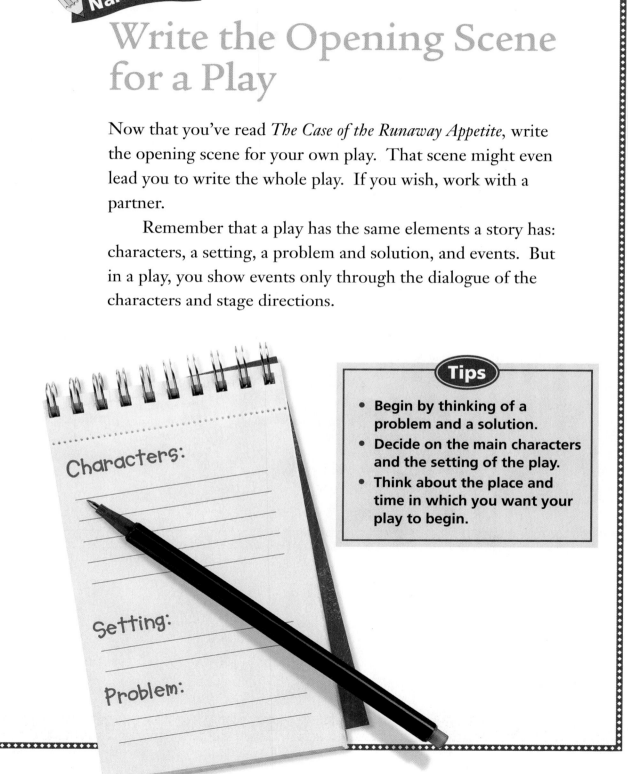

Characters:

Setting:

Problem:

**Tips**

- Begin by thinking of a problem and a solution.
- Decide on the main characters and the setting of the play.
- Think about the place and time in which you want your play to begin.

# One Land, Many Trails

I have heard of a land
Where the earth is red with promises …
Where the imagination has no fences
Where what is dreamed one night
Is accomplished the next day

— *Joyce Carol Thomas*
*from* I Have Heard of a Land

# One Land, Many Trails

## with Joseph Bruchac

Hello, My Friends,

I'm writing you from the place where the western frontier began. I live in upstate New York, where the Mohawk River meets the Hudson. Two centuries ago, the Mohawk was the way pioneers started their long journey west. President Jefferson thought this continent was so big the frontier would last a thousand years. But it took less than a century for the United States to stretch from Atlantic to Pacific.

The frontier meant different things to different people. For poor people from cities and immigrants from overseas, it meant the chance to own land. For Native American nations who didn't think of their lands as empty, it spelled trouble. Some tried sharing that land, but ended up fighting for their homes. Over a hundred Indian nations were sent to the Indian Territories that became Oklahoma. Many settlers were African Americans. To them, the frontier meant freedom and equality. Some new towns in the west were founded entirely by ex-slaves and their children.

Some thought the different races could never learn to live together, but the frontier proved them wrong. Red, white, yellow, brown, and black all became strands in the western cloth of our shared history. The story of the frontier is so full of heroism and tragedy, disappointment and optimism, that it can only be described by one word — America.

Peace,

# The New People
## by Joseph Bruchac

When the new people came
we greeted them as friends,
although they were unknown.

Their faces were white
and yellow and black,
they were looking for a home.

They came on horseback
and on foot, in wagons
white as the clouds in the sky.

They passed our villages,
crossed our plains.
We watched as they went by.

But some of them
did not want to share,
hard as that was to believe.
They said that all our land
was theirs, they said
we had to leave.

We fought to keep our sacred land
through long seasons of sorrow.
At times it seemed that all was lost,
there would be no tomorrow.

But seasons have a healing way
and spring has followed winter.
Today we watch our children
of many colors play together.

# Blaze a Trail

Compare Joseph Bruchac's thoughts of the American frontier with your own. What comes to mind when you think about the people and places of the "Wild West" of the 1800s? Where do you think those images came from?

Scout out the theme selections shown below. As you read them, think about how each one tells a different story of the West from a different point of view. You may also discover that, taken together, these selections tell one big story about America.

**Internet**

To learn about the authors in this theme, visit Education Place. **www.eduplace.com/kids**

**A Boy Called Slow**

**Genre**   **Biography**

**Key Vocabulary**

customs
determination
extended
raid
reputation
respect

**Vocabulary Reader**

Crazy Horse

*e*   **Glossary**

468

# FIRST TRAVELERS OF THE PLAINS

Long before European settlers came, the Great Plains were home to some thirty Native American tribes, including the Lakota Sioux and the Crow, the people you will read about in *A Boy Called Slow*. Each tribe had its own language and **customs**. Each traveled the plains, following the buffalo herds, trading with other tribes and sometimes raiding them for horses and weapons. In a **raid**, a warrior hoped to establish a **reputation** for bravery.

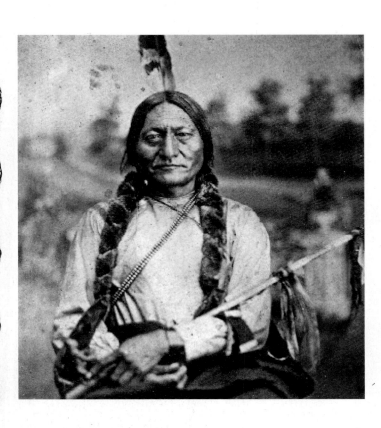

Few chiefs among the Plains Indians earned as much **respect** for courage and **determination** as did Sitting Bull (1831–1890) of the Lakota Sioux.

◄ A warrior might show his bravery by riding up to an enemy and touching him with a coup stick.

Buffalo herds numbering in the millions provided the Plains Indians with food, clothing, and shelter. When the Plains were settled in 1900, fewer than fifty wild buffalo were left.

The homeland of the Plains Indians, the Great Plains, **extended** from the Missouri River to the Rocky Mountains. Sitting Bull grew up in what is now the state of South Dakota.

# A Boy Called Slow

JOSEPH BRUCHAC

ILLUSTRATED BY
ROCCO BAVIERA

## Strategy Focus

Think about the selection title and review the
illustrations. What can you **infer** about the main
character? What do you **predict** will happen?

Many years ago, in the winter of 1831, a boy was born to the family of Returns Again of the Hunkpapa band of the Lakota Sioux.

Though Returns Again loved his daughters — knowing well that women are the heart of the nation — both he and his wife gave thanks to Wakan-Tanka for at last giving them a son. "Now," Returns Again said, "we have one who will hunt for his Hunkpapa people and help to protect them."

But his wife smiled. "Han!" she said. "We have one to follow his father's path."

It was the custom in those days to give a childhood name. Such names came from the way a child acted. So it had been with Returns Again and his father before him.

So the parents of this boy and the other relatives in his tiyospaye, his extended family, watched the first son of Returns Again closely.

If he had tried to swallow everything he could get hold of — as was the case with one of his cousins — they might have called him "Hungry Mouth." But that was not so for this boy.

"If he were to take much longer eating," his uncle Four Horns said, "the food would bite him before he bites it!"

Perhaps, his mother thought, if he were quick in his movements and always watching things they might call him "Mouse." But that was not the case for this boy. He never did anything quickly. This son of Returns Again was always slow.

"U we!" his mother said. "Come here, quickly!" But her son only looked at her.

"Nihwa hwo?" Returns Again would say. "Are you sleepy?" But it was not sleep that made their son act as he did. It was simply the way he was. Every action he took was slow.

"Slon-he," his father said. "That is the name for our son."

His mother agreed. "We will call him Slow."

So that became his name.

Slow's uncle Four Horns would tell Slow how the horses came to the plains only in the time of Slow's grandparents, and how the horses made their lives easier than they had been in the old days. Some said that the horses were brought by the wasicun, the white man. But Four Horns told him a different story.

"Our Creator, Wakan-Tanka, loves the Lakota people," his uncle would tell him. "Wakan-Tanka saw that we had only our dogs to help us pull our travois and hunt buffalo. So Wakan-Tanka sent us a new animal as faithful as our dogs but able to pull our loads and carry us as quick as the whirlwind into the hunt, the Shoog-Ton'kah, the 'Spirit Dog.'"

As Slow grew up, he was not happy with his name. Few boys were given names they wanted to keep. No one wanted to be known as "Hungry Mouth" or "Curly" or "Runny Nose" or "Slow" all of his life. But until a child earned a new name by having a powerful dream or by doing some brave or special deed, it could not be changed.

472

473

Slow wished for this vision of bravery to come to him. He wished for a vision that would allow him to prove himself to his people.

Slow longed to have a name like his uncle Four Horns, or like the strong name his father had earned — Returns Again to Strike the Enemy.

"Your father," Slow's mother said, "was given his name because of his courage in battle. When the Crows raided our village, the others were ready to retreat, but your father was the one who returned. Because of his bravery, the enemies were driven away.

"You must always help and protect your people," she continued. "A true Lakota shares everything with the people."

Slow listened to his mother's words, knowing how true they were. He had often seen his father return from hunting and share what he brought  back with the poorest people in the village. He remembered two winters ago when his father returned from a raid and brought back many horses. Returns Again had given all of those horses away except for one strong gray pony, which he saved for his son.

"The best way," Returns Again told him, "to gain the respect of your people is to be both brave and wise."

Slow understood those words. By the time Slow reached his seventh winter, he had gained a reputation as one of the strongest of the boys. And when it came to riding, none of the small children was more at ease on the back of a pony than the boy called Slow.

Returns Again was a man who could sometimes understand the speech of the animals and the birds. Slow, too, inherited some of his father's gift. He knew that his gray pony understood him, and when he was on its back, it was as if the two of them were one. Slow knew that many of his Lakota people could speak with the birds and animals, and hear their speech as clearly as human words; and the animals understood them, as well. And because he listened to the animals, Returns Again was given four more names.

One summer, Returns Again went hunting with some friends. As they camped at night beside their fire not far from the place called Smoky Butte, they heard a sound approaching them. It was a low sound, like a deep voice talking. Someone was coming along the trail which led

between the low hills. The other men reached for their weapons, but
Returns Again stopped them. There, coming slowly along the trail toward
them, was a big bull buffalo, its head close to the ground. The deep mur-
muring sound came from its throat. The other men could not make out
what the buffalo was saying, but Returns Again heard it clearly. Returns
Again listened carefully as the buffalo spoke, for the words it spoke
were names:

    Tatan'ka Iyota'ke,
    Tatan'ka Psi'ca,
    Tatan'ka Winyu'ha Najin,
    Tatan'ka Wanji'la.

Those were the four names spoken by the great bull buffalo. They were powerful names. As the buffalo slowly passed them and continued on along the trail until it was over the hill and out of sight, Returns Again knew that those names had been given to him. From that day on, he owned not only the name Returns Again to Strike the Enemy, he also owned those four names given him by the old bull buffalo.

Slow was proud to have a father with such names as Returns Again and Tatan'ka Iyota'ke. One day, he promised himself, he too would have such a strong name. But he knew that it would not be easy. So, as Slow wrestled with his friends, as he hunted with his bow and arrows, as he raced his gray pony, he always tried to do his best so that one day he would become a good warrior.

Slow was careful and deliberate in everything he did. It might take him a while to decide, but once he put his head down and went forward, he would not turn back.

At the age of ten, he killed his first buffalo — a yearling calf. His mother skinned the buffalo calf and, with his two sisters helping, tanned its skin and made it into a robe for him to wear. Though he was still called Slow, no one teased him any longer. His name now meant determination and courage to those who knew him.

As the winters passed, Slow grew. He was not as tall as some of the boys his age, but his shoulders were broad and strong.

One evening, he heard word in the camp that his father and some other men were going to ride out against the Crow, who his father called his favorite enemies. Slow knew that the Crow were great warriors and had some of the best horses on the plains. Slow had now seen fourteen winters and was old enough to go along.

He wrapped his robe made of the skin of the buffalo calf around his shoulders. He picked up his bow and his quiver full of blunt-pointed arrows that he used for hunting birds. He quickly brushed his gray pony's tail and plucked a burr from its mane. "Mitakola," he said, "my friend, we are ready to help protect the people."

Determined, he rode through the cottonwood trees until he reached the trail his father's war party had taken. Before long, Slow came to the place where they had chosen to gather and make plans. He rode into their midst and before his father or any of the other men could speak, he jumped from his pony's back and put his arm over the animal's neck.

"We are going," Slow said.

Returns Again looked around at the other men and then looked at his son with pride.

"Han," he said.

The war party began to ride to the place where the Red River meets the Missouri River.

When at last they were close to the place, the men who had been sent ahead as scouts came back.

"Upelo," the scouts said. "They are coming!"

The men began to make preparations. They put on their best clothing and brought out their paint to mark their faces and their horses. They uncovered their war shields and took out their coup sticks and their lances. From behind a small hill, they had a good view of the plain before them and could see the enemy coming from a long way off.

Closer and closer the enemy came, ready for attack.

Everyone waited for Slow's father to give the word. But as he waited, Slow's father looked over to his right. There, already mounted on his horse, was Slow. All that he wore were his moccasins and his breech cloth and he held a coup stick in his hand. He looked over at his father and then he kicked his horse's sides.

"Hiyu'wo!" the boy shouted. His horse leaped forward and over the top of the hill, down toward the enemy. His father and the rest of the war party tried to catch up, but Slow's horse was too far ahead.

481

The Crow war party at the base of the hill looked up to see many men galloping down.

One of the Crow warriors drew an arrow to his bowstring, but before he could let it go, Slow had reached him and struck his arm with the coup stick, spoiling his aim. "Oh-hey," Slow cried in triumph.

At the sight of Slow and the men, the Crow warriors fled.

"Hiyu'wo, Hiyu'wo!"

When the fight was over, not one Hunkpapa warrior had been injured. The Lakota people brought back many horses and weapons from the Crow. The raid was a success.

Slow was a hero.

When they returned to their village, all of the men spoke in loud voices of the brave deeds they had done. But the loudest voice of all was the voice of Slow's father. He painted his son with black paint — a sign of victory.

"My son is brave," he said. "His determination has won the battle for us. I give him a new name. I give him the name that was mine. He is no longer Slon-he. He is now Tatan'ka Iyota'ke."

And so it was that the boy who was once called "Slow" gained the name Tatan'ka Iyota'ke, a name which is known well, for Tatan'ka Iyota'ke means Sitting Bull — one of the greatest of all the Lakota warriors.

And this is his story.

## Meet the Author Joseph Bruchac

Joseph Bruchac's books show the influence of his Native American roots. His grandfather was Abenaki, a member of a Native American group from the Northeastern United States and Canada.

Bruchac has published stories, poetry, and novels including *Eagle Song, The Great Ball Game: A Muskogee Story, Children of the Longhouse,* and *Flying with the Eagle, Racing the Great Bear.* Some of his books draw on his Abenaki heritage. Others, such as *A Boy Called Slow,* deal with Native American cultures very different from his own.

In his writing Bruchac frequently celebrates nature and being true to yourself. He says: "Have pride in what you are and recognize that we as human beings make ourselves. Our possibilities are not limited by what our family was or by what other people say we are."

## Meet the Illustrator Rocco Baviera

In addition to *A Boy Called Slow,* Rocco Baviera has collaborated with Joseph Bruchac on *The Song of the Buffalo.* The illustrator of two other books for children, Baviera lives with his wife in Ontario, Canada.

Internet

To learn more about Joseph Bruchac and Rocco Baviera, visit Education Place.

**www.eduplace.com/kids**

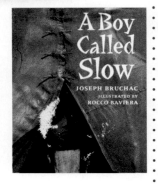

# Think About the Selection

**1.** If you could give yourself a name in the Lakota way, what name would best suit you? Why?

**2.** Think about Slow's boyhood goals. How are they similar to those of a child today? How are they different?

**3.** Do you agree with Returns Again about the best way to gain the respect of others? Why or why not?

**4.** Slow's father calls the Crow his "favorite enemies." What do you think he means?

**5.** What childhood actions and character traits were clues that Slow might grow up to be a great warrior and leader?

**6.** Why do you think Slow used a coup stick in the raid? What did it show about him?

**7.** **Connecting/Comparing** Both Slow and Leigh Botts in *Dear Mr. Henshaw* got advice from older people. Compare the kinds of advice and how they made sense for each boy's life.

Narrating

# Write a Story

Think about how Four Horns might have gotten his name. Then write a story about how it happened. Use what you learned in the selection about Lakota names to help you.

**Tips**

- Put the story's events in order.
- Use details to make the setting real for your readers.
- Include dialogue that suits your characters and the time.

## Social Studies

# Make a Card Quiz

*A Boy Called Slow* contains many facts about the Lakota Sioux and their traditions. Use the selection to create a series of Question and Answer cards giving information about the Lakota and Slow. Challenge classmates to come up with the answers.

**Bonus** Find out more about the history and traditions of the Plains Indians. Make an illustrated report showing what you learned. Present your findings to the class.

## Vocabulary

# Make a Word Banner

Find words in the selection that describe important character traits, such as *determined*. Choose one of those traits and design a word banner on paper or cardboard that defines and illustrates the word. You might choose to draw a scene from the selection or from your own life.

**Internet**

# Complete a Web Word Find

Rediscover some of the words you learned about the Lakota Sioux. You can find them in a puzzle that can be printed from the Education Place Web site.

**www.eduplace.com/kids**

**Genre**

### Fine Arts

### Skill: How to Look at Fine Art

*As you look . . .*

Ask yourself these questions:

- **What** does the artwork show? Look at the whole scene, figure, or portrait. Notice the details.

- **How** did the artist create the artwork? What materials were used? What colors, shapes, lines, and patterns do you notice?

- **Where** and **when** did the artist create the artwork? What does it tell you about that place and period in history?

# Drawn from History

The Indians of the Great Plains have long recorded their lives, visions, and history by drawing and painting. They first painted on rocks and animal hides using paints made from natural pigments and brushes made from bones and sticks. But by the 1860s, Plains Indians were using new materials on a new surface: paper.

Explorers and traders who traveled across the Great Plains brought ledger books and other notebooks with them. Plains Indians began to trade for these notebooks, as well as for colored pencils, crayons, and watercolor paints. Soon, ledger pages once used for lists of numbers became, in the hands of the Lakota, Kiowa, and other Plains tribes, a new art form called Ledger Art.

As you view these drawings, you may notice that the earlier ones, like Sitting Bull's, are simpler in form. By the 1880s, as artists had a wider variety of art supplies to work with, they added scenery and other details. Today the full range of these drawings serves as a valuable record of American Indian life on the Great Plains.

On what is known as the Julian Scott Ledger, an unknown Kiowa artist drew this portrait entitled "Kiowa Couples" in 1880 using pencil, ink, and colored pencil.

This sketch, created by Sitting Bull and copied by his uncle, shows the 14-year-old Slow striking a Crow warrior with his coup stick. The buffalo bull is Sitting Bull's signature.

In 1877, Kiowa artist Wohow represented the new art of photography in "Kiowa Portraits" using pencil and crayon.

Kiowa Chiefs on a visit to the Agent,

▲ The Kiowa artist who drew "Kiowa Couples" also created this group portrait, "Twelve High-Ranking Kiowa Men," in 1880 using pencil, ink, and colored pencil.

◀ This pencil-and-ink drawing was created before 1868 by Little Shield of the Arapaho. It is entitled "Pen-na-tak-er Co-manch."

A Cheyenne artist, Squint Eyes, made this
1876 drawing, "Buffalo Hunt," using pencil
and colored pencil.

The artist Black Hawk, of the Sans-arc Lakota, drew this untitled
group portrait from an unusual perspective in 1881 using ink and
colored pencil.

491

# A Research Report

A research report presents facts about a particular
topic. Use this student's writing as a model when
you write a research report of your own.

## Pioneers

The **introduction**
helps to capture
the attention of
the reader.

The **main idea**
and **topic
sentences**
are usually
placed at the
beginning.

Being a pioneer was an exciting adventure
and involved plenty of hard work for men,
women, boys, and girls. Pioneers from 1780 to
1850 traveled in wagon trains on a long, haz-
ardous journey to the American West. They had
oxen, horses, and even dogs tied to their wagons. Some also traveled by large boats, called
flatboats, that carried two or three families
down a river, along with their livestock and
everything else they owned. More than a million
people and animals traveled. Lots of them died
on their journey.

The pioneers always helped one another while they traveled. Once they reached their destination, they continued this practice. They worked together as a team. The men made tools, carried water, and sawed wood. The women made candles and clothing. The boys and girls ground corn. The pioneers usually ate vegetables such as beans, squash, turnips, potatoes, and cabbages, but they mostly ate corn. They shared their food with one another.

The pioneers needed shelter during their journey and after they reached their destination. The wagons and flatboats provided shelter for the travelers. The flatboats had a large boxlike structure in the center, which the families used as a house when they traveled. Once they reached the end of their journey, the pioneers usually built log cabins, which they could put together quickly.

**Supporting details** show that the writer is using facts.

Good reports have a **logical sequence** of information.

Clothing was harder to provide on the frontier than either food or shelter, because clothing materials were expensive and difficult to get. Linsey-woolsey, a coarse cloth, woven with wool and cotton, was the favorite material of the pioneer housewife for making clothes for herself, her husband, and her children.

When the pioneers farmed, they made their own tools, such as rakes, hoes, and plows. They also built themselves workshops, where they made their tools and household items.

Almost every large pioneer settlement had a church. Parents taught prayers and songs to their children, and kept Sunday as a day of rest and worship.

The **conclusion** satisfies the reader.

Pioneering was challenging, exciting, and very difficult. Only the strong and persistent were able to answer the challenge to find and settle in new territories.

# List of Sources

"Frontier Life." <u>Encyclopedia Americana.</u> 1995 ed.

"Pioneer Life in America." <u>World Book Encyclopedia</u>. 1992 ed.

Youngberg, Florence C., ed. <u>Conquerors of the West:</u> <u>Stalwart Mormon Pioneers,</u> Vol. 1. Agreka Books. 1998.

## Meet the Author

### Cora L.

**Grade:** five
**State:** Massachusetts
**Hobbies:** cooking, baking cakes with her dad
**What she'd like to be when she grows up:** a movie star or a famous singer

**Pioneer Girl**

## Key Vocabulary

claim
discouraged
fertile
homestead
immigrants
pioneers
prairie
sod

**Vocabulary Reader**

*Prairie School*

by Carlynn Trout

*e* ● **Glossary**

496

# Claiming the Land

For years, European **pioneers** thought of the Great Plains as a place to cross, not a place to live. Then in 1862 a new law was passed — the Homestead Act. Settlers could claim a **homestead** on 160 acres of **prairie** land. If they lived on their claims and farmed the land for five years, they would become the owners. Thousands of homesteaders like the family you will meet in *Pioneer Girl* eagerly rushed to settle in Kansas, Nebraska, and the Dakota Territories. Among them were recent **immigrants** from Sweden, Norway, Denmark, France, Germany, and Russia.

◀ With this receipt for a filing fee, a settler officially owned a **claim** on a Nebraska lot — a piece of land the size of eighty city blocks.

The grasslands were **fertile** for growing crops, if the weather cooperated. But many farm families grew **discouraged** living in houses of **sod** , or earth blocks, far from neighbors.
▼

# Andrea Warren

**Childhood:** Warren grew up in a small Nebraska town on the edge of the Great Plains, where she spent hours reading at the local library. Although she loved to read as a child, she didn't think about becoming a writer until she was an adult.

**Work:** Warren had several jobs before she decided to write full time, including teaching, editing, and newspaper reporting. She says that each of those jobs has "in some way connected me to words and the joy of writing, or teaching writing."

**Writing:** Warren has written books for several age groups, including novels for adults and young adults, and books for younger readers. *Pioneer Girl* is her second nonfiction book for children. Her first was *Orphan Train Rider: One Boy's True Story*, which won the *Boston Globe–Horn Book* Award.

To find out more about Andrea Warren, visit Education Place. **www.eduplace.com/kids**

# Pioneer Girl

## GROWING UP ON THE PRAIRIE

### Andrea Warren

## Strategy Focus

As you read about a pioneer family in the 1880s, think of **questions** that you can ask your classmates about details of the pioneer life.

# RICH FARMING LANDS!

## ON THE LINE OF THE

# Union Pacific Railroad!

Located in the GREAT CENTRAL BELT of POPU-
LATION, COMMERCE and WEALTH, and
adjoining the WORLD'S HIGHWAY
from OCEAN TO OCEAN.

# 12,000,000 ACRES!

*3,000,000 Acres in Central and
Eastern Nebraska, in the Platte Valley, now for sale!*

We invite the attention of all parties seeking
a HOME, to the LANDS offered for sale by this Company.

**The Vast Quantity of Land** from which to select, ena-bles every one to secure such a location as he desires, suita-ble to any branch of farming or stock raising.

**The Prices are Extremely Low.** The amount of land owned by the Company is so large that they are determined to sell at the cheapest possible rates, ranging from $1.50 to $8.00 per acre.

**The Terms of Payment are Easy.** Ten years' credit at six per cent interest. A deduction of ten per cent for cash.

**The Location is Central**, along the 41st parallel, the favorite latitude of America. Equally well adapted to corn or wheat; free from the long, cold winters of the Northern, and the hot, unhealthy influences of the Southern States.

**The Face of the Country is** diversified with hill and dale, grain land and meadow, rich bottoms, low bluffs, and undulating tables, all covered with a thick growth of sweet nutritious grasses.

**The Soil** is a dark loam, slightly impregnated with lime, free from stone and gravel, and eminently adapted to grass, grain and root crops; the subsoil is usually light and porous, retaining moisture with wonderful tenacity.

**The Climate** is mild and healthful; the atmosphere dry and pure. Epidemic diseases never prevail; Fever and Ague are unknown. The greatest amount of rain falls between March and October. The Winters are dry with but little snow.

**The Productions** are wheat, corn, oats, barley, rye and root crops, and vegetables generally. Flax, sweet potatoes, sorghum, etc., do well and yield largely.

**Fruits, both Wild and Cultivated,** do remarkably well, The freedom from frosts in May and September, in connec-tion with the dry Winters and warm soil, renders this State eminently adapted to fruit culture.

**Stock Raising** in all its branches, is particularly profita-ble on the wide ranges of rich pasturage. Cattle and sheep feed with avidity and fatten upon the nutritious grasses without grain; hogs thrive well, and wool growing is exceed-ingly remunerative.

**Timber** is found on the streams and grows rapidly.

**Coal** of excellent quality, exists in vast quantities on the line of the road in Wyoming, and is furnished to settlers at reduced rates.

**Market Facilities** are the best in the West; the great mining regions of Wyoming, Colorado, Utah and Nevada, are supplied by the farmers of Platte Valley.

**The Title** given the purchaser is absolute, in fee simple, and free from all incumbrances, derived directly from the United States.

**Soldiers of the Late War** are entitled to a Homestead of one hundred and sixty acres, within Railroad limits, which is equal to a bounty of $400.

**Persons of Foreign Birth** are also entitled to the ben-efits of the Free Homestead Law, on declaring their inten-tions of becoming citizens of the United States; this they may do immediately on their arrival in this country.

**For Colonies,** the lands on the line of the Union Pacific Railroad afford the *best locations* in the West.

**TOWN LOTS FOR SALE VERY CHEAP** in the most important towns on the line of the Road, affording ex-cellent opportunities for business or investments.

Full information in regard to lands, prices, terms of sale, &c., together with pamphlets, circulars and maps, may be obtained from all the Agents of the Department, also the

### "PIONEER."

A handsome ILLUSTRATED PAPER, with maps, etc., and containing the HOMESTEAD LAW. *Mailed free* to all appli-cants. Address

## O. F. DAVIS,
### Land Commissioner, U. P. R. R.

#### OMAHA, NEB.

*Posters like this one, advertising land for sale by the railroad,
drew settlers to the prairie.*

*In 1885, the McCance family of Missouri filed a claim on 160 acres of land in central Nebraska, headed west, and became "homesteaders." Poppie McCance built a house on the windswept prairie out of blocks of earth, or sod. The new farm brought both adventures and hardships for the McCance children – Grace, Florry, and Stella – and their hardworking parents. Grace had a remarkable memory and could recall details from even her very early years. Whenever she is quoted, the words are directly from her memoir.*

During the fall, Grace and Florry played outside whenever they could. Their favorite place was the old buffalo trail that wound over the prairie and out of sight from the house. Their cat liked to go with them. Sometimes they found tiny shells in the soil and would bring them home to Mama. She explained how, millions of years ago, glaciers covered the land. When they melted, they created a sea. That's where the shells had come from.

Later Grace learned that the Midwest was dry because the Rocky Mountains in Colorado blocked moisture blowing inland from the Pacific Ocean. Nebraska was one of the driest Midwest states. The few trees grew mostly along the rivers. Rainfall also affected how tall the grass grew. Travelers going west noticed that the closer they got to the Rocky Mountains, the shorter the grass was. "Shortgrass" grew only six to twelve inches tall.

*The McCance family reunion, 1892: Mama and Poppie are standing to the far right. In front of them are babies Elsie and Nelie.*

On the eastern side of the Midwest, known as the "tallgrass" prairie, native grasses got enough rain to grow six to twelve feet in height. In the shortgrass area where the McCances lived, Poppie planted types of wheat and corn that needed little rainfall. His crops still had to have some rain, however, and like all farmers he kept one eye on the weather.

The weather was always a concern. Hailstorms could pound crops to pieces in a matter of minutes, and injure or kill birds and animals. Hailstones even killed people caught without shelter. Lightning was another danger. Grace once saw a horse that had been killed by lightning. When the weather was dry, lightning, a spark from a campfire, or a gun discharge could start prairie fires, and the wind would spread them.

Settlers banded together to fight the fires. Sometimes they tried setting backfires — burning a strip of land in the fire's path so that when the fire reached the strip, it either burned out or turned in a different direction. Like every settler, Poppie tried to keep firebreaks — grassless ditches the fires could not cross — plowed around his land. But sometimes, if prairie fires

*Seated to the far right are (left to right) Stella, Florry, Grace, and Ethel.*

were moving fast enough, they could jump firebreaks and be stopped only by a river or a creek.

Grace never forgot her first prairie fire. As soon as Poppie saw smoke in the far hills, he took off in the wagon with a barrel of water. Mama, Florry, and Grace watched all morning as the fire drew closer to their land. Grace was frightened.

Mama told the girls that if the fire jumped the firebreak they would run to the middle of the big bare field where the fire would have nothing to burn and would either go around them or die out. When the flames reached the firebreaks, Grace was ready to run. Then she saw that the fire was going out. When Poppie finally came home, his clothes and skin were black from soot.

A few months after the fire, a rainstorm struck the homestead. The howling of the wind woke everyone up. Suddenly "the darkness, black and thick as velvet, was ripped apart by a terrible blue flash of lightning," Grace remembered. "Then there was a cracking, tearing sound, and the soddy seemed to quiver."

The noise was the roof being torn off the kitchen. When the storm finally stopped, the house was "a sorry-looking mess. Every last thing had blown off the walls, and all Mama's little shelves, brackets, whatnots, and pictures were either smashed to bits or gone entirely." Grace remembered that "Mama went around in a kind of a daze, picking some of her torn and broken things out of the hash on the floor and sweeping out the worst of the mud. The hot sun was pouring down on our heads when Poppie, hard put to keep a cheerful expression on his face, offered thanks for the cornmeal mush and fried eggs we finally sat down to."

The girls helped Mama carry water to clean up. Poppie hunted for roof boards that had blown away and set to work rebuilding the roof. Grace and her mother walked through the fields looking for their belongings. They "found half of the marriage certificate, but no part of the frame or glass. Just that half, ripped from the rest, its doves and cupids hardly stained by the mud and rain."

*Storms could destroy a pioneer family's house and fields.*

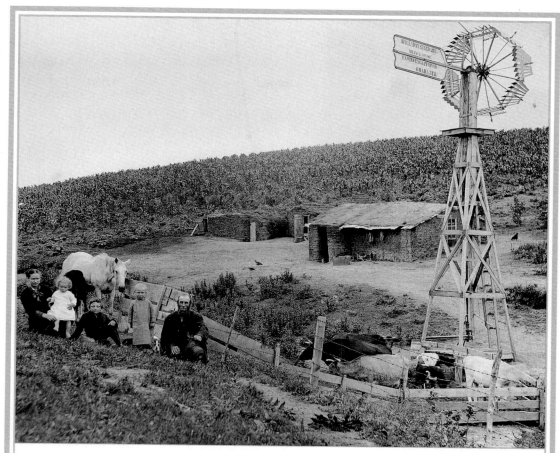

*Windmills built over wells pumped water to the surface and also showed travelers where houses were located.*

Still, Poppie was not discouraged. Like most farmers, he lived on hope, always convinced that the next year would be better.

When early November's chill made it too cold to play outside, Grace and Florry gathered up their cob dolls and settled into the sod house for the winter. "Flour sacks full of beans and dried corn hung in the kitchen corner that winter, and heaps of onions, turnips, pumpkins, cabbage, and potatoes filled the cellar cave."

Just before Thanksgiving, Poppie came home from one of his weekly trips to town with three barrels in the back of the wagon. They had come by railroad from Grandma and Grandpa Blaine, Mama's parents back in Missouri. Grace and Florry and even little Stella were almost beside themselves with excitement when Poppie started to pry off the lids.

*A rare photograph of the crowded interior of a one-room sod house.*

The first one was filled with molasses to sweeten their cereal and Mama's baked goods. The second was full of red apples from Grandpa Blaine's orchard behind the big white house. Grace saw the faraway look in Mama's eyes when she took one and held it in her hands.

The third barrel was the best. First they pulled out bags of black walnuts from Grandpa's nut trees and sweet potatoes from his garden. Then came Grandma's bundles. One contained a dress length of new calico fabric for Mama and each of the girls. The other held clothes from Mama's younger sister, Aunt Ollie, who always wore the latest styles. She had sent along jackets, dresses, and petticoats she did not want anymore.

Mama laid everything out on the bed, and Grace and Florry gazed at the lovely garments. Mama would make over the clothes so the girls would have new outfits. And she promised to have their new calico dresses made in time for Christmas dinner.

That first Christmas, Mama and Poppie could not afford any presents, but Poppie cut down a little wild plum bush and Grace and Florry decorated it with paper chains and strings of popcorn. All three girls wore their new dresses when the neighbors came to feast on a roast turkey dinner. Grace's only complaint was that the table was not big enough. She and Florry and the neighbors' children had to wait until the adults finished at "first table" before it was their turn to eat. "While hard knots of hunger grew and grew inside us, we had to sit back, smelling the good smells, and hoping there would be enough of everything left for us," she recalled. "Homestead children had to put up with a lot of hard things, but one of the hardest was waiting for second table."

## Spring came again, and the prairie turned soft green.

Grace was now four and lingered outside. "The first day of going barefoot was almost as good as Christmas, or the Fourth of July," she recalled. "There is almost no describing it; the good feeling to tender, bare soles of cushiony new buffalo grass, or of the fine, warm dust of a cow trail."

Everything on the homestead was humming and growing. The horse gave birth to a colt. Pearlie the cow had a calf. Little chicks followed the fussy old turkey. Poppie planted his wheat, and then had to use his shotgun to fight off flocks of geese flying north that kept stealing the precious seeds. Mama planted her garden again, a bigger one this year. "Poppie said, for the hundredth time, that he had never seen such a land as this, so rich, so fertile. But Mama said only that she wished we had a well in our own yard."

Poppie kept after the well men, but they had so much business from all the new homesteaders in the area that they raised their rates. Poppie said they did not have enough money. He would have to keep hauling water until he could dig the well himself.

Their second year on the prairie passed much as the first. Grace and Florry still begged to go whenever Poppie loaded up the water barrels. If Mama would relent, "we had fun, jouncing along in the wagon and singing

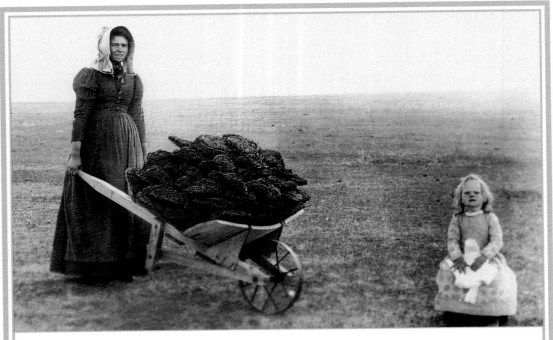

*Pioneers used buffalo or cow chips for fuel because there were few trees on the prairie. The little girl is holding her corn husk doll.*

with Poppie above the rattle and bang of the empty barrels. . . . When we pulled up at the well, our neighbor, Mrs. Totten, would come out to visit with us while Poppie filled the barrels, or maybe she would take us to the house with her."

The Tottens were only a few miles away, but Mama still felt as if she lived in the middle of nowhere. That changed when the Yoders, who had been the McCances' neighbors in Missouri, took a claim nearby. "Their arrival made Mama happier than anything that had happened since we came to Nebraska," Grace realized.

On Mama's birthday in April, Mama decided the family should visit the Yoders since their son's birthday was the same day. Mama began preparing food to take with them. Grace and Florry did their chores and took baths, put on their best petticoats, and tried to stand still while Mama braided their long hair. Then Mama brushed her own hair and arranged it stylishly on her head. Just as they all finished dressing, Mama glanced out the window and cried, "'Merciful heavens, there's the Yoders, the whole family, and look at this house!'"

*Immigrants, like this French family who pioneered in Kansas, played an important role in helping to settle the Midwest.*

Grace and Florry looked — at a tub of cold dirty bathwater, clothes strewn everywhere, and the kitchen not yet tidied from breakfast. While Mama hurriedly picked up, Grace and Florry grabbed the bath basin and dragged it outside, just as their unexpected guests came to the door. They had brought a birthday dinner for Mama and their son, all ready to eat.

The homesteaders settling around the McCances were mostly Swedish immigrants. When the farmers gathered together to help harvest one another's wheat crops, Poppie, whose ancestors were Scottish and Irish, missed out on most of the conversation, which was in Swedish.

Immigrants who settled in the Midwest usually came for the rich farmland. In the countries they left behind, they either could not afford to own land or were not allowed to. Some also came to find religious freedom, to escape paying unfair taxes, or to avoid serving in the military. So many Germans settled in Kansas during the 1860s and 1870s that one tribe of Kansas Indians spoke German as a second language instead of English. In 1870, over half of Nebraska's population was made up of foreign-born immigrants and their American-born children.

Like Poppie, many people born in the United States also wanted to homestead. Some had lost their homes in the Civil War or thought the East was getting too crowded. Freed slaves came because they wanted to leave the South, and homesteading was a way they could own land. Sometimes freed slaves established a community, such as the little Kansas town of Nicodemus.

Most homesteaders were poor. Children were often barefoot because they owned no shoes. One child remembered that his parents used kegs for chairs during family meals and the children stood. Before they had those kegs, they sat on pumpkins.

Everyone worked six days a week, including small children. Three-year-olds could act as human scarecrows to chase grain-eating birds out of the fields and help gather chips for fuel. Four-year-olds ran errands, took water to field-workers, and gathered eggs. Five-year-olds helped break up clods in the fields, pull weeds, feed the cookstove, milk cows, and even plow. One six-year-old boy sent to find stray cattle was gone several days before his father set out to search for him and found him not far from home, returning with the lost cows.

Grace and Florry had always helped out. Grace was five and Florry was seven when they were given a new chore: looking for turkey nests. When chicken and turkey hens turned "broody" in the spring, they stopped laying for several weeks so they could sit on one batch of eggs long enough for them to hatch into baby chicks. But they often laid their eggs far from home, where skunks and snakes could get them and where coyotes could kill the hens. The girls' job was to find the nests and get the hens to "brood" them back at the stable. Grace recalled, "The hens would stroll the prairie for hours, acting as if they had nowhere to go and nothing to do. Sometimes we sat watching a hen for a solid half day, and then somehow missed her when she slipped, like the shadow of a cloud, into some patch of brush or tall grass and disappeared."

The fall of 1887, Poppie bought a small herd of cattle. Since there were no boys in the family, he called on five-year-old Grace, nicknaming her Pete because she would be doing work usually done by a boy. He said, "'You'll have to be my herd boy now, Pete. Mommie needs Florry to help her in the house and you'll have to do it all alone. Think you can?'" Grace was thrilled. She disliked housework and far preferred to work outdoors.

Her job was to drive the cattle to the fields in the morning, stay with them all day, and bring them home in the evening. Herding would have gone fine, had it not been for one mean-tempered heifer who constantly threatened Grace with her sharp horns. Grace had to carry a stout stick to protect herself. One evening the cows turned contrary and wanted to stay inside the cave they had created in the big haystack: "No matter how much I ran and yelled and whacked, they outran me and dodged back into the cave. Finally, I pushed past them into the hole and began pounding on their heads with my stick. The older cows gave up and backed out together, leaving me suddenly face-to-face with the long-nosed, ornery heifer."

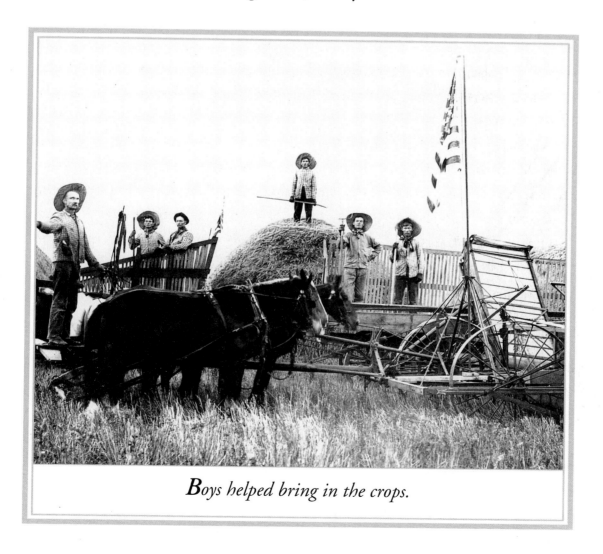

*Boys helped bring in the crops.*

As the heifer rushed her, Grace flattened herself against the hay, but the heifer gouged a deep cut from her hip to armpit. As much as it hurt, Grace got the cows home, even the heifer. When she was finally in the house, she burst into tears. Mama cared for her, then told Poppie he had to get rid of the heifer or Grace could no longer herd. Poppie said he would sell the heifer the next time he went to town. In the meantime, he would keep her in the corral.

A few days later, when Grace was in the barn helping with the milking, she heard a snort behind her. She whirled around and saw the heifer, head down, coming straight for her. Grace made a mad dash, ducking under one of the cows and rolling under the barbed-wire fence. She was unhurt, but she was wearing her favorite calico dress and ripped it so badly it was ruined. That made her cry more than the scare. Poppie sold the heifer in town the next day.

*Even very young pioneer children helped feed animals, milk cows, and do other chores.*

# GRACE McCANCE SNYDER
## 1882–1982

When I was growing up in Newman Grove, Nebraska, I could see a cornfield from my bedroom window, and I marked the seasons by its growth and colors. My view now is of city streets, and I sometimes wish I could still see that cornfield every day as a reminder of the pioneer families who settled the Midwest.

Many pioneer children grew up on hardscrabble homesteads, working alongside their parents in harsh conditions to nurture the growth of crops and cattle. In researching the lives of children on the prairie, however, I did not hear many complaints. These children were needed by their families and had a strong sense of purpose. Because they knew no other life, they did not feel deprived. The prairie was their home. Their optimism, steadfastness, and hard work have given those of us fortunate enough to live in this beautiful part of the world a proud legacy.

When I first read Grace McCance Snyder's memoir, *No Time on My Hands*, I knew I wanted to write about her pioneer childhood. I liked her spunk and spirit. She dared to dream, and she saw her dreams come true.

I hope readers will enjoy her story as it is told here and, through her, will gain new appreciation of what it meant to grow up on the prairie.

— Andrea Warren

*Grace posed on horseback for her ninetieth birthday.*

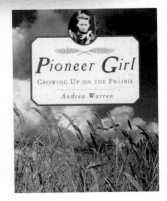

# Think About the Selection

**1.** How do Grace and Florry's chores compare with the chores you do at home?

**2.** The author writes that Poppie and the other farmers "lived on hope." Give examples from the selection that show this.

**3.** What do you think would have been the best and worst things about being a child in a homesteading family? Explain your answer.

**4.** Based on the information in the selection, would you expect the McCance family's farm to become successful? Why or why not?

**5.** Do you think it was fair to lure homesteaders to the prairie with ads promising rich farmland? Explain.

**6.** What can Americans today learn from the experiences of ordinary people of earlier generations, like Grace McCance Snyder?

**7. Connecting/Comparing** Compare how the Lakota people in *A Boy Called Slow* and the McCance family in *Pioneer Girl* adapted to life on the Great Plains.

**Explaining**

# Write Instructions

Think about the chores a child would have to do in a homesteading family. Someone who took over those chores for a few days might need instructions. Write instructions for two of the chores, telling how to do each one.

> **Tips**
> - Use imperative sentences when giving directions.
> - Use words such as *first, then, next,* and *last* to make the order of the steps clear.

## MATH

# Make a Diagram

Draw a diagram of a sod house and the furniture inside it. Use information from the selection to help you decide the size of the living area and the objects in it. Include the approximate measurements of each room.

**Bonus** Suppose you were building a sod house out of sod blocks 3' long by 1' wide by 4" thick. How many blocks would you need for a one-foot-thick wall measuring 12' long by 9' high?

## ART

# Create an Illustration

Use the photographs, events, and descriptions in *Pioneer Girl* to create your own illustration for the story. Think about the clothes the characters might have worn and other details of the landscape and weather.

# Send an E-Postcard

Send a friend an e-postcard telling about the McCance homestead. You might give a few details from the selection, and invite your friend to read *Pioneer Girl*. You'll find the postcard at Education Place. **www.eduplace.com/kids**

# Nicodemus Stakes a Claim In History

By Angela Bates-Tompkins

In 1877, 350 former slaves moved from Kentucky to northwest Kansas. The town in which they settled was given the name Nicodemus. It was named after the first slave to purchase his freedom in the United States. W.R. Hill, a white town builder, and W.H. Smith, an African American homesteader, were partners in organizing this all-black settlement.

*A buffalo soldier demonstration in Nicodemus in 1998.*

*The townspeople of Nicodemus, Kansas, gather on Main Street around 1885 (left). Today fewer than thirty people live in the town.*

*This October 1, 1879 homestead application (below) was submitted by S.P. Roundtree, one of the founders of Nicodemus.*

Hill and Smith were joined by five African American ministers who had been living in Topeka, Kansas. In April 1877, the group founded the Nicodemus Town Company and sought settlers from Kentucky to move to Kansas.

The first 350 recruits arrived in Nicodemus in September 1877 with high hopes. They were soon disappointed. They found themselves surrounded by a treeless landscape. Some of the town organizers even were living in dugouts. As many as sixty families returned to Kentucky. Those who stayed had brought only a few belongings with them. Their supplies soon ran out. Fortunately, some Osage Indians stopped at Nicodemus while on a hunting trip and gave the settlers food to survive the winter.

Though the first year was a struggle, several other groups of settlers soon joined the original bands. By 1885, the population of Nicodemus had grown to nearly seven hundred people. The town had two newspapers, livery stables, a post office, a general store, a doctor, hotels, restaurants, schools, and churches. From the late 1800s to the 1940s, the largest number of black farmers and African American–owned farmland in Kansas was in Graham County, of which Nicodemus was the central city.

In 1887, residents of Nicodemus raised money to try to help bring a railroad through their town. Trains and railroads meant progress. The townspeople hoped that a train station would carry people and goods to the town. The railroad bypassed the town, however. Many settlers became discouraged and began to leave. Some merchants moved their businesses to the newly organized railroad town of Bogue, just six miles to the west.

Difficult years followed, but Nicodemus residents still hoped to succeed. A drought came, making it hard to grow crops. When the crops did flourish, locusts ate them.

In the 1930s, the United States was faced with the Great Depression. In Nicodemus, as elsewhere in the country, people lost their jobs and new jobs were almost impossible to find. Townspeople left for what they hoped would be new starts in better places.

Despite the decline in population, Nicodemus remained a cultural center for African American life. And although people left the town, they did not forget it. They still return for the annual Emancipation Celebration, held during the last weekend of July. Descendants of those first settlers come from all over the United States to reconnect with family and friends.

In 1976, Nicodemus was put on the National Register of Historic Places as a National Historic Landmark. In 1991, efforts by the Nicodemus Historical Society resulted in a proposal to establish Nicodemus as a National Historic Site/Park. The bill was passed by Congress and signed by President Bill Clinton on November 12, 1996. The town is now receiving funds to help restore its five historic buildings.

The National Park Service is providing assistance in interpreting the town's rich African American history and its unique contribution to the economic, social, and political development of Kansas and the West.

*Nicodemus is the oldest and only remaining all-African American town west of the Mississippi River. On August 1, 1998, during the 120th Emancipation Celebration, Nicodemus was dedicated as a National Historic Site/Park.*

# Galloping Free

**Black Cowboy, Wild Horses**

**Genre** Nonfiction

## Key Vocabulary

- bluffs
- herds
- mares
- mustangs
- ravines
- stallion

**Vocabulary Reader**

*e* ● Glossary

Horses were once native to North America. Long ago they disappeared from the landscape, only to return in the 1500s with explorers from Spain. Many of these horses escaped, ran free out into the plains, and lost their tame ways. They became wild horses, or **mustangs**. Before long, **herds** of mustangs were roaming the **bluffs** and **ravines** of the Great Plains and the Southwest, much like the herd in *Black Cowboy, Wild Horses*.

Wild horses are smaller than domestic horses, with harder hooves, to help them survive outdoors. Each herd contains one male, a **stallion**, who leads several females, or **mares**, and their youngsters, or foals. Another stallion may challenge the leader to a fight. If the challenger wins, he becomes the new leader.

Horses were especially valuable to the cattlemen of the plains in the 1870s. Without horses, cowboys could not move their cattle to market. Many cowboys had a talent for rounding up and taming mustangs.

One of the most famous horsemen was Bob Lemmons. In Lemmons's time — especially the 1870s and 1880s — one out of three cowboys was African American or Mexican.

## Meet the Author
# Julius Lester

**Birthplace:** St. Louis, Missouri

**Writing for children:** Lester's own children had a big influence on his writing. He says, "I want them to have books that I would have liked to have had when I was growing up."

**Odd jobs:** Lester was once a professional musician and singer and the host of a radio show in New York.

## Meet the Illustrator
# Jerry Pinkney

**Birthplace:** Philadelphia, Pennsylvania

**Odd job:** Pinkney once worked as a designer and illustrator for a greeting card company.

**Family ties:** Pinkney's wife, Gloria Jean, and his daughter-in-law, Angela Davis Pinkney, are both writers. His son, Brian, is a children's book writer and illustrator, and his son Myles is a photographer whose work also appears in children's books.

**Collaborators:** Lester and Pinkney have worked together on *John Henry* and five books of *The Tales of Uncle Remus.*

To learn more about Julius Lester and Jerry Pinkney, visit Education Place. **www.eduplace.com/kids**

BLACK COWBOY WILD HORSES
*A True Story*
JULIUS LESTER ☆ JERRY PINKNEY

## Strategy Focus

The author tells a true story using words to create pictures in a poetic way. As you read, **evaluate** how well those word pictures help to tell that story.

IRST LIGHT. Bob Lemmons rode his horse slowly up the rise. When he reached the top, he stopped at the edge of the bluff. He looked down at the corral where the other cowboys were beginning the morning chores, then turned away and stared at the land stretching as wide as love in every direction. The sky was curved as if it were a lap on which the earth lay napping like a curled cat. High above, a hawk was suspended on cold threads of unseen winds. Far, far away, at what looked to be the edge of the world, land and sky kissed.

He guided Warrior, his black stallion, slowly down the bluff. When they reached the bottom, the horse reared, eager to run across the vastness of the plains until he reached forever. Bob smiled and patted him gently on the neck. "Easy. Easy," he whispered. "We'll have time for that. But not yet."

He let the horse trot for a while, then slowed him and began peering intently at the ground as if looking for the answer to a question he scarcely understood.

It was late afternoon when he saw them — the hoofprints of mustangs, the wild horses that lived on the plains. He stopped, dismounted, and walked around carefully until he had seen all the prints. Then he got down on his hands and knees to examine them more closely.

Some people learned from books. Bob had been a slave and never learned to read words. But he could look at the ground and read what animals had walked on it, their size and weight, when they had passed by, and where they were going. No one he knew could bring in mustangs by themselves, but Bob could make horses think he was one of them — because he was.

He stood, reached into his saddlebag, took out an apple, and gave it to Warrior, who chewed with noisy enthusiasm. It was a herd of eight mares, a colt, and a stallion. They had passed there two days ago. He would see them soon. But he needed to smell of sun, moon, stars, and wind before the mustangs would accept him.

The sun went down and the chilly night air came quickly. Bob took the saddle, saddlebag, and blanket off Warrior. He was cold, but could not make a fire. The mustangs would smell the smoke in his clothes from miles away. He draped a thick blanket around himself, then took the cotton sack of dried fruit, beef jerky, and nuts from his saddlebag and ate. When he was done, he lay his head on his saddle and was quickly asleep. Warrior grazed in the tall, sweet grasses.

As soon as the sun's round shoulders came over the horizon, Bob awoke. He ate, filled his canteen, and saddling Warrior, rode away. All day he followed the tracks without hurrying.

Near dusk, clouds appeared, piled atop each other like mountains made of fear. Lightning flickered from within them like candle flames shivering in a breeze. Bob heard the faint but distinct rumbling of thunder. Suddenly lightning vaulted from cloud to cloud across the curved heavens.

Warrior reared, his front hooves pawing as if trying to knock the white streaks of fire from the night sky. Bob raced Warrior to a nearby ravine as the sky exploded sheets of light. And there, in the distance, beneath the ghostly light, Bob saw the herd of mustangs. As if sensing their presence, Warrior rose into the air once again, this time not challenging the heavens but almost in greeting. Bob thought he saw the mustang stallion rise in response as the earth shuddered from the sound of thunder.

Then the rain came as hard and stinging as remorse. Quickly Bob put on his poncho, and turning Warrior away from the wind and the rain, waited. The storm would pass soon. Or it wouldn't. There was nothing to do but wait.

Finally the rain slowed and then stopped. The clouds thinned, and there, high in the sky, the moon appeared as white as grief. Bob slept in the saddle while Warrior grazed on the wet grasses.

The sun rose into a clear sky and Bob was awake immediately. The storm would have washed away the tracks, but they had been going toward the big river. He would go there and wait.

By mid-afternoon he could see the ribbon of river shining in the distance. He stopped, needing only to be close enough to see the horses when they came to drink. Toward evening he saw a trail of rolling, dusty clouds.

In front was the mustang herd. As it reached the water, the stallion slowed and stopped. He looked around, his head raised, nostrils flared, smelling the air. He turned in Bob's direction and sniffed the air again.

Bob tensed. Had he come too close too soon? If the stallion smelled anything new, he and the herd would be gone and Bob would never find them again. The stallion seemed to be looking directly at him. Bob was too far away to be seen, but he did not even blink his eyes, afraid the stallion would hear the sound. Finally the stallion began drinking and the other horses followed. Bob let his breath out slowly. He had been accepted.

The next morning he crossed the river and picked up the herd's trail. He moved Warrior slowly, without sound, without dust. Soon he saw them grazing. He stopped. The horses did not notice him. After a while he moved forward, slowly, quietly. The stallion raised his head. Bob stopped.

When the stallion went back to grazing, Bob moved forward again. All day Bob watched the herd, moving only when it moved but always coming closer. The mustangs sensed his presence. They thought he was a horse.

So did he.

The following morning Bob and Warrior walked into the herd. The stallion eyed them for a moment. Then, as if to test this new-comer, he led the herd off in a gallop. Bob lay flat across Warrior's back and moved with the herd. If anyone had been watching, they would not have noticed a man among the horses.

When the herd set out early the next day, it was moving slowly. If the horses had been going faster, it would not have happened.

The colt fell to the ground as if she had stepped into a hole and broken her leg. Bob and the horses heard the chilling sound of the rattles. Rattlesnakes didn't always give a warning before they struck. Sometimes, when someone or something came too close, they bit with the fury of fear.

The horses whinnied and pranced nervously, smelling the snake and death among them. Bob saw the rattler, as beautiful as a necklace, sliding silently through the tall grasses. He made no move to kill it. Everything in nature had the right to protect itself, especially when it was afraid.

The stallion galloped to the colt. He pushed at her. The colt struggled to get up, but fell to her side, shivering and kicking feebly with her thin legs. Quickly she was dead.

Already vultures circled high in the sky. The mustangs milled aimlessly. The colt's mother whinnied, refusing to leave the side of her colt. The stallion wanted to move the herd from there, and pushed the mare with his head. She refused to budge, and he nipped her on the rump. She skittered away. Before she could return to the colt, the stallion bit her again, this time harder. She ran toward the herd. He bit her a third time, and the herd was off. As they galloped away, Bob looked back. The vultures were descending from the sky as gracefully as dusk.

536

It was time to take over the herd. The stallion would not have the heart to fight fiercely so soon after the death of the colt. Bob galloped Warrior to the front and wheeled around, forcing the stallion to stop quickly. The herd, confused, slowed and stopped also.

Bob raised Warrior to stand high on his back legs, fetlocks pawing and kicking the air. The stallion's eyes widened. He snorted and pawed the ground, surprised and uncertain. Bob charged at the stallion.

Both horses rose on hind legs, teeth bared as they kicked at each other. When they came down, Bob charged Warrior at the stallion again, pushing him backward. Bob rushed yet again.

The stallion neighed loudly, and nipped Warrior on the neck. Warrior snorted angrily, reared, and kicked out with his forelegs, striking the stallion on the nose. Still maintaining his balance, Warrior struck again and again. The mustang stallion cried out in pain. Warrior pushed hard against the stallion. The stallion lost his footing and fell to the earth. Warrior rose, neighing triumphantly, his front legs pawing as if seeking for the rungs on which he could climb a ladder into the sky.

The mustang scrambled to his feet, beaten. He snorted weakly. When Warrior made as if to attack again, the stallion turned, whinnied weakly, and trotted away.

Bob was now the herd's leader, but would they follow him? He rode slowly at first, then faster and faster. The mustangs followed as if being led on ropes.

Throughout that day and the next he rode with the horses. For Bob there was only the bulging of the horses' dark eyes, the quivering of their flesh, the rippling of muscles and bending of bones in their bodies. He was now sky and plains and grass and river and horse.

When his food was almost gone, Bob led the horses on one last ride, a dark surge of flesh flashing across the plains like black lightning. Toward evening he led the herd up the steep hillside, onto the bluff, and down the slope toward the big corral. The cowboys heard him coming and opened the corral gate. Bob led the herd, but at the last moment he swerved Warrior aside, and the mustangs flowed into the fenced enclosure. The cowboys leaped and shouted as they quickly closed the gate.

539

Bob rode away from them and back up to the bluff. He stopped and stared out onto the plains. Warrior reared and whinnied loudly. "I know," Bob whispered. "I know. Maybe someday." Maybe someday they would ride with the mustangs, ride to that forever place where land and sky kissed, and then ride on. Maybe someday.

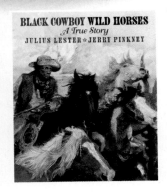

# Think About the Selection

**1.** Choose one of the author's descriptions of nature that you like best. Explain what this description helps you imagine.

**2.** How do you think Bob might have "read" the mustang hoof-prints? How did they provide him with clues about the herd?

**3.** Do you agree with Bob's reason for letting the rattlesnake go after it killed the colt? Why or why not?

**4.** Do you think people should be allowed to round up wild horses or should we not interfere with them? Explain your answer.

**5.** What would you find most difficult about what Bob does for a living? Most rewarding?

**6.** What do you think the author means when he says, "Bob could make horses think he was one of them — because he was."

**7.** **Connecting/Comparing** How are Bob Lemmons and Returns Again alike in their understanding of animals? Compare and contrast their experiences with animals.

## Write a Description

The author uses similes and metaphors to create vivid descriptions. Write a colorful description of a scene or detail from the selection. Use similes and metaphors to enliven your description.

> ### Tips
>
> - Remember that a simile uses *like* or *as* to compare two things. A metaphor compares two things by stating that one thing is the other.
> - Use vivid, exact words.

## Science

# Explain How an Ecosystem Works

Living things, together with the environment they live in, form ecosystems. Use the illustrations and text to write an explanation of the ecosystem in *Black Cowboy, Wild Horses*. What animals, plants, and features of the environment are part of it? How do the horses depend on it?

**Bonus** Draw a diagram to illustrate your explanation.

> Ecosystem of Wild Horses
>
> Animals
>
> Plants
>
> Environmental Features

## Viewing

# Review Illustrations

With a partner, present an oral review of the illustrations in *Black Cowboy, Wild Horses*. Choose ones you especially like and tell what you like about them. How do they help tell Bob Lemmons's story?

---

*Internet*

# Take an Online Poll

Think about the following statement: *It is wrong for people to herd and tame wild horses.* Do you agree or disagree? Find out what other students your age think. Visit Education Place and add your opinion to a poll.

**www.eduplace.com/kids**

# Home on

**Technology has changed life on this giant 145-year-old Texas ranch. But not much.**

*by Johnny D. Boggs*

Calves bawl as a handful of cowboys send the scared animals through narrow, wooden chutes to separate them for tomorrow's branding.

The dust is thick and suffocating, and the afternoon sun bakes man and beast. Saddle leather creaks, spurs jingle, horses snort and sweat-soaked cowboys yell in Spanish and English to keep the cattle moving.

Out of nowhere, high-pitched beeps suddenly sound. In a pickup truck, a cowboy's phone-radio is ringing.

Hey, it's the 1990s — not the 1870s.

# the Range

## A Short History of a BIG Place

Welcome to the King Ranch in south Texas. At 825,000 acres, it's the largest privately owned ranch in the world. How big? At almost 1,300 square miles, it's larger than Rhode Island. Wire fences along the ranch's boundaries could stretch from Denver, Colo., to Boston, Mass.

Riverboat pilot Richard King founded the ranch in 1853. The captain bought cattle in Mexico and convinced an entire village to move to Texas to work for him. These workers became known as *Kiñenos*, Spanish for King's Men.

Today, the King Ranch is run by the heirs of Captain King, and *Kiñenos* still work here. Fourth-generation *Kiñeno* Faustino Montalvo was born on the ranch. "No hospital, no doctor," the 55-year-old says.

Times have changed, though. A public school district falls within the ranch's boundaries, and the town of Kingsville, founded in 1904 and built partly on land donated by Mrs. King, includes a state university and modern facilities. The ranch itself is diverse, with oil exploration, wildlife management and farming.

But cattle remain the ranch's centerpiece. And it still takes real cowboys to look after some 60,000 cattle.

**The "Running W" brand marks the Santa Cruz cattle of the King Ranch.**

Photographs © 1998 by David Nance

545

## The Cowboy Way

Today, nearly 50 cowboys work on the King Ranch, and some things haven't changed since the 1800s. Many hands still live on the ranch. They answer to nicknames like "Chito," "Gallo" and "Leon."

Cowboys still wear leather chaps over their jeans, spurs on their boots and well-worn straw cowboy hats. Some opt for baseball caps and, occasionally, athletic shoes.

Calves get branded with the same "Running W" mark Captain King first used in 1869, using the old, heavy irons. Sometimes the cattle are vaccinated and branded in the chutes.

Often, though, it's done the old-fashioned way. Calves are roped and held down — it's where the calf-roping contest in rodeos comes from — while a cowboy slaps a hot iron above the animal's rear leg. Smoke and dust burn the nostrils. It's a dirty job, just as it was in the 1800s.

"It's not a job you get into for the money," cowboy Steve Shermer says. Indeed. Cowboys don't get paid overtime, and their workday can begin before sunrise and end after dark. "You just work until the job's done," Shermer says.

And there's usually a lot to be done, whether it's checking stock, mending fences or working with horses.

## High-Tech Cowboys

Technology has changed the ways of the ranch. While cowboys continue to drive cattle to the corral on horseback, a pickup truck — air-conditioned, of course — also helps. And though they don't plug branding irons into electrical

**Cowboy Jonathan Hawkins, 19, helps round up the cattle.**

Photographs © 1998 by David Nance

Although technology can help with some tasks, cowboys still rely on the help of dogs to herd cattle (far left). Cowboys (left) lead calves into wooden chutes in order to give them medicine.

outlets, propane tanks make lighting fires and heating branding irons easier.

"It used to take seven to ten days to work the cattle," says Alfredo "Chito" Mendietta. "Now we can work them in two days."

Computers log inventory and keep track of wildlife. Hal Hawkins, King Ranch's animal physiologist, monitors herd research and development with a laptop computer.

## Technology's Drawbacks

Shermer compares the job of today's cowboy to that of a factory worker. "The land's the factory and the cattle are your product," he says. "In a factory, you try to get the most out of your product. And that's what we try to do as land managers."

Technology goes only so far. Computers can't make it rain. Droughts were rough on cowboys and cattle in the 1800s, and they're just as hard today.

"It's tough," unit manager Robert Silguero says. "It can make you think of doing something else."

But not really. The weather can be tough, but cowboys are tougher.

## City Slickers Are Welcome

So you want to be a cowboy? Silguero, Mendietta and Montalvo have been at the King Ranch all of their lives. Others, like Hawkins, Shermer and Knudsen, come from rural areas.

"We've had quite a few hands come out of the city, though," Shermer says. "The trick is you've just got to be willing to learn. I pretty much learn something new every day."

You also have to be willing to spend long days in the sun, working livestock. And it's not all fun and games.

Mendietta certainly didn't think so when a horse landed on his leg and left him in a hospital for ten days.

"This," Shermer says, "is really a job that you have to love."

# A Revolution in Mexico

*Elena*

**Key Vocabulary**

bandit
dictator
frantic
notorious
refugees
transformed

**Vocabulary Reader**

Railroad Revolution

*e* • Glossary

**Rebel leader Pancho Villa was both cheered and feared throughout Mexico.**

The year was 1910. For more than thirty years, the nation of Mexico had suffered under a cruel **dictator**, President Porfirio Díaz. He had taken land from the peasants, or *campesinos*, and given it to wealthy friends, leaving most Mexicans poor and hungry.

Finally, the people had had enough. Rebel leaders all over Mexico, including the **notorious** former **bandit**, Pancho Villa, rose up to overthrow President Díaz. It was the beginning of the Mexican Revolution, but it was far from the end.

For the next ten years, Mexico was **transformed** into a country at war. Groups of Mexicans bitterly fought one another. No one was in charge for long. Innocent people lost their homes and lives.

Tens of thousands of **frantic** citizens fled to the United States with their few possessions. Among them was the family in *Elena,* which is a true story of that dangerous time.

**Many refugees left Mexico for California, following the same route as the one taken by Elena's family.** ▶

**A group of revolutionaries gathers in Mexico City, Mexico in 1915.** ▼

549

# Elena

## DianeStanley

★ Strategy Focus

As you read, think about the characters, their problem, and how they solve it to **summarize** the events of the story.

*Growing up in a wealthy family in rural Mexico, Elena insists on learning to read and do math, skills denied most girls a hundred years ago. She also wins her parents' permission to marry the man she loves — Pablo, a famous sombrero maker. But just before the Mexican Revolution, her peaceful life is disrupted. Elena's true story is told by Rosa, one of Pablo and Elena's four children.*

In the year 1910, when I was about five years old, my father had to go to Guadalajara on business. He went there once or twice a year. It was nothing unusual. As he mounted his horse, my mother went out to say goodbye. "Be careful," she told him. She was worried about who he might meet on the road. We had heard talk of a revolution. There were said to be rough soldiers and armed *campesinos* about. They were dangerous men. But Father just squeezed her hand and smiled. "I will be careful," he said.

Father was joined by several villagers who were making the trip with him. They waved to us and headed off across the rugged countryside, for there were no proper roads. It was just at the end of the rainy season and the path was wet. About an hour after they left, the ground under Father's horse suddenly gave way, creating a landslide. Down they plunged into the ravine below.

The villagers raced back for help, and many men hurried off with ropes to haul my father up to safety.

They brought him to our house and laid him on the bed. The doctor came and dressed my father's wounds. As he was leaving, we asked the doctor, "Will he live?" He shrugged his shoulders. "Who can tell?" he said. "Perhaps Pablo knows."

My mother stood and watched the doctor walk away from our house. "He is right," she thought to herself. "Pablo knows." So she went into the darkened room and knelt down beside the bed. She took his big hand and gently stroked it.

"Husband," she whispered, "how is it? Do you think you will recover?"

For a long time he did not look at her and he did not answer. At last he turned his head and spoke. "No," he said. Then in a weak but steady voice he told her what he knew. He named the very day and hour in which he would die. He said there would be war and that she and the children must leave their home.

"You will always be in my heart," he said. He never spoke again.

Three days later, at the very hour he had spoken, my father died.

Mother went crazy with grief. She ran weeping into the patio, and with a big stick began to swing wildly, knocking down her beautiful flowers. Then she opened all the cages and let the birds free.

After that, my mother grew quiet. Though she went on caring for us just as before, that *chispa*, the bright spark that was always a part of her, went out. Papá's absence filled our house with emptiness. I could not really understand what had happened, because I was so young. It seemed to me that Papá had just gone to where I couldn't see him — perhaps he was in the next room. I kept expecting him to walk in our door one day and make everything good again. But he never came, of course, and in time I understood that he never would.

I remember that it was warm and beautiful at that time, the skies a brilliant cloudless blue, day after day. It was as if nature were mocking us.

One day I was playing upstairs with my brother Luis. I heard the loud clop-clop of horses on the stone pavement outside — not one, but many horses. So I ran to the window to see. Looking down, I saw our street transformed into a river of sombreros. The revolution had reached our little village — it was the army of Pancho Villa riding by! With a gasp, Mother pulled me away from the window, for Pancho Villa was a notorious man. It was true that he was fighting to help free Mexico from the dictator Porfirio Díaz and that he wanted to give back to the campesinos the land that had been stolen from them. He was, in fact, on his way to becoming a genuine folk hero, the Robin Hood of Mexico. But it was also well known that he had once been a bandit and that his men were just as bad as the government soldiers. Neither army respected the law. Wherever they went, they stole from the people, killed anyone who challenged them, and left burned villages in their wake. What would happen to us?

Mother knelt down and gathered us in her arms. She understood in a flash that everything that had happened to her before had been for a reason. The books she had read, the hard numbers she had conquered, the battle she had won over her marriage — all this had made her strong. Now she had no father and no husband to help her. She had, instead, great courage and determination. Had there not always been wars? And in every country and every age, brave men and women had faced terrible dangers. She could do it, too. We saw this understanding pass across her face like a ripple of light. "Children," she said urgently, "we must find Esteban."

She knew that soldiers often took older boys and forced them into the army. My brother was sixteen.

None of us had seen him for hours. We searched the house for him, but he wasn't there. A book lay open on his bed. He had put it down and gone off somewhere. Maybe he was out in the streets among all those men. Maybe they had already taken him. At last María found him — up on the roof watching the soldiers. Boys are so foolish sometimes!

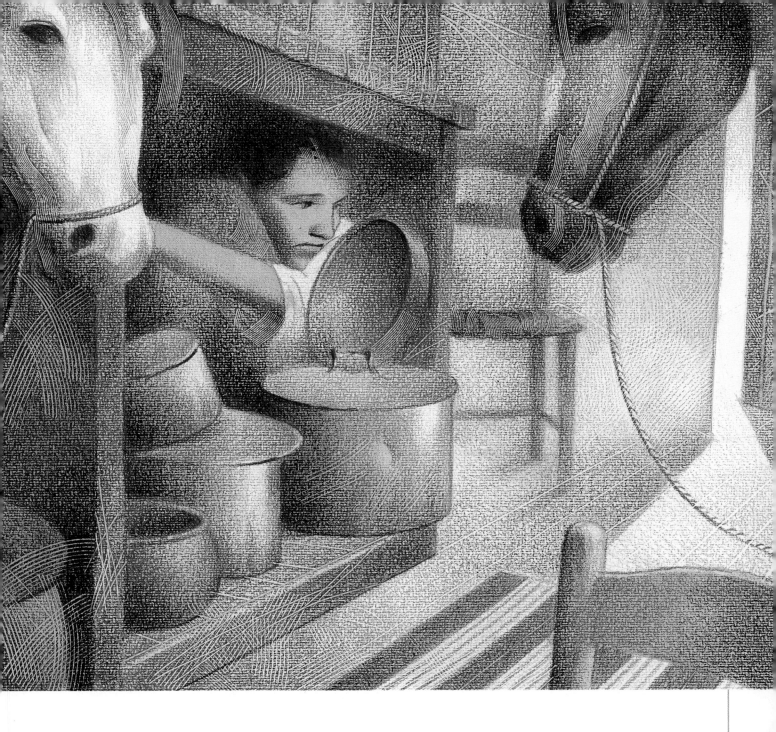

We made a hiding place for him in a kitchen cabinet, behind the big clay pots. Then Mother had another thought — the horses. They were sure to steal the horses. But maybe if they found the stable empty, they would think the horses had already been seized. They would certainly not think to look for them in the kitchen, so she brought the horses in there, too.

Before my mother could hide anything else, there was a loud knock on the door. We could hear deep voices laughing and talking outside. Mother hesitated a moment, wondering what to do. Then she sent us into the back room. We did as we were told but opened the door a crack so we could see what happened. Mother took a deep breath and opened the door.

There stood four or five soldiers, rough men who smelled of sweat and horses. The man in front was stout and wore a huge drooping mustache. *Bandoleras* crossed his chest. We had seen his face before, on a government poster. It was Pancho Villa himself!

"Señora," he said, "is this the house of Pablo, the famous maker of sombreros?" It was the last thing she expected to hear.

"It is," she said. "I am his widow."

"Then please accept my sincere condolences," said the leader of the rebel army, bowing slightly. He paused for a moment and then added almost shyly, "And the hats? The fine hats? Are there no more left?"

My mother actually smiled. "Excuse me a minute," she said. She went to a cupboard in her bedroom and returned with one of Father's beautiful silver-trimmed sombreros. "This is the last one," my mother said.

Pancho Villa was delighted. He put it on right away and actually paid her for it. Not only that, he posted a guard outside our house. As long as Villa's army was there, we were not harmed.

"Pablo was surely watching over us this day," my mother told us later. "But it may not always be so. Before your father died, he told me there would be soldiers. He told me we must leave our home. I wonder how I could have forgotten it."

"You were sad, *Mamacita*," María said.

When the *Villistas* had gone, Mother went to the plaza and opened the shop to the people of the village. She emptied the store of everything, taking down great bolts of manta and giving them to people who had nothing. We took only our money, some clothes, and food for the journey. We were leaving behind our aunts and uncles, our little house, the furniture, the pictures, the pots and pans and dishes. We said good-bye to the friends of a lifetime.

Everyone urged us not to go. "It is not proper for a woman to travel unprotected like that," they said. "It is not safe."

"The world is changing around us," Mother answered. "We must change, too."

We left the village early in the morning. When we reached the train station, we found that it was packed with frantic, pushing people. It seemed as though everyone in Mexico was trying to get on that train. Mother and María managed to make it inside. Then before Esteban got on, he handed Luis and me in through the window, along with the basket of food.

We were lucky to have benches to sit on. Most of the people were in boxcars or crowded in the aisles.

For five days the train chugged north. Through the open windows came soot, dust, and flies. I had worn a beautiful lacy white dress for the trip. Soon it was damp with sweat and covered with dirt.

When we reached Ciudad Juárez, we faced a new problem. What were we to do with Esteban? He was tall, almost a man. The soldiers at the border crossing would not treat him as a child. They might detain him for days, together with the rough men from the train. They might take him for the army.

"I think the answer will come to me," Mother told us. "We must be patient."

So we waited while she thought, but it was not a good place to be. The town was rough and lawless. With thousands of refugees pouring in, desperate to flee homes that were no longer safe, thieves and pickpockets roamed the streets. Hotels and shops charged ridiculous prices that people had to pay, because they had no other choice but to starve or sleep in the streets. For days we ate nothing but fruit.

Mother befriended a Chinese fruit seller who was honest and kind. One day she told him our problem. He smiled, for he knew exactly how to help us. Every day he crossed the border with his fruit wagon. We could dress Esteban in the man's clothes and straw hat. He would pretend to be the fruit seller's helper.

That afternoon we went over the bridge to El Paso together, Mother and the three of us walking along next to the fruit wagon. The cost was one penny each. At last we were safely in the United States.

We headed for California because we had a cousin, Trinidad, who lived there. We didn't have his address, though. In fact, we didn't even know what town he lived in. So we went to San Francisco, which was famous. We made our way to the *barrio*, where many people from Mexico lived. We asked everyone we met there, "Do you know our cousin Trinidad?" No one did. And besides, we didn't like it there. It was damp and cold. In Los Angeles, no one had heard of Trinidad, either. We were happier there, because the weather was warmer. But the city was too big, not like our lovely little village in Mexico. We heard about a place called Santa Ana. There were lemon and orange and walnut groves there and good schools for the children. So that is where we went and that is where we stayed. We never did find Trinidad.

By then, we had spent most of our money. So Esteban got a job picking fruit. Sometimes he was gone for weeks, living in the camps near the farms. When he came home he was sore and tired. He didn't laugh and play with me the way he had before.

Mother ran a boardinghouse, which was hard work. She did the cleaning, made the beds, mopped the floors, and scrubbed the bathtub. She washed and ironed the boarders' clothes. After all that, she went into the kitchen and cooked mountains of rice and beans and *tortillas* and *enchiladas* for them to eat. We all sat down to dinner together at a long pine table. Sometimes the boarders were very nice and became our friends. Some even came from the same part of Mexico as our family had. It made me feel like I wasn't so far from home.

María and I did what we could. We hung the laundry out on the clothesline, and we brought it back in if it rained. We helped wash the dishes and changed all the sheets once a week. And we looked after little Luis.

But Mother said that our real job was to get an education. School and homework always came first. When we were done with that, she said, we could help. I felt bad sometimes, sitting in a chair with a book in my lap while Mother was never still, always bustling about at her chores. She did it with a good spirit, though. If I said to her, "You work too hard, Mamacita," she would just shake her head and smile.

"And what is so bad about work?" she would say. "Work is how I take care of my family. Work is how I keep busy. Work is how I am useful. It is not so bad."

At school we learned to speak English and heard all about George Washington crossing the Delaware and Thomas Jefferson writing the Declaration of Independence. We wrote essays on the American Revolution and the American Civil War, and one day it dawned on me that Americans had suffered in terrible wars just as we had. And not long after that, I realized that Americans weren't "they" anymore. After all, we wore American clothes, read American books, knew American songs, and ate American candy. We had all become *real* Americans — all of us, that is, but Mamá.

She never quite knew what she was. Part of her was still back in Mexico and part of her was with us in California. Sometimes in the evening, after the dishes were done, we all went out on the porch to sit and enjoy the cool night air. At those times, Mother liked to talk about the old days. She told us about growing up in her father's great house in the beautiful mountains of Mexico. She talked of her gentle sisters who sang so beautifully to the guitar. She remembered her own little house full of flowers and birds. But she especially loved to talk about Father — how they fell in love first and got to know each other later, how he was such an artist, making beautiful sombreros, and how he knew things it was impossible to know, yet he knew them just the same. I had been so small when Father died, I could scarcely remember him. Those stories gave him back to me.

In all those years she talked only of happy times. It was much later that we learned what had happened in our little village. Only when we were grown — strong and full of hope — did we find out that it was gone, burned to the ground by the soldiers. And when we heard about the people who had died, people we had known, then we understood what our mother had done. With her courage and daring, she had saved us all.

## Meet the Author **Diane Stanley**

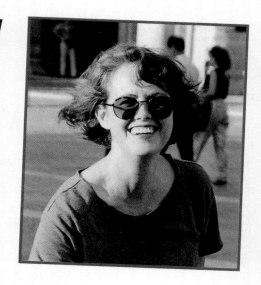

Diane Stanley is best known as an author and illustrator of biographies of historical figures. She was born in Abilene, Texas, and spent her childhood there, in New York City, and Southern California. Although moving was a challenge, she feels that it helped her become a writer by presenting her with new situations and keeping her from looking at things in only one way. *Elena*, Stanley's first work of historical fiction, is based on the family story of one of her grandmother's friends during the Mexican Revolution.

Stanley's other books include: *Shaka: King of the Zulus, Cleopatra*, and *Leonardo Da Vinci*.

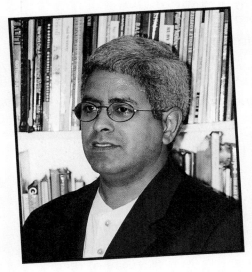

## Meet the Illustrator **Raúl Colón**

Before he began illustrating children's books, Raúl Colón worked in animation, designed puppets, and created theater posters and CD covers. Part of the unique look of Colón's illustrations comes from his use of a tool called a "scratcher" to etch lines and patterns into his paintings and drawings. Colón lives in New York City with his wife and two children.

To find out more about Diane Stanley and Raúl Colón, visit Education Place.

**www.eduplace.com/kids**

563

# Responding

## Think About the Selection

**1.** Compare the way you expected the outlaw Pancho Villa to act with the way he did act in *Elena*. Why do you think he acted this way?

**2.** What part of the family's troubles in *Elena* would you have found most difficult? Why?

**3.** Rosa says that she and her brothers and sister became "*real Americans*" in Santa Ana. What do you think she means by that?

**4.** Mamá says, "The world is changing around us. We must change, too." Do you agree with her? Why or why not?

**5.** Why do you think Mamá believes so strongly in the importance of education? How is your education important to you?

**6.** What do you think Rosa learned from her experiences in *Elena*?

**7.** **Connecting/Comparing** All the main characters in *One Land, Many Trails* demonstrate courage and determination. Compare Elena's courage to that of Slow, Grace McCance, or Bob Lemmons.

Reflecting

## Write a Journal Entry

Think about a scene in *Elena* in which the characters have to make an important decision. Then write a journal entry describing a time in your life when you had to make a decision of similar importance.

**Tips**

- Remember that keeping a journal is a way of recording events, facts, feelings, and ideas.
- Use the first-person point of view when writing a journal entry.

## Social Studies

# Create a Wanted Poster

Think about the descriptions of Porfirio Díaz and Pancho Villa on page 554. Use them to create a wanted poster for either Díaz or Villa. Include a picture of your choice and list the reasons why you think he should be brought to justice.

**Bonus** Work with a partner to find out more about Pancho Villa or Porfirio Díaz. Give an oral report to the class on what you learn.

## Listening and Speaking

# Role-Play a Telephone Conversation

Suppose that Mamá and the children finally locate their cousin Trinidad. With a partner, role-play the first telephone conversation between Trinidad and Mamá, Rosa, or Esteban. Include their stories and their feelings.

### Tips

- Speak clearly and not too fast.
- Be careful not to interrupt while another is talking.
- Pay attention to what is being said or asked.

---

## Internet

# Take an Online Quiz

In this theme, you have read about some of the people who have shaped the United States, and about some of the journeys that helped shape their lives. See how much you learned by taking our online theme quiz at Education Place.

**www.eduplace.com/kids**

# Social Studies Link

## Genre

**True Experiences**

**Skill: How to Take Notes**

*As you read . . .*

- Write down the **topic** or title.

- Note the most important ideas.

- Write down **key words** and phrases as headings. Use a separate note card for each heading, or leave several lines between headings on your paper.

- Write **details** about each key word or phrase beneath the heading.

- Write down the **source** of the information.

# COMING TO GOLDEN MOUNTAIN

*Not all of the trails to California started in the eastern United States or Mexico. Another path for emigrants began in China.*

*Gold!* In 1848, word went out about the discovery of gold near Sutter's Mill, California. From around the world, people flocked to the territory of California — newly acquired from Mexico, but not yet a state — hoping to strike it rich.

The lure of the gold mines was especially strong in China.

During the mid-1800s, millions of Chinese were living in poverty. Chinese farmers were having trouble producing enough food to meet the needs of China's population. And from 1850 to 1864, China was wracked by a civil war that claimed over twenty million lives.

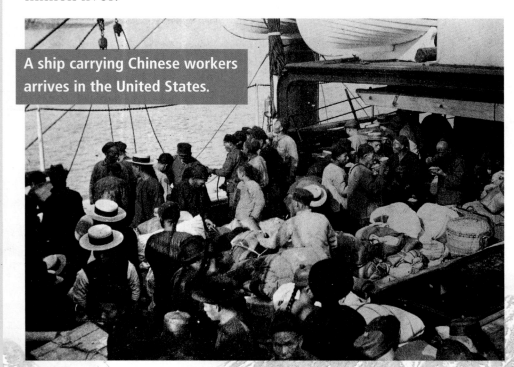

A ship carrying Chinese workers arrives in the United States.

With life in China so difficult, the idea of finding a fortune in America sounded very appealing. Many Chinese were encouraged by newspaper advertisements that confidently stated, "Money is in great plenty and to spare in America." Even the popular Chinese name for California, *Gum Shan*, or "Golden Mountain," gave the impression that riches were there for the taking.

The cost of boat passage from ports such as Guangzhou to San Francisco was very high by the standards of most Chinese. Some managed to save enough to pay for the journey themselves; others borrowed from banks or wealthier family members. Later emigrants from China had the option of working to pay the cost of their tickets once they arrived in America.

The first Chinese gold-seekers arrived in California in 1848, the same year as the gold strike. By 1852, there were around 25,000 Chinese living in the state. Almost all were men. Many had left their wives and children back in China and hoped to return home one day with enough money to live in comfort.

At first the Chinese enjoyed some success in the gold fields. Most worked for Chinese or American mining companies; a few worked on their own claims. Some gained a reputation as skillful miners who could extract gold from claims

Chinese miners join in the search for gold in California.

Railroad workers (above) build a trestle to support train tracks.

Records for track laying (below) were achieved at the cost of many lives.

that other miners had given up as worthless. One story told of a Chinese man who bought a miner's shack for $25, and then collected $300 worth of gold dust that the previous inhabitants had spilled on the floor.

But many American miners resented this success. They used threats and intimidation to force Chinese miners to take up other kinds of work. Some Chinese became merchants. Others took on jobs as cooks or launderers in mining camps.

Starting in 1864, many Chinese laborers began working to help complete the transcontinental railroad, connecting the east and west coasts of the United States. The work was very hard and dangerous. Especially in the mountains, the weather could be harsh, leading to frostbite and death by exposure. In addition, the Chinese were often assigned to blasting crews, whose job it was to clear rock out of the path of the railroad. Accidental explosions were responsible for the death and injury of hundreds

10 MILES OF TRACK, LAID IN ONE DAY. APRIL 28TH 1869

568

of Chinese workers. No group gave so much to the building of the railroad and received so little credit at the time.

There would be more disappointments from Golden Mountain.

New federal laws made it difficult for Chinese to become American citizens. More laws banned all Chinese immigration — laws that were not lifted until 1943. In addition, the hostility that the Chinese faced in the countryside caused most to settle in "Chinatowns" in large cities such as San Francisco and Los Angeles.

Despite the difficulties of life on Golden Mountain, most Chinese-Americans stayed, many relying on their own small businesses to make a living. People helped one another as they had in China. Family or clan associations rose up to help new arrivals find homes and jobs. Through theater, art, holiday celebration, and many other traditions, the Chinese heritage continued.

And the Chinese-Americans who stayed — along with the people of many other countries who followed the Gold Rush — made the state of California culturally all the richer.

Children in San Francisco welcome the Chinese new year.

# Check Your Progress

You have read about the experience of people who lived in the Great Plains and in California in the 1800s. Now return to those trails to read and compare two new selections and sharpen your test-taking skills.

Begin by taking a fresh look at Joseph Bruchac's letter and poem on pages 464–466. What new thoughts or feelings do you have about his words?

In the next two selections, you will meet young people living in the wilderness of the early and late 1800s. As you read, compare Mem's and Robert's adventures and think back to the adventures of other characters in the theme.

# Read and Compare

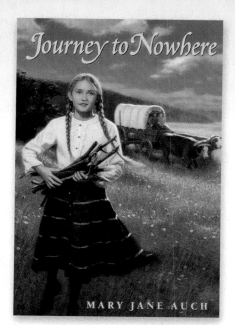

**Historical Fiction**

Join Mem and her family as they travel to the wilds of New York State in 1815.

Try these strategies:
Evaluate
Question

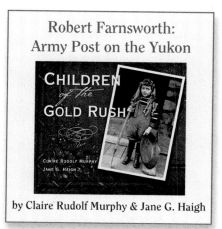

**Nonfiction**

Learn about a boy who lives in an army fort in the territory of Alaska in 1899.

Try these strategies:
Monitor and Clarify
Summarize

**Strategies in Action** *Be sure to use all your reading strategies while you read.*

# Journey to Nowhere

### by Mary Jane Auch, illustrated by Nick Spender

The year is 1815. Remembrance ("Mem") Nye, her parents, and her brother Joshua have left their farm in Connecticut for the wilds of western New York state. After a number of mishaps along the way, their oxen-drawn wagon is finally bringing them close to their destination.

By now, the weather was warm and dry enough so that we could camp every night, instead of staying at taverns. We took most of our meals outdoors, too, with Mama cooking bacon and cornmeal mush over a fire. Then one afternoon we walked up a steep hill, and when we reached the top, there was a sight that took my breath away. A long narrow lake filled the valley below us, with peach orchards on the slopes. And stretching full length across the lake was a bridge.

"Take a good look," Papa said, stopping the team. "That's Cayuga Bridge, the dividing line between the east and the west. It's the longest bridge in the whole United States — over a mile, I believe."

"Let's hurry, Papa," Joshua said. "I want to see the bridge up close."

"This hill is steep," Papa said. "I'll be bringing the team along slowly, but you children can run on ahead if you want. Mind you don't fall in the water, though."

Joshua was so excited, he ran all the way to the bridge. Twice he got going faster than his feet could carry him. He stumbled and rolled a ways, then jumped back up and began running again. I could barely keep up with him, even though my legs were longer than his. Finally, the two of us were gasping for breath at the edge of Cayuga Bridge. It stood on hundreds of wooden legs, like a huge centipede that had stretched across the water to sun itself on the lake.

Joshua's eyes sparkled. "Isn't it wondrous, Mem? Did you ever see such a thing? Can we start across?"

"We have to wait for Mama and Papa."

I leaned on the bridge railing and looked around, while Joshua darted from one side of the bridge to the other. "If you land in the water, I'll not fish you out, Joshua."

There was a cluster of buildings at the edge of the lake — an inn, a few taverns, and some houses. On the far end of the bridge, a stage-coach was just reaching the other shore. By the time Papa and Mama came along with the wagon, Joshua and I were rested and ready to start out.

As soon as the wagon wheels hit the bridge, the sound was like thunder. The oxen hesitated, their eyes rolling wildly from side to side, but Papa calmed them down quickly. Besides, the wagon rolled smoothly on the bridge, making the team's job easier. They soon got used to the hollow noise the wheels made.

I felt like a queen walking across that bridge, as if someone had laid down a wooden carpet so I could walk over the water. It was a powerful, grand sight looking to the south, where the hills dipped to the surface of the lake on either side.

When we were about in the middle, Joshua ran ahead of me and tugged at Papa's sleeve. "I don't see the line. Where is it?"

"What line is that, son?"

"The line between east and west. You said there was a line."

Papa looked from one end of the bridge to the other. "Well, we seem to be about halfway across, so I calculate the line would be right about here."

Joshua stopped. "Now I'm in the east." He took a giant step. "Now I'm in the west, right, Papa?"

"I'd say that's about right, son. From now on, you're a westerner."

In spite of the fact that Mama had thought we'd find nothing but wilderness in the west, we came upon two fine cities. The first was Geneva, on the shores of Seneca Lake. Part of the city was built up high on the hill, while another part curved around the lake's edge. We could see the tall white buildings of the upper city in the distance a long time before we entered the town.

The next city was named Canandaigua and it was on a lake, too. I had never seen so many fine lakes as we passed in this country — all with Indian names.

"Canandaigua is our last stop on the turnpike," Papa said. "From here we strike out to the north toward the great lake of Ontario."

We pulled into Canandaigua and found a bustle of activity. There were others there with all their goods in their wagons, coming west to settle like us. Some of the men and ladies walking through the town looked grand in their store-bought clothes. They weren't new settlers at all, but people who had been here for a good long time, I figured.

I supposed we looked a bit raggedy, with the mud stains and dust on our clothes. I hadn't seen a looking glass for days. Mama must have read my mind, because she smoothed her hair with her hand and licked her fingers to rub a smudge off Joshua's cheek. Then she ran her fingers through my curls. The sight of my short hair still brought a flicker of sadness to her eyes.

Papa slipped a coin into Mama's hand. "I'm going in to settle our papers at the land office, Aurelia. Why don't you take the children into the store to get a treat?"

We went into a general store that had just about everything a person could wish for. There were teas, coffee, sugar, and spices and all kinds of pots and dishes. There was one whole table with nothing but cloth. Mama ran her hand over a bolt of blue silk, checking the price tag.

"That would make a fine gown, Mama," I said.

She smiled. "I know, Mem, but we'll have to use what cloth I can make for this year, at least. Store-bought cloth is a luxury we can't afford right now."

I thought of all the work of making linen. We had to beat the flax to soften it and get it down to the fibers we could spin. And then we had to dye the skeins, set up the loom, and weave it into cloth. The wool was a little easier, but we still had to pick the burrs out of the wool and card it before we could spin, dye, and weave it. No wonder Mama ran her hand so wistfully over the pretty blue silk. How nice it must be to have the money to buy cloth already made, just waiting to be cut out and sewn into a new dress.

Joshua tugged at Mama's skirt. "I know what I want, Mama. There are big glass jars filled with candy at the front counter."

"You children can each pick out one treat," Mama said.

I chose a big, thick peppermint stick, and Joshua looked at everything before he decided he wanted the same. I tucked mine in my pocket, but Joshua went out to sit on the front steps and started right in on his. By the time Mama came outside, Joshua had sticky peppermint all over his face and hands.

We took our time looking in the windows of the shops, then rode the wagon to the shore of the lake to settle in for the night. Just before the sun dipped behind the hills, it turned Canandaigua Lake the color of raspberry jam. "There's a good omen for us," Papa said. "I don't think I've ever seen a prettier sight than that. This is the last leg of our journey. Tomorrow night, we'll be home."

# Robert Farnsworth:
## ARMY POST ON THE YUKON

BY CLAIRE RUDOLF MURPHY AND JANE G. HAIGH

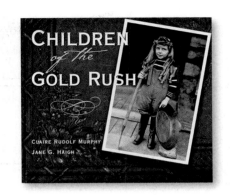

*On December 31, 1899,* an ice storm filled the air with millions of crystals. Northern lights danced in the sky overhead. It was seventy degrees below zero in Tanana, Alaska, but eleven-year-old Robert Farnsworth stood outside to admire the sight. He wore a full suit of fur clothing made by the local Native women to keep him warm. Later, he would write about that night: "The aurora borealis hung in the skies like washing on a line, waving around."

Robert had mushed his own dog team and made friends with an Athabascan chief named Chief Joseph. Sometimes he and his father went caribou hunting on snowshoes with the Native people. Once, they found a herd of more than a thousand caribou and shot thirty-six of them. There was enough meat to feed the whole town and the post throughout the winter.

Robert Farnsworth and friends on the steamer *Humbolt,* bound for Seattle, after leaving Alaska, August 1901

Robert's arrival in Alaska six months earlier already seemed like a distant memory. A scared ten-year-old, he had come north by ship with his stepmother and father. His natural mother had died when he was a baby. His father was the lieutenant commander of Army Company E, which had just been assigned to Alaska. Because of the Klondike gold rush, the North had become a wild place with lots of claim-jumping, robberies, and even murders. The United States Army hoped that a military post on the Yukon River would help maintain order.

When they arrived in St. Michael, Alaska, in July 1899, it was eleven o'clock at night. But the sun was still high in the sky, so Robert refused to go to bed. His parents tried to tell him about the midnight sun and how it did not set during the summer. But Robert would not listen. He stayed up all night just like the Inupiaq Eskimo children he met there who played at night and slept during the day.

Robert feeding his dogs on the Army post, Fort Egbert, at Eagle, Alaska

Soon the family and the soldiers traveled up to the village of Tanana where the Tanana River joins the Yukon. There the soldiers constructed Fort Gibbon. Robert was the only child at the fort. Because there was no school there, his mother taught him lessons.

After the long winter, the first boat to come upriver in May brought fresh fruit and mail. Sadly, Robert learned that his grandfather had died in January. But fortunately, another family, including several children, arrived on the boat. Robert threw his arms around the oldest boy, who instantly gave him a black eye. The family had brought along the first "funny paper" he had ever seen. Robert recovered his pride by reading the "Katzen-jammer Kids" over and over, laughing and crying at their antics.

Orders also arrived from Washington. The Farnsworths and Company E were transferred to Fort Egbert at Eagle, Alaska, 800 miles up the Yukon River. Eagle was a small settlement, not far from the Canadian border and only 120 miles from the boomtown of Dawson. But Robert never managed to visit Dawson because his mother considered it too wild for a young boy.

Eagle, Alaska, in 1900

With its barracks for 102 enlisted men, a gymnasium, baseball fields, a library of 1,200 books, and a large stable for horses and mules, Fort Egbert was much larger than Fort Gibbon. Robert enjoyed his new home and many new activities.

One of his father's responsibilities was to supervise the construction of a telegraph line to connect Eagle with the rest of the world. Then there would be no more waiting for news from outside. In addition, Robert and some of the townspeople helped his father collect specimens of birds and bears for the Smithsonian Institution in Washington, D.C. Years later, Robert would proudly see them on display there.

When ice breakup came in June, Farnsworth was reassigned to Fort Vancouver, Washington. The family sadly left Fort Egbert. Robert had grown out of all his clothing, so his mother cut him a pair of pants out of an old yellow army blanket. He also wore a pair of his mother's old shoes with the heels cut off and an old, shabby coat. When the family reached Seattle, they were such an awful sight that the taxicab driver refused to take them unless they paid in advance.

Robert never again lived in Alaska, but his father and mother returned for another tour of duty in 1910. After his father died, Robert donated his father's Alaskan papers and photographs to the University of Alaska Fairbanks' archives. Later he wrote a manuscript about his adventures in the North country and the interesting people he had met.

Robert Farnsworth and his mother pose with the troops outside a cabin at Fort Gibbon, the first army post on the Yukon River, near the present village of Tanana.

# Think and Compare

1. If Mem Nye visited Robert Farnsworth, how do you think she would compare his setting with hers?

2. Suppose Robert had a conversation with Slow. How do you think their thoughts about Native Americans and white settlers sharing territory might be different or alike?

3. Compare the experiences of Grace and Mem. With whom would you rather trade places? Why?

4. Both Slow and Bob Lemmons have a close relationship with horses. What might they have said to each other about mustangs?

5. Compare the journey Rosa's family takes with the journey Mem and her family take. How are the journeys alike and different?

**Strategies in Action** Think about the reading strategies you used during this theme. How did they help you?

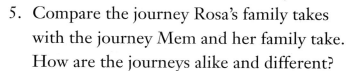

## Persuading

# Write an Advertisement

Write a newspaper advertisement the families of Mem, Robert, Grace, or Rosa might have read persuading them to travel to their new home.

### Tips

- Think about why the family is moving to this new home.
- List features that might be appealing to the family.
- Write the most appealing feature first.

# Writing an Answer to a Question

Some test items ask you to write an answer to a question about something you have read. Usually you can answer the question in a few sentences. Here is a sample test question about *Journey to Nowhere.*

**Write your answer to this question.**

1. In *Journey to Nowhere*, what is the importance of Mem and her family crossing the Cayuga Bridge?

## ① Understand the question.

Find the key words in the question. Use them to understand what you need to do.

## ② Get ready to write.

Skim the selection, using the key words. List the details that can help you answer the question.

Here is a sample list.

### Selection Details

The bridge is the dividing line between east and west.

The bridge is the longest in the United States.

After they're halfway across, Mem and her family feel like westerners.

## 3 Write your answer.

Use details from your list. Write a clear and complete answer.

**Here is a good answer to the test question.**

> When Mem's family goes over the Cayuga Bridge, it is important that they are crossing the line that divides the east from the west. They are changing the way they see themselves. Now Mem and her family think of themselves as westerners.

AUTOBIOGRAPHY

# Autobiography

An **autobiography** is the story of a person's life as told by that person. The writer shares **memories** from childhood to the present day, often adding **insights** about the events. People, animals, places, and experiences that were important to the writer — all might appear in an autobiography.

## CONTENTS

573

In this selection from her autobiography, poet and author Eloise Greenfield describes a place that has played an important part in her life, the neighborhood where she grew up.

# Langston Terrace
## by Eloise Greenfield

I fell in love with Langston Terrace the very first time I saw it. Our family had been living in two rooms of a three-story house when Mama and Daddy saw the newspaper article telling of the plans to build it. It was going to be a low-rent housing project in northeast Washington, and it would be named in honor of John Mercer Langston, the famous black lawyer, educator, and congressman.

So many people needed housing and wanted to live there, many more than there would be room for. They were all filling out applications, hoping to be one of the 274 families chosen. My parents filled out one, too.

I didn't want to move. I knew our house was crowded — there were eleven of us, six adults and five children — but I didn't want to leave my friends, and I didn't want to go to a strange place and be the new person in a neighborhood and a school where most of the other children already knew each other. I was eight years old, and I had been to three schools. We had moved five times since we'd been in Washington, each time trying to get more space and a better place to live. But rent was high so we'd always lived in a house with relatives and friends, and shared the rent.

One of the people in our big household was Lillie, Daddy's cousin and Mama's best friend. She and her husband also applied for a place in the new project, and during the months that it was being built, Lillie and Mama would sometimes walk fifteen blocks just to stand and watch the workmen digging holes and laying bricks. They'd just stand there watching and wishing. And at home, that was all they could talk about. "When we get our new place . . ." "If we get our new place . . ."

Lillie got her good news first. I can still see her and Mama standing at the bottom of the hall steps, hugging and laughing and crying, happy for Lillie, then sitting on the steps, worrying and wishing again for Mama.

Eloise with her brother and father at Langston Terrace in 1938.

Finally, one evening, a woman came to the house with our good news, and Mama and Daddy went over and picked out the house they wanted. We moved on my ninth birthday. Wilbur, Gerald, and I went to school that morning from one house, and when Daddy came to pick us up, he took us home to another one. All the furniture had been moved while we were in school.

Eloise's sisters Vera (left) and Vedie Little, at Langston Terrace in 1949.

Langston Terrace was a lovely birthday present. It was built on a hill, a group of tan brick houses and apartments with a playground as its center. The red mud surrounding the concrete walks had not yet been covered with black soil and grass seed, and the holes that would soon be homes for young trees were filled with rainwater. But it still looked beautiful to me.

We had a whole house all to ourselves. Upstairs and downstairs. Two bedrooms, and the living room would be my bedroom at night. Best of all, I wasn't the only new person. Everybody was new to this new little community, and by the time school opened in the fall, we had gotten used to each other and had made friends with other children in the neighborhood, too.

I guess most of the parents thought of the new place as an in-between place. They were glad to be there, but their dream was to save enough money to pay for a house that would be their own. Saving was hard, though, and slow, because each time somebody in a family got a raise on the job, it had to be reported to the manager of the project so that the rent could be raised, too. Most people stayed years longer than they had planned to, but they didn't let that stop them from enjoying life.

They formed a resident council to look into any neighborhood problems that might come up. They started a choral group and presented music and poetry programs on Sunday evenings in the social room or on the play-ground. On weekends, they played horseshoes and softball and other games. They had a reading club that met once a week at the Langston branch of the public library, after it opened in the basement of one of the apartment buildings.

The library was very close to my house. I could leave by my back door and be there in two minutes. The play-ground was right in front of my house, and after my sister Vedie was born and we moved a few doors down to a three-bedroom house, I could just look out of my bedroom window to see if any of my friends were out playing.

There were so many games to play and things to do. We played hide-and-seek at the lamppost, paddle tennis and shuffleboard, dodge ball and jacks. We danced in fireplug showers, jumped rope to rhymes, played "Bouncy, Bouncy, Bally," swinging one leg over a bouncing ball, played baseball on a nearby field, had parties in the social room and bus trips to the beach. In the playroom, we played Ping-Pong and pool, learned to sew and embroider and crochet.

For us, Langston Terrace wasn't an in-between place. It was a growing-up place, a good growing-up place. Neighbors who cared, family and friends, and a lot of fun. Life was good. Not perfect, but good. We knew about problems, heard about them, saw them, lived through some hard ones ourselves, but our community wrapped itself around us, put itself between us and the hard knocks, to cushion the blows.

Eloise with her future husband, Bobby Greenfield, in 1948.

It's been many years since I moved away, but every once in a long while I go back, just to look at things and remember. The large stone animals that decorated the playground are still there. A walrus, a hippo, a frog, and two horses. They've started to crack now, but I remember when they first came to live with us. They were friends, to climb on or to lean against, or to gather around in the evening. You could sit on the frog's head and look way out over the city at the tall trees and rooftops.

Nowadays, whenever I run into old friends, mostly at a funeral, or maybe a wedding, after we've talked about how we've been and what we've been doing, and how old our children are, we always end up talking about our childtime in our old neighborhood. And somebody will say, "One of these days we ought to have a Langston reunion." That's what we always called it, just "Langston," without the "Terrace." I guess because it sounded more homey. And that's what Langston was. It was home.

In this brief autobiography, Jane Goodall, one of the world's foremost experts on chimpanzees, tells how her childhood interest in animals led her to doing research in Africa.

# Jane Goodall

I have been interested in animals since before I can remember. From the time I was very small, I was fascinated with creepy, crawling, furry, flying creatures. When I was quite young, my mother found me in my room with a handful of worms in my bed, watching as they went around and around. She didn't say, "Yuk!" and threw them out the window. She said, "Jane, if you leave them in here, they'll die. They need the air." And so I let them go free.

In fact, my mother is the most important reason for my doing what I've done and being who I've been. When I was four years old, I stayed on a farm, where I helped collect hens' eggs. I became puzzled and asked those around me, "Where is the hole big enough for the eggs to come out?" When no one answered to my satisfaction, I hid in a small, stuffy henhouse for four hours to find out. While I watched and waited, my mother looked frantically for me in the house and garden. She even called the police to help locate me. But when my mother saw me rushing toward the house in excitement, she didn't scold me for disappearing for so long. She sat down and listened to me tell the wonderful story of how a hen lays eggs.

Two orphaned chimpanzees (above) make friends in the Congo's Tchimpounga Sanctuary.

**Goodall's study of chimpanzees, which began in 1960, is now in its fifth decade.**

Even my first books were about animals. I read *The Story of Dr. Doolittle, The Jungle Book*, and *Tarzan*. Looking back, I see that the original Tarzan was terribly hard on animals. But I didn't realize it then. Books are a great source of inspiration. They lure your mind to be imaginative. By the time I was eight or nine, I was dreaming of going to Africa. And my mother, a very special person, would say, "Jane, if you really want something and if you work hard, take advantage of opportunities, and never give up, you will somehow find a way."

In those days you had to learn a foreign language to get a schol-arship to a university. But I couldn't do it — I couldn't speak French, couldn't speak German, couldn't speak Latin. So Mum said, "Why not take a secretarial course, then you can get a job anywhere in the world." So that's what I did.

But that didn't lead me directly to Africa. After I finished my sec-retarial class I began working for a documentary film company — a wonderful job, but with very low pay. When a school friend invited me to visit her family in Kenya, I readily accepted. I quit my job with the film company to begin work as a waitress in order to save the money. Finally, at age 23, with only enough money for boat fare to Africa (that was the cheapest way to travel in those days), I went off by myself to an unknown continent.

After two months in Africa I met the man who made all my dreams come true. Louis Leakey was an anthropologist and paleontologist who was interested in animals and early man. I made an appointment to meet him. Because I had studied animals throughout my childhood, I was able to answer many of his questions about the natural world, and he gave me a job as his assistant. I traveled with Louis and his wife, Mary, on one of their fossil-hunting expeditions to Olduvai Gorge. After some time, Louis decided I was the person he had been looking for to study the chimpanzees

living near the shore of Lake Tanganyika, in what is now called Tanzania. And when the British authorities refused to let a young, untrained girl venture into the wilds of Africa on her own, who should volunteer to accompany me for the first three months but my own amazing mother.

**Louis Leakey (1903-1972)**

And so my work began. After several years in Africa I returned to England to work for my Ph.D. in ethology from Cambridge University, and then I returned to the paradise of Gombe Stream, Tanzania, to continue my research.

**Goodall extends a hand to a young chimpanzee named Flint.**

Before becoming a children's author and illustrator, Bill Peet worked as an animator at Walt Disney Studios. In this excerpt, Peet has just arrived in Los Angeles. His fiancée, Margaret, is back in Indiana. Peet's hope for a job rests on a letter from Disney inviting him to participate in a tryout.

# BILL PEET: AN AUTOBIOGRAPHY

The Disney Studios were closed in by a high cement wall, and the only view was through the wrought-iron front gate. What I could see of the complex looked most inviting. There was a flagstone walk across a grass courtyard to an archway in front of what appeared to be the main building — a quaint, cozy look appropriate for a company dealing with fun and fantasy.

Just a block from the studios I ran across a rooming house, a big barn of a place with the second floor and the attic sectioned off into narrow compartments with a small cot in each one. The landlady was a little mouse of a woman who explained apologetically that the two dollars a week rent need not be paid until I could afford it.

582

Her tenants were mostly Disney beginners or else newcomers like me who had no guarantee of a job. That dear little lady, Mrs. Beson, was well aware of our situation, and no
doubt she had seen many come and go who could never pay
the rent.

The next morning at the appointed time of nine o'clock I
was at the Disney front gate. It was the wrong place. I was
told to check in at a one-story stucco building across the
street called the Disney Annex. The tryout group had already
lined up at the front door to sign in, and I was the last of the
fifteen to arrive.

Most of them were fresh out of art school as I was, and
they came from all parts of the country in response to the
special delivery letter, not knowing what to expect.

The boss of the Annex, George Drake, was a tall, scrawny
fellow with a shock of rusty hair and extremely large ears.

He started things off with a stern lecture warning us that the one-month tryout would be no bed of roses. And more than once he reminded us how fortunate we were to get an opportunity to work for Disney. "There are plenty of people waiting out on the street to get a job here" was his last warning.

After the lecture we were given model sheets, guides to drawing Mickey, Donald, and Goofy so we could practice the roundish Disney drawing style. During that one-month period Drake kept us on edge by continually pacing the hall and popping in on us at odd moments. Every few days one or two of the group were let go, and as it came down to the last week we wondered if Drake would fire all of us. I was warned many times about leaving the buttons off of Mickey's pants, but even so I was one of the three survivors at the end of the month.

We were put to work as in-betweeners, with the tedious, painstaking job of adding hundreds of drawings in between hundreds of other drawings to move Donald or Mickey from here to there.

It was a matter of enduring the job with the hope of making it to the promised land across the street where big exciting things were going on.  They were making *Snow White and the Seven Dwarfs,* the very first feature-length animated film.

I wrote to Margaret immediately to let her know I made it through the tryouts and was on the job.  And even though it was assembly-line work there would be all kinds of opportunities if *Snow White* was a success.

I didn't mention all the dire predictions coming from Hollywood bigwigs and movie columnists.  They called *Snow White* Disney's Folly.  The picture would be a box-office flop! People would never sit through a full-length cartoon feature! Disney was getting too big for his britches!  And so on.

Those ominous predictions made me wonder if I had arrived just in time to board the Disney *Titanic*. And I'm sure those voices of doom haunted the people working with a frenzy to complete *Snow White* in time for the grand premiére before Christmas. I even got in on the last-minute effort, working nights tracing dwarves on something called a rotoscope machine.

Margaret came out on the train the last week of November and we were married on the thirtieth, then moved into a dingy little apartment about a half-hour walk from the studio. A few weeks later, we attended the gala première of *Snow White*. All Disney employees and their wives or husbands were invited, along with hundreds of special guests and newspeople. As we moved through the mob toward the marquee of the Carthay Circle Theater, I caught my first glimpse of Walt Disney. He was addressing the crowd from a podium, but his voice was lost in all the hubbub.

Very few people who worked on the film had seen it all in one piece, so it was a new experience for most of the audience. Of course the overwhelming success of *Snow White* is motion picture history, and as I write about it now, it is out in the theaters for the seventh time, having celebrated its fiftieth anniversary in 1987.

I believe everyone in that first *Snow White* audience could have predicted the enormous success of the film. They were carried away by the picture from the very beginning, and as it went along everyone was bubbling over with enthusiasm and frequently bursting into spontaneous applause. At the end, the audience exploded into a thunderous ovation — and the voices of doom were silenced for good.

In this selection, athlete Alex Rodriguez tells about an important period in his career, his first two years in professional baseball with the Seattle Mariners.

# Hit a Grand Slam!

*by* Alex Rodriguez

My first spring training opened my eyes to how hard pro athletes work. The posted time for practice was ten o'clock in the morning. Every day for a month I showed up at 9:30, figuring being early would show my dedication. One day I decided to arrive at 7:00 A.M. I walked in and saw a few guys already in the clubhouse.

I turned the corner into the weight room and saw second baseman Joey Cora pumping iron. I then went to the batting cage and found two-time batting champion Edgar Martinez hitting off a batting tee into a net.

"Edgar, what are you doing here so early?"

"I have to hit. I have to work!"

Most guys would go home at about two o'clock in the afternoon. One day I forgot my pager. I returned to the clubhouse and found Edgar in the batting cage at 6:00 P.M. Those veterans showed me that success in anything begins with dedication and hard work. I met NBA coach Pat Riley recently, and he told me a key to success is enjoying your sweat. That means you have to find joy in practice and working out to reach your highest athletic potential.

I started my first season at the bottom of the Mariners' minor leagues with Wisconsin's Class A Appleton Foxes. Players tell horror stories about the minor leagues, but playing in Appleton gave me cherished memories.

The town embraced me with a welcoming hug.

Within two months, I moved up to Class AA at Jacksonville. Three weeks later, I got the call to join the big-league team, that week playing in Boston.

I stayed up late calling family, friends, and old coaches — "I'm going to the show!"

At 18, I became the youngest Major League player in a decade. The lights, reporters, and crowds were unbelievable.

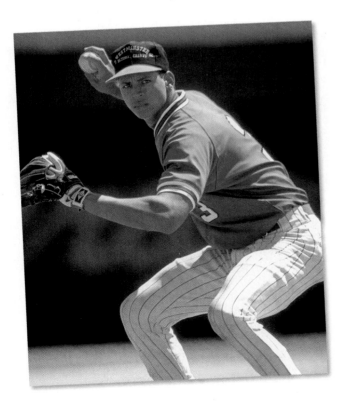

I remember preparing for my first at-bat in the on-deck circle. Ken Griffey, Jr. walked by and said: "It's showtime."

My body felt jittery, and my knees buckled. I could barely stand. I went hitless in three tries that first night, but I had a solid fielding night.

The next night I broke out with two hits. Still, I was nervous for days. I didn't want to make a mistake. I arrived early at the ballpark, hoping not to be noticed.

After 26 days, the Mariners sent me down to their Class AAA team in Calgary, Canada. That gave me the rare glimpse of playing in all four pro levels in one season.

I started the 1995 season with the Tacoma Rainiers, the M's new Class AAA affiliate. The 31-mile trip between Tacoma and Seattle became all too familiar. I was called up to Seattle on May 6th and stayed 21 days, enduring the rookie razzing.

The Mariners have a special rookie tradition for the team's first series in Kansas City. When I got out of the shower after the last game, all my clothes were gone. Instead, I had to sign 30 autographs while wearing a silver dress and balancing in high-heeled shoes. If that wasn't bad enough, I had to wear them on the flight home and listen to all the teasing jokes. I laughed along with them.

Much of that season was no laughing matter to me. I became a human yo-yo going between Tacoma and Seattle. Three times the M's sent me back to Tacoma. Each demotion chipped away at me. The last time, in mid-August, I sat at my Seattle locker with my head down, in tears. I felt drained, defeated.

"Come on, relax, you're going to get through this," teammates said.

Hurt and angry, I seriously thought about driving back to Miami. Instead, I called Mom.

"Forget them. I hate them all. I don't want to be here. I'm coming home," I said.

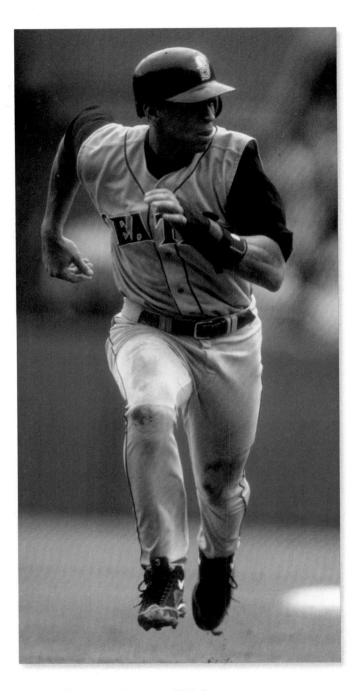

"No you're not!" Mom answered. "You don't have a house here if you come home. You have to stay out there. You are GOING TO MAKE IT!"

Wanting to quit during tough times is natural. There are times you should quit and try something else. But quitting out of frustration is rarely the right time. I'm so thankful Mom talked me out of it. I know now the adversity made me stronger.

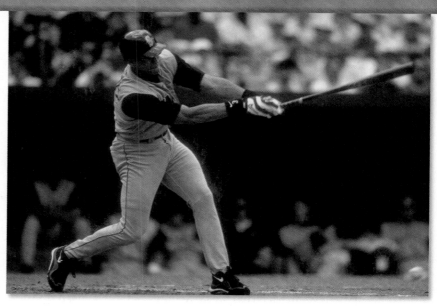

If I had quit, I would have missed the Mariners' remarkable "Refuse To Lose" playoff run. In August, Seattle trailed California by 13 games. A magical string of victories closed the gap as I rejoined the team August 31st.

The playoff race excited me as much as the guys playing.

I saw it as a learning experience. I prepared myself each day to play. I paid attention to every detail, as if my life depended on it.

The season ended with us tied with California. We won the one-game playoff in dramatic fashion for the M's first-ever play-off spot.

I hit three times in the hard-fought playoff series against New York. What a thrill! What I'll remember most, though, is being on-deck in the roaring Kingdome when Edgar drove home Junior in the 11th inning to beat New York 6-5 in the deciding division play-off game. That's the best feeling I've had in baseball. There's nothing like winning. The same could be said for losing.

Cleveland dashed our World Series visions 4–2 in the American League Championship Series.

With the season-ending loss at the Kingdome, Seattle fans gave us a thunderous moving ovation after the game to show their thanks for the season's incredible ride.

# *Think About the* AUTOBIOGRAPHIES

1. Eloise Greenfield writes about a place, while Jane Goodall covers many events. Compare these two ways of telling about a life. Do you think one is better than another? Explain.

2. What do Jane Goodall, Bill Peet, and Alex Rodriguez want you to think is most important about their work? Why?

3. Think about Eloise Greenfield's neighborhood of Langston Terrace. What place would you write about in your life?

4. What are some of the details that helped you "see" the places or events the writers tell about?

5. How would you describe what makes a good autobiography?

**Internet**

## Play a Trivia Game

Show what you learned about the people who told about their lives in the four autobiographies. Play an online trivia game at Education Place.

**www.eduplace.com/kids**

**Narrating**

# Write a Chapter of Your Autobiography

You've read a few examples of autobiography. Now write a chapter from your own autobiography. Focus on a time or event in your life that has been important to you. Choose something that you think other people would be interested in reading about.

> **Tips**
>
> - Before beginning, think about your topic. Write down details that you think would be interesting.
>
> - Think about how you will begin and end your chapter.
>
> - Provide background. People and places that are familiar to you may not be to your readers.

# Animal Encounters

The great hurrah about wild animals is that they exist at all, and the greater hurrah is the actual moment of seeing them.

— *Annie Dillard*
*from* Pilgrim at Tinker Creek

# Animal Encounters

## with George Ancona

Dear Reader,

This theme shows how people get close to, and sometimes are able to help, wild animals.

As a photographer I have learned to be patient, especially when taking pictures of animals in the wild. Waiting is a very useful experience. It's never a waste of time.

At first I listen to the people who know about the animals I'm interested in and who teach me by showing me their world. These can be scientists who study animals or a farmer who has learned about the creatures in the forest surrounding his farm. Often children teach me about the animals they are familiar with.

Then I begin to look for what I will photograph. But animals don't wait for you. You can't tell them to stop, turn around, and smile. So I wait.

While I wait I listen to the sounds around me, the birds of the forest, the rain pattering on the leaves, the buzzing of the insects, or the crow of a rooster in the distance. I feel the ground I'm sitting on, the heat of the tropics, and the sweat running into my eyes. I become aware of the smells that the breezes carry past me. All these sensations will help me to write the story that will accompany the photographs I'm there to take.

**great egret**

**golden lion tamarin**

**red panda**

**common marmoset**

Sometimes days will pass and no animals appear. One never knows when something will happen. If what I am looking for doesn't appear, often the unexpected will astonish me.

Then, holding my breath, I begin to take pictures and hope that my camera is working. When that moment ends I am happy.

I think, *I got it, I hope,* since I won't know until the film is developed. Then I have the pictures for my book.

You will see moments like that in this theme, when people and animals discover each other. And as a reader, you will also take part in that discovery.

Yours truly,

George Ancona

# Your Animal Encounters

Take a minute to remember encounters you have had with animals. Think about how your experiences were like or different from those of George Ancona.

Each of the selections in this theme, shown below, gives its own meaning to the title *Animal Encounters*. As you read, think about how the animals and the people in each selection were changed by the encounter.

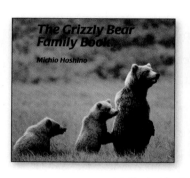

*The Grizzly Bear Family Book*
Michio Hoshino

MY SIDE OF THE MOUNTAIN
Jean Craighead George

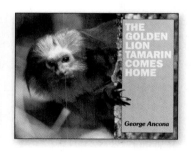

THE GOLDEN LION TAMARIN COMES HOME
George Ancona

토끼의 심판
**The Rabbit's Judgment**
Suzanne Crowder Han · Illustrated by Yumi Heo

*Interrupted Journey*
Saving Endangered Sea Turtles
Kathryn Lasky · photographs by Christopher G. Knight

**Internet**

To learn about the authors in this theme, visit Education Place. **www.eduplace.com/kids**

*The Grizzly Bear
Family Book*
Michio Hoshino

**The Grizzly Bear
Family Book**

Genre  **Nonfiction**

## Key Vocabulary

abundant
caribou
territory
tundra
wariness
wilderness

**Vocabulary Reader**

Animals of
ALASKA

*e* **Glossary**

# Wild Alaska

The state of Alaska, the setting of *The Grizzly Bear Family Book*, includes huge areas of **wilderness**. Two great mountain ranges span the state.

The Brooks Range, in the north, lies above the Arctic Circle. The Alaska Range, in the south, arcs up to include Mt. McKinley, also called Denali, the highest mountain in North America, located in Denali National Park. At over 7,300 square miles, the park is larger than Connecticut and Rhode Island combined.

The land in the park is a rich environment of mountains, glaciers, and grassy, treeless Arctic **tundra**, home to **abundant** wildlife. Over thirty species of mammals live there, ranging in size from tiny shrews and voles to the grizzly bears featured in the selection. Other large animals in the park include Dall sheep, moose, and **caribou**, also known as reindeer.

Human beings who visit the wild habitats of Alaska need to remember that they are entering the **territory** of wild animals. The creatures who make their homes there are likely to view humans with **wariness**. In return, the humans should view the wild inhabitants with respect.

**Caribou**

**Alaska**

Brooks Range

Denali National
Park

Alaska ★ Range

Dall Sheep

Grizzly Bears

601

# The Grizzly Bear Family Book

Michio Hoshino

## Strategy Focus

The author of this selection spent a year photographing grizzly bears. As you read, **evaluate** how his personal involvement enhances the story he tells.

Imagine meeting a grizzly bear in the wild. Not at the zoo, not in a book, but out in the open — a chance encounter with the real thing. Just you and the bear, face to face.

It happened to me once, when I was camping near Mount McKinley in Alaska. For more than half of each year, I hike through the mountains and plains of Alaska, the Great Land, with my tent on my back, taking pictures of the land which has attracted me since my teens.

Around four o'clock one morning I was awakened by something brushing against my tent. Wondering what it was, I rubbed my eyes and opened the tent flap. There, right in front of me, was a bear's face. I was startled, but the bear must have been even more surprised. It took one look at me and clumped hastily away.

I had never before been so close to a bear. And I knew that I wanted to use my camera to record one year in the lives of the Alaskan grizzlies.

In midwinter the temperature here may fall to fifty degrees below zero. During this harsh time, a grizzly bear will sleep in a snug underground den, the entrance covered by a blanket of snow.

While the mother bear sleeps, her tiny cubs are born. They nurse and snuggle next to her until longer days and warmer temperatures signal the arrival of spring.

One day in April, as I hiked through the mountains called the Alaska Range, I noticed fresh bear tracks on the snowy slope. Following them with my binoculars, I spotted a mother bear and her cub walking through the snow.

The cold, biting wind was already giving way to spring breezes. When the bears come out of their dens, it's a sure sign that the long winter is over.

As the snow melts and shrinks into patches of crusty ice, wildflowers push their faces towards the sky. In the far north, the flowers are very small. But each blossom possesses tremendous strength. I am moved when I come upon these tiny shapes, living their lives to the fullest extent.

In early spring, grizzly bears also enjoy life to its fullest. Once I watched as a mother and her cub played tag on a slope across from me. The mother chased her cub across the grassy hillside. When she caught the youngster, she took it in her arms and hugged it to her gently, and they began to roll down the slope together. They seemed to be having such a wonderful time, I couldn't help but burst out laughing.

A nursing bear will often lie on her back and offer milk to her cub. If she has two, she will cradle one in each arm. I'm not sure that nursing tires her out, but afterwards the mother often spread-eagles on the ground, sound asleep.

People have such fearful images of bears. But is the affection and care of a human mother for her children so different from the love and tenderness the mother bear shows her cubs?

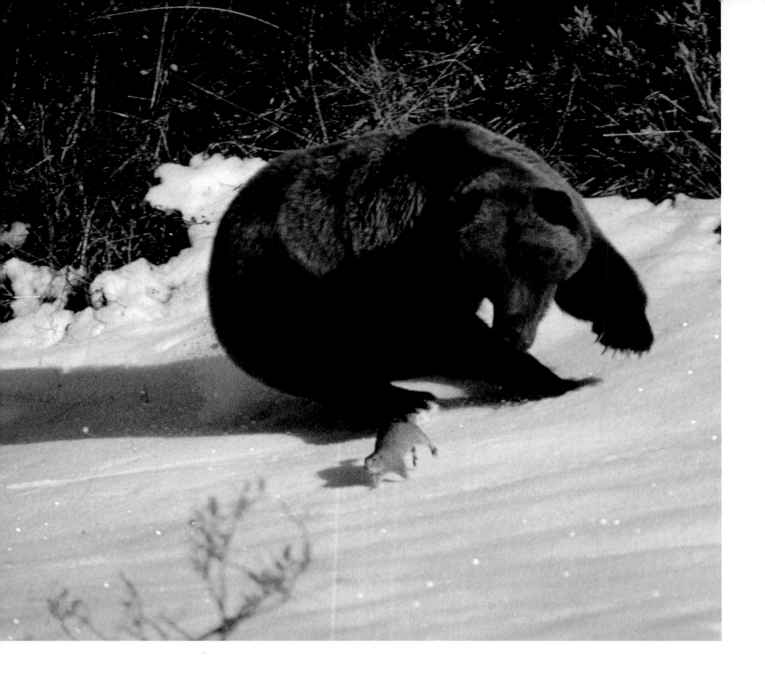

Grizzlies just emerging from their winter dens are as thin as they will be all year.  They have not eaten for months, and in the snow-covered landscape, their first meal may be the carcass of a moose or caribou that did not survive the winter.  Near the sea, bears may find a beached whale, or a dead sea lion or walrus.

After the snow melts and the earth turns green, bears begin to eat roots and grasses.  Sedges — grasses that grow in wetlands — are particularly important, because they grow rapidly in the early spring and are rich in protein.

Arctic ground squirrels are a popular food for bears, but it takes real work to catch one. An 850-pound bear chasing a 2-pound squirrel is a truly comical sight. When the squirrel dives into its hole, the bear begins digging furiously with its front paws. But there may be many holes, all connected underground. Sometimes the squirrel

will pop out of a hole behind the bear and watch it dig away.

Of course, many squirrels do get caught and eaten by bears. Scientists at Denali National Park in Alaska found that each grizzly bear eats about 400 ground squirrels a year.

Caribou, wolves, Dall sheep, moose, and many other animals give birth in the spring. They must keep constant watch over their newborns to protect them from danger.

One June afternoon I was sitting on a mountain slope looking down at a moose with her two young calves. For some reason the moose was uneasy, her ears pulled far back to the sides. A bear suddenly appeared from the bushes and rushed towards the calves.

The moose turned to confront the powerful bear. The bear stopped and the two faced off, staring at each other intently. A moment later the moose charged. The startled bear took off, with the moose close behind.

The moose had risked her life to protect her calves. And the bear retreated rather than risk being injured by the slashing hooves of the determined cow.

The bear will try again, of course, and next time it may be successful. But I have come to understand that when a bear catches a moose calf, it is not a sad event. The bear may have cubs of her own who will share in the meal. There will be new moose calves and new bear cubs next year, and life in the wilderness will go on. In nature, all living things, including humans, depend on other lives for their existence.

As summer nears, the daylight hours lengthen quickly until the nights are completely gone.

Imagine having no night at all.  The sun moves around the sky in a big circle, always staying just above the horizon.  Without a watch, it's hard to know when one day ends and the next begins.  You may forget what day of the week it is, and even what month.  And all the while, the sun's energy feeds the trees, grasses, and shrubs of the Alaskan wilderness.

In June salmon swim upstream in Alaska's rivers and streams, and bears are drawn to choice fishing spots.  Grizzlies avoid contact with other bears during most of the year, but fishing season brings them shoulder to shoulder along the streams.  With food temporarily abundant, they seem to tolerate one another more, but first a dominance order — an understanding of who bosses whom — must be established.

The stronger, more aggressive bears, usually males, command the best places.  When a new bear joins a group, a brief struggle for dominance is often the result.  Bears avoid fighting if at all possible, but two bears of nearly equal strength may wage a fierce battle.  When two bears who have already fought meet again, the loser will automatically give up its place to the victor, avoiding another fight.

Bears use body language to express dominance or subservience within the temporary community at the river. By observing bears as they fish, I have learned some useful clues about the safest way to behave around bears in the wild.

One time I watched a mother bear with one cub, and another mother with two cubs, approach a river. While the mothers fished for salmon in the river, the cubs waited on the riverbank. Curiosity drew all three cubs together. Suddenly the mother of the two cubs rushed up the bank. Would she kill the stranger? But the mother bear simply sniffed the cub that was not her own. Then the mother of the single cub realized what was happening, and charged out of the water to defend her young. Again it seemed as if there might be trouble. The cubs looked on nervously, staying near their mothers. In the end, the two families parted peacefully. Mother bears are usually quite tolerant of the cubs of others, even to the point of adopting strays and orphans.

I was surprised the first time I saw a bear catch a salmon, hold it briefly as if examining it, and then release it in the river. When salmon are rare, grizzlies will hungrily devour every one they catch. But at the height of the salmon season, a bear may capture ten salmon an hour and can afford to be selective. Sometimes bears just eat the head and eggs, discarding the rest. The uneaten portion of the fish doesn't go to waste, however, because gulls swarm nearby, ready to grab the leftovers.

When a bear catches a salmon with its paws and mouth, it can probably smell the difference between a male fish and a female fish. The bear I saw catching and releasing salmon may have been selecting only the female fish with their delicious eggs.

First-year cubs wait on the riverbank for their mothers to bring freshly caught salmon. By their second year, cubs wade in to fish for themselves. Although rarely successful at first, they learn by watching and imitating their mothers.

With the end of the salmon run, the bears' temporary society breaks up, each bear returning to its own mountain territory, where autumn food sources are now maturing.

The bugling of sandhill cranes sweeping south in great ragged Vs announces autumn across Alaska. The animals of the Arctic grow lovely, thick winter coats. Moose and caribou antlers are now very large. Aspen and birch forests turn golden, and the tundra blazes red.

Blueberry, cranberry, and crowberry bushes blanket the ground, offering a rich harvest for bears.

"Don't bump heads with a bear when you go blueberry picking!" This frequently heard advice is no joke in Alaska. Both humans and bears become so engrossed in berry picking that they scarcely take a moment to lift their heads and look around. While you probably won't actually bump heads with a bear, it's wise to check your surroundings now and then.

Bears seem to like soapberries best of all. Wondering how they taste, I picked a ripe red one and popped it in my mouth. It didn't taste very good to me, but then I don't like fish heads, either.

It's wonderful to observe a huge bear holding a thin soapberry branch, gently stripping it of the delicate fruit.

As the days shorten, bears must put on a large store of fat to take them through winter. Berries are high in sugar, and the autumn feast can be critical to a bear's survival. With their shiny coats rippling as they move across the tundra, grizzlies consume an enormous amount of berries.

How many berries would you guess a grizzly can eat in one day? The bears in Denali National Park eat berries for twenty hours a day in late summer, hardly stopping to sleep. One bear may consume 200,000 berries in a single day! Bear droppings at this time of year consist mainly of partially digested berries. From the seeds in these droppings new bushes will grow to feed a new generation of bears.

One autumn day as I was hiking through the Brooks Range near the Arctic Circle, I suddenly noticed two bears running towards me from a riverbank. Were they coming at me on purpose, or did they not realize I was there? They appeared to be siblings, just old enough to leave their mother's care, but already powerful. Closer and closer they came, loping gracefully. My heart beat like a drum. When they were about twenty yards away, I raised my arms and shouted, "*Stop!*"

The two bears skidded to a halt as if in complete surprise. They stood up on their hind legs, wagging their heads from side to side, sniffing the air. I was so excited, I thought my heart would burst.

Then, as if they had finally become aware of my existence, they turned and raced off in the direction they'd come from. It had been a pretty frightening experience for me, but it must have been equally startling for the bears.

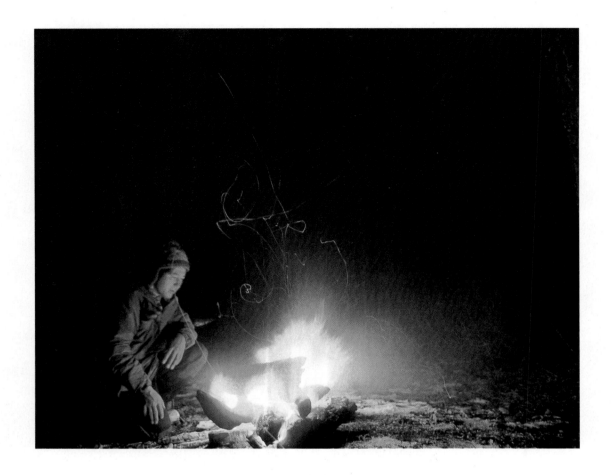

That night I couldn't fall asleep.  The two grizzlies might be close by.  Very few bears are interested in pursuing people, but still I felt somewhat uneasy.  Unable to sleep, I thought about bears, about people, and about Alaska.

If there wasn't a single bear in all of Alaska, I could hike through the mountains with complete peace of mind.  I could camp without worry.  But what a dull place Alaska would be!

Here people share the land with bears.  There is a certain wariness between people and bears.  And that wariness forces upon us a valuable sense of humility.

People continue to tame and subjugate nature.  But when we visit the few remaining scraps of wilderness where bears roam free, we can still feel an instinctive fear.  How precious that feeling is.  And how precious these places, and these bears, are.

Trophy hunters from the lower United States and from Europe come to Alaska to shoot grizzlies. They smile for the camera and stand, gun in hand, over the body of a dead bear. They hang their trophy on the wall — the head of a bear with its fangs bared, as if it was killed while attacking the heroic hunter. In truth, a high-powered rifle was fired from a great distance at a bear that was peacefully eating berries.

Just imagine: You're alone and unarmed on the Arctic plain with a bear. You and the bear feel the same breeze pass over your faces. You — a human being — are on an equal footing with the bear.

How wonderful that would be. No matter how many books you read, no matter how much television you watch, there is no substitute for experiencing nature firsthand. If you cannot meet a bear in the wild, then you must try to imagine it — for even if you only imagine it, the feeling can be real. And it is the feeling that is important.

Today's snowfall marks the advent of winter. The daylight hours are shorter now. The aurora dances in the clear night sky. A mother bear and her half-grown cubs trace footprints in the new snow as they climb up the mountain to their den. The cubs will spend the long winter with their mother snug beneath the snow.

The snow continues to fall, and finally the tracks are gone. Alaska, the Great Land, settles down for a quiet winter sleep.

## Meet the Author/Photographer
# Michio Hoshino

Michio Hoshino grew up in Tokyo, Japan. When he was a young man he saw a picture of a remote Inuit village in a book. He sent a letter to the village's mayor, who invited him to Alaska to spend the summer living with a family in the village. He accepted.

Hoshino was fascinated by the Alaskan wilderness, and his photographs of the state's wildlife were published in many books, and in magazines including *National Geographic* and *Smithsonian*. In addition, Hoshino wrote several books, including *Grizzly*, an award-winning book of bear photography.

After a career of almost twenty years as a wildlife photographer, Hoshino's life was cut short. In the early morning of August 8th, 1996, he was pulled from his tent and killed by a brown bear at a camp in a wildlife refuge in Siberia. Witnesses said the bear had begun behaving aggressively towards human beings as a result of being given food by visitors to the refuge.

Learn more about Michio Hoshino by visiting Education Place. **www.eduplace.com/kids**

# Think About the Selection

**1.** A surprise encounter caused the author to want to learn more about grizzlies. Would you have had the same reaction? Explain.

**2.** Why do you think the author compares bear mothers to human mothers on page 605?

**3.** Why do you think the author includes so much information about the grizzly bears' habitat?

**4.** The author writes on page 607: ". . . when a bear catches a moose calf, it is not a sad event." Do you agree? Why or why not?

**5.** Based on the selection, what generalizations can you make about bears? Think about their family life, growth, and feeding habits.

**6.** Has reading this selection changed your feelings about bears? Why or why not?

**7. Connecting/Comparing** Compare the relationship of Michio Hoshino and the bears he photographs with that of Bob Lemmons and the horses he rounds up in *Black Cowboy, Wild Horses*.

## Write About Bears

Choose two photographs of grizzly bears from the selection. Write a paragraph about each photograph. Describe the setting and season, how fully grown the bears are, and what the bears are doing.

**Tips**

- **Include a topic sentence in each paragraph.**
- **Make each paragraph more interesting by using different sentence types and lengths.**

## Math

# Make a Graph

Make a list of all the animals mentioned in the selection. Then take a poll of your class or school. Find out how many people have seen each kind of animal the author mentions. Create a graph that shows the results.

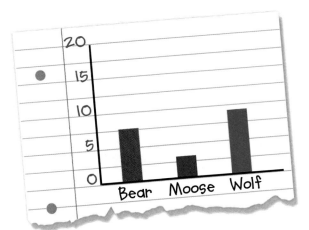

## Health and Safety

# Make a Safety Poster

Humans in bear territory need to be educated about grizzlies, for both their own and the bears' protection. Use information from the selection about bear behavior to make a safety poster especially for people who pick wild berries or people who fish for salmon.

# Go on a Web Field Trip

Connect to Education Place and explore a part of the world where grizzlies roam.

**www.eduplace.com/kids**

**Skill: How to Compare Poems**

When you read two or more poems together, ask these questions:

- What is the **subject** of each poem? How are the subjects or images in the poems alike or different?

- What is the **mood** of each poem? Light and funny? Dark and serious? How are the moods alike or different?

- How are the **sounds** and **rhythms** alike or different?

- If the poems are by the same poet, what **elements** (subject, sound, images, mood) tell you that the same person wrote them?

# Three Poems by Joseph Bruchac

## Above Jackson Pond

Long-winged, it circled
slow as a heron
yet shoulders broader in flight.

Seeking an updraft
to lift it higher,
it flapped wings
darker than clouds,
tail fanned, catching light.

An Eagle.

I whistled its way
and on my third whistle
it folded wings,
dove and rolled in answer
before flying on
past the tallest pines
which sentinel
the hill above Jackson Pond.

Valleys widen with green,
with the flow of spring,
rivers and lakes
veins pulsing the heart
of the land
held under those wide wings.

Thinking now of that great bird
praising its return,
my own vision opens
to see this earth
more gift than we humans
can give.

# Raccoons on the Shore at Paradox Lake

From the lake shore
greyed in by trails of mist
from the warm evening water
bright eyes flash at me
in the beam of the lantern
as I lift my paddle
and let the boat drift.

Six small raccoons, cubs of this year.
One curious one edges too close
and, nudged by a brother or a sister,
splashes off the dock,
comes up like a cork
and scrambles back onto the land.

They watch me,
until the canoe bumps in
to the dock, then after
a quick glance at each other,
they scoot to the base
of the big basswood tree
and hand over hand
up to its thin branches
which arch over water.

Their small paws
break free twigs
which rain about me
as a sudden wind
cuts across the lake,
cutting through the low
grey clouds above me,
so that there,
above their lifting heads I see
the shoulder of the mountain
and then, just before the mist
closes in again, high above
on the night trail of the Milky Way.

There, too, beyond Great Bear
and The Hunter
are the Northern Lights,
the ones my old people
called the spirits who dance.
They ripple the edge of the sky.

Stars reflect around me
in the lake's dark mirror
and between the shapes of the dancing stars
and that rippling form of my canoe cutting its wake
across the stars, I see again
those small raccoons,
looking up and down
in wonder.

# A Thousand Geese

Geese have flown over
for twelve days now.
I've counted each flock
lying on my back
at the edge of the old field
where sumacs edge in.

All that they carry
is all that they are.
They travel far
in need of nothing
but fair weather,
food and a safe place to rest,
their wide wings linking
winter and spring.

As the last flight passes
they take with them
my weariness
which had no reason
yet held me back
from doing the real work
half of my life.

Now, like those geese,
today all I seek
is warmth enough,
food and light enough
to sustain myself and
those whose lives
are close to mine
as we journey
the seasons.

# A Persuasive Essay

The purpose of a persuasive essay is to convince the reader to think or act in a particular way. Use this student's writing as a model when you write a persuasive essay of your own.

## Why People Should Get a Dog

I think people should get dogs because they are good companions. I also think pets, especially dogs, help you and improve your life. Some people say their dogs changed their lives because when you take care of a dog you need to learn to be unselfish. People also say dogs help them communicate better. When you have a dog, you have to try to find out what it wants, and that can help you find out how to talk to other people.

An important thing about getting a dog is to find one that suits you. When I had my dog Simba, he was my best friend. He was my favorite mammal to be with besides my mom. He always made my family and me laugh. Sometimes he got all mixed up and ran into the wall. When we played music, he tried to sing. I loved him very much. I could tell him anything in the world as if he was my best friend.

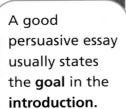

A good persuasive essay usually states the **goal** in the **introduction.**

The persuasive goal should be supported by **strong reasons.**

Dogs help you because your personality is one of the many important parts of your life, and dogs help improve it. My dog helped me improve my personality by making me be more open because it wasn't always about me. He also improved my knowledge because I did not know dogs needed so many things to be satisfied. I had to learn how to react to him and find out when to feed him and what he liked to eat.

Some people say that dogs need too much care. You have to feed them and take them for walks. My dog Simba was worth any work I had to do because he was my friend.

I think everyone should have a dog because they may improve your life. Simba and every other pet I had taught me a valuable lesson I will need to know later in life. By getting a dog, you too can learn a valuable lesson or two.

It's important to state **facts** and give **examples.**

A good persuasive essay **answers objections.**

The **conclusion** should bring the essay to a satisfactory close.

## Meet the Author

Michiala L.

**Grade:** five
**State:** Massachusetts
**Hobbies:** playing softball, making friendship bracelets, listening to music, and riding her bike
**What she wants to be when she grows up:** a veterinarian

## Background and Vocabulary

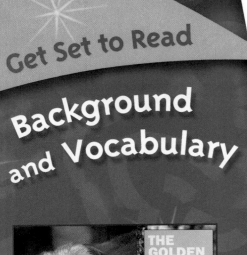

**The Golden Lion Tamarin Comes Home**

THE GOLDEN LION TAMARIN COMES HOME

George Ancona

### Key Vocabulary

captive
dilemma
extinction
habitat
reintroduction

Vocabulary Reader

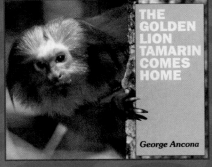
ANIMALS OF THE AMAZON

*e* Glossary

# Rescue in the Rain Forest

The "home" in *The Golden Lion Tamarin Comes Home* is the coastal rain forest of Brazil. It provides a **habitat** for a great variety of animals, even though, as the map on the right shows, the rain forest has been reduced to a fraction of its original size. How did this happen?

When human beings move into an area, their need for food and shelter may conflict with the needs of animals who make their home there. As they lose their habitat to human development, animals like the golden lion tamarin may even face **extinction**. This creates a **dilemma**: how to allow for development without threatening wildlife?

There is hope. The **reintroduction** of **captive** tamarins into the wild may help their numbers grow in what remains of the rain forest. Who is doing this work? Where does the work begin and end? The answers are in *The Golden Lion Tamarin Comes Home*.

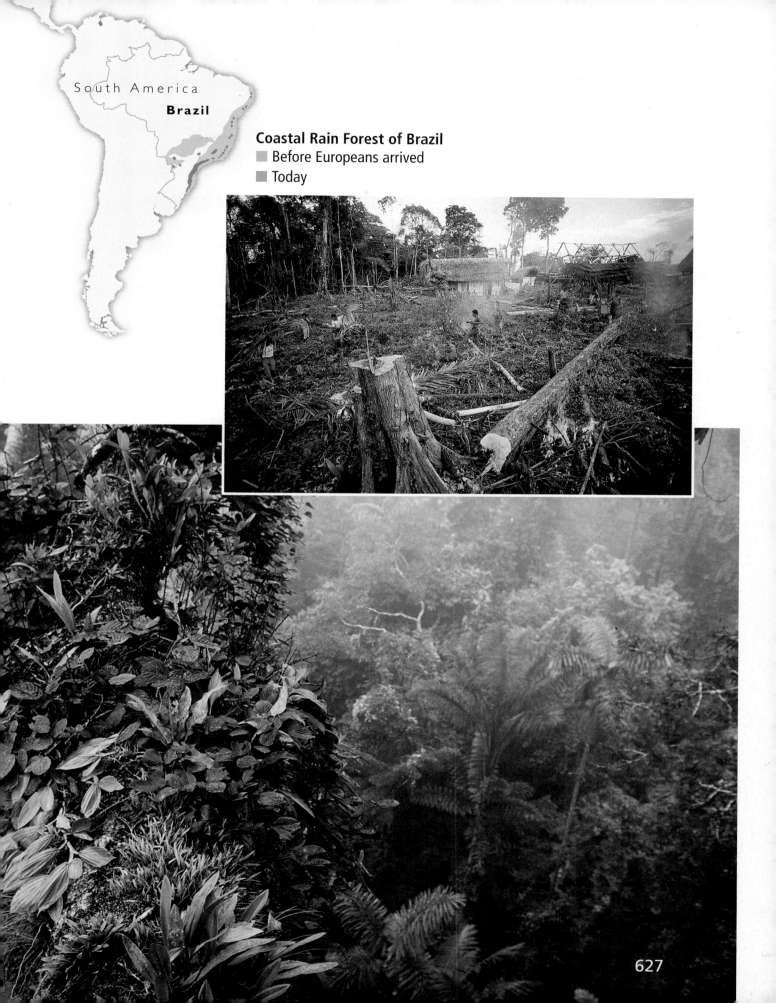

South America

**Brazil**

**Coastal Rain Forest of Brazil**
Before Europeans arrived
Today

627

# Meet the Author/Photographer

# George Ancona

**Future Traveler:** As a boy, Ancona visited the East River docks in New York City with his father. Watching freighters from around the world sparked an interest in other countries.

**Study Abroad:** While in art school, Ancona traveled to southern Mexico, where he met his parents' families for the first time.

**Early Work:** Before Ancona became a photographer, he worked for a carpenter, a mechanic, and at an amusement park.

**In His Own Words:** "I think people are fascinating and I love to find myself in strange places, meeting people, getting to know them and learning about them. This helps me to learn about myself."

**Other Titles:** Ancona's books reflect his love of travel and other cultures. *Turtle Watch* and *Carnaval* also take place in Brazil, and *Pablo Remembers* was photographed in Mexico.

To find out more about George Ancona, log on to Education Place. **www.eduplace.com/kids**

# THE GOLDEN LION TAMARIN COMES HOME

*George Ancona*

## Strategy Focus

As you read, **monitor** your understanding of how people are trying to help the golden lion tamarin. If necessary, reread or read ahead to **clarify**.

629

Whistling softly as she scans the upper canopy of leaves, Andreia Martins leads her sister Carolina and brother Renato through the rain forest. It is hot and humid. The small group is surrounded by the teeming life of the tropical forest.

Birds sing, insects buzz, cicadas chirp. Nearby they hear a tractor engine, cattle lowing, a rooster, and men at work on a *fazenda*, or "farm." They pick their way carefully along the narrow path to avoid the sharp spines of leaves and the tangle of vines underfoot.

Andreia raises her hand, and the group stops. Above them the leaves rustle and branches sway as streaks of orange-gold flash in the speckles of sunlight. "*Micos*," she whispers to the children, and points to the cluster of golden lion tamarins staring down at them from the branches of the trees. Their high-pitched whistles and squeaks pierce the air.

"Mico" is short for *mico leão dourado*, the Portuguese name for the golden lion tamarin of Brazil. About the size of a squirrel, the monkey is named for its color and lionlike mane.

The golden lion tamarin is found only in the coastal rain forest of southeastern Brazil. Flanked by a mountain range on the west and the Atlantic Ocean on the east, the forest once stretched for 1,500 miles.

When the first Europeans arrived, they cut down the trees to build their homes and towns. They burned the rest of the forest to clear the land for settlements, for coffee and sugar plantations, and for pastures on which to graze livestock. The city of Rio de Janeiro grew and spread. Today only 2 percent of the original rain forest remains, scattered like small islands in a sea of farms and towns.

As its native habitat disappeared, so did the golden lion tamarin. By 1960 there were so few left that Dr. A. Coimbra-Filho, a Brazilian biologist, warned of its imminent extinction. He urged the Brazilian government to set aside the remaining forest as a wildlife refuge. The Poço das Antas Biological Reserve, a protected habitat, was established in 1973.

The tall trees in the tropical rain forest offer the tamarins food, protection from predators, and a network of routes through their territories. The cupped centers of bromeliads, plants that live in host trees, hold water and insects for the monkeys to drink and eat. Tamarins are omnivorous. They eat not only fruits, seeds, and nuts but also bird eggs, insects, frogs, and snakes, which provide additional protein.

The rain forest is alive both day and night with a diversity of wildlife. Among the trees can be seen sloths and other species of monkeys.

Tamarins must always be on guard for predators. Above them fly owls, while on the ground prowl ocelots, feral dogs, and — the most dangerous of all — humans. Poachers trap the tamarins and sell them in illegal animal markets for high prices. If discovered, these pets are confiscated and returned to the reserve.

Today golden lion tamarins are bred in many zoos around the world. These animals do not have the skills to survive in the wild on their own. A captive tamarin lives in a confined space, climbs sturdy poles that don't move, and is served its food in a bowl at regular hours by a familiar keeper. It has never leaped from a vine to a delicate tree branch that sways under its weight. It doesn't know how to forage for its food. It hasn't experienced weather changes — cold, rain, thunder, and lightning. It would be killed by predators or get lost and starve. It needs the help of humans and that of native-born tamarins to learn to survive independently in its original habitat.

Since 1983, Dr. Benjamin Beck and his staff at the National Zoological Park in Washington, D.C., have been trying to find ways to prepare captive-born tamarins for their return to the rain forest. Dr. Beck coordinates the reintroduction of the tamarins into their natural habitat for the Golden Lion Tamarin Conservation Program.

The tamarins being reintroduced often come from other zoos and are examined carefully when they arrive at the National Zoo. A different number is tattooed onto each animal's leg and entered into a record of all the tamarins born in captivity.

As an experiment, tamarins are being permitted to live free in a wooded section of the zoo. Because they are territorial, they stay close to their nesting boxes, which are wired vertically high in the trees. The nesting box is a modified picnic cooler with two chambers inside, one above the other. In the top chamber is a hole through which the tamarins enter and leave. Should a predator attack, the tamarins huddle in the lower chamber, where a groping paw cannot reach them.

A tamarin claims its territory by rubbing a scent from its body onto tree limbs. The ones that will someday be reintroduced into the wild wear radio collars that transmit a constant beep, enabling the keepers to locate them in the woods. The tamarins are fed by food trays raised to the height of their nesting boxes.

Ropes are hung to simulate vines and to provide a network of treetop highways for the monkeys. The ropes and the nesting boxes are often changed while the tamarins are asleep to help prepare them for the unexpected.

The dilemma for the zoo is how to protect the animals and still expose them to the experiences and dangers they will meet in the wild.

Observers watch and record everything the monkeys do.  To tell the tamarins apart, they mark the tails with hair dye.  Each member of the tamarin family has its own distinctive tail marking.

When the time is right, the monkeys are shipped by air from Washington, D.C., to Rio de Janeiro.

Andreia Martins is one of the many people in Brazil and abroad working to save the golden lion tamarin.  She coordinates a team of observers who roam the rain forest, tracking tamarins and observing their behavior.  The team's notes are sent to the National Zoo, where scientists in the conservation program use them to help prepare captive-born tamarins for their reintroduction into the rain forest.

In Rio de Janeiro, Andreia and Dionizio Moraes Pessamilio, director of the reserve, carry bags of fruit when they meet a shipment of seven tamarins that arrives from Washington, D.C.

After the overnight flight, the squealing monkeys are hungry, and they gobble up the pieces of fruit that Andreia and Dionizio squeeze into the cages. Then the noisy cages are loaded into a van for the two-hour trip to the reserve.

Golden lion tamarins tend to be monogamous, which means a male and female will live together and mate only with each other. This shipment includes a family of four from one zoo: the mother, the father, and a pair of one-year-old twins, one male and one female. The other three tamarins come from three different zoos and will be used to create new families.

Because there are so few tamarins left in the wild, they keep reproducing among themselves. Introducing animals that are born in distant zoos helps to strengthen the gene pool of the native tamarins. Genes carry the characteristics of a species from one generation to the next.

The van and the observation team meet on a narrow road in the forest. The tamarins are unloaded and carried into the woods, where large cages await the immigrants. They are released into the cages, where they will grow accustomed to their new surroundings.

Everything is different: the heat, the tall trees, the noises. The tamarins will get to know their potential prey, such as the insects and small reptiles and mammals that scoot in and out of their cages. Beyond the cages stalk their predators, which they must learn to avoid.

The reserve is located a few kilometers from the town of Silva Jardim, where Andreia lives with her mother and ten brothers and sisters. Every morning Andreia and her sister Arleia, who is also an observer, cut up fruit and canned marmoset food. The canned food, which provides needed protein, is exactly what the tamarins ate in the zoo.

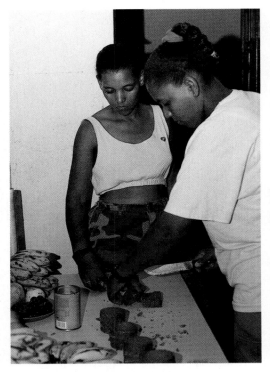

The pieces of food are then stuffed into feeders made of plastic tubes wired together to make a square, with holes drilled along the tubes. Andreia crams bits of food into the holes. This encourages the tamarins to use their long fingers and nails to extract the food, just as they will probe in trees and rotted logs once they are released.

Meanwhile, Arleia fills canteens with water. By 7:30 A.M. the van is loaded with feeders and canteens. The sisters tuck their camouflage pants into their socks to keep out insects and jump into the van.

The Golden Lion Tamarin Conservation Program has provided many jobs for people in Silva Jardim. A small town, it is located near the main highway to Rio. The *praça*, or "plaza," with its tall shade trees, band-stand, and playground, sits in the center of town.

Andreia stops at the plaza to pick up more of the observation team. While waiting for them to arrive, she works out the assignment for each one. Every day, an observer is assigned to a different group of tamarins.

The observation team is split into two groups. One group goes to the reserve, while the other goes to the fazendas where tamarins have been reintroduced. Originally the *fazenderos*, or "farmers," were hesitant about accepting the monkeys on their forest-land. But now they speak of them as "my micos."

Andreia drives through the forest, stopping every so often to drop off an observer. Each carries a canteen and a machete on a belt, as well as a backpack with food, rain gear, a snakebite kit, and mosquito repellent. Everyone carries a compass, a digital watch, a notebook, and an antenna and radio receiver for tracking the tamarins. A full tamarin feeder, carried on the shoulder, completes the equipment each observer takes into the woods.

Today the newly arrived tamarin family of four will be released. They have spent enough time in the large cage to become accustomed to the climate of the rain forest. In addition to its own tail marking, each monkey has another mark on its body that identifies the family to which it belongs. One tamarin in the group wears a new radio collar.

Andreia and Paulo Caesar, another observer, carry the nesting box into the woods. They have selected a tree in an area that the tamarin family can claim as its own. Paulo Caesar nimbly climbs the tree with a rope and wire on his shoulder. When he reaches a fork about twenty feet above the ground, he drops one end of the rope to Andreia. She ties the end to the nesting box, and Paulo Caesar hoists it up and wires it in place. With the rope draped over a branch, he drops both ends to Andreia so she can raise a feeder up to the box. Finally, Paulo Caesar uncovers the opening of the nesting box and slides down to the ground. Then they both sit down to see what will happen.

A young tamarin pokes its head out of the box, looks around, and squeals. Then the other golden heads appear to take a look. After some tentative moves, the juvenile darts out to the feeder, pokes into it, and stuffs food into its mouth.

Below, Andreia glances at her watch and writes in her notebook. For the first hour, she describes what the entire group is doing — the way they eat, socialize, and rest, and the sounds they make. Then she notes what each member of the family does.

In order not to give the tamarins human characteristics, the observers do not give them names. Instead they identify the monkeys by letters that represent the zoo they came from and numbers that symbolize their position in the group. For example, KO1 is the adult female from the zoo in Cologne, Germany, KO2 is the adult male, and KO3 and KO4 are their offspring.

At first the newcomers stay close to their nesting box. Away from their new home, they may become disoriented and get lost. Alone, a newly reintroduced tamarin can die of starvation, become injured, or fall prey to a predator.

This is when the tamarins need the most help. They are given plenty of food and water. Oranges and bananas are hung on branches for them. Because the tamarins have always eaten chopped fruit, they don't know how to peel whole fruit. The bananas are partially opened for them, and the oranges have "windows" cut into them.

As the months go by, the feeder is placed farther from the nesting box. Fruits are placed on saplings that will sway when the tamarins leap onto them.

When the tamarins begin to forage and eat natural foods, the observers reduce their visits to three times a week, then to once a week, and finally to once a month. When the tamarins become independent, all feeding is stopped.

Bit by bit, the family becomes familiar with the rain forest, the younger ones adapting faster than the parents. But only about 30 percent of all reintroduced tamarins survive more than two years. Some die by eating poisonous fruits or snakes. Some are killed by Africanized, or "killer," bees, which sometimes take over a nesting box to make a hive. The infants that are born in the wild fare much better than the reintroduced tamarins. They are more acrobatic and confident as they leap from limb to limb. They are able to deal with surprises, and they don't have to unlearn behaviors that were adequate for zoo life but are useless in the forest.

*The goal of the Golden Lion Tamarin Conservation Program is to have two thousand tamarins living in the wild by the year 2025. For this to happen, the people who live in and around the rain forest have to help protect the tamarins and their environment. That way, human beings and tamarins will be able to share the Brazilian landscape for years to come.*

## Think About the Selection

**1.** Do you think the settlers' reasons for cutting down the rain forest were good ones? Why or why not?

**2.** Why do you think tamarins born in the wild do better than tamarins who return to the rain forest after living in captivity?

**3.** Find evidence in the text to support this idea: Tamarins need the most help just after they return to the rain forest.

**4.** Do you agree with the observers' decision on page 639 not to name the tamarins? Why or why not?

**5.** Would you want to be part of a conservation program? If so, what would you like to do? If not, why not?

**6.** Do you think the efforts to return tamarins to the forest are worthwhile, even though only 30% of them survive? Explain.

**7. Connecting/Comparing** Which animal's survival do you feel more hopeful about — the grizzly's or the golden lion tamarin's? Why?

**Informing**

## Write a Fax Message

A conservation team leader might send a fax to tamarin observers. Write a fax that tells what jobs they will do, what equipment they will need, and where and when they will be picked up.

**Tips**

- Keep your message brief and clear.
- Include a cover page giving your name and the name of the person you're faxing.

# Make a Fact Chart

Use the information in the selection to make a chart of facts about the golden lion tamarin. Create rows with category headings such as *Size, Color, Habitat, Food, Predators,* and *Family.* Then fill in the rows to show what you have learned.

**Bonus** Make a similar fact chart for another kind of monkey, and then compare the two animals.

| Golden Lion Tamarin | |
|---|---|
| Size | |
| Food | |
| Color | |

# Give a Talk

Are you concerned about the golden lion tamarin? Do you agree that it should be returned to the rain forest? Use the selection to prepare a talk about the Golden Lion Tamarin Conservation Program and present it to your class.

**Tips**

- Use note cards instead of writing out your whole talk. Practice using your notes.
- Speak at an even pace. Be sure that everyone in your audience can hear you.

**Internet**

# E-Mail a Friend

What did you learn from reading *The Golden Lion Tamarin Comes Home?* What did you think about what you read? Send an e-mail message to a friend, telling about the selection.

# Technology Link

**Genre**

**Technology Article**

**Skill: How to Read a Technology Article**

*Before you read . . .*

- Identify the **topic** of the article.

- Look through the article for **diagrams** or **illustrations** that help explain the technology.

*As you read . . .*

- If you come to an unfamiliar **term**, try rereading or reading ahead to find its definition.

- If you come to an unfamiliar **abbreviation**, scan back to the first time it appears. The full name is usually given there.

# Tuning in on Animals

**Golden lion tamarins are not the only species scientists are listening to. New technologies have changed the way we keep in touch with animals, and have taught us surprising things about their behavior.**

In the fall of 1994, a Florida manatee, an endangered sea mammal, was spotted off the coast of Maryland. Scientists know that manatees migrate north over the summer, but they were puzzled that this one had not returned south yet. Clearly there was a lot more they needed to know about manatees. They caught the animal, but before bringing it back to Florida waters, they fitted it with a special radio collar around the base of its tail. From this collar, the scientists could track the manatee's movements and location and learn more about manatee migration.

Animal tracking means following the location of an animal as it walks, runs, swims, or flies. By tracking many single animals over time, scientists can learn how a whole species migrates with the seasons. They also learn details about animal behavior that may help them in protecting endangered species.

## Tags and Telemetry

The simplest way to track an animal is to follow one and keep it in view. But physically tracking an animal is not always possible. (Think of how quickly a bird can fly out of sight.) So, almost two hundred years ago, researchers began catching individual animals, fitting them with tags, and letting them go. This method was better, but still flawed: if scientists wanted to learn about the animal, they would have to catch it again later.

The next development was *telemetry* — using radio signals to track animals.

Here's an example of how it works. A single animal, such as a lynx, is fitted with a small device that transmits a radio signal. Using a receiver, scientists pick up the signals from a distance on land or from an airplane. Over days or weeks, they chart where the lynx goes. This method is still used today, but it has limitations. The receiver must be within a few hundred yards of the transmitter. And telemetry won't work everywhere. Radio signals cannot penetrate heavy jungle vegetation or below the surface of the ocean.

Once this lynx is fitted with a radio transmitter (left), it can be tracked using a portable radio antenna and receiver (above).

## Satellite Signals

Perhaps the most accurate and powerful type of animal tracking today is the Global Positioning System (GPS). This system uses 26 satellites orbiting 11,000 miles above the earth to follow the animals being tracked.

Instead of carrying a transmitter, a waved albatross, for example, would be fitted with a receiver. At regular intervals, the receiver automatically selects the four GPS satellites that are closest to the albatross. The receiver picks up the signals from these satellites and passes them on to a computer. The computer then calculates the position of the albatross by processing the information collected from the four satellites. The location that the GPS system calculates is accurate, on average, to within 30 meters (33 yards).

Satellite tracking has revealed fascinating and important information about many kinds of animals. Scientists have learned that albatross parents fly thousands of miles to find food for a single chick.

They have discovered that leatherback turtles swim more than a thousand miles in the open sea, along routes that they return to again and again. And studies have shown that great white sharks hunt around the clock, not just in the daytime as researchers had previously believed.

Scientists are constantly working on improvements in animal tracking. One group of researchers fits sharks with special tags that relay information to receivers on buoys floating in the water. Radio transmitters as light as seven-tenths of an ounce can be attached to even very small birds, and scientists are working to make them still lighter.

Perhaps the most exciting aspect of present-day animal tracking is that, using the Internet, anyone can find out the most up-to-date information that scientists are gathering. By logging onto the Web sites of animal trackers, you can learn where an animal goes each month or week, or even every day. And maybe the next time a manatee surfaces in an unusual place, you'll be one of the first to know.

**To feed their young, albatrosses scan the ocean for fish. Trackers scan for albatrosses.**

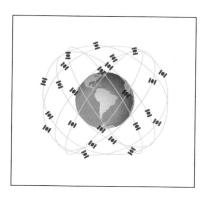

In GPS tracking, 26 satellites with transmitters orbit the Earth (left). At regular intervals, the four satellites closest to a waved albatross (below) send signals to the bird's receiver, which records its location.

Using this data, biologists with the Albatross Project are able to track the flights of waved albatrosses with great accuracy from the birds' breeding site on tiny Española, one of the Galapagos Islands off the coast of Ecuador.

**My Side of the Mountain**

**Genre** **Realistic Fiction**

## Key Vocabulary

cache
fashion
harsh
harvesting
storehouse
survival

**Vocabulary Reader**

Keeping Warm in Winter
By Susan M. Bauer

*e* • Glossary

# Living on the Land

**I**n *My Side of the Mountain*, a boy chooses to "live on the land" in a forest. His **survival** depends on being able to use what he finds in nature to meet his needs.

Think about what those needs would be. A person living on the land would need to give a lot of attention to food, clothing, and shelter. How would someone go about **harvesting** food from edible plants in the area? How much work would it be to build up a **cache** of food that would last through the winter? Or to create a **storehouse** where food would not spoil or be eaten by wild animals?

Naturally, a forest dweller would also need a place to live. What kind of shelter would that person **fashion** out of materials found in the woods? What qualities in a shelter would help keep out a **harsh** winter? What would make the warmest clothing?

There is one more need to think about. Even if food, shelter, and clothing were taken care of, a person would need to keep from being lonely. What kind of friendship might someone find in the forest?

# Jean Craighead George

Jean Craighead George's family lived in Washington, D.C., and her father often took her and her brothers into the surrounding countryside to teach them about plants and animals. She also learned some of the survival skills that Sam Gribley uses, including building a lean-to, and making a fishhook and line out of wood and wood fiber. Of her writing, George says, "I write for children. Children are still in love with the wonders of nature, and I am too."

Among over seventy other books dealing with nature, George has extended the story of *My Side of the Mountain* in two sequels: *On the Far Side of the Mountain* and *Frightful's Mountain*.

MEET THE ILLUSTRATOR

# Gary Aagaard

Gary Aagaard grew up in Seattle, Washington. He remembers being energetic as a child and full of curiosity. To illustrate *My Side of the Mountain*, Aagaard traveled to upstate New York, where the story takes place. There he took pictures of the outdoors, using a friend's son as a model for Sam. Aagaard currently lives in New York City.

Learn more about Jean Craighead George and Gary Aagaard at Education Place. **www.eduplace.com/kids**

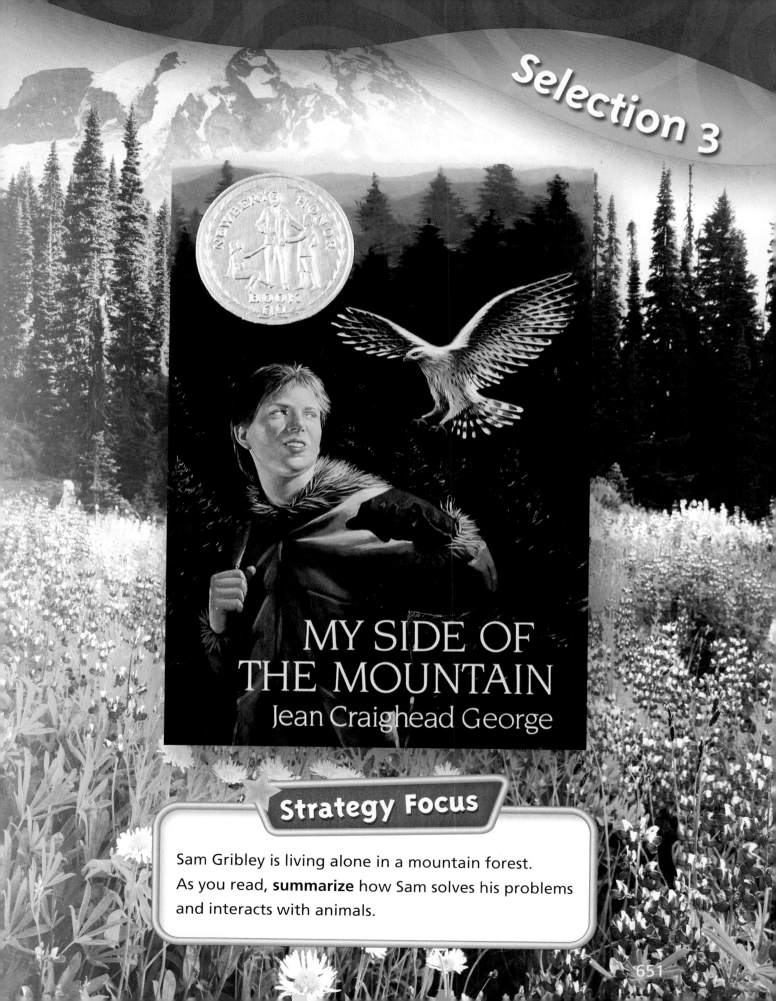

# MY SIDE OF THE MOUNTAIN
Jean Craighead George

## Strategy Focus

Sam Gribley is living alone in a mountain forest.
As you read, **summarize** how Sam solves his problems
and interacts with animals.

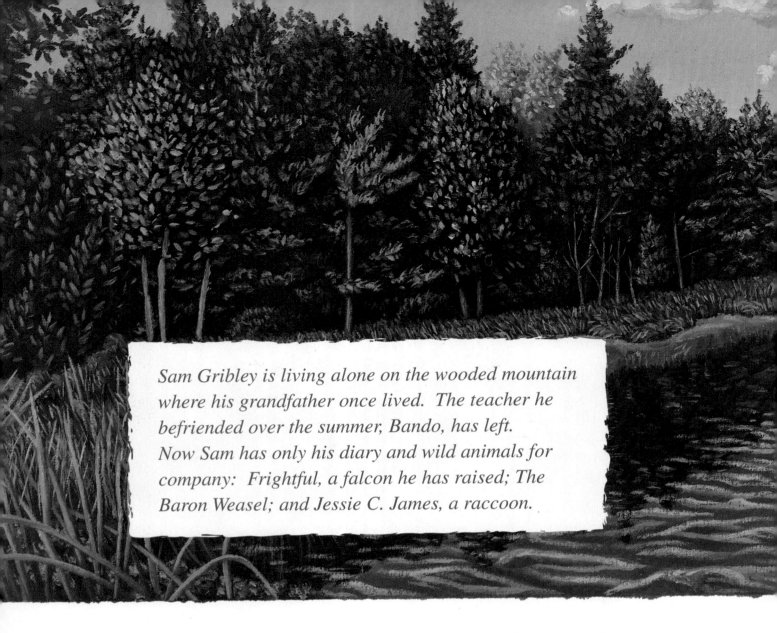

*Sam Gribley is living alone on the wooded mountain where his grandfather once lived. The teacher he befriended over the summer, Bando, has left. Now Sam has only his diary and wild animals for company: Frightful, a falcon he has raised; The Baron Weasel; and Jessie C. James, a raccoon.*

## IN WHICH
### *The Autumn Provides Food and Loneliness*

September blazed a trail into the mountains. First she burned the grasses. The grasses seeded and were harvested by the mice and the winds.

Then she sent the squirrels and chipmunks running boldly through the forest, collecting and hiding nuts.

Then she frosted the aspen leaves and left them sunshine yellow.

Then she gathered the birds together in flocks, and the mountaintop was full of songs and twitterings and flashing wings. The birds were ready to move to the south.

And I, Sam Gribley, felt just wonderful, just wonderful.

I pushed the raft down the stream and gathered arrowleaf bulbs, cattail tubers, bulrush roots, and the nutlike tubers of the sedges.

And then the crop of crickets appeared and Frightful hopped all over the meadow snagging them in her great talons and eating them. I tried them, because I had heard they are good. I think it was another species of cricket that was meant. I think the field cricket would taste excellent if you were starving. I was not starving, so I preferred to listen to them. I abandoned the crickets and went back to the goodness of the earth.

I smoked fish and rabbit, dug wild onions by the pouchful, and raced September for her crop.

"October 15

"Today The Baron Weasel looked moldy. I couldn't get near enough to see what was the matter with him, but it occurs to me that he might be changing his summer fur for his white winter mantle. If he is, it is an itchy process. He scratches a lot."

Seeing The Baron changing his mantle for winter awoke the first fears in me. I wrote that note on a little birch bark, curled up on my bed, and shivered.

The snow and the cold and the long lifeless months are ahead, I thought. The wind was blowing hard and cool across the mountain. I lit my candle, took out the rabbit and squirrel hides I had been saving, and began rubbing and kneading them to softness.

The Baron was getting a new suit for winter. I must have one too. Some fur underwear, some mittens, fur-lined socks.

Frightful, who was sitting on the foot post of the bed, yawned, fluffed, and thrust her head into the slate-gray feathers of her back. She slept. I worked for several hours.

I must say here that I was beginning to wonder if I should not go home for the winter and come back again in the spring. Everything in the forest was getting prepared for the harsh months. Jessie Coon James was as fat as a barrel. He came down the tree slowly, his fat falling in a roll over his shoulders. The squirrels were working and storing food. They were building leaf nests. The skunks had burrows and plugged themselves in at dawn with bunches of leaves. No drafts could reach them.

As I thought of the skunks and all the animals preparing themselves against the winter, I realized suddenly that my tree would be as cold as the air if I did not somehow find a way to heat it.

"notes:

"Today I rafted out into the deep pools of the creek to fish. It was a lazy sort of autumn day, the sky clear, the leaves beginning to brighten, the air warm. I stretched out on my back because the fish weren't biting, and hummed.

"My line jerked and I sat up to pull, but was too late. However, I was not too late to notice that I had drifted into the bank — the very bank where Bando had dug the clay for the jam pots.

"At that moment I knew what I was going to do. I was going to build a fireplace of clay, even fashion a little chimney of clay. It would be small, but enough to warm the tree during the long winter.

"Next day

"I dragged the clay up the mountain to my tree in my second best pair of city pants. I tied the bottoms of the legs, stuffed them full, and as I looked down on my strange cargo, I thought of scarecrows and Halloween. Suddenly I was terribly lonely. The air smelled of leaves and the cool wind from the stream hugged me. The warblers in the trees above me seemed gay and glad about their trip south. I stopped halfway up the mountain and dropped my head. I was lonely and on the verge of tears. Suddenly there was a flash, a pricking sensation on my leg, and I looked down in time to see The Baron leap from my pants to the cover of fern.

"He scared the loneliness right out of me. I ran after him and chased him up the mountain, losing him from time to time in the ferns and crowfeet. We stormed into camp an awful sight, The Baron bouncing and screaming ahead of me, and me dragging that half scarecrow of clay.

"Frightful took one look and flew to the end of her leash. She doesn't like The Baron, and watches him — well, like a hawk. I don't like to leave her alone. End notes. Must make fireplace."

It took three days to get the fireplace worked out so that it didn't smoke me out of the tree like a bee. It was an enormous problem. In the first place, the chimney sagged because the clay was too heavy to hold itself up, so I had to get some dry grasses to work into it so it could hold its own weight.

I whittled out one of the old knotholes to let the smoke out, and built the chimney down from this. Of course when the clay dried, it pulled away from the tree, and all the smoke poured back in on me.

So I tried sealing the leak with pine pitch, and that worked all right, but then the funnel over the fire bed cracked, and I had to put wooden props under that.

The wooden props burned, and I could see that this wasn't going to work either; so I went down the mountain to the site of the old Gribley farmhouse and looked around for some iron spikes or some sort of metal.

I took the wooden shovel that I had carved from the board and dug around what I thought must have been the back door or possibly the woodhouse.

I found a hinge, old hand-made nails that would come in handy, and finally, treasure of treasures, the axle of an old wagon. It was much too big. I had no hacksaw to cut it into smaller pieces, and I was not strong enough to heat it and hammer it apart. Besides, I didn't have anything but a small wooden mallet I had made.

I carried my trophies home and sat down before my tree to fix dinner and feed Frightful. The evening was cooling down for a frost. I looked at Frightful's warm feathers. I didn't even have a deer hide for a blanket. I had used the two I had for a door and a pair of pants. I wished that I might grow feathers.

I tossed Frightful off my fist and she flashed through the trees and out over the meadow. She went with a determination strange to her. "She is going to leave," I cried. "I have never seen her fly so wildly." I pushed the smoked fish aside and ran to the meadow. I whistled and whistled and whistled until my mouth was dry and no more whistle came.

I ran onto the big boulder. I could not see her. Wildly I waved the lure. I licked my lips and whistled again. The sun was a cold steely color as it dipped below the mountain. The air was now brisk, and Frightful was gone. I was sure that she had suddenly taken off on the migration; my heart was sore and pounding. I had enough food, I was sure. Frightful was not absolutely necessary for my survival; but I was now so fond of her. She was more than a bird. I knew I must have her back to talk to and play with if I was going to make it through the winter.

I whistled. Then I heard a cry in the grasses up near the white birches.

In the gathering darkness I saw movement. I think I flew to the spot. And there she was; she had caught herself a bird. I rolled into the grass beside her and clutched her jesses. She didn't intend to leave, but I was going to make sure that she didn't. I grabbed so swiftly that my hand hit a rock and I bruised my knuckles.

The rock was flat and narrow and long; it was the answer to my fireplace. I picked up Frightful in one hand and the stone in the other; and I laughed at the cold steely sun as it slipped out of sight, because I knew I was going to be warm. This flat stone was what I needed to hold up the funnel and finish my fireplace.

And that's what I did with it. I broke it into two pieces, set one on each side under the funnel, lit the fire, closed the flap of the door and listened to the wind bring the first frost to the mountain. I was warm.

Then I noticed something dreadful. Frightful was sitting on the bedpost, her head under her wings. She was toppling. She jerked her head out of her feathers. Her eyes looked glassy. She is sick, I said. I picked her up and stroked her, and we both might have died there if I had not opened the tent flap to get her some water. The cold night air revived her. "Air," I said. "The fire-place used up all the oxygen. I've got to ventilate this place."

We sat out in the cold for a long time because I was more than a little afraid of what our end might have been.

I put out the fire, took the door down and wrapped up in it. Frightful and I slept with the good frost nipping our faces.

"notes:

"I cut out several more knotholes to let air in and out of the tree room. I tried it today. I have Frightful on my fist watching her. It's been about two hours and she hasn't fainted and I haven't gone numb. I can still write and see clearly.

"Test: Frightful's healthy face."


# IN WHICH
## *We All Learn About Halloween*

---

"October 28

"I have been up and down the mountain every day for a week, watching to see if walnuts and hickory nuts are ripe. Today I found the squirrels all over the trees, harvesting them furiously, and so I have decided that ripe or not, I must gather them. It's me or the squirrels.

"I tethered Frightful in the hickory tree while I went to the walnut tree and filled pouches. Frightful protected the hickory nuts. She keeps the squirrels so busy scolding her that they don't have time to take the nuts. They are quite ter-rified by her. It is a good scheme. I shout and bang the tree and keep them away while I gather.

"I have never seen so many squirrels. They hang from the slender branches, they bounce through the limbs, they seem to come from the whole forest. They must pass messages along to each other — messages that tell what kind of nuts and where the trees are."

A few days later, my storehouse rolling with nuts, I began the race for apples. Entering this race were squirrels, raccoons, and a fat old skunk who looked as if he could eat not another bite. He was ready to sleep his autumn meal off, and I resented him because he did not need my apples. However, I did not toy with him.

I gathered what apples I could, cut some in slices, and dried them on the boulder in the sun. Some I put in the storeroom tree to eat right away. They were a little wormy, but it was wonderful to eat an apple again.

Then one night this was all done, the crop was gathered. I sat down to make a few notes when The Baron came sprinting into sight.

He actually bounced up and licked the edges of my turtle-shell bowl, stormed Frightful, and came to my feet.

"Baron Weasel," I said. "It is nearing Halloween. Are you playing tricks or treats?" I handed him the remains of my turtle soup dinner, and, fascinated, watched him devour it.

"note:

"The Baron chews with his back molars, and chews with a ferocity I have not seen in him before. His eyes gleam, the lips curl back from his white pointed teeth, and he frowns like an angry man. If I move toward him, a rumble starts in his chest that keeps me back. He flashes glances at me. It is indeed strange to be looked in the eye by this fearless wild animal. There is something human about his beady glance. Perhaps because that glance tells me something. It tells me he knows who I am and that he does not want me to come any closer."

The Baron Weasel departed after his feast. Frightful, who was drawn up as skinny as a stick, relaxed and fluffed her feathers, and then I said to her,

660

"See, he got his treats. No tricks." Then something occurred to me. I reached inside the door and pulled out my calendar stick. I counted 28, 29, 30, 31.

"Frightful, that old weasel knows. It is Halloween. Let's have a Halloween party."

Swiftly I made piles of cracked nuts, smoked rabbit, and crayfish. I even added two of my apples. This food was an invitation to the squirrels, foxes, raccoons, opossums, even the birds that lived around me to come have a party.

When Frightful is tethered to her stump, some of the animals and birds will only come close enough to scream at her. So bird and I went inside the tree, propped open the flap, and waited.

Not much happened that night. I learned that it takes a little time for the woodland messages to get around. But they do. Before the party I had been very careful about leaving food out because I needed every mouthful. I took the precaution of rolling a stone in front of my store tree. The harvest moon rose. Frightful and I went to sleep.

At dawn, we abandoned the party. I left the treats out, however. Since it was a snappy gold-colored day, we went off to get some more rabbit skins to finish my winter underwear.

We had lunch along the creek — stewed mussels and wild potatoes. We didn't get back until dusk because I discovered some wild rice in an ox bow of the stream. There was no more than a handful.

Home that night, everything seemed peaceful enough. A few nuts were gone, to the squirrels, I thought. I baked a fish in leaves, and ate a small, precious amount of wild rice. It was marvelous! As I settled down to scrape the rabbit skins of the day, my neighbor the skunk marched right into the campground and set to work on the smoked rabbit. I made some Halloween notes:

"The moon is coming up behind the aspens. It is as big as a pumpkin and as orange. The winds are cool, the stars are like electric light bulbs. I am just inside the doorway, with my turtle-shell lamp burning so that I can see to write this.

"Something is moving beyond the second hemlock. Frightful is very alert, as if there are things all around us. Halloween was over at midnight last night, but for us it is just beginning. That's how I feel, anyhow, but it just may be my imagination.

"I wish Frightful would stop pulling her feathers in and drawing herself up like a spring. I keep thinking that she feels things.

"Here comes Jessie C. James. He will want the venison.

"He didn't get the venison. There was a snarl, and a big raccoon I've never seen walked past him, growling and looking ferocious. Jessie C. stood motionless — I might say, scared stiff. He held his head at an angle and let the big fellow eat. If Jessie so much as rolled his eyes that old coon would sputter at him."

It grew dark, and I couldn't see much. An eerie yelp behind the boulder announced that the red fox of the meadow was nearing. He gave me goose bumps. He stayed just beyond my store tree, weaving back and forth on silent feet. Every now and then he would cry — a wavery owl-like cry. I wrote some more.

"The light from my turtle lamp casts leaping shadows. To the beechnuts has come a small gray animal. I can't make out what — now, I see it. It's a flying squirrel. That surprises me, I've never seen a flying squirrel around here, but of course I haven't been up much after sunset."

When it grew too dark to see, I lit a fire, hoping it would not end the party. It did not, and the more I watched, the more I realized that all these animals were familiar with my camp. A white-footed mouse walked over my woodpile as if it were his.

I put out my candle and fell asleep when the fire turned to coals. Much later I was awakened by screaming. I lifted my head and looked into the moonlit forest. A few guests, still lingering at the party, saw me move, and dashed bashfully into the ground cover. One was big and slender. I thought perhaps a mink. As I slowly came awake, I realized that screaming was coming from behind me. Something was in my house. I jumped up and shouted, and two raccoons skittered under my feet. I reached for my candle, slipped on hundreds of nuts, and fell. When I finally got a light and looked about me, I was dismayed to see what a mess my guests had made of my tree house. They had found the cache of acorns and beechnuts and had tossed them all over my bed and floor. The party was getting rough.

I chased the raccoons into the night and stumbled over a third animal and was struck by a wet stinging spray. It was skunk! I was drenched. As I got used to the indignity and the smell, I saw the raccoons cavort around my fireplace and dodge past me. They were back in my tree before I could stop them.

A bat winged in from the darkness and circled the tallow candle. It was Halloween and the goblins were at work.

Having invited all these neighbors, I was now faced with the problem of getting rid of them. The raccoons were feeling so much at home that they snatched up beechnuts, bits of dried fish and venison and tossed them playfully into the air. They were too full to eat any more, but were having a marvelous time making toys out of my hard-won winter food supply.

I herded the raccoons out of the tree and laced the door. I was breathing "relief" when I turned my head to the left, for I sensed someone watching me. There in the moonlight, his big ears erect on his head, sat the red fox. He was smiling — I know he was. I shouted, "Stop laughing!" and he vanished like a magician's handkerchief.

All this had awakened Frightful, who was flopping in the dark in the tree. I reached in around the deer flap to stroke her back to calmness. She grabbed me so hard I yelled — and the visitors moved to the edge of my camp at my cry.

Smelling to the sky, bleeding in the hand, and robbed of part of my hard-won food, I threw wood on the fire and sent an enormous shaft of light into the night. Then I shouted. The skunk moved farther away. The raccoons galloped off a few feet and galloped back. I snarled at them. They went to the edge of the darkness and stared at me. I had learned something that night from that very raccoon bossing Jessie C. James — to animals, might is right. I was biggest and I was oldest, and I was going to tell them so. I growled and snarled and hissed and snorted. It worked. They understood and moved away. Some looked back and their eyes glowed. The red eyes chilled me. Never had there been a more real Halloween night. The last bat of the season darted in the moonlight. I dove on my bed, and tied the door. There are no more notes about Halloween.

# Think About the Selection

**1.** What does Sam's solution for staying warm through the winter tell you about him?

**2.** Think about Sam's loneliness on page 655. What are some ways a time of year can affect a person's feelings?

**3.** On page 665, Sam says that he has never experienced a "more real" Halloween night. What do you think he means?

**4.** How do you think Sam feels about the wild woodland creatures that live around him? Use details from the story to support your answer.

**5.** If it were up to you, would you have tried to persuade Sam to leave the wilderness? Why or why not?

**6.** Do you think you would enjoy a wilderness experience similar to Sam's? Why or why not?

**7. Connecting/Comparing** Compare Sam's fictional woodland adventure with the real-life wilderness experiences of Michio Hoshino and Andreia Martins in this theme. How are they different? How are they alike?

## Explaining

# Write Directions

A person who relies on food from the forest would need to know what food to eat and how to prepare it. Use information in the selection to write directions for making a wilderness meal. Include choices for a main course, side dish, and dessert.

---

**Tips**

- List the ingredients needed for each course of the meal.
- Use a sequence of steps to explain how to gather and prepare the food.

## Social Studies

# Make a Picture Map

With a partner, take notes about Sam's camp and the trees, animals, and land he describes. Then make a picture map, using small pictures to show the camp and its surroundings. Include a key that explains the pictures you have used.

**Bonus** Give a presentation in which you compare a picture map to another kind of map, such as a road map or a contour map. Tell in what situation each map would be useful.

## Viewing

# Update an Illustration

Choose an illustration from the selection. Study it carefully. Then show in a drawing or describe in a paragraph how the scene in that illustration might look hours later, one month later, or one year later.

### Tips

- Ask yourself how the illustration would look in a different season.
- If the illustration shows the day, consider how it might look at night — or vice versa.

## Internet

# Complete a Web Word Find

You've learned a lot of vocabulary words related to Sam's experience living on the land. Try finding those words in a puzzle that can be printed from Education Place. **www.eduplace.com/kids**

# Robin Hughes: Wildlife Doctor

*Dr. Robin Hughes could give Sam Gribley advice. She formerly worked as wildlife veterinarian at the Virginia Living Museum in Newport News, Virginia.*

by Susan Yoder Ackerman

As I walked into her office, Robin was on the phone. "Yes," she was saying, "hummingbirds need more than sugar water. They need protein. Fruit flies are perfect for them!"

Robin's understanding of small wild birds is no wonder, growing up as she did with the name Robin. While her friends were selling Kool-Aid on hot days, little Robin set up a veterinary stand. She stocked it with her stethoscope, long sticks for splints, and lots of gauze. The neighborhood pets showed up with their sore paws and torn ears.

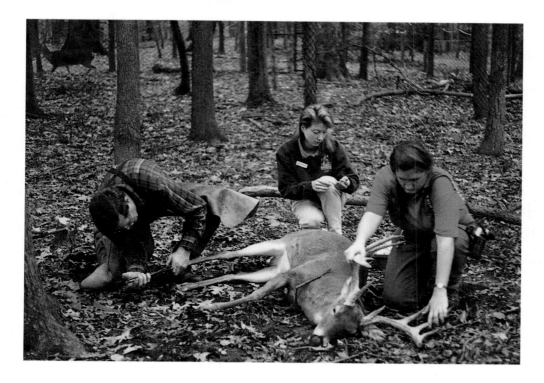

Sometimes Dr. Hughes's work takes her out of the office and into the woods. After tranquilizing this deer to work on its overgrown hoof, Dr. Hughes (center) administers medicine to wake him up.

As she got older, Robin decided to go to veterinary school to learn all she could about dogs and cats and horses. But she didn't stop there. Pursuing her interest in wild animals, she cared for gazelles at the Kansas City Zoo. She learned to know the white ibises who feed on fiddler crabs on Pumpkin Seed Island in South Carolina. She worried over the growth on a Gila monster's tongue in California's Living Desert.

So, when Robin finally became Dr. Robin Hughes, she wasn't content in private practice treating mostly cats and dogs. She came to the Virginia Living Museum, where she has the care of live-animal exhibits that reflect Virginia's wildlife in its native habitat. And though she uses all the training she's had, sometimes she feels as if she's writing her own medical book. How do you medicate a sick beaver? Just figure out the dosage for a very large guinea pig! What about an otter? Try what's good for ferrets. A skunk with heart disease? Perhaps the treatment for a small dog would be most appropriate. Robin studies diet, behavior, tooth structure, and anatomy to figure out the best way to treat her patients. Has she ever treated a wild animal she couldn't match to a domestic one?

"A possum!" she said with a laugh. "Possums are clearly in a class of their own! *The Care and Treatment of Possums* is a book nobody has written yet."

Besides nursing raccoons and giving advice on the diet of hummingbirds, what does Robin do in the course of a day? Happily for her, every day is different. As curator of animals and a veterinarian, she may find herself out on a trawler in the York River, using a seine net to find new fish for the aquarium display. She might be rescuing injured waterfowl to bring to the outdoor wetlands aviary. She might travel to a distant wooded lake and release half-grown beavers into the wild. Other days she adjusts the diets for all the animals on the museum grounds.

And then there are the days when Robin really shows her stuff. Such as the day she needed to operate on an eastern diamondback rattlesnake to remove a mass growing under its eye. A fungal infection was causing inflammatory tissue to form into a granuloma. Robin said that snakes in the wild often get abscesses and tumors, but she didn't want any snake under her care to crawl off into a corner to die. So she scrubbed up and got started.

Robin vented anesthetic gas through a small hose in the lid of a sealed aquarium until the snake was asleep. (Since a sleeping snake doesn't look a whole lot different from a snake that's awake, this was the tricky part.) Then, taking the snake out of the aquarium, she put a tube down its windpipe to control the amount of anesthesia until the procedure was over.

Cutting into the skin so near the venomous fangs was also risky. Just to be safe, Robin placed corks over the fangs during surgery. And, to save herself a lot of trouble, she closed the incision with sutures that would dissolve all by themselves. A rattlesnake might not want to hold still to get its stitches taken out.

Sometimes Robin finds herself running a maternity ward. A couple of newborn baby otters stole the show at the museum for months, and black-crowned night herons hatched their young in the outdoor aviary. One year Robin and everyone else tiptoed around the bald eagle enclosure for thirty-eight days, hoping that the eggs the pair was guarding would hatch. They never did, but Robin hopes that the adult birds, injured by hunters in the wild, will someday produce perfect little bald eagles that can fly wherever they wish.

Then there are the exciting outdoor dramas that take place when the larger animals get vaccinated. The deer, foxes, and otter don't like injections any more than people do, so Robin has to come prepared. Sometimes she uses a dart gun to carry the vaccine; sometimes she'll throw a net around the animal to hold it still. Even so, there can be surprises, such as the time the thirty-pound bobcat leaped onto Robin's back when she turned to get the vaccine ready! She wasn't injured, but the incident made her aware that he was still a wild animal, even though he'd been hand-raised as an orphan. She never turns her back to him now if she has to enter his enclosure.

Bobcat, rattlesnake, hummingbird, raccoon — Dr. Robin is there for them. She also cares about the half million people who visit the Virginia Living Museum each year. Robin wants visitors to walk away with a greater appreciation and concern for Virginia's wildlife.

## Career File

# Veterinarian

Do you like taking care of animals? If so, consider becoming a veterinarian. As a vet, you'll have a chance to help house pets, wild animals, farm or zoo animals by . . .

- caring for them when they're sick or injured
- making sure they eat healthy diets
- giving them the medicine or vitamins they need
- studying diseases that could affect them

After college, you'll need a degree from a four-year veterinary school. You'll also need to pass a state exam in the state where you want to work. In the meantime, you can learn more about what a veterinarian does by volunteering at a local animal hospital, humane society, zoo, or farm.

# Check Your Progress

In this theme you have been reading about how people meet — and often help — wild animals. The next two selections bring you new animal encounters to read about and compare.

Before you begin, return to George Ancona's letter on pages 596–598. Think about how other characters in the theme show the patience and awareness he writes about.

People helping animals is the subject of the following selections. Compare the kinds of help the humans give, and the results of that help. Then give some thought to what all the theme selections tell about how people should act toward wild animals.

# Read and Compare

A boy finds an endangered sea turtle and brings in others to help save its life.

**Try these strategies:**
Monitor and Clarify
Summarize

**Nonfiction**

In this Korean folktale, a man helps an ungrateful tiger and needs to be saved by a clever rabbit.

**Try these strategies:**
Predict and Infer
Question

**Fiction**

**Strategies in Action** *Remember to put all your reading strategies to work as you read.*

# Interrupted Journey

## Saving Endangered Sea Turtles

by Kathryn Lasky
photographs by Christopher G. Knight

The young turtle has been swimming for three months now in the same warm shallow bay, grazing on small crabs and plankton, basking in an endless dream of calm water and plentiful food. But as the days begin to shorten and the light drains out of the sky earlier and earlier, the water grows colder. It drops to fifty degrees Fahrenheit. The turtle is confused. Swimming is harder. Its heartbeat slows — and almost stops.

Ten days before Thanksgiving, on a beach where Pilgrims once walked, Max Nolan, a ten-year-old boy, and his mother begin their patrol. The Nolans are among volunteers who walk Cape Cod's beaches during November and December to search for turtles who are often cold and stunned and seem dead — turtles whose lives they may be able to save.

It is a blustery day on Ellis Landing Beach. At twenty-five knots the bitter northwest wind stings Max's face like sharp needles. It makes his eyes water but he keeps looking — looking above the high-water mark through the clumps of seaweed, looking below the tide line where the sand is hard and sleek and lapped by surf — looking for a dark greenish-brown mound about the size of a pie plate, looking for a Kemp's ridley turtle that is dying and perhaps can be saved.

Max and his mother and the other volunteers work for a vital cause. All sea turtles are threatened or endangered; Kemp's ridleys are the most endangered of all. Right now on our planet there are fewer than eight thousand Kemp's ridley turtles left. They are a vanishing species.

On Ellis Landing Beach, snow squalls begin to whirl down. The waves are building, and as they begin to break, the white froth whips across their steep faces. So far there is no sign of a turtle.

Max is far ahead of his mother when he sees the hump in the sand being washed by the surf. He runs up to it and shouts to his mom, "Got one!" The turtle is cold. Its flippers are floppy. Its eyes are open, but the turtle is not moving at all. It might be dead, but then again, it might not.

Max remembers the instructions given to all rescuers. He picks up the turtle, which weighs about five pounds, and moves it above the high-tide mark to keep it from washing out to sea. Then he runs to find seaweed to protect it from the wind. He finds a stick to mark the spot, and next, he and his mother go to the nearest telephone and call the sea-turtle rescue line of the Massachusetts Audubon Society.

Within an hour the turtle has been picked up and taken to the Wellfleet Bay Wildlife Sanctuary on Cape Cod. Robert Prescott, the director of the Sanctuary, examines the turtle. "It sure does look dead," he says softly. "But you can never tell." If the turtle is really alive, it must be brought out of its cold, stunned condition. That is a task for the New England Aquarium with its medical team who, over the years, have made a specialty of treating turtles.

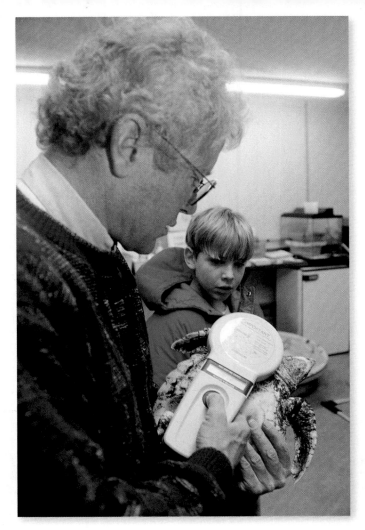

Robert puts the new turtle in a plastic wading pool with another turtle that is quite lively. Max crouches by the edge and watches his turtle. It is as still as a stone. He gently touches a flipper. Nothing moves. Then after about twenty minutes, he thinks he might see a flicker in the turtle's left eyelid. He leans closer. "Hey, it's moving!" It wasn't just the eyelid. He saw the right rear flipper move a fraction of an inch. Over the next five minutes, he sees the turtle make three or four microscopically small motions with its right rear flipper. Soon, the rescue team from the New England Aquarium arrives.

Beth Chittick is a vet at the New England Aquarium. When the turtles arrive she is ready for them. The turtles are taken immediately into the examination room. Beth is joined by head veterinarian, Howard Crum. They insert a thermometer into the cloaca, the opening under the turtle's tail. The temperature of the turtle Max found is fifty degrees Fahrenheit. Normal temperature for a turtle is usually about seventy-five degrees. Howard next tries to find a heartbeat. He listens intently. "I think I can hear a faint sound . . ." He holds the stiff turtle against his ear as one might hold a seashell. "Why, gee whiz, I can hear the ocean," he jokes.

Howard is still not convinced that the turtle is dead. "With turtles," Howard says, "death is a relative term." Turtles can operate, can survive, even when their hearts slow down for periods of time. Events that might damage the larger, more complicated brains of other animals will not always prove fatal to turtles.

In fact, a turtle's heartbeat naturally slows down at times to just one or two beats per minute in order to conserve oxygen and keep vital organs like the brain working. So Howard won't give up on this turtle yet. The turtle does not seem dehydrated. The skin on its limbs is not wrinkled — a good sign.

An assistant swabs down an area on the turtle's neck, from which a blood sample will be taken. By analyzing the blood, Howard and Beth will be able to see how the turtle's kidneys and other organs are functioning.

Next the turtle is cleaned. The algae are washed and wiped from its shell. The doctors detect movement in its tail and then see some of the same movements that Max saw in its flippers. They are the motions a turtle makes when it swims. They do not necessarily mean that it is alive, though. It has been speculated that these movements could be what are sometimes called vestigial motions, echoes of long-ago actions, fossil behaviors embedded in the brain of an ancient creature. The turtle could be swimming in death or swimming toward life.

Nonetheless, the vets hook up the turtle to an intravenous needle through which fluids will be pumped very slowly at a temperature slightly higher than the turtle's body. Beth and Howard have learned much about the condition of this turtle but they are still not sure if it is really alive or dead.

Finally the turtle is tagged with a yellow-blue band. It will be known as Yellow-Blue. It is put in the Intensive Care Unit, a large temperature-controlled stainless steel box with a glass window. Inside, the turtle is placed on a soft pile of towels so its shell is supported and it will not have to rest on its ventrum, or bottom shell.

Then the team turn their attention to another turtle, which is definitely alive. Howard picks up the turtle and talks to it as its flippers thrash madly. "Okay, little man!" This turtle's temperature is sixty-two degrees. When they take its blood, the sample appears much redder than the nearly brownish blood of Yellow-Blue, which indicates that there is more oxygen in it.

But as lively as this one is, Howard gives it only a fifty-percent survival rate. There is a good chance that pneumonia could still develop. They insert an intravenous tube for rehydration. Then they tag the animal with a plain yellow band. There are other turtles also being treated. One, Orange, needs to have its eyes lubricated and then be weighed and examined. The turtle is feisty and needs to be sedated. This is done without drugs, simply by shielding the top of its head from the ceiling lights. There is a gland inside a turtle's head that is sensitive to light, and it is speculated that when the gland is covered, it helps the turtle settle down into a relaxed, near-sleeping state.

In this peaceful state, Orange begins to "swim" on the table, its flippers making the paddling motions that have since birth propelled it through thousands of miles of sea. Its heart rate, at thirty-six beats a minute, is good. Its respiration rate is still slow. It takes only one breath every minute. Its temperature is near seventy degrees. Orange is x-rayed for signs of pneumonia. The lungs are clear.

Whatever the outcome for these three turtles, Beth, Howard, Robert, Max, and his mother all know they are doing their part to help return the turtles to health, to help return them to the sea.

# The Rabbit's Judgment

## by Suzanne Crowder Han • illustrated by Yumi Heo

Long, long ago, when plants and animals talked, a tiger fell into a deep pit while roaming through the forest in search of food. He tried over and over to get out but the walls were too steep for him to climb and he could not jump high enough to reach the opening. He called for help but none came.

The next morning he called for help until he was hoarse. Hungry and exhausted, he slumped down on the ground, thinking that he was doomed to die in the pit. But then he heard footsteps.

"Help! Help!" he cried desperately.

"Oh! A tiger!" said a man, peering over the side of the pit.

"Please! Please help me out of here!" pleaded the tiger. "If you help me, I won't forget you as long as I live."

The man felt sorry for the tiger but he was afraid of being eaten. "I would like to help you but, I'm sorry, the thought of what might happen makes me refuse. Please forgive me. I must be on my way," said the man and he began walking down the path.

"No! No! Please don't think like that! Please help me!" cried the tiger. "You don't have to worry, I promise. I won't hurt you. Please help me out. Please! I beg you! If you get me out, I'll be forever grateful to you. Please!"

The tiger sounded so pitiful that the man turned around and walked back to the pit. He looked around until he found a big log. "Here, climb up this," he said, lowering the log into the pit.

The tiger climbed up the log and came face to face with the man. His mouth watered and he began circling him.

"Hey! Wait a minute! Didn't you promise not to hurt me? Is this your idea of gratefulness? Is this how you repay a kindness?"

"What do I care about a promise when I'm starving! I haven't eaten for days!"

"Wait! Wait!" cried the man. "Let's ask that pine tree if it is right for you to eat me."

"All right," said the tiger. "But I'm awfully hungry."

The tiger and the man explained the situation to the pine tree.

"What do men know about gratefulness?" said the pine tree. "Why, your kind take our leaves and limbs to make fires to heat your homes and cook your food. And it takes us years to grow big but when we finally do, you cut us down and cut us up to make timber and planks for houses and furniture and the like. Moreover, it was a man that dug that pit. Gratefulness, indeed! Don't give it another thought, Tiger. You just go ahead and satisfy your hunger!"

"Now what do you think of that?" asked the tiger, smacking his lips loudly and slinking toward the man.

Just at that moment an ox wandered by. "Wait! Wait!" cried the man. "Let's ask that ox to judge."

The tiger agreed, so they explained everything to the ox and asked his opinion.

"Well, as far as I'm concerned, there's no question about what to do," said the ox, turning to the tiger. "You should eat him up!"

"You see, from the time we're born we oxen work diligently for men. We carry heavy loads on our backs and plow up the ground so they can grow food. But what do they do when we're old? They kill us and eat our flesh and use our hides to make all kinds of things. So don't talk to me about being grateful to him. Just eat him!"

"See! Everyone agrees. Now get ready to die," said the tiger, crouching to pounce.

The man thought that it must surely be his time to die. But then a rabbit came hopping by.

"Wait, Tiger! Wait!" shouted the man.

"Now what?" roared the tiger.

"Please give me one last chance," begged the man. "Let's ask that rabbit to judge whether I should be eaten or not."

"Oh, what's the use? You know the answer will be the same."

"Please, please," pleaded the man.

"Oh, all right. But this is the last time. I'm starving!"

So the tiger and the man told the rabbit their story. The rabbit listened carefully. Then he closed his eyes and stroked one of his long ears. After a few seconds he opened his eyes and spoke slowly and deliberately. "I well understand what the two of you have said. But if I am to make a wise judgment we should go to that pit and you should tell me again what happened. So lead the way."

The tiger and the man led the rabbit the few short steps to the pit.

"Well, it certainly is deep," said the rabbit, looking down into the pit. "Let's see, you say you were down there, and you were standing here like this?" he said to the tiger and then to the man. "Well, if you get in those positions, then I can make a judgment."

Without giving it a second thought, the hungry tiger jumped down into the pit. The man peered over the edge.

"So, that is how the two of you were," said the rabbit. "Now I can judge. The problem started when this man helped that tiger out of this pit. In other words, if the man had not shown any kindness and had left the tiger in the pit, there wouldn't be a problem. So I think the man should continue his journey and the tiger should remain in the pit.

"Now, a good day to the both of you," said the clever rabbit and he hopped away.

# Think and Compare

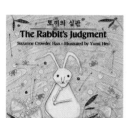

1. Compare Max's encounter with the sea turtle and the man's encounter with the tiger. How are the encounters alike and different?

2. Compare the efforts to save the sea turtle and the efforts to save the tamarins in *The Golden Lion Tamarin Comes Home.* Do you think the efforts will be successful? Why or why not?

3. The ox and the pine tree don't have good things to say about people in *The Rabbit's Judgment.* What do you think the grizzly bear, the tamarin, and Sam Gribley's animal neighbors would say about people?

4. Do you agree with the ox and the pine tree's opinions? How would you respond to them?

5. Think about the different ways people interact with animals in the theme. Which person would you most like to trade places with? Explain why.

**Strategies in Action** Tell about two or three places in *Interrupted Journey* where you used reading strategies.

# Write an Essay

Write a brief essay telling what kind of responsibility people should have toward wild animals. Use examples from the selections.

> **Tips**
> - **Think of a sentence stating the main point you want to make.**
> - **Think of reasons to back up that main point.**
> - **Think of details that support those reasons.**

# Writing an Opinion Essay

Some tests may prompt you to write your opinion about a topic. Read this sample test prompt. Use the steps when you write an opinion essay.

> Write an essay that gives your opinion about why people should or should not help wild animals. Include at least three reasons. Support each reason with details.

## ① Read the prompt.

Find the key words that tell the topic and the kind of writing. Restate in your own words what you need to do. Decide what to write about.

## ② Explore and plan.

Brainstorm reasons and details to support your opinion. Organize your reasons and details in a chart.

Here is a sample chart.

| Opinion: People should help wild animals. | | |
|---|---|---|
| **Reason and Details** | **Reason and Details** | **Reason and Details** |
| Without our help, many animals might vanish. (Ridley sea turtles, golden lion tamarins) | People should fix problems they have caused. (loss of habitat, pollution) | Wild animals share the planet with us. (Helping is good; animals enrich our lives.) |

### ③ Write your paper.

Draft your opinion essay. Follow the chart you made. Revise your paper. Look for places to add exact words and details. Proofread your essay to correct errors.

Here is the beginning of a sample essay, showing the first reason and details.

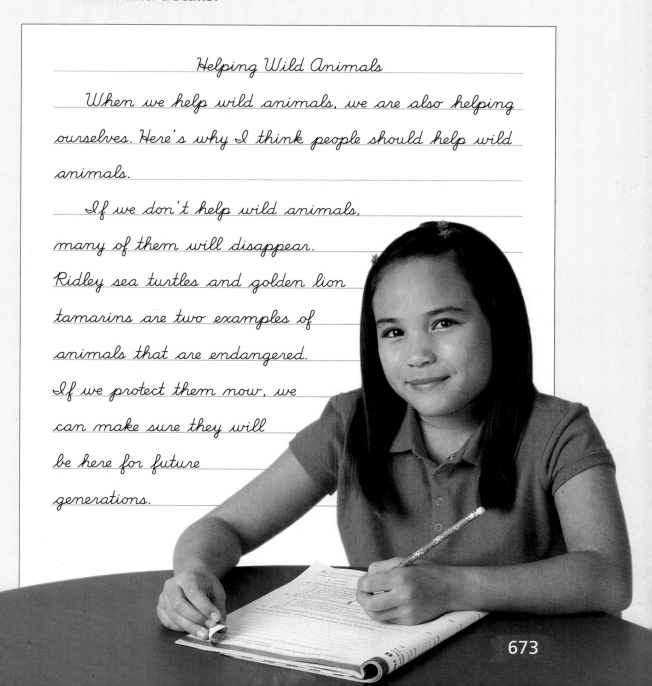

Helping Wild Animals

When we help wild animals, we are also helping ourselves. Here's why I think people should help wild animals.

If we don't help wild animals, many of them will disappear. Ridley sea turtles and golden lion tamarins are two examples of animals that are endangered. If we protect them now, we can make sure they will be here for future generations.

# Glossary

Visit **www.eduplace.com** for
*e* • Glossary **and** *e* • Word Game.

This glossary contains meanings and pronunciations for some of the words in this book. The Full Pronunciation Key shows how to pronounce each consonant and vowel in a special spelling. At the bottom of the glossary pages is a shortened form of the full key.

# Full Pronunciation Key

## Consonant Sounds

| | | | | | |
|---|---|---|---|---|---|
| b | **b**i**b**, ca**bb**age | kw | **ch**oir, **qu**ick | t | **t**ight, stopp**ed** |
| ch | **ch**ur**ch**, sti**tch** | l | **l**id, need**l**e, ta**ll** | th | ba**th**, **th**in |
| d | **d**ee**d**, mail**ed**, pu**dd**le | m | a**m**, **m**an, du**mb** | *th* | ba**th**e, **th**is |
| f | **f**ast, **f**i**f**e, o**ff**, **ph**rase, rou**gh** | n | **n**o, sudd**en** | v | ca**v**e, val**v**e, **v**ine |
| | | ng | thi**ng**, i**n**k | w | **w**ith, **w**olf |
| g | **g**a**g**, **g**et, finger | p | **p**op, ha**pp**y | y | **y**es, **y**olk, on**i**on |
| h | **h**at, **wh**o | r | **r**oar, **rh**yme | z | ro**s**e, si**z**e, **x**ylophone, **z**ebra |
| hw | **wh**ich, **wh**ere | s | mi**ss**, **s**au**c**e, **sc**ene, **s**ee | zh | gara**g**e, plea**s**ure, vi**s**ion |
| j | **j**ud**g**e, **g**em | sh | di**sh**, **sh**ip, **s**ugar, ti**ss**ue | | |
| k | **c**at, **k**i**ck**, s**ch**ool | | | | |

## Vowel Sounds

| | | | | | |
|---|---|---|---|---|---|
| ă | p**a**t, l**au**gh | ŏ | h**o**rrible, p**o**t | ŭ | c**u**t, fl**oo**d, r**ou**gh, s**o**me |
| ā | **a**pe, **ai**d, p**ay** | ō | g**o**, r**ow**, t**oe**, th**ough** | û | c**i**rcle, f**u**r, h**ea**rd, t**e**rm, t**u**rn, **u**rge, w**o**rd |
| â | **ai**r, c**a**re, w**ea**r | ô | **a**ll, c**augh**t, f**o**r, p**aw** | | |
| ä | f**a**ther, k**o**ala, y**a**rd | oi | b**oy**, n**oi**se, **oi**l | | |
| ĕ | p**e**t, pl**e**asure, **a**ny | ou | c**ow**, **ou**t | yŏŏ | c**u**re |
| ē | b**e**, b**ee**, **e**asy, pian**o** | ŏŏ | f**u**ll, b**oo**k, w**o**lf | yōō | ab**u**se, **u**se |
| ĭ | **i**f, p**i**t, b**u**sy | ōō | b**oo**t, r**u**de, fr**ui**t, fl**ew** | ə | **a**go, sil**e**nt, penc**i**l, lem**o**n, circ**u**s |
| ī | r**i**de, b**y**, p**ie**, h**igh** | | | | |
| î | d**ea**r, d**ee**r, f**ie**rce, m**e**re | | | | |

## Stress Marks

Primary Stress ´: bi·ol·o·gy [bī **ŏl´** ə jē]
Secondary Stress ´: bi·o·log·i·cal [bī´ ə **lŏj´** ĭ kəl]

Pronunciation key and definitions © 1998 by Houghton Mifflin Company. Adapted and reprinted by permission from *The American Heritage Children's Dictionary.*

# A

**ab·o·li·tion·ist** (ăb´ ə lĭsh´ ə nĭst) *n.* · A person who felt that slavery should be against the law. *Quakers and other **abolitionists** believed that owning slaves was wrong.*

**a·bun·dant** (ə bŭn´ dənt) *adj.* More than enough; plentiful. *Fish and game were **abundant** along the coast.*

**ac·com·pa·ni·ment** (ə kŭm´ pə nĭ mənt) *n.* A musical part, usually played on an instrument, that goes along with the performance of a singer or musician. *Victoria sang to the **accompaniment** of a guitar.*

**ad·ven·ture** (əd vĕn´ chər) *n.* An unusual or exciting experience. *Greg thought that sailing to Africa would be a real **adventure**.*

**ag·gres·sive** (ə grĕs´ ĭv) *adj.* Ready and quick to fight; bold. *The bear cub snarled in an **aggressive** way.*

**am·a·teur** (ăm´ ə chər) *n.* Someone who performs a sport or other activity without being paid. *You must be an **amateur** to compete in high school sports.*

**a·maz·ing·ly** (ə mā´ zĭng lē) *adv.* In a way that causes surprise or wonder. *The test questions were **amazingly** easy.*

**ap·plause** (ə plôz´) *n.* The clapping of hands to show approval. *Adam's speech was greeted with loud **applause**.*

**ap·pren·tice** (ə prĕn´ tĭs) *n.* Someone who works for another person in order to learn a trade. *The blacksmith helped the **apprentice** learn how to use the tools.*

**arm** (ärm) *v.* To equip with weapons. *The rebels were **arming** themselves as the British troops approached the town.*

**ar·ti·fi·cial** (är´ tə fĭsh´ əl) *adj.* Created by humans rather than occuring in nature. *The zookeepers built an **artificial** den for the lion to live in.*

**ar·tis·tic** (är tĭs´ tĭk) *adj.* Showing imagination and skill in creating something beautiful. *The dancers gave an **artistic** performance.*

**as·tro·naut** (ăs´ trə nôt) *n.* A person trained to fly in a spacecraft. *Neil Armstrong was the first **astronaut** to walk on the moon.*

**at·tach·ment** (ə tăch´ mənt) *n.* A feeling of closeness and affection. *The two cousins have a strong **attachment** to one another.*

**amateur**
*Amateur* comes from the Latin word *amare*, which means "to love." Someone who is an amateur takes part in an activity for the love of it.

**apprentice**
*Apprentice* comes from the Latin word *apprehendere*, which means "to grasp." An apprentice is a learner who must grasp what to do in a profession.

**astronaut**
This word was created in 1929 by combining two ancient Greek word parts, *astro-* and *nautes*, which translate as "star sailor."

---

ōō b**oo**t / ou **ou**t / ŭ c**u**t / û f**u**r / hw **wh**ich / th **th**in / *th* **th**is / zh vi**s**ion / ə **a**go, sil**e**nt, penc**i**l, lem**o**n, circ**u**s

**braille**
Louis Braille (1809–1852) was a French inventor who lost his sight at the age of three and as a student of fifteen created the unique writing system that bears his name.

**canopy**
The Greek word *konopeion,* a bed with a netting to keep out mosquitoes, gave us the word for the covering created by treetops in a rain forest.

**caribou**
*Caribou* is the Canadian French version of a Native American word — the Micmac *khalibu,* which means "snow scraper."

**au·di·ence** (ô´ dē əns) *n.* People who gather to see and hear a performance. *The audience cheered loudly as the singer bowed.*

# B

**ban·dit** (băn´ dĭt) *n.* An outlaw, especially one who robs. *The bandit demanded that the passengers hand over their wallets.*

**bluff** (blŭf) *n.* A high cliff or bank. *From the top of the bluff, he could see the entire valley.*

**braille** (brāl) *n.* A system of writing that uses raised dots, for people who are visually impaired. *Angela ran her fingers over the braille letters on the page.*

# C

**cache** (kăsh) *n.* A store of hidden goods. *The bear dug up the campers' cache of food.*

**can·o·py** (kăn´ ə pē) *n.* The highest layer of a forest, formed by the treetops. *Many kinds of parrots and monkeys live in the dense canopy of the rain forest.*

**cap·tive** (kăp´ tĭv) *n.* A prisoner. *The soldiers brought their captives back to the fort.* — *adj.* Captured; held against one's will. *The captive squirrel managed to escape from the trap.*

**car·cass** (kär´ kəs) *n.* The dead body of an animal. *The wolves fed on the carcass of a deer.*

**car·go** (kär´ gō) *n., pl.* **cargoes**. The freight carried by a ship or other vehicle. *The ship's cargo included molasses from the West Indies.*

**car·i·bou** (kăr´ ə bōō´) *n., pl.* **caribou**. A large deer found in northern North America, related to the reindeer. *The herd of caribou swam across the river.*

**cau·tious** (kô´ shəs) *adj.* Careful; not taking chances. *It is best to be cautious when crossing a busy street.*

**cel·e·bra·tion** (sĕl´ ə brā´ shən) *n.* A special activity that honors a person, event, or idea. *I invited ten friends to my birthday celebration.*

**cin·der** (sĭn´ dər) *n.* A partly burned piece of coal or wood. *A pile of cinders lay at the bottom of the fire pit.*

**claim** (klām) *n.* A piece of land that someone reserves for ownership. *The settlers took a claim that bordered on the river.*

**col·lide** (kə līd´) *v.* To come together with forceful impact. *When warm and cold air masses collide, the weather becomes stormy.*

---

ă rat / ā pay / â care / ä father / ĕ pet / ē be / ĭ pit / ī pie / î fierce / ŏ pot / ō go / ô paw, for / oi oil / ōō book

# D

**col·o·ny** (kŏl´ ə nē) *n., pl.*
**colonies** A territory ruled by or
belonging to another country.
*The thirteen colonies no longer
wanted to be taxed by England.*

**com·pete** (kəm pēt´) *v.* To take
part in a contest. *The runners
hoped to compete in the Boston
Marathon.*

**con·cen·trate** (kŏn´ sən trāt´) *v.*
To give full attention to. *It is difficult to concentrate on my book
when the television is on.*

**con·flict** (kŏn´ flĭkt´) *n.* A struggle; a war. *The United States had
a second conflict with England
in 1812.*

**con·vinced** (kən vĭnsd´) *adj.*
Persuaded; certain. *They were
convinced that the bridge was
strong enough to carry their
weight.*

**cra·ter** (krā´ tər) *n.* A hollow
bowl-shaped area at the mouth of
a volcano. *The hikers peered
down into the deep rocky crater
below.*

**crust** (krŭst) *n.* The hard outer
layer of the earth. *Cracks in the
earth's crust help create volcanoes.*

**cus·tom** (kŭs´ təm) *n.* Something that members of a group
usually do. *One of the customs
of people in the desert is to offer
visitors refreshment and shade.*

**de·bris** (də brē´) *n.* The remains
of something broken or destroyed;
rubble. *The bulldozer pushed the
debris into the corner of the lot.*

**de·but** (dā byōō´) *n.* First public
performance. *The actor made his
stage debut as Peter Pan.*

**dec·o·rate** (dĕk´ ə rāt´) *v.* To
make festive or beautiful. *We will
decorate the room with flowers
and streamers.*

**dem·on·stra·tion** (dĕm´ ən strā´
shən) *n.* A showing and explanation of how something works.
*The teacher gave a demonstra-
tion of how to operate a camera.*

**de·scrip·tion** (dĭ skrĭp´ shən) *n.*
A statement that uses words to
tell about something. *Debbie
wrote an exciting description of
the game.*

**de·tain** (dĭ tān´) *v.* To delay; to
hold back. *If you detain us much
longer, we will miss the bus.*

**de·ter·mi·na·tion** (dĭ tûr´ mə nā´
shən) *n.* Firmness in carrying
out a decision. *The team's determination to do better showed in
how well they played.*

**dev·as·ta·tion** (dĕv´ ə stā´ shən)
*n.* Destruction or ruin. *The
floods brought devastation to
much of the coast.*

crater

---

ōō b**oo**t / ou **ou**t / ŭ c**u**t / û f**u**r / hw **wh**ich / th **th**in / *th* **th**is / zh vi**si**on / ə **a**go,
sil**e**nt, penc**i**l, lem**o**n, circ**u**s

**dex·ter·i·ty** (děk **stěr´** ĭ tē) *n.* Skill in the use of the hands, body, or mind. *The juggler showed great dexterity in keeping the oranges in the air.*

**di·a·ry** (**dī´** ə rē) *n., pl.* **diaries**. A daily record of a person's thoughts and experiences. *Every night Marta wrote about the day's events in her diary.*

**dic·ta·tor** (**dĭk´** tā tər) *n.* A ruler who has complete power over a country. *The dictator would not allow any citizens to travel outside the country.*

**di·lem·ma** (dĭ **lěm´** ə) *n.* A situation in which one has to choose between two or more difficult options. *Sara's dilemma was whether to wake up her father or try to figure out the problem herself.*

**dim sum** (dĭm´ sŏŏm´) *n.* A type of traditional Chinese meal where small portions of different foods are served one after another. *Many Chinese restaurants serve dim sum on Sunday mornings.*

**dis·ap·point·ed** (dĭs´ ə **point´** əd) *adj.* Unhappy because of an unsatisfied hope or wish. *Tanya was disappointed when her team lost the game.*

**dis·com·fort** (dĭs **kŭm´** fərt) *n.* A feeling of mild distress. *Noah always feels discomfort when people ask him about his famous brother.*

**dis·cour·aged** (dĭ **skûr´** ĭjd) *adj.* Not hopeful or enthusiastic. *Sam felt discouraged when he learned that he had not won a prize.*

**dis·mayed** (dĭs **mād´**) *adj.* Filled with sudden concern or distress. *They were dismayed to learn that the bus had left without them.*

**dog guide** (dôg gīd) *n.* A dog especially trained to lead visually impaired people. *May's dog guide waited until it was safe to cross the street.*

**dom·i·nance** (**dŏm´** ə nəns) *n.* The greatest control within a group. *Wolves compete for dominance in the pack.*

**dread** (drěd) *n.* Great fear. *The panther's roar filled the villagers with dread.*

**drill** (drĭl) *v.* To perform training exercises. *The soldiers were drilling all morning.*

**du·o** (**dōō´** ō) *n.* Two people performing together. *The sisters performed in the show as a singing duo.*

# E

**earth·quake** (**ûrth´** kwāk´) *n.* A trembling or shaking of the ground caused by sudden movements in rock below the earth's surface. *The earthquake caused buildings to topple.*

**dominance**

The root of this word is the Latin word *domus*, meaning "house." The head of a household often had control, or dominance, over a large staff of people.

**dim sum**

---

ă rat / ā pay / â care / ä father / ě pet / ē be / ĭ pit / ī pie / î fierce / ŏ pot / ō go / ô paw, for / oi oil / ŏŏ book

**el·e·ment** (ĕl´ ə mənt) *n.* A basic part of a whole. *Spirals, spins, and jumps are **elements** of a figure skating program.*

**em·bar·rassed** (ĕm băr´ əsd) *adj.* Made to feel self-conscious and ill at ease. *Josh felt **embarrassed** when he realized he had called her by the wrong name.*

**en·cour·age** (ĕn kûr´ ĭj) *v.* To give support to; to inspire. *Hal's parents **encouraged** him to become a skater.*

**en·slave·ment** (ĕn slāv´ mənt) *n.* The process by which one person becomes the property of another. *After years of **enslavement** by cruel owners, the men were set free.*

**e·rup·tion** (ĭ rŭp´ shən) *n.* A volcanic explosion or large flow of lava. *The newspaper showed photos of the **eruption** of a volcano in Nicaragua.*

**ex·cite·ment** (ĭk sīt´ mənt) *n.* A stirred-up feeling. *The fire caused a lot of **excitement** in our neighborhood.*

**ex·per·i·ence** (ĭk spîr´ ē əns) *n.* An event that someone takes part in or lives through. *Camping was a new **experience** for the children.*

**ex·press** (ĭk sprĕs´) *adj.* Fast, direct, and often nonstop. ***Express** services promise overnight deliveries.*

**ex·tend·ed** (ĭk stĕn´ dĭd) *adj.* Including more; broadened. *Your **extended** family includes your aunts, uncles, and cousins.*

**ex·tinc·tion** (ĭk stĭngk´ shən) *n.* The condition of having died out. *No one knows for sure what caused the **extinction** of the dinosaurs.*

# F

**fash·ion** (făsh´ ən) *v.* To give a form or shape to; to make. *Ralph was able to **fashion** a waterproof cape from a large plastic bag.*

**fault** (fôlt) *n.* A break in a rock mass caused by a shifting of the earth's crust. *An active **fault** runs through the center of our town.*

**fer·tile** (fûr´ tl) *adj.* Rich in material needed to grow healthy plants. *Wheat and corn grew well in the prairie's **fertile** soil.*

**fes·tive** (fĕs´ tĭv) *adj.* Joyful; merry. *The party guests were in a **festive** mood.*

**fierce** (fîrs) *adj.* Intense; ferocious. *The lion gave a **fierce** roar.*

**for·ty-five re·cord** (fôr´ tē fīv´ rĕk´ ərd) *n.* A small phonograph record that is played at forty-five revolutions per minute. *The **forty-five record** has one song on each side.*

**eruption**

**fierce**
The Latin word *ferus* ("wild and savage") is the origin of the words *ferocious* and *fierce.*

oo b**oo**t / ou **ou**t / ŭ c**u**t / û f**u**r / hw **wh**ich / th **th**in / *th* **th**is / zh vi**s**ion / ə **a**go, sil**e**nt, penc**i**l, lem**o**n, circ**u**s

**funnel cloud**

**fran·tic** (**frăn´** tĭk) *adj.* Very upset, as from fear or worry. *When she couldn't find her backpack anywhere, Julie became* **frantic.**

**fright·ened** (**frīt´** nd) *adj.* Scared, alarmed. *Billy was* **frightened** *as he stepped out on the diving board.*

**fun·nel cloud** (**fŭn´** əl kloud´) *n.* A storm cloud that is wide at the top and narrow at the bottom, often becoming a tornado. *Whenever the settlers saw* **funnel clouds***, they hurried toward storm shelters.*

# G

**gene** (jēn) *n.* A tiny part of a plant or animal cell that determines a characteristic passed on to the next generation. *Lucy has blue eyes like her parents because of their* **genes.**

# H

**hab·i·tat** (**hăb´** ĭ tăt´) *n.* The type of environment where an animal or plant naturally lives and grows. *Sloths and jaguars live in the rain forest* **habitat.**

**harsh** (härsh) *adj.* Demanding and severe; unpleasant. *Winter is a* **harsh** *season for most animals.*

**har·vest** (**här´** vĭst) *v.* To gather a crop. *The workers were* **harvesting** *apples.*

**heif·er** (**hěf´** ər) *n.* A young cow that has not yet had a calf. *Sally's cow has been winning blue ribbons since it was a* **heifer.**

**herd** (hûrd) *n.* A group of animals of a single kind. *A* **herd** *of wild horses galloped across the plain.*

**her·i·tage** (**hěr´** ĭ tĭj) *n.* Traditions, practices, and beliefs passed down from earlier generations. *Yinglan celebrates her Chinese* **heritage** *in her choice of music, clothes, and food.*

**home·stead** (**hōm´** stěd´) *n.* A piece of land given to settlers for farming and building a home. *The Andersens'* **homestead** *lay near Blackberry Creek.*

**hon·or** (**ŏn´** ər) *v.* To show respect for; to accept. *They will* **honor** *their mother's request to dress up for Thanksgiving dinner.*

**hu·mid** (**hyōō´** mĭd) *adj.* Containing a large amount of water vapor; damp, sticky. *The air is often* **humid** *before a storm.*

# I

**im·mi·grant** (**ĭm´** ĭ grənt) *n.* A person who moves to a new country. *Many* **immigrants** *from Norway made their homes on the Great Plains.*

---

ă rat / ā pay / â care / ä father / ě pet / ē be / ĭ pit / ī pie / î fierce / ŏ pot / ō go / ô paw, for / oi oil / ŏŏ book

**im·mo·bile** (ĭ mō´ bəl) *adj.* Fixed in one place; unable to move. *He stood **immobile** against the cliff face as the hikers passed by.*

**im·pact** (ĭm´ păkt´) *n.* The striking of one object against another. *The **impact** of the bike hitting the fence knocked the flowerpots to the ground.*

**im·press** (ĭm prĕs´) *v.* To have a strong, favorable effect on someone's feelings. *His piano playing **impressed** the audience.*

**in·flu·en·tial** (ĭn´ flōō ĕn´ shəl) *adj.* Having the power to affect events or sway opinions. *The **influential** Women's League brought the problem to the mayor's attention.*

**in·her·it** (ĭn hĕr´ ĭt) *v.* To receive something from a parent or ancestor. *They **inherited** their mother's talent for music.*

**in·stinct** (ĭn´ stĭngkt´) *n.* An inner feeling or way of behaving that is automatic, not learned. *A newly hatched sea turtle's **instinct** is to crawl toward the water.*

**in·tense** (ĭn tĕns´) *adj.* Very strong; focused. *Patrice put in hours of **intense** study to get ready for the test.*

# J

**jag·ged** (jăg´ ĭd) *adj.* Having a ragged or pointed edge or outline. *Jamal cut his hand on a **jagged** piece of tin.*

**jar** (jär) *v.* To bump or cause to shake from impact. *By **jarring** Matthew, I caused him to drop the ball.*

**jolt** (jōlt) *n.* A sudden jerk or bump. *When the car went over the speed bump, the passengers got quite a **jolt**.*

**judge** (jŭj) *n.* A person who decides who wins a contest. *The **judges** awarded first prize to my grandfather's pumpkin pie.*

**just** (jŭst) *adj.* Honorable and fair. *It is **just** to listen to both sides of an argument.*

# K

**kin** (kĭn) *n.* Relatives; family. *Your father's cousins are your **kin**, too.*

# L

**launch** (lônch) *v.* To forcefully send upward. *A powerful blast **launches** the rocket into the sky.*

**la·va** (lä´ və) *n.* Hot melted rock that flows from a volcano. *As the **lava** moved down the hillside, it set fire to the trees in its path.*

**lava**
People from Naples, Italy, near Mt. Vesuvius, used the Italian word *lava*, meaning "a stream caused suddenly by rain" for the molten rock that flowed down the volcano. It became an English word in 1750.

ōō b**oo**t / ou **ou**t / ŭ c**u**t / û f**u**r / hw **wh**ich / th **th**in / *th* **th**is / zh vi**si**on / ə **a**go, sil**e**nt, penc**i**l, lem**o**n, circ**u**s

**lay·out** (lā´ out´) *n.* The way something is arranged. *The layout of the office building confuses visitors.*

**lib·er·ty** (lĭb´ ər tē) *n.* Freedom from the control of others; inde-pendence. *The colonists won their liberty from England.*

**light·ning** (līt´ nĭng) *n.* The flash of light when electricity builds up in storm clouds. *A bolt of light-ning lit up the night sky.*

**lime·light** (līm´ līt´) *n.* The cen-ter of public attention. *Ana's per-formance in the play brought her into the limelight.*

# M

**mag·ma** (măg´ mə) *n.* Molten rock underneath the earth's sur-face. *Magma boiled up through cracks deep inside the mountain.*

**mare** (mâr) *n.* A female horse. *Some of the mares were followed by their colts.*

**mas·ter** (măs´ tər) *v.* To become expert in a skill or art. *Ramón mastered the violin through years of practice.*

**ma·ture** (mə tyŏŏr´) *adj.* Fully grown or mentally developed. *A mature dog is calmer than a puppy.*

**mem·o·rize** (mĕm´ ə rīz´) *v.* To learn by completely remember-ing. *The hikers are memorizing the landmarks along their route.*

**mi·gra·tion** (mī grā´ shən) *n.* A movement of animals to a differ-ent habitat, especially in response to the change of seasons. *Scientists have mapped the spring migration of the whales.*

**mill** (mĭl) *v.* To move around in confusion. *The impatient crowd milled in front of the theater doors.*

**mis·sion** (mĭsh´ ən) *n.* An opera-tion that attempts to achieve cer-tain goals or carry out specific tasks. *The astronauts' mission included bringing back samples of moon rocks.*

**mol·ten** (mōl´ tən) *adj.* Made liquid by heat. *The molten lava glowed red-orange.*

**mus·tang** (mŭs´ tăng´) *n.* A wild horse of the plains of west-ern North America. *Joe could not ride as fast as the herd of mustangs.*

# N

**no·ble** (nō´ bəl) *adj.* Showing greatness of character by unselfish behavior. *It was noble of Karen to share her prize money with her teammates.*

**no·to·ri·ous** (nō tôr´ ē əs) *adj.* Well known for something bad. *Billy the Kid was a notorious outlaw.*

ă rat / ā pay / â care / ä father / ĕ pet / ē be / ĭ pit / ī pie / î fierce / ŏ pot / ō go / ô paw, for / oi oil / ŏŏ book

# O

**o·be·di·ence** (ō bē´ dē əns) *n.* Willingness to follow orders. *Mr. Yee expects* **obedience** *from his crew.*

**ob·ser·va·tion** (ŏb´ zûr vā´ shən) *n.* The act of paying careful attention. *You can learn a lot about nature through* **observation.**

**ob·sta·cle** (ŏb´ stə kəl) *n.* A thing that stands in one's way. *The horse had to jump over such* **obstacles** *as bushes and fences.*

**op·er·a** (ŏp´ ə rə) *n.* A form of theater in which the dialogue is sung to musical accompaniment. *The actors in the* **opera** *wore beautiful costumes.*

**op·pose** (ə pōz´) *v.* To be against something or someone. *The neighbors* **oppose** *the plan to turn the park into an office building.*

**or·bit** (ôr´ bĭt) *n.* The path of a spacecraft around the earth. *Shannon Lucid spent six months in* **orbit** *aboard the spacecraft Mir.*

**o·ver·take** (ō´ vər tāk´) *v.* To catch up with. *If we continue at this pace, we will* **overtake** *Billie's group.*

# P

**pan·to·mime** (păn´ tə mīm´) *n.* The use of movements and facial expressions instead of words to convey meaning. *Jean used* **pantomime** *to show us how she caught the fish.*

**Pa·tri·ot** (pā´ trē ət) *n.* A colonist who was against British rule in the time of the Revolutionary War. *Patrick Henry spoke as a* **Patriot** *when he said "Give me liberty or give me death!"*

**peer** (pîr) *v.* To look at with concentration. *Mom* **peered** *at Paul suspiciously as he told his story.*

**pi·o·neer** (pī´ ə nîr´) *adj.* Describing a person who is first or among the first to settle in a region. *Our town was settled by three* **pioneer** *families in the 1800s.*

**prai·rie** (prâr´ ē) *n.* A large area of flat or rolling grassland. *The treeless* **prairie** *stretched for miles in all directions.*

**pred·a·tor** (prĕd´ ə tər) *n.* An animal that hunts other animals for food. *Small lizards must always be on the alert for hungry* **predators.**

**pres·en·ta·tion** (prĕz´ ən tā´ shən) *n.* Performance. *Although the actor knew his lines, his* **presentation** *was flat.*

**pioneer**
This word comes from the French word *peonier,* meaning "foot soldier." Those who marched into unknown territory were often soldiers on an expedition.

---

ōō b**oo**t / ou **ou**t / ŭ c**u**t / û f**u**r / hw **wh**ich / th **th**in / *th* **th**is / zh vi**si**on / ə **a**go, sil**e**nt, penc**i**l, lem**o**n, circ**u**s

**pres·sure** (**prĕsh´** ər) *n.* A strong influence or force. *Sandra felt* *pressure to finish the book over the weekend.*

**pri·va·teer** (prī´ və **tîr´**) *n.* A privately owned ship that is ordered by the government to attack enemy ships during a war. *The privateers captured several merchant ships without firing a shot.*

**pro·gram** (**prō´** grăm´) *n.* In figure skating, the routine that one performs in front of judges or an audience. *The young skater spent hours getting his program ready for the competition.*

**prose** (prōz) *n.* Ordinary spoken or written language, in contrast to poetry. *Most fiction and nonfiction books are written in prose.*

# R

**raid** (rād) *n.* A sudden attack, often with the goal of taking property. *The men brought back horses after their raid on their neighbors' village.*

**ra·vine** (rə **vēn´**) *n.* A narrow, deep valley, usually formed by the flow of water. *A small stream trickled at the bottom of the ravine.*

**reb·el** (**rĕb´** əl) *n.* A person who opposes or defies the government in power. *The rebels refused to obey King George's laws.*

**ref·u·gee** (rĕf´ yo͞o **jē´**) *n.* A person who flees to find protection from danger. *As the fighting in the hills grew worse, refugees streamed into the city.*

**re·hear·sal** (rĭ **hûr´** səl) *n.* A session of practicing for a public performance. *The cast needed one more rehearsal before the play opened.*

**re·in·tro·duc·tion** (rē´ ĭn trə **dŭk´** shən) *n.* The process of returning animals to their native habitats. *The zoo's tamarins are doing well since their reintroduction into the rain forest.*

**re·ject** (rĭ **jĕkt´**) *v.* To refuse to accept. *The magazine rejected her poem.*

**re·luc·tant** (rĭ **lŭk´** tənt) *adj.* Unwilling to take an action. *Emily was reluctant to get out of the swimming pool.*

**re·morse** (rĭ **môrs´**) *n.* A feeling of regret or guilt for having done something wrong. *Jennie felt remorse for the trouble she had caused her sister.*

**rep·u·ta·tion** (rĕp´ yə **tā´** shən) *n.* What others think about someone's character, behavior, and abilities. *Alex had a reputation for getting along well with everyone.*

**re·quired** (rĭ **kwīrd´**) *adj.* Needed. *Kayla has all of the training required for this job.*

**ravine**

---

ă rat / ā pay / â care / ä father / ĕ pet / ē be / ĭ pit / ī pie / î fierce / ŏ pot / ō go / ô paw, for / oi oil / o͝o book

**re·spect** (rĭ **spĕkt´**) *n.* A feeling of admiration and approval. *Mr. García won the **respect** of all his students.*

**re·us·a·ble** (rē **yo͞oz´** ə bəl) *adj.* Able to be used again. *April's family never throws away **reusable** paper bags.*

**rev·o·lu·tion·ar·y** (rĕv´ ə **lo͞o´** shə nĕr´ ē) *adj.* Connected with complete change. *The American colonists fought for their independence from England during the **Revolutionary** War.*

**rhyth·mic** (**rĭth´** mĭk) *adj.* Having a noticeable beat with a pattern to it. *It is easy to dance to **rhythmic** music.*

**ro·tate** (**rō´** tāt) *v.* To turn around on a center or axis. *It takes twenty-four hours for the earth to **rotate** once.*

**rug·ged** (**rŭg´** ĭd) *adj.* Having a very rough and uneven surface. *The valley was surrounded by **rugged** mountains.*

# S

**sat·el·lite** (**săt´** l īt´) *n.* A human-made device that orbits a planet. *A weather **satellite** sends weather photos and data back to earth.*

**sen·try** (**sĕn´** trē) *n., pl.,* **sentries**. A guard who is posted at a spot to keep watch. *Two **sentries** guarded the gates of the city.*

**se·vere** (sə **vîr´**) *adj.* Serious or extreme in nature. ***Severe** thunderstorms caused flooding in parts of the Midwest.*

**shud·der** (**shŭd´** ər) *v.* To suddenly shake, vibrate, or quiver. *The house **shuddered** every time a heavy truck drove by.*

**siz·zling** (**sĭz´** lĭng) *adj.* Crackling or hissing with intense heat. *The tree trunk was **sizzling** after the lightning bolt hit it.*

**skir·mish** (**skûr´** mĭsh) *n.* A small, short fight; a minor battle. *The soldiers galloped away after a brief **skirmish** with the rebels.*

**skit·ter** (**skĭt´** ər) *v.* To move lightly and quickly, especially with many changes of direction. *The mice **skittered** across the floor.*

**skit·tish** (**skĭt´** ĭsh) *adj.* Nervous and jumpy. *The cat was **skittish** during the thunderstorm.*

**snoop** (sno͞op) *n.* Someone who tries to find out about other people's doings in a sneaky way. *Maria's brother is such a **snoop** that she must keep her diary locked.*

**sod** (sŏd) *n.* A chunk of grass and soil held together by matted roots. *Settlers built houses out of blocks of **sod** because wood was scarce.*

**satellite**
In the Middle Ages the French used the word *satellite* to refer to an attendant who waits upon an important person. That same idea is in the modern meaning of a small device circling around a planet.

---

o͞o b**oo**t / ou **ou**t / ŭ c**u**t / û f**u**r / hw **wh**ich / th **th**in / *th* **th**is / zh vi**s**ion / ə **a**go, sil**e**nt, penc**i**l, lem**o**n, circ**u**s

**sombrero**
The name of the broad-brimmed hat that shades the wearer's eyes came from the Spanish word for shade, *sombra.*

**shuttle**
*Shuttle* started out as an Old English word, *scytel,* meaning "dart." It came to mean a weaving device that carried thread back and forth, and from that, a vehicle going back and forth over a short route.

**som·bre·ro** (sŏm **brâr´** ō) *n.* A tall hat with a wide brim, worn in Mexico and the American Southwest. *The farmers wore* **sombreros** *to shade their eyes from the sun.*

**space shut·tle** (spās **shŭt´** l) *n.* A reusable spacecraft that is launched like a rocket and can be landed like a plane. *The* **space shuttle** *landed safely after a seven-day flight.*

**space·craft** (**spās´** krăft´) *n.* A vehicle designed for travel beyond the earth's atmosphere. *The* **spacecraft** *carried astronauts to the moon.*

**spe·cial·ist** (**spĕsh´** ə lĭst) *n.* Someone who is an expert in a particular field. *A pediatrician is a medical* **specialist** *who treats only children.*

**spec·ta·tor** (**spĕk´** tā´ tər) *n.* A person who watches an event or performance. *The* **spectators** *cheered when Jessie hit a home run.*

**splen·did** (**splĕn´** dĭd) *adj.* Excellent. *The actor gave a* **splendid** *performance.*

**stal·lion** (**stăl´** yən) *n.* An adult male horse. *Lizzie rode a black* **stallion** *at the horse show.*

**stam·i·na** (**stăm´** ə nə) *n.* The strength needed to keep doing something tiring or difficult. *A young child lacks the* **stamina** *for a ten-mile hike.*

**store·house** (**stôr´** hous´) *n.* A place or building where supplies are stored for future use. *The settlers'* **storehouse** *contained dried fruit and hams.*

**sub·mit** (səb **mĭt´**) *v.* To offer one's work to someone for their judgment or approval. *She* **submitted** *an article to the student newspaper.*

**sub·ser·vi·ence** (səb **sûr´** vē əns) *n.* Willingness to give in to others' power. *Letting the tail droop is a sign of* **subservience** *in a wolf.*

**sum·mit** (**sŭm´** ĭt) *n.* The top of a mountain. *Carolyn and I cheered when we finally reached the* **summit** *of Mount Rainier.*

**sur·viv·al** (sər **vī´** vəl) *n.* The preservation or continuation of one's life. *Quick thinking is often necessary for* **survival** *in the wilderness.*

**sus·pect** (sə **spĕkt´**) *v.* To believe without being sure; to imagine. *Scott* **suspects** *that we are planning a surprise party for him.*

# T

**tack** (tăk) *v.* To change the course of a boat. *The sailing ship was* **tacking** *in order to return to the harbor.*

ă rat / ā pay / â care / ä father / ĕ pet / ē be / ĭ pit / ī pie / î fierce / ŏ pot / ō go / ô paw, for / oi oil / ŏŏ book

**tal·ent** (tăl´ ənt) *n.* A natural ability to do something well. *She has a talent for playing the violin.*

**tax** (tăks) *n.* Money that people must pay in order to support a government. *England insisted that the colonists pay taxes on tea, stamps, and many other items.*

**tech·ni·cal** (tĕk´ nĭ kəl) *adj.* Showing basic knowledge of a complex task. *The acrobat performed the triple somersault with great technical skill.*

**ter·ri·fy** (tĕr´ ə fī´) *v.* To fill with overpowering fear. *The angry bear terrified the campers.*

**ter·ri·to·ry** (tĕr´ ĭ tôr´ ē) *n., pl.* **territories.** An area inhabited by an animal or animal group and defended against intruders. *The mountain lion hunted within its own territory.*

**To·ry** (tôr´ ē) *n., pl.* **Tories.** An American who sided with the British during the American Revolution. *As the British troops departed, most of the city's Tories followed.*

**tor·na·do** (tôr nā´ dō) *n.* A violent, whirling wind in a funnel-shaped cloud that can cause great destruction. *Many tornadoes form in Kansas and Oklahoma.*

**tra·di·tion** (trə dĭsh´ ən) *n.* The passing down of customs and beliefs from one generation to the next. *There is a long tradition of helping others in our family.*

**train·ing** (trā´ nĭng) *n.* The process of learning how to behave or perform. *Guide dogs must go through a long period of training before they can help people.*

**trans·form** (trăns fôrm´) *v.* To change greatly in appearance or form. *The make-up transformed the actor into the character of an old man.*

**tun·dra** (tŭn´ drə) *n.* A treeless Arctic region where very few plants can grow. *Large plants cannot put down roots in the frozen subsoil of the tundra.*

# U

**un·der·stand** (ŭn´ dər stănd´) *v.* To get the meaning of. *After the teacher explained it again, Ivan could understand the problem.*

**un·du·lat·ing** (ŭn´ jə lāt´ ĭng) *adj.* Moving in waves or with a smooth, wavy motion. *The undulating water raised and lowered the rowboat.*

**un·sure** (ŭn shoor´) *adj.* Not certain; having doubts. *She was unsure of whether to bring her umbrella.*

---

**tornado**
*Tornadoes* were unknown and unnamed in Britain, so Americans borrowed and adapted the Spanish word *tronada,* meaning "thunderstorm."

**tradition**
Our word for the passing down of customs from one generation to another comes from the Latin verb *tradere,* which means "to hand down."

**undulate**
The Latin word for a wave, *unda,* contributes the sense of rising and falling in *undulate.*

---

o͞o b**oo**t / ou **ou**t / ŭ c**u**t / û f**u**r / hw **wh**ich / th **th**in / *th* **th**is / zh vi**si**on / ə **a**go, sil**e**nt, penc**i**l, lem**o**n, circ**u**s

**up·heav·al** (ŭp hē′ vəl) *n.* A lifting or upward movement of the earth's crust. *The mountain range was created by a great* **upheaval**.

**ur·gent·ly** (ûr′ jənt lē) *adv.* In a way that calls for immediate action. *The team* **urgently** *needs someone to take Kate's place.*

# V

**vol·un·teer** (vŏl′ ən tîr′) *v.* To offer to do something of one's own free will, usually without being paid. *He* **volunteered** *to make the posters for the show.*

# W

**war·i·ness** (wâr′ ē nĭs) *n.* Extreme caution. *Wild animals show* **wariness** *with people they don't know.*

**wilderness**

**weight·less·ness** (wāt′ lĭs nĭs) *n.* The condition of experiencing little or no pull of gravity. *Astronauts experience* **weightlessness** *in outer space.*

**wil·der·ness** (wĭl′ dər nĭs) *n.* A region in its natural state, unsettled by human beings. *Grizzly bears live in the Alaskan* **wilderness**.

**wound** (wo͞ond) *n.* Injury in which the skin is cut or broken. *The soldier's* **wounds** *were not serious.*

ă rat / ā pay / â care / ä father / ĕ pet / ē be / ĭ pit / ī pie / î fierce / ŏ pot / ō go /
ô paw, for / oi oil / o͝o book

# Acknowledgments

## Main Literature Selections

*And Then What Happened, Paul Revere?* by Jean Fritz, illustrated by Margot Tomes. Text copyright © 1973 by Jean Fritz. Illustrations copyright © 1973 by Margot Tomes. Reprinted by permission of the Putnam & Grosset Group, a division of Penguin Putnam Inc.

*Black Cowboy, Wild Horses: A True Story,* by Julius Lester, illustrated by Jerry Pinkney. Text copyright © 1998 by Julius Lester. Illustrations copyright © 1998 by Jerry Pinkney. Reprinted by permission of Dial Books for Young Readers, a division of Penguin Putnam Inc.

Selection from *Blizzard!,* by Jim Murphy, published by Scholastic Press, a division of Scholastic Inc. Copyright © 2000 by Jim Murphy. Reprinted by permission of Scholastic Inc.

*A Boy Called Slow: The True Story of Sitting Bull,* by Joseph Bruchac, illustrated by Rocco Baviera. Text copyright © 1994 by Joseph Bruchac. Illustrations copyright © 1994 by Rocco Baviera. Reprinted by permission of the Putnam Grosset Group, a division of Penguin Putnam Inc.

Selection from *Dear Mr. Henshaw,* by Beverly Cleary, illustrated by Paul O. Zelinsky. Text copyright © 1983 by Beverly Cleary. Reprinted by permission of HarperCollins Publishers.

Selection from *Earthquake Terror,* by Peg Kehret. Copyright © 1996 by Peg Kehret. Reprinted by permission of Dutton Children's Books, a division of Penguin Putnam Inc.

Selection from *Elena,* by Diane Stanley. Copyright © 1996 by Diane Stanley. Reprinted by permission of Hyperion Books for Children.

*Eye of the Storm: Chasing Storms with Warren Faidley,* by Stephen Kramer, photographs by Warren Faidley. Text copyright © 1997 by Stephen Kramer. Photographs copyright © 1997 by Warren Faidley. Reprinted by permission of G. P. Putnam's Sons, a division of Penguin Putnam Inc.

Selection from *The Fear Place,* by Phyllis Reynolds Naylor. Copyright © 1994 by Phyllis Reynolds Naylor. Reprinted by permission of Atheneum Books for Young Readers, an imprint of Simon & Schuster Children's Publishing Division. Cover copyright © 1994 by Doron Ben Ami. Reprinted by permission of the author and illustrator.

*The Golden Lion Tamarin Comes Home* by George Ancona. Copyright © 1994 by George Ancona, except photographs of frog, snake and sloth by James M. Dietz and map by Isabel Ancona. All rights reserved. Reprinted with permission of Simon & Schuster Books for Young Readers, an imprint of Simon & Schuster Children's Publishing Division.

*The Grizzly Bear Family Book,* by Michio Hoshino, translated by Karen Collier-Taylor. Copyright © 1992 by Michio Hoshino. Reprinted by permission of North-South Books Inc., New York. All rights reserved.

Selection from *Iditarod Dream,* by Ted Wood. Copyright © 1996 by Ted Wood. Reprinted by arrangement with Walker & Co.

Selection from *Interrupted Journey,* by Kathryn Lasky, photographs by Christopher Knight. Text copyright © 2001 by Kathryn Lasky. Photographs copyright © 2001 by Christopher Knight. Reproduced by permission of Candlewick Press Inc., Cambridge, MA.

*"James Forten"* from *Now Is Your Time: The African-American Struggle for Freedom,* by Walter Dean Myers. Copyright © 1991 by Walter Dean Myers. Reprinted by permission of HarperCollins Publishers.

Selection from *Journey to Nowhere,* by Mary Jane Auch. Copyright © 1997 by Mary Jane Auch. Jacket illustration copyright © 1997 by Bob Crofut. Cover and excerpt reprinted by permission of Henry Holt and Company, LLC.

*Katie's Trunk,* by Ann Turner, illustrated by Ron Himler. Text copyright © 1992 by Ann Turner. Illustrations copyright © 1992 by Ron Himler. All rights reserved. Reprinted by permission of Simon & Schuster Books for Young Readers, an imprint of Simon & Schuster Children's Publishing Division.

*"La Bamba"* from *Baseball in April and Other Stories,* by Gary Soto. Copyright © 1990 by Gary Soto. Reprinted by permission of Harcourt Inc. The song "La Bamba" adaptation and arrangement by Ritchie Valens © 1958 Picture Our Music (Renewed). All rights for U.S.A. administered by EMI Longitude Music (BMI). All rights for the World except U.S.A. administered by Warner-Tamerlane Publishing Corp. All rights reserved. Reprinted by permission of Warner Bros. Publications U.S. Inc.

*Mae Jemison: Space Scientist,* by Gail Sakurai. Copyright © 1995 by Gail Sakurai. Reprinted by permission of Childrens Press Inc., a division of Grolier Publishing.

Selection from *Mariah Keeps Cool,* by Mildred Pitts Walter, illustrated by Pat Cummings. Text copyright © 1990 by Mildred Pitts Walter. Cover illustration copyright © 1990 by Pat Cummings. Reprinted by permission of Simon & Schuster Books for Young Readers, an imprint of Simon & Schuster Children's Publishing Division.

*"Mary Redmond, John Darragh, and Dicey Langston: Spies"* from *We Were There, Too!: Young People in U.S. History,* by Phillip Hoose. Copyright © 2001 by Phillip Hoose. Reprinted by permission of Farrar, Straus and Giroux, LLC.

Selection from *Me, Mop, and the Moondance Kid,* by Walter Dean Myers. Copyright © 1988 by Walter Dean Myers. Used by permission of Random House Children's Books, a division of Random House, Inc.

Selection from *Michelle Kwan: Heart of a Champion, An Autobiography.* Copyright © 1997 by Michelle Kwan Corp. Reprinted by permission of Scholastic Inc. and Momentum Partners Inc.

*Mom's Best Friend,* by Sally Hobart Alexander, photographs by George Ancona. Text copyright © 1992 by Sally Hobart Alexander. Photographs copyright © 1992 by George Ancona. Text reprinted by permission of the Author and Bookstop Literary Agency. Photographs reprinted by permission of the Photographer.

Selection from *My Side of the Mountain,* by Jean Craighead George. Copyright © 1959 by Jean Craighead George. Reprinted by permission of Dutton Children's Books, a division of Penguin Putnam Inc.

Selection from *Night of the Twisters,* by Ivy Ruckman. Text copyright © 1984 by Ivy Ruckman. Reprinted by

## Focus Selections

## Links and Theme Openers

Cheatwood, Florida; Diana Davis, North Carolina; Kathy Driscoll, Massachusetts; Linda Evers, Florida; Heidi Harrison, Michigan; Eileen Hoffman, Massachusetts; Julia Kraftsow, Florida; Bonnie Lewison, Florida; Kanetha McCord, Michigan.

# Credits

## Photography

**3** (t) © Ed Young/Corbis. (m) Hemera Technologies Inc. (b) C Squared Studios/PhotoDisc Green/Getty Images. **5** © Ed Young/Corbis. **8** Hemera Technologies Inc. **9** (t) © PhotoDisc/Getty Images. **11** Hemera Technologies Inc. **13** Hemera Technologies Inc. **16** © 2001 Werner Forman/Art Resource, NY. **17** (l) Courtesy HarperCollins Publishers. (ml) Hugo Van Lawick/National Geographic Image Collection. (mr) © The Walt Disney Company, courtesy The Kobal Collection. (r) Bill Frakes/Life Magazine © Time Inc. **19** C Squared Studios/Photodisc Green/Getty Images. **20—21** (bkgd) ©Byron Aughenbaugh/ The Image Bank/Getty Images. **21** (m) © Ed Young/ Corbis. **22** (mr) © Warren Faidley/Weather Stock. (b) Aaron Horowitz/Corbis. **22—23** (bkgd) Gary Williams/ Liaison. **23** (m) © Warren Faidly/Weather Stock. **24—25** (m) Gary Williams/Liaison. **24** (t) © Warren Faidly/ Weather Stock. **27** © Kevin Schafer/Allstock/ PictureQuest. **28—9** (bkgd) © Roger Ressmeyer/Corbis. **45** (t) Jeff Reinking/Mercury Pictures. (m) Courtesy Phil Boatwright. (b) © PhotoDisc/Getty Images. **48** ©Vince Streano/CORBIS. **49** (t) Mauro Andino/AP/Wide World Photos. (m) Topi Lyambila/AP/Wide World. (b) Geoff Spencer/AP/Wide World. **51** Library of Congress (LC-USZ62-11491). **52** Digital Vision/PictureQuest. **54** (t) © PhotoDisc/Getty Images. (b) © Johnny Autery. **55** L.M. Otero/AP Photo. **56—7** (bkgd) © Vittoriano Rastelli/ Corbis. **56** (t) Christine Kramer. (b) AP/Wide World Photos./Lennox McLendon. **58—77** Warren Faidley/ WeatherStock. **79** (tl) National Center for Atmospheric Research/University Corporation for Atmospheric Research/National Science Foundation. (tr) National Climactic Data Center. (bl) ©Peter Jarver/Wildscape Australia. (br) ©Mark C. Burnett/Photo Researchers, Inc. **80—1** (bkgd) © Bill Bachman/ Photo Researchers, Inc. **82—3** Dr. Peter W. Sloss/NOAA/NESDIS/NGDC. **82** (b) Photo by J.D. Griggs/U.S. Geological Survey. **83** (tl) Photo by Lyn Topinka, U.S. Geological Survey. (tr) ©Nik Wheeler/CORBIS. (b) © Stephen and Donna O'Meara/ Volcano Watch International. **84—5** (bkgd) © Tom Ives/ Corbis **85** National Park Service, Hawaii Volcanoes National Park. **86** Terraphotographics/BPS. **86—7** Gary Rosenquist/Earth Images. **88** Terraphotographics/BPS. **90** Solarfilma. **91—2** J. D. Griggs/U.S. Geological Survey. **93** Seymour Simon. **94** (t) National Park Service, Hawaii Volcanoes National Park. (b) John K. Nakata/ Terraphotographics/BPS. **95** Terraphotographics/BPS. **96** Carl May/Terraphotographics/BPS. **97** Terraphotographics/BPS. **98** Seymour Simon. **99** (l) Courtesy Seymour Simon. (r) © PhotoDisc/Getty Images. **106—6A** (bkgd) © First Light/CORBIS. **106** (b) © Ed Young/Corbis. **106L—M** Culver Pictures. **128** from *Larger Than Life: The American Tall-Tale Postcard 1905–1915* by Cynthia Elyce Rubin and Morgan Williams. Compilation

copyright © 1990 by Abbeville Press, Inc. **130—1** (bkgd) © Zoran Milich/Allsport Concepts/Getty Images. **131** (m) Hemera Technologies Inc. **132** Courtesy of Phyllis R. Naylor. **136** AP/Wide World Photos. **137** (t)Thomas Zimmermann/Stone/Getty Images. (m) © Agence Vandystadt/Allsport. (b) ©Tim Defrisco/Allsport. **138—9** (bkgd) Spike/Stone/Getty Images. **139** Courtesy of the Kwan family. **141** (t) Courtesy of the Kwan family. (b) © Dave Black. **142** © Cindy Lang. **143** Courtesy of the Kwan family. **145** (t) ©Kevin R. Morris/CORBIS. (m) ©Mike Powell/Allsport. (b) Associated Press AP. **146** (l) © Dave Black. (r) ©1997 Gerard Chataigneau. **149** © Dave Black. **151** Momentum Partners, Inc. **154** © 1985 Jose Azel/AURORA. **155** © Photonews/Liaison Agency Inc. **156** (l) © Photonews/ Liaison Agency Inc. (r) ©1985 Jose Azel/AURORA. **157** ©Peter Wouda/Persbureau Noordoost, The Netherlands **162—3** (bkgd) Aaron Jones Studios/Stone/Getty Images. **162** (t) Courtesy Carolyn Soto. (b) Lorraine Parrow/ Mercury Pictures. **178** (t) Archive Photos. (b) U.S. Department of the Interior, National Park Service, Edison National Historic Site/Photo Researchers, Inc. **179** (tl) (tc) Brown Brothers. (tr) Popperfoto/Archive Photos. (mr) © CORBIS. (bl) Smithsonian Institution/National Museum of American History (SI #: 69857). **180** (tl) Archive Photos. (tc) Hulton Getty/Stone/Getty Images. (ml) Comstock Klips. (bl) Archive Photos/John V. Dunigan. (br) © Bettmann/CORBIS. **181** (tc) Leonard Lessin/Peter Arnold, Inc. (r) © PhotoDisc/Getty Images. (bl) Courtesy of Sony Electronics, Inc. **182** © Robert Holmgren/ Stone/Getty Images. **182—3** ©Andrew J.G. Bell, Eye Ubiquitous/CORBIS **183** Stephen Cooper/Allstock/ PictureQuest. **184—5** (bkgd) Norbert Rosing/National Geographic/Getty Images. **184** (t) Dennis Crews/Mercury Pictures. (b) Michael Justice/Mercury Pictures. **188—9** (b) © David Muench/CORBIS. **191** (b) © David Muench/ CORBIS. **194—5** (b) © David Muench/CORBIS. **199** (b) © David Muench/CORBIS. **202** (b) © David Muench/ CORBIS. **204—7** Jamie Bloomquist, American Foundation for the Blind. **208—9** (bkgd) NASA/Ames Research Center. **208—9** (inset) NASA. **208** (bl) NASA. **208** (c) Sovfoto/ Eastfoto. **209** NASA. **210—1** (bkgd) © Pli/Taxi/Getty Images. **211—2** NASA. **214—5** CORBIS–Bettmann/UPI. **216—21** NASA. **222** AP/Wide World Photos. **223** Mike Williams/Mercury Pictures. **226—9** (bkgd) © PhotoDisc/ Getty Images. **227** ©1995 Marty Snyderman. **228—9** © Bruce H. Robison. **230—0A** (bkgd) © PhotoDisc/Getty Images. **230** (b) Hemera Technologies Inc. **230B—D** Ted Wood. **230E** Ted Levin/Animals Animals. **230F—I** Ted Wood. **234** NonStock/PictureQuest. **235** © PhotoDisc/ Getty Images. **236** W.A. Sharman/Milepost 92 1/2 /CORBIS. **237** © PhotoDisc/Getty Images. **238—9** Roy Corral/CORBIS. **240** Craig Lovell/CORBIS. **242** (t) William Amos/Bruce Coleman. (b) Gossi/Bruce Coleman. **243** Gary Meszanos/Bruce Coleman. **245** Telegraph Colour Library/FPGInternational. **246** © PhotoDisc/ Getty Images. **249** © PhotoDisc/Getty Images. **250** NonStock/PictureQuest. **251** Nancy Ney/Corbis. **252** Ron Rovtar/Photonica. **254—5** (bkgd) The Colonial Williamsburg Foundation. **255** (m) Hemera Technologies Inc. **256—8** (bkgd) Siede Preis/Photodisc/Getty Images. **256** (tl) Courtesy of Walter Dean Myers, (mr) Joseph Sohm; Visions of America/Corbis, (bl) Carl & Ann Purcell/

694